THE REAL WAR

THE REAL WAR

THE REAL WAR
1914–1918

BY

CAPTAIN B. H. LIDDELL HART

With Twenty-Five Maps

LITTLE, BROWN AND COMPANY
BOSTON NEW YORK TORONTO LONDON

First published 1930

Re-issued 1964

20   19

MV-NY

To
JOHN BROWN
AND
THE LEGION

ACKNOWLEDGMENT

I wish to acknowledge the kindness of those who read various parts of this book in proof, and their helpfulness in contributing criticisms and suggestions. They include Lieutenant-Colonel H. G. de Watteville, especially, who read the whole volume; Mr. H. C. Bywater, Mr. E. G. Hawke, and one unnamed whose knowledge of sources was as boundless as the trouble he took to aid me.

PREFACE

On finishing this book I am conscious of its imperfections — some consolation comes from the reflection that every book worth reading is imperfect. This book may at least claim one merit, and one contrast to most war "histories." I have as little desire to hide its imperfections as to hide the imperfections of any who are portrayed in its pages. Hence in writing it my pursuit of the truth has not been interrupted by recourse to the pot of hypocritical varnish that is miscalled "good taste." In my judgment of values it is more important to provide material for a true verdict than to gloss over disturbing facts so that individual reputations may be preserved at the price of another holocaust of lives. Taking a long view of history, I cannot regard the repute of a few embodied handfuls of dust as worth more than the fate of a nation and a generation.

On the other hand, I have equally little desire to exaggerate the imperfections of individuals for the sake of a popular effect, or to shift on to them the weight of folly and error which should be borne by the people as a whole.

The historian's rightful task is to distill experience as a medicinal warning for future generations, not to distill a drug. Having fulfilled this task to the best of his ability, and honesty, he has fulfilled his purpose. He would be a rash optimist if he believed that the next generation would trouble to absorb the warning. History at least teaches the historian a lesson.

The title of this book, which has a duality of meaning, requires a brief explanation. Some may say that the war depicted here is not "the real war" — that this is to be discovered in the torn bodies and minds of individuals. It is far from my purpose to ignore or deny this aspect of the truth. But for anyone who seeks, as I seek here, to view the war as an episode in human history, it is a secondary aspect. Because the war affected individual lives so greatly, because these individuals were numbered by millions, because the roots of their fate lay so deep in the past, it is all the more necessary to see the war in perspective, and to disentangle its main threads from the accidents of human misery. Perhaps this attempt is all the more desirable by reason of the trend of recent war literature, which is not merely individualistic, but focuses attention on the thoughts and feelings of some of the pawns of war. The war was, it is true, waged and decided in the minds of individuals more than in the physical clash of forces. But these decisive impressions were received and made in the cabinets and in the military headquarters, not in the ranks of the infantry nor in the solitude of stricken homes.

The other — and more intentional — meaning of the title is that the time has come when a "real" history of the war is possible. Governments have opened their archives, statesmen and generals their hearts, with an unparalleled philanthropy. It is safe to say that most of the possible documentary evidence on the war has now been published or is available for the student. But it has not yet been collated for the information of the public.

The flood of documents, diaries, and memoirs has one outstanding advantage. They have come when they can still be tested by the personal witness of those who took part in the crises and critical discussions of the war. A few years hence would be too late. Yet in the application of this test lies the only chance that history may approximate to truth. The more that any writer of history has himself been at hand when history is being made, or in contact with the makers, the more does he come to see that a history based solely on formal documents is essentially superficial. Too often, also, it is the unwitting handmaiden of "mythology."

CONTENTS

Preface ix

I The Origins of the War 3

II The Opposing Forces and Plans . . . 36

III 1914 — The Clinch 54
    Scene 1. The Battle That Was Not, Yet Turned
        the Tide — The Marne 82
    Scene 2. The Field of Legend — Tannenberg . 103

IV 1915 — The Deadlock 115
    Scene 1. The Birth of a "Plan" — The Dardanelles 143
    Scene 2. The Slip 'twixt Lip and Cup — The Land-
        ing on Gallipoli, April 25, 1915 . . 159
    Scene 3. The Gas Cloud at Ypres — April 22, 1915 175
    Scene 4. The Unwanted Battle — Loos, September
        15, 1915 186

V 1916 — The "Dog-Fall" 199
    Scene 1. The Mincing Machine — Verdun . . 214
    Scene 2. The Brusilov Offensive 224
    Scene 3. The Somme Offensive 227
    Scene 4. The Growing Pains of the Tank . . 249
    Scene 5. Rumania Swallowed 261
    Scene 6. The Capture of Baghdad . . . 267
    Scene 7. The Battle of Blind Man's Buff — Jutland 271

VI 1917 — The Strain 296
    Scene 1. The Halt and Lame Offensive — Arras,
        April 1917 321
    Scene 2. The Siege-War Masterpiece — Messines . 330
    Scene 3. The "Road" to Passchendaele . . 337
    Scene 4. The Tank Surprise at Cambrai . . 344
    Scene 5. "Caporetto" 357

VII   1918 — THE BREAK   364
  Scene 1. The First Break-Through . . . 387
  Scene 2. The Break-Through in Flanders . . 403
  Scene 3. The Break-Through to the Marne . . 411
  Scene 4. The Second Battle of the Marne, July 1918 419
  Scene 5. The "Black Day" of the German Army,
     August 8 429
  Scene 6. Megiddo — The Annihilation of the Turk-
     ish Armies 439
  Scene 7. The Battle of a Dream — St. Mihiel . 449
  Scene 8. The Battle of a Nightmare — The Meuse-
     Argonne 461

 EPILOGUE 470

 BIBLIOGRAPHY 477

 INDEX 497

MAPS

THE WESTERN FRONT	60
THE MARNE, 1914	89
TANNENBERG, 1914	106
THE EASTERN FRONT	132
MESOPOTAMIA	140
GALLIPOLI	162
YPRES, 1915	177
LOOS, 1915	193
VERDUN, 1916	219
SOMME, 1916	229
RUMANIA	263
JUTLAND: APPROACH OF THE RIVAL FLEETS	276
JUTLAND: THE CONTACT	289
ARRAS, APRIL 1917	323
YPRES, 1917	335
CAMBRAI, 1917	349
CAPORETTO	361
GERMAN OFFENSIVE, MARCH 1918	395
THE LYS, APRIL 1918	407
THE BREAK-THROUGH TO THE MARNE	414
SECOND BATTLE OF THE MARNE	426
AMIENS, AUGUST 8, 1918	433
MEGIDDO, 1918	442
ST. MIHIEL	455
MEUSE-ARGONNE	465

THE REAL WAR

I

THE ORIGINS OF THE WAR

FIFTY years were spent in the process of making Europe. Five days were enough to detonate it. To study the manufacture of the explosive materials — which form the fundamental causes of the conflict — is within neither the scope nor the space of a short history of the World War. On the one side we should have to trace the influence of Prussia on the creation of the Reich, the political conceptions of Bismarck, the philosophical tendencies in Germany, and the economic situation — a medley of factors which transmuted Germany's natural desire for commercial outlets, unhappily difficult to obtain, into a vision of world power. We should have to analyze that heterogeneous relic of the Middle Ages known as Austria-Hungary, appreciate her complex racial problems, the artificiality of her governing institutions, the superficial ambitions which overlay a haunting fear of internal disruption and frantically sought to postpone the inevitable end.

On the other side we should have to examine the strange mixture of ambition and idealism which swayed Russia's policy, and the fear it generated beyond her frontiers, especially among her German neighbors — perhaps the deadliest of all the ingredients in the final detonation. We should have to understand the constant alarms of fresh aggression which France had suffered since 1870, study the regrowth of confidence which fortified her to resist further threats, and bear in mind the cancerous remains left in her side by Germany's surgical excision of Alsace-Lorraine. Finally, we should have to trace Britain's gradual movement from a policy of isolation into membership of the European system and her slow awakening to the reality of German feeling towards her.

In such a study of European history during half a century, a generalization can for once be closer to exactness than the most detailed history. The fundamental causes of the conflict can be epitomized in three words — fear, hunger, pride. Beside them, the international "incidents" that occurred between 1871 and 1914 are but symptoms.

All that is possible, and sensible, here is to trace the most significant turning points in the trail of causation which led to combustion. This trail runs through the structure of alliances which Bismarck built after 1871. Ironically, Bismarck intended it as a shelter for the peaceful growth of his creation, the German Empire, and not as a magazine for explosives. For although his philosophy was epitomized in his 1868 phrase, "The weak were made to be devoured by the strong," his own hunger was satiated, after three meals, by the war of 1870–71. It cannot be charged against him that his eyes were larger than his stomach; feeling that Germany now was, as he said, a "saturated" state, his governing idea henceforth was not expansion but consolidation. And to secure time and peace for this consolidation of the new Germany he aimed to keep France in a state of permanent powerlessness to wage a war of revenge. But the result was to prove that two wrongs do not make a Reich.

Apart from frequent direct menaces to France, he sought to counteract her annoyingly rapid recovery by the indirect method of depriving her of friends or supporters. To this end his first effort was to bring Austria and Russia together by forging a common link with Germany, while he strove to ensure peace in the Balkans as a means to avoid any dangerous strain on the link. For some years his policy was that of acting as the "honest broker" in the diplomatic exchange of Europe, without committing himself to any party. But friction with the Russian Chancellor, Gortchakov, and the complications caused by the Russo-Turkish war of 1877, led him to make a defensive alliance with Austria in 1879, despite the objections of the old Emperor William I, who regarded it as "treachery" to Russia and even threatened to abdicate. This definite commitment was to have infinite consequences. Nevertheless, Bismarck temporarily regained his central position by his diplomatic master stroke of 1881, the famous "three emperors' alliance," whereby Russia, Austria, and Germany undertook to act together in all Balkan affairs. And although it lapsed in 1887, Germany's connection with Russia was strengthened in compensation by the secret "Reinsurance Treaty," by which the two powers agreed to maintain benevolent neutrality towards each other in case of war with a third. It was not, however, to apply if Germany attacked France or Russia attacked Austria. By this second master stroke, executed with great duplicity, Bismarck averted the risk, then imminent, of an alliance between Russia and France.

Meantime, the alliance between Germany and Austria had been enlarged by the inclusion of Italy in 1882. The object was to safeguard Austria against a stab in the back if at war with Russia, and in return Italy's new allies would come to her assistance if attacked by France. But as a safeguard to her old friendship with Britain and to her own coasts, Italy had a special protocol appended to the treaty stating that it was in no case to be directed against Britain. In 1883, Rumania, through her King's personal and secret act, was attached to the new Triple Alliance. Even Serbia was temporarily linked on by a separate treaty with Austria, and Spain by an agreement with Italy.

In regard to Britain, Bismarck's aim seems to have been to keep her in friendly isolation from Germany and unfriendly isolation from France. His feelings towards Britain oscillated between friendship and contempt, and the political party system formed the pivot. For the "old Jew," Disraeli, he had genuine respect, but he could not understand the point of view of the Gladstonian Liberals, and their wavering actions he despised. While Disraeli was in power Bismarck toyed with the idea of linking Britain to his chain of alliances, but although Queen Victoria was plaintively "sure that Germany would be the safest ally in every way," she was less sure of Bismarck's safety as a repository of trust, and Disraeli shared her doubts. Hence Bismarck continued, with equal satisfaction, his policy of playing off Britain against Russia and France in turn. And with shrewd calculation he favored Britain's occupation of Egypt because it embroiled her with France, and resisted the growing clamor in Germany for colonial expansion ("Our colonial jingos' greed is greater than we need or can satisfy") because it threatened future trouble with Britain, yet made his support to Britain in Egypt a means of extracting oversea concessions as morsels with which he could assuage the colonial hunger of a body of German interests too powerful even for him to ignore. The Conservatives' return to power in Britain, and the intensified friction with France, led to a fresh tightening of the links with Germany, and Bismarck's offer of a formal alliance was eagerly welcomed by Lord Salisbury's Cabinet, who seem only to have held back from fear of Parliamentary objection to foreign entanglements. Bismarck, however, profited from the informal entente to secure the cession of Heligoland — so vital to German naval operations a generation later — at a paltry price.

Thus at the end of the eighties Bismarck's great structure seemed complete. Germany was buttressed by the Triple Alliance, while the attached yet semi-detached position of Russia and Britain gave her advantages without encumbrances. From this secure base she was ready to develop her commercial expansion. And Bismarck had placed France in the combined solitude and circumscription of a political isolation ward.

But with the beginning of the nineties the first crack appeared in the structure, close upon the dismissal of the builder. The accession in 1888 of the young Emperor William II was disagreeable to the Tsar, Alexander III, who disliked his "aggressive amiability" and distrusted his intentions. Yet the breach came not from Alexander, but from William. Bismarck's control irked him just as it irked the General Staff, and in the soldiers, among whom he had been brought up, he so naturally found allies that in linking himself with them he did not realize that he was forging fresh fetters for himself.

The first effect, after the dismissal of the "pro-Russian" Chancellor, was his successor's refusal to renew the "Reinsurance Treaty" with Russia. The second effect, a natural sequel to the first, was that the Tsar swallowed his aversion to republicanism and in 1891 made an agreement with France which a year later was developed into a military convention for mutual assistance in case of attack. In this convention a significant point was that if any member of the Triple Alliance mobilized its forces both France and Russia were instantly to mobilize. The Tsar at least could not complain that he did not understand the meaning, for the French negotiator, General Boisdeffre, took pains to explain that "mobilization means declaration of war."

In the Tsar's case, the draught was swallowed under the fear that Britain was about to ally herself with Germany; it lay heavy on his stomach, so that it was long in producing any diplomatic value for France.

Nevertheless, France had left "quarantine." Henceforth there was not one political group, but two, in Europe. Although one was loose, the other compact, the two groups formed a balance of power, if their power was not yet balanced evenly.

A doubly significant sidelight upon Germany's renunciation of the Russian secret treaty is that the council in Berlin which reviewed the matter decided against the treaty on the ground that it was disloyal not only to Austria but to Britain. Whatever the Kaiser's failings, he was more sincere than Bismarck, and the insincerity apparent in his contradictory utterances seems to have been due to his combination of excessive frankness with a quick-changing mind. An essential difference between the two men was that the one sought security through consistent dishonesty, and the other gained insecurity through spasmodic honesty. The consideration shown for Britain was in accord with the Kaiser's views. For, although he had reversed Bismarck's attitude towards Russia, he maintained Bismarck's policy of friendship towards Britain, perhaps owing to more sincere and less political motives. The one personal source of cleavage lay in the mutual antipathy of the Kaiser and his uncle, the Prince of Wales — later King Edward VII. And, curiously, it was the Bismarck family who worked to widen this personal breach.

But this could not have developed into a national cleavage without greater causes being at work. More truly, it was one

cause with sundry accretions. Its origin and its foundation
lay in Germany's change of policy from internal to external
expansion. The growth of her commerce and influence to a
world-wide scale inevitably brought her interests and those
of Britain into contact at many points. Under tactful or
even Bismarckian guileful handling this contact might not
have caused such friction as to strike sparks, for British states-
manship was peculiarly insensitive. The party most conscious
of Britain's imperial estate happened to be the party most
sympathetic to imperial Germany. But Bismarck had gone,
and tact did not fill his place. As so commonly happens with
great men, his disciples forgot his principles and remembered
only his method — the mailed fist. Yet the Kaiser himself
could also exert charm, and through it succeeded not only in
maintaining his popularity in England despite repeated irritation, but in gaining a strong hold on the new and weakly
amiable Tsar Nicholas II. For a time he thereby acquired
influence without obligation.

The first friction with Britain came over Turkey — a shadow
cast on the future. A Liberal government was in power again
in 1892, when, as Grey relates, "suddenly there came a sort
of ultimatum from Berlin, requiring us to cease competition"
with Germans "for railway concessions in Turkey." And in
the years that followed the Kaiser lost no opportunity to
emphasize that the spreading web of German commerce had
a sharp-fanged spider at its centre. In 1895 his intervention
made it possible for Russia to deprive Japan of her spoils in
the war with China. In 1896 came the next, and more serious,
friction with Britain. Ironically, its source was an Englishman's too ardent admiration for Bismarckian imperialism.
The Kaiser, unsoothed by Rhodes's equal admiration for himself, became more and more irritated by Rhodes's schemes of
British expansion in South Africa, frustrating his own. After
several sour complaints, and sweet encouragement of the
Transvaal Boers, he found a tempting pretext in the Jameson
raid into the Transvaal. At a council on January 3, 1896,
he suggested that Germany should proclaim a protectorate
over the Transvaal and send troops thither. When the Chan-

cellor, Caprivi, objected that "that would be war with England," the Kaiser ingenuously replied, "Yes, but only on land." As a less drastic alternative the Kaiser was encouraged to send a congratulatory telegram to President Kruger, so worded as not only to be highly offensive to Britain, but to deny her suzerainty over the Transvaal.

Popular feeling boiled over in both countries, due in the one case to ill-suppressed jealousy and in the other to pained surprise at discovering a fresh rival in a traditional friend. Germans felt a natural chagrin that Britain, with already so many colonies, should be gaining more in the one part of the world where a late-comer might hope to stake a claim. Englishmen had made such a habit of colonization that they blandly assumed it could only fit John Bull's figure, and could not understand that anyone, save the traditional rivals, France and Russia, might be anxious. However unconsciously provoking in ordinary intercourse, this calm assurance was a sedative in a crisis, and it largely saved this one. Warlike measures were actually ordered by Germany, and she suggested to France and Russia a combination against Britain. But lack of response from these countries, the calmness of Lord Salisbury's government, and a sense of her own naval weakness, restrained Germany and averted the immediate danger to peace.

But a danger put off by lack of power is not a danger removed. From this moment dates the real growth of German naval ambition, expressed in the Kaiser's words of 1897, "The trident must be in our fist," and in the Kaiser's action of summoning Admiral Tirpitz to manufacture the trident. That year saw the first large naval programme. It also heard the Kaiser proclaim himself, during his visit to Damascus, the protector of all Mahomedans throughout the world — a direct provocation to Britain and France. And not only to them. For the Kaiser's undisguised assumption of the rôle of patron saint of Turkey was fatal to his accord with Russia. His shadow now obscured Russia's view of Constantinople, the goal of her dreams. Like the opponents whom Napoleon derided, the Kaiser failed in policy because he "saw too many things at once," and forced the other powers, whom Bismarck had played off against each other, to see only one thing — the fist of Germany — wherever they looked. Nevertheless, the affront to Britain in South Africa was followed, in 1898, by the offer from Britain of that very alliance which Bismarck had sought in vain. But it was now the turn of Germany to be suspicious of the offer. On the British side the offer was impelled by a new and uncomfortable consciousness of isolation and weakness, while based on the old consciousness of natural affinity with Germany. But it looked, as it was in part, a confession of weakness, and weakness was not a quality to appeal to the new Germany. And one of Bismarck's few legacies to his successors was the habit of underrating Britain's strength and overrating Russia's.

In Germany's repeated rejections of Chamberlain's proposals between 1898 and 1901, the dominant factor was a personal factor — the concealed figure of Holstein. This crabbed, suspicious, and miserly official of the Foreign Office, who loved obscurity because its dimness enhanced his real power in the pursuit of "real policy," who would not buy himself a new suit although he did not shrink from using his official knowledge for private speculation, who had intrigued for his master's dismissal while posing as his pupil, was now viewed with awe as the spiritual heir of Bismarck when he had only inherited his immoral methods. Above all, he lacked Bismarck's confidence.

In consequence, although he would have liked to accept the British offers, he shrank back from fear that Germany would become Britain's cat's-paw, and be converted into her shock-absorber against Russia. On the other hand he felt that Britain's weakness might now be exploited for Germany's benefit by holding Britain at arm's length and wringing concessions from her, while still keeping her hopeful of closer ties. In this view at least he was supported by the Chancellor, Bülow, and the Kaiser, whose outlook was well summed up in his words to Bülow: "I have now got the British, despite their twisting and wriggling, where I want them." And the German navy, expanded afresh in 1900, was the means of putting the screw on harder.

During the next few years, and especially during the South African crisis and war, the British Government had to pay heavily, not for German support, but merely for the privilege that German threats and insults should not be pressed to action. Over the Portuguese colonies, over Samoa, over China, Lord Salisbury's government showed such contemptible weakness as almost to justify the Kaiser's description of them as "unmitigated noodles"; the revelations from the diplomatic archives of these years are sorry reading. To them, indeed, can be traced an indirect responsibility for the eventual conflict, for it was natural that the Kaiser and his advisers should be confirmed in their good opinion of the mailed-fist method. He can be acquitted of a desire to press his method as far as actual war, not only because of the evidence of his distaste for it, but because of his tendency to superficial judgment. The limited menace was so obviously yielding the profits of war without the hazards that the too obvious deduction was just the one to appeal to his mentality.

His responsibility for the war lies in these years. And it is a large responsibility — indeed, the largest. By the distrust and alarm which his bellicose utterances and attitude created everywhere he filled Europe with gunpowder. It is as irrational to fix the chief blame on those who eventually struck the sparks as it is to concentrate investigation of the war's origins on the brief month when the sparks were struck.

In reaction from the unhistorical propaganda which pictured the Kaiser as seeking, or even planning, the war, the pendulum has swung too far the other way. To recognize his erratic good intentions should not lead us to underestimate his bad effects. And they came essentially from the fact that he was too well pleased with the reflection of his acts and himself. He saw himself arrayed in "shining armor" when actually he was wearing the garb of Puck. He proved that making mischief makes war.

In delaying any acceptance of British overtures the Kaiser and Bülow felt secure. They underrated the effect of a common uneasiness in making easy bedfellows. With undue assurance they argued that there could be no real union "between the whale and the bear," and by their acts they compelled this union. In retrospect, the most extraordinary feature is the number of kicks required to drive Britain away from Germany and into the awkward embrace of the Dual Alliance. Germany had at least full warning, for Chamberlain warned her in 1898 and again in 1901 that "the period of England's splendid isolation is past. . . . We should prefer adherence to Germany and the Triple Alliance. But if this proves impossible, then we, too, contemplate a *rapprochement* with France and Russia."

The German belief in its impossibility proved a fallacy. That belief was summed up in Holstein's words: "The threatened understanding with Russia and France is purely an English swindle. . . . A reasonable agreement with England can, in my opinion, only be attained when the feeling of compulsion over there has become more general." He was too clever. By his "reasonable agreement" he meant not an alliance between equals, but the relation of master and servant. Weakly as the British Government had behaved, and weaker still as it appeared to one imbued with the "blood and iron" philosophy, this weakness is not sufficient to explain Holstein's amazing presumption. This is, indeed, an illustration that the real trouble in Germany, and the cause of her troubles, was not any true Machiavellian design, but merely the complaint summed up in the schoolboy phrase "swelled head."

Britain's first attempt to strengthen her position in other directions was her alliance with Japan in 1902. Its European significance is that it did not carry Britain away from Germany, but tended to raise a fresh barrier between Britain and the Dual Alliance. It sprang from Chamberlain's original proposal of a treaty between Britain, Germany, and Japan, in close touch with the United States. Germany held back and so almost did Japan. For the Japanese statesman, Marquis Ito, preferred to seek an alliance with Russia, and was only turned from his purpose because his arrival in St. Petersburg was outstripped by the progress of the negotiations in London between Baron Hayashi, the Japanese ambassador, and Lord Lansdowne, the Foreign Secretary. Even then, the

Japanese Council of Elder Statesmen wavered, under Ito's pressure, before accepting the British alliance — whose indirect result was thus to precipitate the Russo-Japanese War, a result neither desired by nor palatable to Britain.

For by 1904 a dramatic change had occurred in the European situation. Only five years before, France had been so bitter against Britain over Fashoda that she had almost forgotten Alsace-Lorraine. But fear of Germany, more deep-seated, made her statesmen open to approach when, in 1901, Chamberlain fulfilled his warning to Germany. The first step in the eventual negotiations between Lansdowne and Paul Cambon, the French ambassador, was to remove causes of friction at the most sensitive point — overseas. The greatest obstacle was Egypt, still a cherished object of French ambition, and it was no mean diplomatic feat that recognition of Britain's actual occupation was exchanged for recognition of French right to occupy Morocco if she could. The agreement was signed in April 1904. Although the popular idea of King Edward VII's responsibility for the agreement is purely legendary, — still more so the popular German idea of him as spinning a Machiavellian web around Germany, — his visit to Paris created the atmosphere in which agreement was possible. At first his reception was frigid, but his tact and understanding of the French combined with their truly republican love of royalty to hasten a thaw, and succeeding visits uncovered common ground. Thus, if it is not true that he made the new *entente*, he undoubtedly made it *cordiale*.

But the Kaiser also helped. Deeply chagrined that the lover whose advances Germany had spurned had dared to woo another, his mischief-making was now redoubled. His efforts were directed to break up the Franco-British entente. And the coincident Russo-Japanese War provided the opportunity. His first move was a failure, for the peace-loving Tsar rejected his advice to send the Black Sea Fleet through the Dardanelles in defiance of Britain. But when the Baltic Fleet, Russia's last naval trump, sailed for the Far East it received false information — the Russians later alleged that it came from German sources — that Japanese torpedo craft were lying in wait in the North Sea. Through a panic mistake they fired on British trawlers, and made no effort to redeem their error, which brought Russia and Britain momentarily to the brink of war. For some days the British Channel Fleet shadowed the Russians, until the tension was eased by a message of regret from the Tsar, against the wishes of the war party in Russia. The Tsar, bitter at his humiliation, now, to the Kaiser's delight, proposed a combination of Russia, Germany, and France "to abolish English and Japanese arrogance and insolence." The Kaiser promptly dispatched a draft treaty between Russia and Germany, but urged the Tsar not to divulge it to the French, arguing that, the "Treaty once a *fact*, our combined powers will exert a strong attraction on France," and adding that "an excellent expedient to cool British insolence and overbearing would be to make some military demonstration on the Perso-Afghan frontier. . . ." But it was the Tsar who cooled, on reflection.

The next German move was singularly inapt, and for it the Kaiser was not responsible. Now, too late, he wanted to woo France instead of trying to separate her from Britain by threat. But he was sent off by Bülow and Holstein to Tangiers, there to "throw down the glove to France" by a speech which challenged French claims in Morocco. Bülow followed it up by calling for a conference to review the future of Morocco. The challenge came at an awkward moment. The French army was suffering one of its periodical crises, Russia was entangled with Japan, and the French Prime Minister, Rouvier, doubted both the assurance and value of British support. Thus the foreign minister, Delcassé, was sacrificed and France accepted the demand. The mailed fist had scored afresh, but the alarm had driven Britain and France closer together.

The third move was the Kaiser's own. In July 1905, when on board the Tsar's yacht at Bjorko, he suddenly produced the draft treaty, and in his hybrid "Willy-Nicky" English asked, "Should you like to sign it? It would be a very nice souvenir of our *entrevue*." The Kaiser relates that when Nicholas answered "Yes, I will," "tears of joy filled my eyes — a thrill ran down my spine," and he felt that all his ancestors, including "Grandpapa" and the "old Prussian God," were giving him their benediction. This phase of royal diplomacy, however serious its implication, was not without its humorous relief. There is a delightful commercial touch in one of his letters to "Dearest Nicky": "Now that the programme for the renewal of your fleet has been published, I hope you won't forget to remind your authorities to remember our great firms at Stettin, Kiel, etc. They will, I am sure, furnish fine specimens of line of battleships." Melodrama marks his aggrieved letter to Bülow, who, as the treaty ran counter to his own anti-French aims in Morocco, threatened resignation: "The morning after your resignation reaches him, the Kaiser will no longer be in this world! Think of my poor wife and children."

But when the Tsar's ministers saw the treaty, they objected that it could not be reconciled with the French alliance, and sufficient hint of it leaked out to cause strong protests from France. Thus the "masterpiece" was quietly dropped into the diplomatic waste-paper basket.

In justice to the Kaiser it must be mentioned that at the time he had some cause for personal grievance against Britain, even though it was largely the reaction to his long-standing habit of seeking his end by threats. His forceful impulsiveness had a counterpart in Sir John Fisher, just become First Sea Lord, who constantly talked of a preventive war and freely aired suggestions that if Germany would not limit her naval expansion her fleet should be "Copenhagened" — on the Nelson model. Such wild suggestions naturally made more impression in Berlin than in London. King Edward VII's share as a cause of irritation was social and personal rather than political. A little more tolerance towards his nephew's *gaucherie* might have helped to smoother relations. Lord Lansdowne records that "the King talks and writes about his royal brother in terms which make one's flesh creep." These personal antipathies and pin-pricks, of little account on the British side, where the King was a constitutional ruler and also had a sense of humor, had a deeper reaction on the German side of the North Sea, where the ruler could influence policy decisively and had no sense of humor. And by inciting the Kaiser to further mischief-making intrigues and menaces they had an ultimate reaction in Britain, where even the new Liberal government of Campbell-Bannerman could not ignore them, and was unwillingly forced closer into the arms of France.

While the government refused to commit Britain to a formal alliance with France, it held out the hope that British public opinion might favor intervention if France was attacked. And when the French logically argued that emergency aid would be no use unless its method of application had been thought out, Campbell-Bannerman authorized discussions between the two general staffs. While these had no effect upon the eventual decision for war, they were to have a great influence on the conduct of the war. It is significant also that in 1905 the new German war plan made allowance for a British expeditionary force of 100,000 men — the very figure the French asked for — being present on the French side.

Baulked of his idea of drawing France, with Russia, into a combination against Britain, the Kaiser now reverted to the idea of action against France over Morocco. He decided, however, that "from a technico-military standpoint" conditions were not suitable, and that an alliance with Turkey, "which would place the forces of Mahomedanism to the furthest extent—under Prussian leadership — at my disposal," and a secure internal position were necessary preliminaries. This illuminating example of his unbalanced mind is contained in a letter of December 31, 1905, to Bülow, which concludes, "First shoot the Socialists down, behead them, render them impotent — if necessary per Blood bath — and then war abroad! But not before, and not à tempo."

Yet the next change in the European situation was not to strengthen his foundations, but to weaken them, by weakening his influence over Russia in the person of the Tsar. With supreme irony the change came in the most unlikely way — by the drawing together of the new British Government and its antipathy, despotic Russia. Impelled partly by its general pacifism and partly by its natural reaction to German menaces, the Liberal government continued the effort begun by Lansdowne to remove the traditional sources of friction with Russia. And in 1907 the points of difference at the points of contact were settled by an arrangement. While there was no definite agreement, the natural effect was to smooth the way to coöperation in Europe. Although Britain was not tied either to France or Russia by any formal agreement, she was tied to their side by the bonds of loyalty, and so could no longer impose a check upon them without suspicion of disloyalty. Thus her old independent influence in a crisis had slipped away.

The dilemma was realized and well summed up by the Foreign Secretary, Sir Edward Grey, in a memorandum of February 20, 1906 : —

"There would, I think, be a general feeling in every country that we had behaved meanly and left France in the lurch. The United States would despise us, Russia would not think it worth while to make a friendly arrangement with us about Asia, Japan would prepare to reinsure herself elsewhere, we should be left without a friend and without the power of making a friend and Germany would take some pleasure in exploiting the whole situation to our disadvantage. . . . On the other hand the prospect of a European War and of our being involved in it is horrible."

Henceforth the great powers were in fact, if not in name, divided into two rival groups. During the next few years Germany, whose aggressive and impolitic policy had created the counter-group, so curiously assorted, was also to help and be helped by Austria in hardening it, as a snowball is hardened when squeezed. But she was also to suffer from her own creation. Britain's adhesion to the new group weakened the old, by making Italy a doubtful partner. Hence Germany was compelled to cling more closely to her other partner, Austria, whom formerly she had led. If Germany wished for war, this bondage was an advantage, but if she wished for peace she would be hampered even as Britain was hampered.

The new grouping of Europe was not the old balance of power but merely a barrier between powers. That barrier, moreover, was charged with explosives — the armaments which the several countries, now driven more by fear than

by ambition, hurriedly augmented. Another ill consequence
was that fear of a sudden detonation led the autocratic powers
at least to give the military custodians of these armaments a
dangerously free hand in disposing them. Fear had taken
charge of reason long before July 1914.

The first spark came from the Balkans in 1908. The
revolution in Turkey was seized upon by Bulgaria to throw
off Turkish suzerainty and by Austria to annex the provinces
of Bosnia and Herzegovina, which she had administered
since 1879. This annexation had been discussed between the
Austrian and Russian foreign ministers, Aehrenthal and
Isvolsky, and Isvolsky had been willing to assent to it in return
for Austrian support in securing the opening of the Dardanelles.
But before Isvolsky could sound France and Britain, the
annexation was declared. In Italy it was justly felt to be
an affront, and in Serbia to be a menace. But in Russia the
effect was made worse by the German ambassador's peremptory
demand that Russia should recognize it under pain of a
combined Austrian and German attack.

Russia, caught when she had been acting single-handed,
and threatened by a two-handed combination, gave way
from fear, and was left with resentment, aggravated by the
sense of having forfeited her standing in the Balkans. Isvolsky
felt that he had been not only browbeaten but duped, and,
resigning soon after, went to the Paris embassy as an embittered
foe of the Germanic powers. Another personal factor. And
Austria, flattered by this first success in imitating Germany's
mailed-fist method of diplomacy, was encouraged to continue it.

This Bosnian deceit of Aehrenthal's stands out predomi-
nantly among the immediate origins of the war. Its intervention was the more unfortunate because the years 1906–
1914 saw an improvement in Germany's official relations, at
least, with France and Britain. It would have been more
marked but for the continued ominous increase in the German
navy. It is easy to appreciate now that the Kaiser's encouragement to Tirpitz's anti-British naval ambitions was due largely
to vanity, but then it looked more naturally a consistently
designed challenge. And even when he tried to repair the

damage the Kaiser was unhappy in his method. His way
of conciliating British feeling was to declare, in the famous
Daily Telegraph interview of 1909, that the British were "mad
as March hares" not to recognize his friendship, and that he
was in a minority in a land "not friendly to England." Without soothing British fears, it caused an outcry in Germany,
a public repudiation by Bülow. And it thus weakened the
Kaiser's own power to check the war party in Germany.

But it at least led to the Kaiser's replacement of Bülow
as Chancellor by the well-meaning Bethmann-Hollweg, who
was more desirous of peace if less capable of preserving it.
He promptly opened negotiations for an Anglo-German agreement, and met with an eager response from the Liberal government, now renewed in power by the elections of 1910. But
practical results were barred, first, by Tirpitz's opposition
to any naval adjustment, and, second, by the German demand
that any agreement must be so worded as to bar Britain from
coming to the aid of France.

This was too obviously a strategic move. Sir Edward Grey
made the only possible reply: "One does not make new
friendships worth having by deserting old ones."

Nevertheless the tension was eased. The German public,
press, and Kaiser — as shown by his documentary comments
— still suffered from Anglophobia, owing largely to the feeling
of thwarted aims and the much propagated idea that King
Edward VII had planned a vast hostile encirclement of Germany. Perhaps the most illuminating reaction was the belief
that the King's 1908 visit to the Emperor Francis Joseph was a
move to detach Austria from Germany, whereas we now know
from the Austrian archives that the King actually asked Francis
Joseph's assistance towards reducing the friction between
Britain and Germany, and valued the alliance as a common
link. But the discussions helped the relations between the
British and German foreign ministries and led them to coöperate in settling several points of dispute. Relations were also
helped by the settlement between France and Germany over
Morocco.

Characteristically, this settlement followed a new crisis.

The crisis, curiously enough, was provoked by the otherwise pacific Foreign Minister, Kiderlen-Wächter, and opposed by the Kaiser, another instance of that incalculable double-headedness which was so dangerous a feature of German policy. As a means of encouraging France to grant concessions in Africa, in June 1911, Kiderlen-Wächter dispatched a gunboat to Agadir. In reply, Lloyd George, the former opponent of the Boer War and the leading pacifist in the British Cabinet, warned Germany in a public speech against such threats to peace. The effect, in conjunction with firm indication of a readiness to support France, was to damp the war-spark. But resentment made public opinion in Germany more combustible than ever, and it enthusiastically approved yet another increase in the German navy. Nevertheless, the subsequent settlement over Morocco removed a serious source of friction between France and Germany, and thus indirectly contributed to the better official atmosphere in which Haldane's 1912 mission to Germany took place. Yet even Haldane had to confess that his "spiritual home" had become a "powder magazine," although he communicated his fears only to his colleagues in the Cabinet. The growth of the war party in Germany, however, was accompanied by a consolidation of the peace elements, most marked among the Socialists, and the presence of a pacifically-minded Chancellor kept open a possible avenue for further negotiations.

But at this very time a fresh powder trail was laid — in the Balkans. The weakness of Turkey, and the example of Italy in occupying Tripoli, encouraged Bulgaria, Serbia, and Greece to claim autonomy for Macedonia as a step to ejecting the Turks from Europe. The Turks were quickly defeated. Serbia's share of the spoils was to be Northern Albania. But Austria, already fearful of Serb ambitions, had no intention of allowing a Slav state to gain access to the Adriatic. She mobilized her troops, and her threat to Serbia was naturally answered by Russia's similar preparations. Fortunately, Germany joined with Britain and France to forestall the danger. Less fortunately, their settlement was the cause of a fresh crisis. For, by setting up Albania as an independent state, they upset the division of the spoil. Serbia now claimed part of Macedonia; Bulgaria refused not only by word but by blow, only to be overcome by the combined weight of Serbia and Greece, while Rumania joined in, and Turkey slipped back to recover her lost property under cover of the dust raised by the "dog-fight."

As a result Serbia was the chief gainer and Bulgaria the chief loser. This was much to Austria's distaste, and in the summer of 1913 she proposed an immediate attack on Serbia. Germany restrained her, counseling moderation, but herself gave Russia a fresh cause of offense by extending German control of the Turkish army. Russia saw her dream of the Dardanelles fading, and her ministers came to the conclusion that it could only be revived if a general European war occurred — a dangerful attitude of mind. Their immediate aim was now to recover their shaken influence in the Balkans, and they sought to win over Rumania as a first step towards building a new Balkan alliance. The prospect created fresh alarm in Austria, already distracted by the internal strain of her diverse racial parts.

Force was her method to suppress the dissatisfaction of her Serb and Croat subjects in the annexed provinces and of her Rumanian subjects in Transylvania. And her desire was to apply the same remedy in time to the external state — Serbia — which formed a natural rallying point for all the dissatisfied elements within. Her leaders felt that war beyond her frontiers would be the best way to silence discord within. In this feeling they were not alone. The popular unrest in Russia, only half stifled by the use of knout and exile, and the clamor for universal suffrage in Germany, made the war parties in both countries look to war as a safety-valve.

During the last year incitements multiplied on all sides — bellicose speeches, articles, rumors, frontier incidents. President Wilson's confidant, Colonel House, left Berlin with the conviction that the military party was determined on war, at the earliest opportunity, and would force the Kaiser to abdicate if he opposed their desire. Their excitement was certainly aggravated by the three years' service act which

France had passed as a remedy for her inferior man-power in face of recent developments in the German army. But the German ambassador reported to Bethmann-Hollweg that, "in spite of the chauvinistic attitude of many circles and the general dream of a recovery of the lost provinces, the French nation as a whole could be described as desirous of peace." The most that could be said, even of Poincaré, the President, was what Poincaré himself expressed, "that France did not want war, but did not fear it. . . ." Elsewhere, however, the surface of the Continent was now strewn with powder. And everywhere the air was heavy with fatalism.

The fatal spark was struck at Serajevo, the Bosnian capital, on June 28, 1914. Its first victim marked the irony of destiny. The fiery Slav nationalists who sought to advance their cause by murdering the Archduke Franz Ferdinand, the heir to Francis Joseph, singled out the one man of influence in Austria who was their friend. For Franz Ferdinand also had dreams — of a reconstructed empire in which the several nationalities were held together, not in bondage, but in federation. But to most of the Bosnian Slavs he was merely the symbol of the oppressor, and to the extreme nationalists who plotted his death he was the more to be hated because his dream of reconciliation within the empire might thwart theirs of breaking away from the empire, to join with Serbia in creating a wider Yugoslav state.

The handful of youthful conspirators sought and received help from the Serbian secret society known as the "Black Hand." This was largely composed of army officers, who formed a group hostile to the existing civil government in Serbia. Rumors of the conspiracy seem to have reached the ears of ministers, and orders were sent to the frontier to intercept the conspirators, but as the frontier guards were members of the "Black Hand" the precautions naturally failed. It seems also, but is not certain, that a vague warning was sent to Vienna. What is certain is the amazing carelessness of the Austrian authorities in guarding the Archduke, and their cynical indifference to the fate that befell this highly unpopular heir to the throne. Potiorek, the military governor of Bosnia and future commander of the offensive against Serbia, could not have done more to facilitate the task of the assassins if he had connived at it. Hence there must always be a suspicion that he did.

After a first attempt, on the Archduke's passage to the city hall, had failed, Potiorek so clumsily directed the return journey that the Archduke's car had to pull up, and two shots rang out, mortally wounding the Archduke and his court-despised morganatic consort. He died at 11 A.M. — a prophetic hour.

The news of the crime caused horror and indignation in all countries save two — Austria and Serbia. The Serbian press made little effort to conceal its pleasure, and the Serbian public still less, while the government which, exhausted by the Balkan wars, had every incentive for peace in order to consolidate its gains was foolishly remiss in making or offering an investigation into the complicity of its subjects.

Austrian police investigation was also leisurely, and after a fortnight Wiesner, who was deputed to conduct it, reported that, while Serbian societies and officials were implicated, there were "no proofs of the complicity of the Serbian Government. . . . On the contrary there are grounds for believing it quite out of the question."

But Austrian decision was prompt, although any outward appearance of action was long delayed. Count Berchtold, the Foreign Minister, — who had added an air of elegance to the tradition of deceit bequeathed by Aehrenthal, — gracefully and gratefully seized the opportunity to retrieve Austria's and his own lost prestige. The day after the crime he declared to the Chief of the General Staff that the time had come to settle with Serbia once for all — words that seemed to Conrad von Hötzendorf the echo of his own repeated promptings to war. But Berchtold met an unexpected obstacle in Count Tisza, who objected strongly, on the score of expediency, not of morality: "There can be no difficulty in finding a suitable *casus belli* whenever it is needed." Conrad also considered expediency and remarked to Berchtold, "We must above all ask Germany whether she is willing to safeguard us against Russia." Berchtold, too, had no wish to meet a rebuff from

Germany such as so damaged his prestige two years before. Hence the aged Emperor was induced to sign a memorandum for the Kaiser, accompanied by a personal letter.

But the Kaiser needed no appeal. For when the German ambassador, Tschirschky, had sent off a report of his conversation with Berchtold on June 30, saying that he had given a warning against hasty steps, the Kaiser scribbled in the margin, "Who authorized him to do this? It is idiotic. It is none of his business. . . . Tschirschky must be good enough to stop this lunacy. We must clear the Serbians out of the way, and that too forthwith." Poor Tschirschky! He was not equal to his master's somersaults. Formerly energetic in incitement, he presumably remembered his master's voice, urging restraint two years before, and now thought that he was fulfilling the Kaiser's wish by changing his own tune — only to find that the Kaiser had also changed. How shall we explain it? Most probably by the Kaiser's fear of being again reproached with weakness and by his characteristic indignation that royal blood had been shed, if also by the more creditable motive of his friendship with the murdered man.

Thus to Count Hoyos, the Austrian letter-bearer, he gave the assurance, on July 5, that Austria "could depend on the complete support of Germany." "In the Kaiser's opinion there must be no delay. . . . If it was to come to a war between Austria-Hungary and Russia she could be assured that Germany would stand at her side," although he added that Russia "was in no way ready for war." Germany was — so he was assured. In a series of hasty consultations with his military and naval advisers, various precautionary measures were ordered. Meantime, the Kaiser left, as arranged, to visit Norway. A few days later, on the seventeenth, Waldersee, the Assistant Chief of the General Staff, reported to the Foreign Minister, "I shall remain here ready to jump. We are all prepared."

This blank check, endorsed by the Chancellor, and given with full recognition of the consequences, stands out predominant among the immediate causes of the war. Austria hurried to cash it, and Tschirschky was only too eager to repair his blunder in urging caution. Unlike later decisions, this was taken in a calm if not a cool atmosphere, a fact which gives it special significance in assessing the will to war. Significant also is the care taken by Germany and Austria to lull suspicion of any impending move — in Conrad's words, "peaceful intentions should be simulated." While giving no advice to Austria to keep her demands within moderation, the German Government showed its anxiety that the support of Italy, Bulgaria, Rumania, and Turkey should be ensured for a war. Italy was to be given no hint of the action intended, but Austria was urged to be ready with a price for her support when war came.

Now assured of Germany's backing, Berchtold's next problem is so to draft the ultimatum to Serbia that it will be unacceptable. This takes some thought, and on July 10 Berchtold confesses to Tschirschky that he is still considering "what demands could be put that it would be wholly impossible for Serbia to accept." The only dissenting voice is that of Tisza, but he is told, "A diplomatic success would be valueless." He threatens to withhold his support, but suddenly veers round — after Berchtold has warned him of "the military difficulties which would be caused by a delay," and has impressed the fact that "Germany would not understand any neglect on our part to use this opportunity for striking a blow." Austria might forfeit her partnership with Germany if she showed weakness.

The ultimatum is drawn up, and after reading it the old Emperor says, "Russia cannot accept this . . . this means a general war." But its delivery is delayed until various war preparations are complete — and Poincaré has sailed from St. Petersburg, where he has been visiting the Tsar. The Russian ambassador in Vienna is also induced to go on leave by peaceful assurances. But the German steamship lines are warned of the date on which the Austrian note would be delivered, and that they must be ready for swift "developments."

At 6 P.M. on July 23 the ultimatum is presented to the Serbian Government — when the Prime Minister is away. Its terms not only demand the repression of all propaganda against Austria, but Austria's right to order the dismissal of any Serbian officials that she cares to name and to post her own officials in Serbia. This directly violates Serbia's status as an independent country. Only forty-eight hours are allowed for acceptance. Next day the German Government delivers notes in St. Petersburg, Paris, and London, which state that the Austrian demands are "moderate and proper" — the German Government had not even seen the ultimatum when it light-heartedly wrote this — and add the threat that "any inter-ference . . . would be followed by incalculable consequences." In London the note caused stupefaction, in Russia fierce indignation.

But, two minutes before the ultimatum expired, the Serbian reply was handed to the Austrian ambassador. Without waiting to read it, he broke off relations and caught the train from Belgrade, in accordance with his instructions. Formal orders were issued three hours later for Austria's partial mobilization — on the Serbian front. Simultaneously pre-paratory measures for mobilization took place in Germany and Russia.

Yet the Serbian note had accepted all the Austrian demands except the two which definitely violated her independence. When the Kaiser read it, on July 18, after his return, he wrote the comment, "A brilliant performance for a time-limit of only forty-eight hours. . . . A great moral victory for Vienna; but with it every reason for war drops away." And in reference to Austria's partial mobilization he adds, "On the strength of this I should never have ordered mobilization." Once more the mailed fist has triumphed, and the Kaiser, having shown the doubters that he is a strong man, is eager to rest on his laurels. Royal honor is satisfied. But he unwisely suggests that Austria might well occupy part of Serbia until her demands are fulfilled — an act that Russia could never be expected to permit. Bethmann-Hollweg agreed with the Kaiser's view, and on the morning of the twenty-eighth the advice was sent to Vienna, adding that, "If Austria continues her refusal to all proposals for mediation or arbitration, the odium of being responsible for a world war will in the eyes of the German people fall on the German Government."

But the changed tone was fatally belated. Germany had herself blocked these proposals during the most auspicious period. When the German note was delivered, on July 24, Russia was at once assured of France's support, and Grey was pressed by his allies to declare Britain's solidarity with them. But his parliamentary responsibility and the divided views of the Cabinet, as well as the uncertainty of public support, hindered any such declaration. He feared, too, that any such action might strengthen the war parties in Russia and Germany. Instead, he tried to open a path to mediation. His first move, on the twenty-fourth, was to urge through Berlin an extension of the Austrian time-limit. It received no support in Berlin and was tardily passed on to Vienna, where it arrived two hours before the expiration, when it was at once rejected. On the twenty-fifth and twenty-sixth he made further proposals for joint mediation by Germany, Britain, France, and Italy, while Austria, Russia, and Serbia were to abstain from military operations. Prompt acceptance came at once from Paris and Rome. Sazonov in St. Petersburg, who had originally mooted the idea, now agreed in principle, but preferred first to try direct discussions with Vienna. Berlin refused. The Kaiser scribbled his usual incendiary comments on the reports that came to him: "That is a tremendous piece of British insolence. I am not called upon to prescribe à la Grey to H.M. the Emperor [of Austria] how to preserve his honor." There is much evidence that German opinion was encouraged by Britain's attitude to count on her neutrality in case of war. But in the newspapers of July 27 the British Government published the news that the fleet, assembled for manœuvres, had been ordered not to disperse. This hint, in combination with the nature of Serbia's reply, caused a change of official tone in Berlin, where, the day before, the General Staff had sent to the Foreign Office the ultimatum they had drafted in readiness for delivery to Belgium.

Thus, later on July 27, the German Government decided to pass Grey's proposals on to Vienna. They sent Grey word that this action implied that they "associate themselves to a certain extent with your hope." But, after seeing the German Foreign Minister, the Austrian ambassador telegraphed to Vienna: "The German Government offers the most un-qualified assurances that it in no way identifies itself with them, but on the contrary is decidedly opposed to their consideration, and only communicates them in order to satisfy the English. . . . The German Government is so acting because its point of view is that it is of the utmost importance that England, at the present moment, should not make common cause with Russia and France." On the twenty-eighth, after the Kaiser had seen Serbia's reply, there was a further cooling of tone as we have seen. But Bethmann-Hollweg's cautionary message, his first, to Vienna that day was too late and too tepid.

For, at 11 A.M. — again! — on July 28, Austria's telegraphed declaration of war was delivered to Serbia. And the same day Berchtold refused Sazonov's proposal for direct conversations, giving as his reason the fact that war was now declared! A grim humor underlies both the cause and method of Austria's precipitate decision. Militarily there was every reason for delay in the actual declaration, as the army could not be ready to move until August 12. But messages from Germany had been inciting Austria to haste; Berchtold and Conrad feared to lose her support and the chance of war if they dallied. Berchtold cynically summed up the position to the Emperor on July 27: "I think that a further attempt by the Entente Powers to bring about a peaceful solution remains possible only so long as a new situation has not been created by the declaration of war." And in obtaining the Emperor's signature to the declaration of war he quenched any doubts by incorporating the justification that Serbian had attacked Austrian troops. Having achieved his end, he then deleted the sentence referring to this imaginary attack!

The rush to the abyss now gathered unbrakable speed — driven by the motor of "military necessity." In constructing their huge and cumbrous machines the general staffs of Europe had forgotten the first principle of war — elasticity. Alike in mobilization and in use the conscript armies of the Continent were almost unmanageable. Events were soon to show that they could be set in motion, but could not be effectively guided; their steering gear was inadequate. In this deficiency, now a danger to peace, they afforded a contrast both to the fleets of the time and to the small professional armies of the past.

The one thought of the generals during these critical days was to start their machines. Desire for war, and fear of being caught at a disadvantage, reacted on each other. Thus in Germany and Russia, as already in Austria, any desire among the statesmen for peace suffered the counter-pull of the generals' entreaties to action, and predictions of dire consequences if their technical advice was disregarded. Already in Austria the generals shared with Berchtold the sombre distinction of having initiated the war.

Their next success was in Russia — also a land of military mediocrity. There, the news of the Austrian declaration of war wrought a decisive change. Hitherto Sazonov had kept the generals in hand. Now he begins to succumb to inevitability, and suggests that partial mobilization shall be carried out — of the troops on the Austrian front only. The General Staff argue that for "technical reasons" this is impracticable, and urge that only a general mobilization can avoid upsetting the machine. Unwilling to yield to their arguments, yet unwilling to override them, Sazonov makes a compromise. Two ukases are prepared for the Tsar's signature, one for partial and one for general mobilization, and a decision between them is put off.

But the General Staff are working on the second. Next morning the chief of the mobilization branch receives the order for general mobilization signed provisionally by the Tsar, and goes round to obtain the necessary signature of the Ministers. One of them cannot be found until the evening. Meantime the German ambassador calls on Sazonov, about 6 P.M., and gives him a message from Bethmann-Hollweg, that "if Russia continues her mobilization measures Germany will mobilize, and mobilization means war." The message is delivered with the assurance that it is "not a threat, but a friendly opinion"; to Sazonov it sounds more like a threat, and it seems to prohibit even partial mobilization on the Austrian frontier. His opposition to his own clamorous General Staff weakens, and after a conference with its chief, Yanushkevich, he apparently consents to general mobilization and obtains the Tsar's approval.

Let us shift our gaze for a moment to Berlin. There the same nervous tension exists and the same tug of wills is in progress. But the Kaiser and his political advisers are now seriously alarmed that Austria's action will make them appear the guilty party, and so cost them the support of Italy while ensuring the entry of Britain against them. Thus a demand of the General Staff for immediate mobilization is refused, and late in the evening Bethmann-Hollweg sees the British ambassador. He tries to bargain for Britain's neutrality and suggests that in return Germany would not annex any part of France, but he "cannot give him such an assurance" as regards the French colonies. The ambassador tells him that acceptance of the offer is highly improbable, wherein he proves a true prophet. Lichnowsky's warnings from London that British opinion is hardening send the Kaiser into a paroxysm of frightened rage. He scrawls abusive epithets about "English pharisaism," calling Grey "a mean deceiver," and, rather oddly in view of Bethmann-Hollweg's offer, terms the British a "pack of base hucksters." But Lichnowsky's report of Grey's renewed proposals for mediation at least induces Bethmann-Hollweg to send a string of telegrams to Vienna exhorting the Austrians not to continue their open refusal, lest they drag Germany into war at a disadvantage. The Kaiser, also, telegraphs to the Tsar saying that he is trying to persuade Vienna to agree to "frank negotiations." This message crosses a similar conciliatory telegram from the Tsar, and is answered by a second, suggesting that "it would be right to give over the Austro-Serbian problem to the Hague Conference. I trust in your wisdom and friendship." The fact that the Kaiser's marginal comment is "Rubbish" casts a doubt upon his sincerity. But the Kaiser has also sent a second telegram of appeal to check military measures which "would precipitate a calamity. . . ." This produces an actual effect.

The Tsar, about 10 P.M., rings up the Chief of Staff, and, despite Yanushkevich's horrified protests that the orders have now gone out, directs him to cancel them and substitute a partial mobilization.

But the General Staff, though discomfited, are not defeated. Next morning, in order to retrieve the position, they bring fresh arguments and all their weight to bear. First, they try to approach the Tsar, but he takes refuge from their pressure by refusing to see the Minister of War. Yanushkevich then seeks out Sazonov, and insists that any further delay in general mobilization will "dislocate" the army organization and endanger Russia's safety. He further contends that partial mobilization will give the French the impression that, when war comes, Russia will be unable to help her in resisting Germany's onslaught. Sazonov, now resigned to the certainty of war, agrees to visit the Tsar that afternoon. The Tsar, pale and worried, gives way and gives the order — after Sazonov has soothingly assured him that, whatever happens, his conscience will be clear. Sazonov telephones the order to Yanushkevich, and advises him to "disappear for the rest of the day," as a safeguard against the Tsar's vacillation. Sazonov first thinks of trying to keep the general mobilization as secret as possible, without issuing any proclamation, but finds it technically impossible, and the ukase is posted up next morning, July 31. That same day, but a few hours later, the Austrian order for general mobilization is given. Henceforth the "statesmen" may continue to send telegrams, but they are merely waste paper. The military machine has completely taken charge.

Indeed, it had done so on the thirtieth — not only in Russia. At 2 P.M. Moltke, the Chief of the German General Staff, had sent a message to the Austrian General Staff through their attaché that Russia's military measure "will develop into a *casus foederis* for Germany. . . . Decline the renewed advances of Great Britain in the interest of peace. A European war is the last chance of saving Austria-Hungary. Ger-

many is ready to back Austria unreservedly." Subsequently
he sent a telegram direct to Conrad: "Mobilize at once against
Russia. Germany will mobilize. Persuade Italy, by offering
compensation, to do her duty as an ally." Thus Moltke
counteracted the irresolute telegrams of Bethmann-Hollweg.
The Austrian military and civil leaders needed no urging,
merely the assurance of Germany's support, and had no
intention of acceding to any proposals for mediation unless
Germany threatened to withdraw that support. And "Germany" now meant the General Staff.

As soon as news reached Berlin of the Russian order, a
"state of danger of war" was proclaimed, which comprised
the first step of mobilization — a neat military device to gain a
lead without giving away a trick. At the same time ultimatums were dispatched both to St. Petersburg and Paris. The
ultimatum to Russia demanded that she "must suspend every
war measure against Austria and ourselves within twelve
hours," and "definitely notify us of this." Sazonov, in reply,
said that it was technically impossible to stop the mobilization, but that so long as negotiations continued Russia
would not attack. The Tsar reënforced this statement with
another telegram to the Kaiser: "Understand that you are
obliged to mobilize, but wish to have the same guarantee from
you as I gave you that these measures do not mean war, and
that we shall continue negotiating. . . ." But, without waiting
to hear the reply to their ultimatum, the German Government dispatched a formally worded declaration of war to
their ambassador in St. Petersburg, who duly delivered it,
after the expiry of the time-limit, in the early evening of
August 1. Almost coincidently German mobilization began.

Yet General von Chelius had shrewdly reported from St.
Petersburg: "People have mobilized here through fear of
coming events with no aggressive purpose, and are already
terrified at the result." And the Kaiser had made the note:
"Right; that is the truth." But the Kaiser, now equally
frightened, and willing, could not stop his own military
machine. For Moltke was insistent that "the unusually
favorable situation should be used to strike," pointing out

that "France's military situation is nothing less than embarrassed, that Russia is anything but confident; moreover, the time of year is favorable." The rashness of the Russian General Staff might at least be excused by "nerves," but hardly Moltke's. If three men can be singled out as the main personal causes of the war, at this time, they are Berchtold, Conrad, and Moltke. But Moltke was really a limited company — the Great General Staff.

Yet, if their action was deliberate, fear was the background of their thought, not merely militaristic ambition. Fear, among the Austrian General Staff, of the doubling of the Serbian army in consequence of Serbia's gain of territory in the Balkan war. Fear, among the German General Staff, of the Russian army's unexpectedly rapid recovery from its 1905 sickness under the ministrations of Sukhomlinov. Like a hard-pressed hero of the towpath, Moltke now pushed Austria into war so that he could jump in to her rescue, and then be sure of her help in return.

The German ultimatum to France demanded to know whether France would remain neutral "in a Russo-German war," gave her eighteen hours for a reply, and added the menace, "Mobilization will inevitably mean war." In case she offered to remain neutral, the German ambassador was instructed to make the impossible demand that France must hand over the fortresses of Verdun and Toul as a pledge. For Moltke's plans were made for a two-front war, and his aim would be upset if only one target appeared! Could military folly go further?

The German ambassador called for his answer on August 1, and was simply told that France "would act as her interests required." That afternoon the French mobilization was ordered, but in Republican France the civil government was still superior to the General Staff, and since July 30 the frontier forces had been withdrawn to a line ten kilometres inside the frontier as a pacific gesture and a safeguard against the danger that a frontier skirmish might provide an excuse for war. If a military handicap, the political wisdom of this withdrawal was seen in the fact that German patrols crossed the actual frontier on the thirtieth and again, by German official admission, on the thirty-first. Thus when, on August 3, Germany declared war on France, she could only allege the one concrete excuse that a French aviator had "thrown bombs on the railway near Karlsruhe and Nuremberg" — a rumor already contradicted in Germany before the declaration was delivered.

Why was the actual declaration delayed two days in delivery? First, because of the fresh suggestion from Grey that, so long as there was any chance of agreement between Russia and Austria, Germany and France should refrain from any attack. The suggestion was vaguely worded, and Lichnowsky, in his eager desire for peace, enlarged it in telegraphing to Berlin that "this would appear to mean that, in case we did not attack France, England would remain neutral and would guarantee France's neutrality." The Kaiser and his Chancellor clutched at the straw. The former said to Moltke, "We march, then, with all our forces, only toward the East." Moltke, as his memoirs relate, replied "that this was impossible. The advance of armies formed of millions of men . . . was the result of years of painstaking work. Once planned, it could not possibly be changed." The Kaiser bitterly retorted, "Your uncle would have given me a different reply." Moltke gained his way as regards the continued concentration against France, but a twenty-four-hour brake was ordered to be put on the actual crossing of the frontier of France and Luxembourg. Moltke pathetically records, "It was a great shock to me, as though something had struck at my heart." However, his heart attack was soon relieved, for late that evening further telegrams from London showed that Britain was not promising neutrality. The brake was released. And, if it had caused some check on Moltke's arrangements, some of his advanced troops had actually entered Luxembourg that day in advance of time-table!

Nevertheless the British Cabinet was still wavering. A majority of its members were so anxious for peace and uncertain of the public attitude that they had failed to give a clear warning which might have strengthened Bethmann-Hollweg in his feeble efforts to withstand his own war party. Now it was too late and the military machine was in control. Nothing could have averted war after July 31. Thus the British Cabinet's continued uncertainty, however natural and creditable, merely increased the anxiety of France, fearful of desertion.

Germany came to the rescue. Her long-prepared ultimatum to Belgium, demanding a free passage for her troops as required by her still-longer-prepared war plan, was delivered on the evening of August 2. The Belgian Government sturdily refused to allow its neutrality to be violated. On the morning of August 4, the German troops began their invasion. The threat, even before the act was known, was decisive in hardening British opinion to the point of intervention, even though that intervention was already inevitable, as the German Staff had correctly calculated. An ultimatum was delivered that Germany should respect Belgian neutrality, and was received by Bethmann-Hollweg with the pitiful complaint that Britain was going to war "just for a scrap of paper." At 11 P.M. — by German time — the ultimatum expired. Britain also was in the war — and Italy was out of it, having already decided for neutrality on July 31.

Thus in the final act, as in the earlier acts, "technical military arguments" were decisive. The German army must go through Belgium, even though with the certainty that Britain would thereby be drawn in against Germany. Military technique — how competent in peace to gain war; how impotent in war to gain victory, so it was soon to prove!

II

THE OPPOSING FORCES AND PLANS

THE nations entered upon the conflict with the conventional outlook and system of the eighteenth century merely modified by the events of the nineteenth century. Politically, they conceived it to be a struggle between rival coalitions based on the traditional system of diplomatic alliances, and militarily a contest between professional armies — swollen, it is true, by the Continental system of conscription, yet essentially fought out by soldiers while the mass of the people watched, from seats in the amphitheatre, the efforts of their champions. The Germans had a glimpse of the truth, but — one or two prophetic minds apart — the "Nation in Arms" theory, evolved by them during the nineteenth century, visualized the nation as a reservoir to pour its reënforcements into the army, rather than as a mighty river in which are merged many tributary forces of which the army is but one. Their conception was the "Nation in Arms," hardly the "Nation at War." Even to-day this fundamental truth has yet to be grasped in its entirety and its full implications understood. Progressively throughout the years 1914-1918 the warring nations enlisted the research of the scientist, the inventive power and technical skill of the engineer, the manual labor of industry, and the pen of the propagandist. For long this fusion of many forces tended to a chaotic maelstrom of forces; the old order had broken down, the new had not yet evolved. Only gradually did a working coöperation emerge, and it is a moot point whether even in the last phase coöperation of forces had attained to the higher level of coördination — direction by unity of diversity.

The German army of 1914 was born in the Napoleonic Wars, nursed in infancy by Gneisenau and Scharnhorst, and guided in adolescence by the elder Moltke and Roon. It reached maturity in the War of 1870, when it emerged triumphantly from a trial against the ill-equipped and badly led long-service army of France. Every physically able citizen was liable to service; the State took the number it desired, trained them to arms for a short period of full-time service, and then returned them to civil life. The feature, as also the object, of the system was the production of a huge reserve by which to expand the active army in war. A man served two or three years full-time, according to his branch of the service, followed by five or four years in the regular reserves. He then served in the Landwehr for twelve years, and finally passed into the Landsturm from the age of thirty-nine till forty-five. Further, an Ersatz reserve was formed of those who were not called on for service with the colors.

In this organization and in the thoroughness of the training lay the secret of the first great surprise of the war, one which almost proved decisive. For instead of regarding their reservists as troops of doubtful quality, fit only for an auxiliary rôle or garrison duty, the Germans during mobilization were able to duplicate almost every first-line army corps with a reserve corps — and had the courage, justified by events, to use them in the opening clash. This surprise upset the French calculations and thereby dislocated their entire plan of campaign.

The Germans have been reproached for many miscalculations; less than justice has been done to the correctness of many of their intuitions. They alone realized what is to-day an axiom — that, given a highly trained *cadre* of leaders, a military machine can be rapidly manufactured from short-time levies, like molten liquid poured into a mould. The German mould was a long-service body of officers and N. C. O.'s who in their standard of technical knowledge and skill had no equal on the Continent. But, if the machine was manufactured by training, it gained solidity from another process. The psychological element plays an even greater part in a "national" than in a professional army. *Esprit de corps* is not enough; the stimulus of a great moral impulse to action is necessary, a deep-rooted belief in the policy for which citizens are called on to fight. The leaders of Germany had worked for generations to inspire their people with a patriotic conviction of the grandeur of their country's destiny. And if their opponents went forth to battle in 1914 with as intense a belief in their country's cause, this flaming patriotism had not the time to consolidate such a disciplined combination as years of steady heat had produced in Germany. The German people had an intimacy with and a pride in their army, notwithstanding the severity of its discipline, that was unknown elsewhere.

This unique instrument was handled by a general staff which, by rigor of selection and training, was unmatched for professional knowledge and skill, if subject to the mental "grooves" which characterize all professions. Executive skill is the fruit of practice; and constant practice, or repetition, tends inevitably to deaden originality and elasticity of mind. In a professional body, also, promotion by seniority is a rule difficult to avoid. The Germans, it is true, tended towards a system of staff control which in practice usually left the real power in the hands of youthful general staff officers. As war memoirs and documents reveal, the chiefs of staff of the various armies and corps often took momentous decisions with hardly a pretense of consulting their commanders. But such a system had grave objections, and from it came the grit in the wheels which not infrequently marred the otherwise well-oiled working of the German war-machine.

Tactically the Germans began with two important material advantages. They alone had gauged the potentialities of the heavy howitzer, and had provided adequate numbers of this weapon. And if no army had fully realized that machine-guns were "concentrated essence of infantry," or fully developed this preponderant source of fire-power, the Germans had studied it more than other armies, and were able to exploit its inherent power of dominating a battlefield sooner than other armies. In this anticipation of the value of heavy artillery and machine-guns the German General Staff seems to have been largely influenced by the acute diagnosis of Captain Hoffmann, its youthful attaché with the Japanese army in Manchuria. Strategically, also, the Germans had brought the study and development of railway communications to a higher pitch than any of their rivals.

The Austro-Hungarian army, if patterned on the German model, was a vastly inferior instrument. Not only had it a tradition of defeat rather than of victory, but its racial mixture prevented the moral homogeneity that distinguished its ally. This being so, the replacement of the old professional army by one based on universal service lowered rather than raised its standard of effectiveness. The troops within the borders of the empire were often racially akin to those beyond, and this compelled Austria to a politically instead of a militarily based distribution of forces, so that kinsmen should not fight each other. And her human handicap was increased by a geographical one — namely, the vast extent of frontier to be defended.

Nor were her leaders, with rare exceptions, the professional equals of the Germans. Moreover, if common action was better understood than among the Entente Powers, Austria did not accept German direction gladly.

Yet despite all its evident weaknesses the loosely knit conglomeration of races withstood the shock and strain of war for four years, in a way that surprised and dismayed her opponents. The explanation is that the complex racial fabric was woven on a stout Germanic and Magyar framework.

From the Central we turn to the Entente Powers. France possessed but 60 per cent of the potential man-power of Germany (5,940,000 against 9,750,000), and this debit balance had forced her to call on the services of practically every ablebodied male. A man was called up at twenty, did three years' full-time service, then eleven in the reserve, and finally two periods of seven years each in the Territorial Army and Territorial Reserve. This system gave France an initial war strength of some 4,000,000 men, equal to her German rival, but, in contrast, she placed little reliance on the fighting value of reservists. The French Command counted only on the semi-professional troops of the first line, about 1,500,000 men, for the short and decisive campaign which they expected and prepared for. Moreover, they assumed a similar attitude on the part of their enemy — with dire result.   But, this initial surprise apart, a more profound handicap was the lesser capacity of France for expansion, in case of a long war, due to her smaller population — under 40,000,000 compared with Germany's 65,000,000. Colonel Mangin, later to become famous, had advocated tapping the resources in Africa, the raising of a huge native army, but the Government had considered the dangers to outweigh the advantages of such a policy, and war experience was to show that it had military as well as political risks.

The French General Staff, if less technically perfect than that of Germany, had produced some of the ablest military thinkers in Europe, and its level of intelligence could well bear comparison.   But the French military intelligence tended to lose in originality and elasticity what it gained in logic. In the years preceding the war, too, a sharp division of thought had arisen which did not make for combined action.   Worse still, the new French philosophy of war, by its preoccupation with the moral element, had become more and more separated from the inseparable material factors.   Abundance of will cannot compensate a definite inferiority of weapons, and the second factor, once realized, inevitably reacts on the first.   In material, the French had one great asset in their quick-firing 75mm. field gun, the best in the world, but its very value had led them to undue confidence in a war of movement and a consequent neglect of equipment and training for the type of warfare which came to pass.

Russia's assets were in the physical sphere, her defects in the mental and moral.   If her initial strength was no greater than that of Germany, her man-power resources were immense.   Moreover the courage and endurance of her troops were famous.   But corruption and incompetence permeated her leadership, her rank and file lacked the intelligence and initiative for scientific warfare, — they formed an instrument of great solidity but little flexibility, — while her manufacturing resources for equipment and munitions were far below those of the great industrial powers.   This handicap was made worse by her geographical situation, for she was cut off from her allies by ice- or enemy-bound seas, and she had to cover immense land frontiers. Another radical defect was the poverty of her rail communications, which were the more essential as she relied for success on bringing into play the weight of her numbers. In the moral sphere Russia's condition was less clear. Her internal troubles were notorious and must be a brake on her efforts unless the cause was such as to make a crusade-like appeal to her primitive and incoherent masses.

Between the military systems of Germany, Austria, France, and Russia there was a close relation; the differences were of detail rather than fundamental; and this similarity threw into greater contrast the system of the other great European power — Britain. Throughout modern times she had been essentially a sea-power, intervening on land through a traditional policy of diplomatic and financial support to allies whose military efforts she reënforced with a leaven from her own professional army. This regular army was primarily maintained for the protection and control of the overseas dependencies — India in particular — and had always been kept down to the minimum strength for this purpose. The reason for the curious contrast between Britain's determination to maintain a supreme navy and her consistent neglect, indeed starvation, of the army lay partly in her insular position, which caused her to regard the sea as her essential life-line and main defense, and partly in a constitutional distrust of the army, an illogical prejudice, which had its almost forgotten source in the military government of Cromwell. Small as to size, it enjoyed a practical and varied experience of war without parallel among the Continental armies. Compared with them, its professional handicap was that the leaders, however skilled in handling small columns in colonial expeditions, had never directed large formations in *la grande guerre*.

But the bitter lessons of the South African War had brought much profit, and exerted an influence which to some extent counteracted that inelasticity of mind and ritualism of method which have increased with the increasing professionalization of armies. For the progress in organization in the years before

1914 the British army owed much to Lord Haldane, and to
him also was due the creation of a second line of partially
trained citizens — the Territorial Force. Lord Roberts had
pleaded for compulsory military training, but the voluntary
principle was too deeply embedded in the national mind for
this course to be adopted, and Haldane wisely sought to develop
Britain's military effectiveness within the bounds set by
traditional policy. As a result, 1914 found England with an
Expeditionary Force of some 160,000 men, the most highly
trained striking force of any country — a rapier among scythes.
To maintain this at strength the old militia had been turned
into a special reserve for drafting. Behind this first line stood
the Territorial Force, which, if only enlisted for home defense,
had a permanent fighting organization, unlike the amorphous
volunteer force which it superseded. The British army had
no outstanding asset in war armament, but it had developed
a standard of rifle-shooting unique among the world's armies.

The reforms by which the army had been brought into
line with Continental models had one defect, accentuated by
the close relations established between the British and French
General Staffs since the Entente. It induced a "Continental"
habit of thought among the General Staff, and predisposed
them to the rôle, for which their slender strength was unsuited,
of fighting alongside an Allied army. This obscured the
British army's traditional employment in amphibious operations through which the mobility given by command of the
sea could be exploited. A small but highly trained force
striking "out of the blue" at a vital spot can produce a strategical effect out of all proportion to its slight numbers.

The last argument brings us to a comparison of the naval
situation, which turned on the balance between the fleets of
Britain and Germany. Britain's sea supremacy, for long
unquestioned, had in recent years been challenged by a Germany which had deduced that a powerful fleet was the key to
that colonial empire which she desired as an outlet for her
commerce and increasing population. This ambition was
fostered, as its instrument was created, by the dangerous
genius of Admiral von Tirpitz. To the spur of naval com-

petition the British people eventually responded, determined at any cost to maintain their "two-power" standard. If this reaction was instinctive rather than reasoned, its subconscious wisdom had a better foundation than the catchwords with which it was justified, or even than the need of defense against invasion. The industrial development of the British Isles had left them dependent on overseas supplies for food, and on the secure flow of sea-borne imports and exports for industrial existence. For the navy itself this competition was a refining agency, leading to a concentration on essentials. Gunnery was developed, and less value attached to polished brasswork. Warship design and armament were transformed; the "Dreadnought" ushered in the new era of the all-big-gun battleship. By 1914 Britain had twenty-nine such capital ships and thirteen building, to the eighteen built and nine building of Germany. Further, Britain's naval strength had been soundly distributed, the main concentration being in the North Sea.

More open to criticism, in view of the forecasts of several naval authorities, was her comparative neglect of the potential menace of the submarine. Here German opinion was shown rather by the number building than by those already in commission. It is to Germany's credit that though lacking a sea tradition, her fleet an artificial rather than a natural product, the technical skill of the German navy made it a formidable rival to the British ship for ship, and perhaps its superior in scientific gunnery.

But in the first stage of the struggle the balance of the naval forces was to affect the issue far less than the balance on land. For a fleet suffers one inherent limitation — it is tied to the sea, and hence cannot strike direct at the hostile nation. The fundamental purpose of a navy is therefore to protect a nation's sea communications and sever those of the enemy; although victory in battle may be a necessary prelude, blockade is its ultimate purpose. And as blockade is a weapon slow to take effect, its influence could only be decisive if the armies failed to secure the speedy decision on land upon which all counted.

In this idea of a short war lay also the reason for the comparative disregard of economic forces. Few believed that a modern nation could endure for many months the strain of a large-scale conflict. The supply of food and of funds, the supply and manufacture of munitions, these were problems that had been studied only on brief estimates. Of the belligerents all could feed themselves save Britain and Germany, and Germany's deficit of home-grown supplies could only be serious in the event of a struggle of years. But Britain would starve in three months if her outside supplies were cut off.

In munitions and other war material Britain's industrial power was greatest of all, though conversion to war production was a necessary preliminary, and all, again, depended on the security of her sea communications. France was weak, and Russia weaker still, but the former, unlike the latter, could count on outside supplies so long as Britain held the seas. As Britain was the industrial pivot of the one alliance, so was Germany of the other. A great manufacturing nation, she had also a wealth of raw material, especially since the annexation of the Lorraine iron fields after the 1870 war. But the stoppage of outside supplies must be a handicap in a long war, increasing with its duration, and serious from the outset in such tropical products as rubber. Moreover, Germany's main coal and iron fields lay dangerously close to her frontier, in Silesia on the east and in Westphalia and Lorraine on the west. Thus for the Central Alliance a quick decision and an offensive war were more essential than for the Entente.

Similarly, financial resources had been calculated on a short-war basis, and all the Continental Powers relied mainly on large gold reserves accumulated specially for war purposes. Britain alone had no such war chest, but she was to prove that the strength of her banking system and the wealth distributed among a great commercial people furnished the "sinews of war" in a way that few pre-war economists had realized.

If the economic forces were neglected in the war calculations of the powers, the psychological forces were an unexplored region, except in their purely military aspect. And even here little study had been devoted to the moral element compared with the physical element. Ardant du Picq, a soldier-philosopher who fell in the 1870 war, had stripped battle of its aura of heroic fictions, portraying the reaction of normal men in the presence of danger. Several German critics had described from experience the reality of battle morale as shown in 1870, and had deduced how tactics should be based on the ever-present and balancing elements of fear and courage. At the close of the century a French military thinker, Colonel Foch, had demonstrated how great was the influence of the moral element in the higher sphere of command, although his teaching was concerned rather with fortifying the will of the commander than with unhinging the will of the opponent. But only the surface of the subject had been penetrated. Its civil aspects were untouched, and in the opening weeks of the conflict the general misunderstanding of national psychology was to be shown in the muzzling of the press — in Britain due mainly to Kitchener, followed by the equally stupid practice of issuing *communiqués* which so veiled the truth that public opinion became distrustful of all official news and rumor was loosed on its infinitely more damaging course. The true value of wisely calculated publicity and the true application of the propaganda weapon were only to be learned after many blunders.

The Opposing Plans. In this survey the German plan justly takes priority, for not only was it the mainspring which set in motion the hands of the war clock in 1914, but it may even be said to have governed the course of the war thereafter. It is true that from the autumn of 1914 onwards this course outwardly seemed to be of the nature of a stupendous "siege" of the Central Powers, an idea incompatible with the terms we have used. But the conception of the Germanic Alliance as a besieged party, although true of the economic sphere, suggests a loss of initiative which their strategy contradicts. Although the initial German plan miscarried, even in its failure it dictated the general trend of operations thereafter. Tactically, most of the fighting resembled siege operations, but the actual strategy on land long erred rather by its disregard of these tactical conditions than by its conformity with them.

The Germans were faced with the problem that the combined forces of themselves and Austria were decidedly inferior to those of France and Russia. To offset this adverse balance, however, they had a central position and the anticipation that Russia's mobilization would be too slow to allow her to exert serious pressure in the opening weeks. While this assumption might suggest a decisive blow at Russia before she was ready, it was equally probable that she would concentrate her main forces too far back for such a German blow to reach — and the experience of Napoleon was not an example to encourage an advance deep into the interior of Russia, with its vast distances and poor communications. The plan long since adopted by Germany was, therefore, to deliver a rapid offensive against France while holding the Russian advanced forces at bay, and later, when France was crushed, to deal with the Russian army. But this plan, in turn, was complicated by the great natural and artificial barriers which the French frontier offered to an invader. It was narrow, only some 150 miles across, and so afforded little room to manœuvre or even to deploy the masses that Germany planned to launch against her foe. At the southeastern end it abutted on Switzerland, and after a short stretch of flat country known as the Gap of Belfort the frontier ran for 70 miles along the Vosges Mountains. Behind and prolonging this natural rampart ran an almost continuous fortress system, based on Epinal, Toul, Verdun, and twenty miles beyond the last-named lay not only the frontiers of Luxembourg and Belgium, but the difficult Ardennes country. Apart from the strongly defended avenues of advance by Belfort and Verdun, the only feasible gap in this barrier was the Trouée de Charmes between Epinal and Toul, left open originally as a strategic trap in which the Germans could be first caught and then crushed by a French counter-stroke.

Faced with such a mental and physical blank wall, the logical military course was to go round it — by a wide manœuvre through Belgium. Graf Schlieffen, Chief of the German General Staff from 1891 to 1906, conceived and developed the plan by which the French armies were to be enveloped and a rapid decision gained, and as finally formulated it came into force in 1905. To attain its object Schlieffen's plan concentrated the mass of the German forces on the right wing for a gigantic wheel and designedly took risks by reducing the left wing, facing the French frontier, to the slenderest possible size. The swinging mass, pivoting on the fortified area Metz-Thionville, was to consist of fifty-three divisions, backed up as rapidly as possible by Landwehr and Ersatz formations, while the secondary army on the left wing comprised only eight divisions. Its very weakness promised to aid the main blow in a further way, for if a French offensive pressed the left wing back towards the Rhine, the attack through Belgium on the French flank would be all the more difficult to parry. It would be like a revolving door — if a man pressed heavily on one side the other side would swing round and strike him in the back. Here lay the real subtlety of the plan, not in the mere geographical detour.

The German enveloping mass was to sweep round through Belgium and northern France, and, continuing to traverse a vast arc, would wheel gradually east. With its extreme right passing south of Paris and crossing the Seine near Rouen, it would then press the French back towards the Moselle, where they would be hammered in rear on the anvil formed by the Lorraine fortresses and the Swiss frontier.

Schlieffen's plan allowed ten divisions to hold the Russians in check while the French were being crushed. It is a testimony to the vision of this remarkable man that he counted on the intervention of Britain, and allowed for an expeditionary force of 100,000 "operating in conjunction with the French." To him also was due the scheme for using the Landwehr and Ersatz troops in active operations and fusing the resources of the nation into the army. His dying words are reported to have been: "It must come to a fight. Only make the right wing strong."

Unhappily for Germany, if happily for the world, the younger Moltke, who succeeded him, lacked his moral courage and grasp of strategy. Moltke retained Schlieffen's plan, but he whittled away the essential idea. Of the nine new divisions which became available between 1905 and 1914, Moltke allotted eight to the left wing and only one to the right. True, he added another from the Russian front, but this trivial increase was purchased at a heavy price, for the Russian army of 1914 was a more formidable menace than when Schlieffen's plan came into force. In the outcome two army corps were taken from the French theatre at the crisis of the August campaign, in order to reënforce the eastern front. Schlieffen's death-bed entreaty was lost on his successor.

Moltke also made a change of great political significance in the plan. Schlieffen had intended that the right wing should deploy along not only the Belgian but also the Dutch frontier, as far north as Crefeld. By crossing the strip of Dutch territory known as the "Maastricht Appendix" it would be able to turn the flank of the Liége forts, which barred the way through the narrow Belgian gateway north of the Ardennes. He hoped that German diplomacy might secure permission for this passage through Holland, but he did not wish to violate the territory of either Belgium or Holland if he could avoid the moral reproach. For it was his calculation that the undisguised deployment there of part of his force would so alarm the French as to induce them to cross the southern frontier of Belgium and occupy the natural defensive position in the Meuse Valley, south of Namur. Thereby they would provide a pretext for his own advance into neutral territory. Even should this subtle trap fail, Schlieffen calculated that he would be able to capture Liége in time to avoid any check on his main advance. And he was willing to cut his margin of time so close as to afford German statecraft the fullest chance to escape the charge of rape.

Such vision and boldness were beyond Moltke's capacity, and he decided that Liége must be taken by a *coup de main* immediately after the outbreak of war. Thus for a fancied addition to military security he deliberately invited the condemnation of neutrals, provoked Belgium to resistance, and drew the weight of Britain into the scales against his own forces. Moltke's method of "drawing" the enemy was certainly the antithesis of Schlieffen's. And it is a glaring example of the dangers, even the military dangers, which may ensue if strategy is allowed to dominate policy.

If the fault of the final German plan was a lack of courage, that of the French plan was due to an excess. In their case, also, a miasma of confused thought seemed to creep over the leadership in the years just before the war. Since the disasters of 1870 the French Command had planned an initial defensive, based on the frontier fortresses, followed by a decisive counter-stroke. To this end the great fortress system had been created and gaps like the Trouée de Charmes left to "canalize" the invasion ready for the counter. But in the decade before 1914 a new school of thought had risen, who argued that the offensive was more in tune with French character and tradition, that the possession of the "75" — a field gun unique in mobility and rapidity of fire — made it tactically possible, and that the alliance with Russia and Britain made it strategically possible. Forgetful of the lessons of 1870, they imagined that *élan* was proof against bullets. Napoleon's much quoted saying that "the moral is to the physical as three to one" has much to answer for; it has led soldiers to think that a division exists between the two, whereas each is dependent on the other. Weapons without courage are ineffective, but so also are the bravest troops without sufficient weapons to protect them and their morale. Courage soon oozes when soldiers lose confidence in their weapons.

The outcome was disastrous. The new school, who found their prophet in Colonel de Grandmaison, found in General Joffre, appointed Chief of the General Staff in 1912, a lever for their designs. Under the cloak of his authority, the advocates of the *offensive à outrance* gained control of the French military machine, and, throwing aside the old doctrine, formulated the now famous, or notorious, Plan XVII. It was based on a negation of historical experience, indeed of common sense, and on a double miscalculation — of force and place, the latter more serious than the former. Accepting the possibility that the Germans might employ their reserve formations at the outset, the strength of the German army in the west was estimated at a possible maximum of sixty-eight infantry divisions. The Germans actually deployed the equivalent of eighty-three and a half, counting Landwehr and Ersatz troops. But French opinion was, and continued to be, doubtful of this contingency, so much so that during the crucial days when the rival armies were concentrating and moving forward the French Intelligence counted only the active divisions in its estimates of the enemy strength — a miscalculation by half! If the plan had been framed on a miscalculation less extreme, this recognition does not condone but rather increases its fundamental falsity, for history affords no vestige of justification for a plan by which a frontal offensive was to be launched with mere equality of force against an enemy who would have the support of his fortified frontier zone, while the attackers forswore any advantage from their own.

The second miscalculation — of place — was that although the possibility of a German move through Belgium was recognized, the wideness of its sweep was utterly misjudged. The Germans were expected complaisantly to take the difficult route through the Ardennes in order that the French might conveniently smite their communications! Based on the idea of an immediate and general offensive, the plan ordained a thrust by the First and Second Armies towards the Saar into Lorraine. On their left were the Third Army opposite Metz and the Fifth Army facing the Ardennes, which were either to take up the offensive between Metz and Thionville, or, if the Germans came through Luxembourg and Belgium, to strike northeast at their flank. The Fourth Army was held in strategic reserve near the centre and two groups of reserve divisions were disposed in rear of either flank — relegation to such a passive rôle expressing French opinion on the capacity of reserve formations.

Britain's contingent share in this plan was settled less by calculation than by the "Europeanization" of her military organization during the previous decade. This Continental influence drew her insensibly into a tacit acceptance of the rôle of acting as an appendix to the French left wing, and away from her historic exploitation of the mobility given by sea-power. At the council of war after the outbreak, Lord Roberts, summoned from retirement, suggested the dispatch of the expeditionary force to Belgium — where it would have stiffened the Belgian resistance and threatened the flank of the wheeling German mass. But the plan did not provide for variations, and in any case the British General Staff, through General Wilson, had virtually pledged themselves to act in direct coöperation with the French. When the General Staffs of the two countries conducted their informal negotiations between 1905 and 1914, they were paving the way for a reversal of England's centuries-old policy, for a war effort such as no Englishman had ever conceived.

Lord Kitchener, who had just been made War Minister in the emergency, had a remarkably accurate intuition of the German plan and tried to avert the danger by advocating that the expeditionary force should concentrate near Amiens, where it would be less exposed. But the vehement support given by the Commander, Sir John French, and his staff to the French plan induced Kitchener to give way. Later he lamented his consent as a mistaken weakness. Kitchener, however, gave French instructions which, designed to reduce the risks, were in the issue to complicate and even to increase them. For while French's assigned purpose was "to support, and coöperate with, the French army," it was qualified by the somewhat contradictory statement "that the gravest consideration will devolve upon you as to participation . . . where your force may be unduly exposed. . . ." Further, "you will in no case come in any sense under the orders of any Allied General."

On the Russian front, the plans of campaign were more fluid, less elaborately worked out and formulated, although they were to be as kaleidoscopic in their changes of fortune as in the western theatre. The calculable condition was geographical; the main incalculable, Russia's rate of concentration. Russian Poland was a vast tongue of country projecting from Russia proper, and flanked on three sides by German or Austrian territory. On its northern flank lay East Prussia with the Baltic Sea beyond. On its southern flank lay the Austrian province of Galicia with the Carpathian Mountains to the south, guarding the approach to the plain of Hungary. On the west lay Silesia. As the Germanic border provinces were provided with a network of strategic railways, while Poland, as well as Russia itself, had only a sparse system of communications, the Germanic Alliance enjoyed a great advantage, in power of concentration, for countering a Russian advance. But if its armies took the offensive, the further they progressed into Poland or Russia proper the more would they lose this advantage. Hence their most profitable strategy was to lure the Russians into a position favorable for a counter-stroke rather than to inaugurate an offensive themselves. The one drawback was that such a Punic strategy gave the Russians time to concentrate and set in motion their cumbrous and rusty machine.

From this arose an initial cleavage between German and Austrian opinion. Both agreed that the problem was to hold the Russians in check during the six weeks which must elapse before the Germans should have crushed France, and so could switch their forces eastwards to join the Austrians in a decisive blow against the Russians. The difference of opinion turned on the method. The Germans, intent on a decision against France, wished to leave a minimum force in the East, and only a political dislike of exposing national territory to invasion prevented them from evacuating East Prussia and standing on the Vistula line. But the Austrians, under the influence of Conrad von Hötzendorf, Chief of their General Staff, were anxious to throw the Russian machine out of gear by an immediate offensive, and, as this promised to keep the Russians fully occupied while the campaign in France was being decided, Moltke fell in with this strategy. Conrad's plan was that of an offensive northeastwards into Poland by two armies, protected by two more on their right, further east. Complementary to it, as originally designed, the Germans in East Prussia were to strike southeast, the two forces converging to cut off the Russian advanced forces in the Polish "tongue." But Conrad failed to induce Moltke to provide sufficient German troops for this offensive thrust.

On the opposing side, also, the desires of one Ally virtually affected the strategy of the other. The Russian Command, both for military and for racial motives, wished to concentrate first against Austria, while the latter was unsupported, and leave Germany alone until later, when the full strength of the Russian army would be mobilized. But the French, anxious to relieve the German pressure against themselves, urged the Russians to deliver a simultaneous attack against Germany, and persuaded the Russians to consent to an extra offensive for which they were ready neither in numbers nor in organization. On the southwestern front two pairs of two armies each were to converge on the Austrian forces in Galicia; on the northwestern front two armies were to converge on the German forces in East Prussia. Russia, whose proverbial slowness and crude organization dictated a cautious strategy, was about to break with tradition and launch out on a gamble that only an army of high mobility and organization could have hoped to bring off.

III

1914 — THE CLINCH

THE German invasion of France was designed as a methodical sweep, in which unexpected checks should not upset the time-table. The railway system in Germany had been developed under military guidance and supervision — so strict that not even a narrow-gauge line or road rail could be laid without the approval of the Chief of the General Staff. As a result the number of double lines running to the western frontier had been increased from nine to thirteen between 1870 and 1914. On August 6 the great deployment began; 550 trains a day crossed the Rhine bridges, and altogether 3,120,000 men were carried to the front in eleven thousand trains. Over the Hohenzollern bridge at Cologne a train passed about every ten minutes during the first fortnight of war. This vast railway movement was a masterpiece of organization, but when the deployment, completed on August 17, merged into the forward march, the friction of war soon revealed weaknesses in the German military machine and its control.

To meet the case of Belgian resistance the German plan, as revised by Moltke, provided an instantly available detachment, under General von Emmich, to clear a passage through the Meuse gateway into the Belgian plain north of the Ardennes, ready for the ordered advance of the main armies concentrating behind the German frontier. The ring fortress of Liége commanded this channel of advance, but, after an initial check on August 5, a German brigade penetrated between the forts and occupied the town. The interest of this feat is that it was due to the initiative of an attached staff officer, Ludendorff, whose name ere long was to be world-famous. The forts themselves offered a stubborn resistance and forced the Germans to await the arrival of their heavy howitzers, whose destructive power was to be the first tactical surprise of the World War.

The very success of the Belgians' early resistance cloaked the weight of the main German columns and misled the Allies' Intelligence. The Belgian field army lay behind the Gette covering Brussels, and even before the Liége forts fell the advanced guards of the German First and Second Armies were pressing against this line. The Belgians, deprived of support owing to the mistaken French plan and British conformity with it, decided to preserve their army by falling back on the entrenched camp of Antwerp — where its location would at least make it a latent menace to the German communications. The Germans, their immediate passage now clear, entered Brussels on August 20, and on the same day appeared before Namur, the last fortress barring the Meuse route into France. It must be noted that, despite the Belgian resistance, the German advance was slightly ahead of its time-table. But if the Belgian withdrawal to a flank momentarily expedited, it ultimately hindered the German progress, far more than any sacrifice in battle could have done.

Meanwhile, away on the other flank, the French offensive had opened on August 7 with the advance of a detached army corps into Upper Alsace, a move intended partly as a military distraction and partly for its political effect. Its actual goal was the destruction of the German station at Basel and the Rhine bridges below. Soon brought to a halt, it was renewed on the nineteenth by a larger force under General Pau, which actually reached the Rhine. But the pressure of disasters elsewhere compelled the abandonment of the enterprise and the dissolution of the force — its units being dispatched westward as reënforcements. Meantime the main thrust into Lorraine by the French First (Dubail) and Second (de Castelnau) Armies, totaling nineteen divisions, had begun on August 14 and been shattered in the battle of Morhange-Sarrebourg, August 20, where the French discovered that the material could subdue the moral, and that in their enthusiasm for the offensive they had blinded themselves to the defensive power of modern weapons, a condition which was to throw out of balance the whole mechanism of orthodox warfare. Yet it is fair to add that this abortive French offensive had an indirect effect on the German plan, although this would hardly have occurred if a Schlieffen or a Ludendorff had been in charge at German Headquarters instead of the vacillating opportunist Moltke.

The fact that Moltke had almost doubled the strength of his left, compared with Schlieffen's plan, meant that it was unnecessarily strong for a yielding and "enticing" defensive such as Schlieffen had conceived, while lacking the superiority necessary for a crushing counter-offensive. But when the French attack in Lorraine developed, and Moltke appreciated that the French were leaving their fortified barrier behind, he was tempted momentarily to postpone the right-wing sweep, and instead seek a decision in Lorraine. This impulse led him to divert thither the six newly formed Ersatz divisions that should have been used to increase the weight of his right wing. He had hardly conceived this new plan before he abandoned it and, on August 16, reverted to Schlieffen's "swing-door" design.

But he also told his left-wing commanders somewhat ambiguously that they must detain as many French troops as possible, and when the Crown Prince Rupprecht of Bavaria argued that he could only do this by attacking, Moltke left the decision to him. We may suspect that Rupprecht was loth to forfeit the opportunity of glory by retiring while the German Crown Prince was advancing. But nothing could have been more foolishly ambiguous than the Supreme Command's attitude. For when Rupprecht refused to refrain unless given a clear order, Moltke's deputy, Stein, said on the telephone to Krafft von Delmensingen, Rupprecht's Chief of Staff, "No, we won't oblige you by forbidding an attack. You must take the responsibility. Make your own decision as your conscience tells you." Conscience seems a curious basis for strategy. And when Krafft retorted, "It is already made. We attack," Stein fatuously exclaimed, "Not really! Then strike, and God be with you."

Thus, instead of continuing to fall back and draw the French on, Rupprecht halted his Sixth Army on the seventeenth, ready to accept battle. Finding the French attack slow to develop, he planned to anticipate it by one of his own. He struck on August 20 in conjunction with the Seventh Army (Heeringen) on his left, but although the French were taken by surprise and rolled back from the line Morhange-Sarrebourg, the German counter-stroke had not the superiority of strength (the two armies now totaled twenty-five divisions) or of strategic position to make it decisive. Further, the attempt to envelop the French right flank by a movement through the Vosges was begun too late and failed. Thus the strategic result was merely to throw back the French on to a fortified barrier which both restored and augmented their power of resistance. And thereby they were enabled to dispatch troops to reënforce their western flank — a redistribution of strength which was to have far-reaching results in the decisive battle, on the Marne.

With similar disregard of superior authority, the German Crown Prince, commanding the pivotal Fifth Army between Metz and Thionville, attacked when he had been ordered to stand on the defensive. The lack of what Colonel Foch had termed "intellectual discipline" was to be a grave factor in Germany's failure, and for this the ambitions and jealousies of generals were to be largely responsible.

While this "seesaw" campaign in Lorraine was taking place, more decisive events were occurring to the northwest. The attack on Liége awakened Joffre to the reality of a German advance through Belgium, but not to the wideness of its sweep. And the sturdy resistance of Liége confirmed him in the opinion that the German right would pass south of it, between the Meuse and the Ardennes. Plan XVII had visualized such a move, and prepared a counter. Grasping once more at phantoms, the French Command embraced this idea so fervently that they transformed the counter into an imaginary *coup de grâce*. Their Third Army (Ruffey) and the reserve Fourth Army (de Langle de Cary) were to strike northeast through the Ardennes against the rear flank of the Germans advancing through Belgium, and thus dislocate their enveloping manœuvre. The left-wing (Fifth) Army, under Lanrezac, was moved further to the northwest into the angle formed by the

Sambre and Meuse between Givet and Charleroi. With the British Expeditionary Force coming up on its left, it was to deal with the enemy's forces north of the Meuse and to converge on the supposed German main forces in conjunction with the attack through the Ardennes. Here was a pretty picture — of the Allied pincers closing on the unconscious Germans! Curiously, the Germans had the same idea of a pincer-like manœuvre, with rôles reversed, and with better reason.

The fundamental flaw in the French plan was that the Germans had deployed twice as many troops as the French Intelligence estimated, and for a vaster enveloping movement. The French Third and Fourth Armies (twenty-three divisions), pushing blindly into the Ardennes against a German centre supposedly denuded of troops, blundered against the German Fourth and Fifth Armies (twenty divisions) in a fog on August 22, and were heavily thrown back in encounter-battles around Virton-Neufchâteau. The troops attacked blindly with the bayonet and were mown down by machine-guns. Fortunately the Germans were also too vague as to the situation to exploit their opportunity.

But to the northwest the French Fifth Army (thirteen divisions) and the British (four divisions) had, under Joffre's orders, put their heads almost into the German noose. The German masses of the First and Second Armies were closing on them from the north, and the Third Army from the east — a total of thirty divisions. Lanrezac alone had an inkling of the hidden menace. All along he had suspected the wideness of the German manœuvre, and it was through his insistence that his army had been permitted to move so far northwest. It was due to his caution in hesitating to advance across the Sambre, to the arrival of the British on his left unknown to the German Intelligence, and to the premature attack of the German Second Army, that the Allied forces fell back in time and escaped from the trap.

The Retreat to the Marne. The first four British divisions, after concentrating near Maubeuge, had moved up to Mons on August 22, ready to advance further into Belgium as part of the offensive of the Allied left wing. On arrival, however,

Sir John French heard that Lanrezac had been attacked on the twenty-first and deprived of the crossings of the Sambre. Although thus placed in an exposed forward position, he agreed to stand at Mons to cover Lanrezac's left. But next day, the twenty-third, Lanrezac had word of the imminent fall of Namur and of the appearance of the German Third Army (Hausen) on his exposed right flank near Dinant, on the Meuse. In consequence, he gave orders for a retreat that night. The British, after resisting the attacks of six German divisions during the day, fell back on the twenty-fourth in conformity with their Allies. Not a moment too soon in view of the fact that the rest of the German First Army was marching still further westward to envelop their open left flank.[1]

But if the British had begun to retreat later than their Allies, they continued faster and further. This less happy effect was mainly due to Sir John French's sudden revulsion of mind and emotion. He had gone forward almost too eager to fulfill the task given in Kitchener's instructions. He came back with his mind concentrated on the qualifying clause. And the change was due more to the French than to the Germans. The trouble began when Lanrezac, irritated by Joffre's blindness to the close-looming danger, vented on his newly arrived neighbor the indignation he could not show to his superior. This feeling was illustrated in the greeting which Lanrezac's Chief of Staff gave to Huguet, who came with French to visit Lanrezac: "At last you 're here; it 's not a moment too soon. If we are beaten we shall owe it all to you!" And when French, on being excitedly told that the Germans had reached the Meuse at

---

[1] Happily, the task of reducing Namur absorbed six German divisions and five hundred guns from August 20 to 25 — when these last forts succumbed. This detachment, added to that already left to stand guard over Antwerp, seriously weakened the German right wing during the critical days when it fell upon and sought to overwhelm the Allied left wing in the battles of Charleroi and Mons. The delay, apparently so slight, imposed by the obsolete and neglected defenses of Namur, contributed in turn to the resistance of the equally neglected French fortress of Maubeuge, which did not capitulate until September 7 and detained one and a half divisions from the battlefield of the Marne. Less happily, this detachment was set free just in time to reach the Chemin des Dames ridge north of the Aisne — filling part of the gap between Kluck and Bülow (see page 98) — a few hours before the British advanced guards came up on September 12.

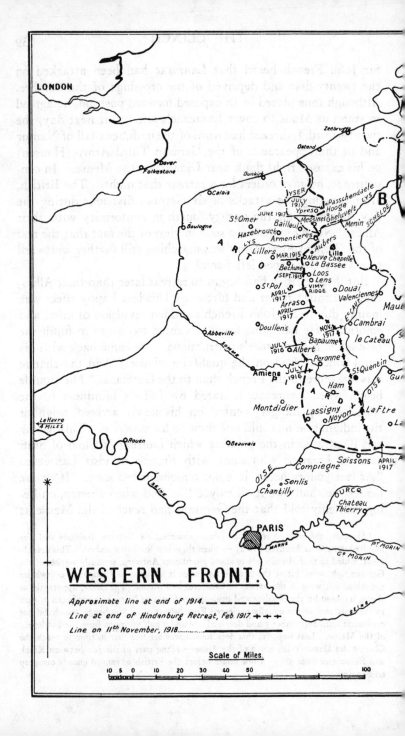

LONDON

Dover
Folkestone
Calais
Boulogne

Ostend
Dunkirk
Zeebrugge

St Omer
Hazebroucko
Lillers
Bethune
SEPT. 1915
St Pol
APRIL
1917
Arras
APRIL
1917
Doullens
Abbeville

YSER
JULY
1917
Ypres
JUNE 1917
Bailleul
Armentieres
MAR. 1915
Neuve Chapelle
La Bassee
Loos
Lens
VIMY
RIDGE

Passchendaele
Hooge
Messines Gheluvelt
Menin
Aubers
Lille

SCHELDE

LYS
LYS

B

A R T O

Douai
Valenciennes
ECAUTRENNES
Maus

Cambrai
le Cateau
S

NOV.
1917
Bapaume
JULY
1916
Albert
Peronne

St Quentin
Ham
Lassigny
Noyon
La Ftre
Gur

OISE
La

JULY
1916
C
A R D O

Amiens
Montdidier

LeHavre
4 MILES
Rouen
Beauvais

Soissons APRIL
1917
Compiegne
Senlis
Chantilly
OISE

OURCQ
Chateau
Thierry

PT. MORIN

SEINE

PARIS

MARNE

Gd MORIN

SEINE

WESTERN FRONT.

Approximate line at end of 1914. _____

Line at end of Hindenburg Retreat, Feb. 1917. + + +

Line on 11th November, 1918. ....

Scale of Miles.

10 5 0   10   20   30   40   50   100

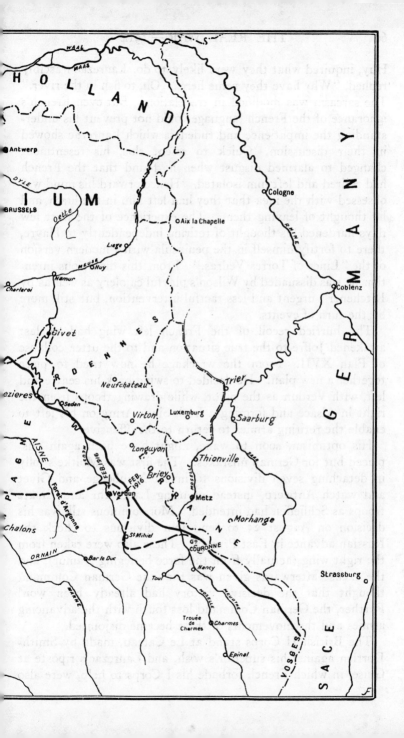

Huy, inquired what they were likely to do, Lanrezac irascibly replied, "Why have they come here? Oh, to fish in the river." The sarcasm was modified in translation. But even French's ignorance of the French language could not prevent his understanding the impatience and rudeness which Lanrezac showed in their discussion. Quick to resent this, his resentment changed to alarmed disgust when he found that the French had retired and left him isolated. Henceforward his mind was obsessed with the idea that they had left him in the lurch, and he thought of leaving them. The experience of the next few days hardened his thought of retiring independently to Havre, there to fortify himself in the peninsula with a modern version of the "Lines of Torres Vedras." From this disastrous intention he was dissuaded by Wilson's playful cajolery as well as by Kitchener's urgent and less tactful intervention, but still more by the turn of events.

The hurried recoil of the French left wing had at last awakened Joffre to the true situation and to the utter collapse of Plan XVII. From the wreckage he now tried to piece together a new plan. He decided to swing back his centre and left, with Verdun as the pivot, while drawing troops from the right in Alsace and forming a fresh Sixth Army on his left to enable the retiring armies to return to the offensive.

His optimism, soon to wane, might have been again misplaced but for German mistakes. The first was Moltke's folly in detaching seven divisions to invest Maubeuge and Givet and watch Antwerp, instead of using Landwehr and Ersatz troops as Schlieffen had intended. More ominous still was his decision on August 25 to send four divisions to check the Russian advance in East Prussia. These also were taken from the right wing (actually from the force besieging Namur), and the excuse afterwards given was that the German Command thought that the decisive victory had already been won! Further, the German Command lost touch with the advancing armies and the movements of these became disjointed.

The British II Corps stand at Le Cateau, made by Smith-Dorrien against his superior's wish, and Lanrezac's riposte at Guise, in which French forbade his I Corps to help, were also factors in checking the German enveloping wing, and each had still greater indirect effects. For Le Cateau apparently convinced the German First Army Commander, Kluck, that the British army could be wiped from the slate, and Guise led Bülow (Second Army) to call on Kluck for support, whereupon Kluck wheeled inwards, thinking to roll up the French left. The idea of a Sedan was an obsession with the Germans, and led them to pluck the fruit before it was ripe. This premature wheel before Paris had been reached was an abandonment of the Schlieffen plan, and exposed the German right to a counter-envelopment.

This rash movement was in progress when Moltke also sacrificed the conception of Schlieffen to the dream of Sedan — in a different sector. His centre and left were ordered to close like pincers round either side of Verdun, while the right wing was to turn outwards and face Paris as a shield to these pincers. This sudden reversal of direction and inversion of rôle was akin to the folly of a driver who jams on his brakes and slews his front wheels hard round on a greasy road. One further factor must be mentioned, perhaps the most significant of all: the Germans had advanced so rapidly, outrunning their time-table, that their supplies failed to keep pace, so that the fatigue of the troops was increased by hunger. Indeed, when the chance of battle came, their fighting power was practically numbed by physical exhaustion — a condition much aggravated by the thorough demolitions which the French had carried out as they fell back. Thus, in sum, so much grit had worked into the German machine that a slight jar would suffice to cause its breakdown. This was delivered in the battle of the Marne.

The Tide Turns. The opportunity was perceived, not by Joffre, who had ordered a continuance of the retreat, but by Galliéni, the Military Governor of Paris, where the newly formed Sixth Army had assembled in shelter. On September 3 Galliéni realized the meaning of Kluck's wheel inwards, directed the Sixth Army (Maunoury) to be ready to strike at the exposed German right flank, and the next day with difficulty won Joffre's sanction. Once convinced, Joffre acted with decision. The whole left wing was ordered to turn about and return to a general offensive beginning on September 6. Maunoury was already off the mark on the fifth, and as his pressure developed on the German's sensitive flank, Kluck was constrained to draw off first one part and then the remaining part of his army to support his threatened flank guard. Thereby a thirty-mile gap was created between Kluck's and Bülow's armies, a gap covered only by a screen of cavalry. Kluck was emboldened to take the risk because of the rapid retreat of the British opposite, and still with their backs to this gaping sector. Even on the fifth, when the French on either flank were turning about, the British continued a further day's march to the south. But in this "disappearance" lay the unintentional cause of victory. For when the British retraced their steps, it was the report of their columns advancing into the gap which, on September 9, led Bülow to order the retreat of his army. The temporary advantage which Kluck's First Army, already isolated by its own act, had gained over Maunoury was thereby nullified, and it fell back the same day. By the eleventh the retreat had extended, independently or under orders from Moltke, to all the German armies.

The attempt at a partial envelopment, pivoting on Verdun, had already failed, the jaw formed by the Sixth and Seventh Armies merely breaking its teeth on the defenses of the French eastern frontier. The attack by Rupprecht's Sixth Army on the Grand Couronné, covering Nancy, was a particularly costly failure. It is difficult to see how the German Command could have reasonably pinned their faith on achieving as an improvised expedient the very task which, in cool calculation before the war, had appeared so hopeless as to lead them to take the momentous decision to advance through Belgium as the only feasible alternative.

Thus, in sum, the battle of the Marne was decided by a jar and a crack, the jar administered by Maunoury's attack on the German right flank causing a crack in a weak joint of the German line, and the penetration of this physical crack in turn producing a moral crack in the German Command.

The result was a strategic but not a tactical defeat, and the

German right wing was able to reknit and stand firmly on the line of the Aisne. That the Allies were not able to draw greater advantage from their victory was due in part to the comparative weakness of Maunoury's flank attack, and in part to the failure of the British and the French Fifth Army (now under Franchet d'Esperey) to drive rapidly through the gap while it was open. Their direction of advance was across a region intersected by frequent rivers, and this handicap was intensified by a want of impulsion on the part of their chiefs — each politely looking to his neighbor and, timorously, to his own flanks. Their feelings can best be described by the apt verse: —

> Lord Chatham with his sword undrawn
> Kept waiting for Sir Richard Strachan:
> Sir Richard, longing to be at 'em,
> Kept waiting too — for whom? Lord Chatham.

It seems, too, that greater results might have come if more effort had been made, as Galliéni urged, to strike at the German rear flank instead of the front, and to direct reënforcements to the northwest of Paris for this purpose. This view is strengthened by the sensitiveness shown by the German Command to reports of landings on the Belgian coast, which might threaten their communications. The alarm caused by these reports had even led the German Command to contemplate a withdrawal of their right wing before the battle of the Marne was launched. When the moral effect of these phantom forces is weighed with the material effect — the detention of German forces in Belgium — caused by fears of a Belgian sortie from Antwerp, the balance of judgment would seem to turn heavily in favor of the strategy which Roberts had tentatively suggested. By it the British Expeditionary Force might have had not merely an indirect but a direct influence on the struggle, and might have made the issue not merely negatively but positively decisive.

But, considering the battle of the Marne as it shaped, the fact that twenty-seven Allied divisions were pitted against thirteen German divisions on the decisive flank is evidence, first, of how completely Moltke had lapsed from Schlieffen's intention; second, of how well Joffre had reshuffled his forces under severe pressure; third, of how such a large balance afforded scope for a wider envelopment than was actually attempted.

The frontal pursuit was checked on the Aisne before Joffre, on September 17, seeing that Maunoury's attempts to overlap the German flank were ineffectual, decided to form a fresh army under de Castelnau for a manœuvre *round and behind* the German flank. By then the German armies had recovered cohesion, and the German Command was expecting and ready to meet such a manœuvre, now the obvious course.   The Allied chiefs, however, if cautious in action, were incautious in speculation.   Critics may complain that they were not sufficiently ingenious, but they were certainly ingenuous.   Wilson and Berthelot, the guiding brains of French and Joffre, were discussing on September 12 the probable date when they would cross the German frontier.   Wilson modestly estimated it at four weeks hence; Berthelot thought that he was pessimistic and reckoned on reaching the frontier a week earlier.

Flux and Stagnation.   Unhappily for their calculations, on the Aisne was reëmphasized the preponderant power of defense over attack, primitive as were the trench lines compared with those of later years.   Then followed, as the only alternative, the successive attempts of either side to overlap and envelop the other's western flank, a phase known popularly, but inaccurately, as the "race to the sea."   This common design brought out what was to be a new and dominating strategical feature — the lateral switching of reserves by railway from one part of the front to another.   Before it could reach its logical and lateral conclusion, a new factor intervened. Antwerp, with the Belgian Field Army, was still a thorn in the German side, and Falkenhayn, who had succeeded Moltke on September 14, determined to reduce it while a German cavalry force swept across to the Belgian coast as an extension of the enveloping wing in France.   One of the most amazing features, and blunders, of the war on the German side is that while the Allied armies were in full retreat, Moltke had made no attempt to secure the Channel ports, which lay at his mercy. The British had evacuated Calais, Boulogne, and the whole coast as far as Havre; even transferred their base to St. Nazaire on the Bay of Biscay, a step which not only revealed the measure of their pessimism, but delayed the arrival of the reënforcing 6th Division until the German front had hardened on the Aisne. And, during the Allied retreat, German Uhlans had roamed at will over the northwest of France, settled down in Amiens as if they were permanent lodgers, yet left the essential ports in tranquil isolation. A month later the Germans were to sacrifice tens of thousands of their men in the abortive effort to gain what they could have secured initially without cost.

We must pause here to pick up the thread of operations in Belgium from the moment when the Belgian Field Army fell back to Antwerp, divergently from the main line of operations. On August 24 the Belgians began a sortie against the rear of the German right wing to ease the pressure on the British and French left wing, then engaged in the opening battle at Mons and along the Sambre. The sortie was broken off on the twenty-fifth when news came of the Franco-British retreat into France, but the pressure of the Belgian army (six divisions) led the Germans to detach four reserve divisions, besides three Landwehr brigades, to hold it in check. On September 7 the Belgian Command learned that the Germans were dispatching part of this force to the front in France; in consequence King Albert launched a fresh sortie on September 9 — the crucial day of the battle on the Marne. The action was taken unsolicited by Joffre, who seems to have shown curiously little interest in possibilities outside his immediate battle zone. The sortie led the Germans to cancel the dispatch of one division and to delay that of two others to France, but the Belgians were soon thrown back. Nevertheless the news of it seems to have had a distinct moral effect on the German Command, coinciding as it did with the initiation of the retreat of their First and Second Armies from the Marne. And the unpleasant reminder that Antwerp lay menacingly close to their communications induced the Germans to undertake, preliminary to any fresh attempt at a decisive battle, the reduction of the fortress and the seizure of potential English landing places along the Belgian coast.

The menace to Britain, if the Channel ports fell into German hands, was obvious. It is a strange reflection that, inverting the German mistake, the British Command should hitherto have neglected to guard against the danger, although the First Lord of the Admiralty, Winston Churchill, had urged the necessity even before the battle of the Marne. When the German guns began the bombardment of Antwerp on September 28, England awakened, and gave belated recognition to Churchill's strategic insight. He was allowed to send a brigade of marines and two newly formed brigades of naval volunteers to reënforce the defenders, while the Regular 7th Division and 3rd Cavalry Division under Rawlinson were landed at Ostend and Zeebrugge for an overland move to raise the siege. Eleven Territorial divisions were available in England, but, in contrast to the German attitude, Kitchener considered them still unfitted for an active rôle. The meagre reënforcement delayed, but could not prevent, the capitulation of Antwerp, October 10, and Rawlinson's relieving force was too late to do more than cover the escape of the Belgian Field Army down the Flanders coast.

Yet, viewed in the perspective of history, this first and last effort in the west to make use of Britain's amphibious power applied a brake to the German advance down the coast which just stopped their second attempt to gain a decision in the west. It gained time for the arrival of the main British force, transferred from the Aisne to the new left of the Allied line, and if their heroic defense at Ypres, aided by the French and Belgians along the Yser to the sea, was the human barrier to the Germans, it succeeded by so narrow a margin that the Antwerp expedition must be adjudged the saving factor.

How had the main battle-ground come to be shifted from France to Flanders? The month following the battle of the Marne had been marked by an extremely obvious series of attempts by each side to turn the opponent's western flank. On the German side this pursuit of an opening was soon replaced by a subtler plan, but the French persevered with a straightforward obstinacy curiously akin to that of their original plan. By September 24, de Castelnau's outflanking attempt had come to a stop on the Somme. Next, a newly formed Tenth Army, under de Maudhuy, tried a little further north, beginning on October 2, but, instead of being able to pass round the German flank, soon found itself struggling desperately to hold Arras. The British Expeditionary Force was then in course of transfer northwards from the Aisne, in order to shorten its communications with England, and Joffre determined to use it as part of a third effort to turn the German flank. To coördinate this new manœuvre he appointed General Foch as his deputy in the north.

Foch sought to induce the Belgians to form the left of this wheeling mass, but King Albert with more caution, or more realism, declined to abandon the coastal district for an advance inland that he considered rash. It was. For on October 14, four days after the fall of Antwerp, Falkenhayn planned a strategic trap for the next Allied outflanking manœuvre which he foresaw would follow. One army, composed of troops transferred from Lorraine, was to hold the expected Allied offensive in check while another, composed of troops released by the fall of Antwerp and of four newly raised corps, was to sweep down the Belgian coast and crush in the flank of the attacking Allies. He even held back the troops pursuing the Belgians in order not to alarm the Allied Command prematurely.

Meanwhile the new Allied advance was developing piecemeal, as corps detrained from the south and swung eastwards to form a progressively extended "scythe." The British Expeditionary Force, now three corps[1] strong, deployed in turn between La Bassée and Ypres — where it effected a junction with Rawlinson's force. Beyond it the embryo of a new French Eighth Army was taking shape, and the Belgian continued the line along the Yser to the sea. Although the British right and centre corps had already been held up, Sir John French, discounting even the underestimate of the German strength furnished by his Intelligence, ordered his left corps (Haig) to begin the offensive from Ypres towards Menin. The effort was still-born, for it coincided with the opening of the German offensive,

[1] At this time a corps consisted of two divisions, although later of three or even four divisions.

on October 20, but for a day or two Sir John French persisted in the belief that he was attacking while his troops were barely holding their ground.   When enlightenment came he swung to the other extreme and anxiously urged the construction of a huge entrenched camp near Boulogne "to take the whole Expeditionary Force."   But his recurrent desire to retreat was overborne by the greater will-power and perhaps the more consistent self-delusion of Foch, who by flattering deference, as well as forceful personality, had now gained a strong influence over French.   And French's regard was increased when Foch let him know privately that Kitchener had proposed — in imagined privacy — to replace him by Sir Ian Hamilton. In this happy way did the leaders fight each other while the troops fought the foe.

The failure of the higher commanders to grasp the situation left the real handling of the battle to Haig and his divisional commanders.   And they for want of reserves could do little more than cement the crumbling parts of the front, by scraping reserves from other parts, and encourage the exhausted but indomitable troops to hold on.   Thus Ypres was essentially, like Inkerman, a "soldier's battle."   Already, since the eighteenth, the Belgians on the Yser had suffered growing pressure which threatened a disaster that was ultimately averted, by the end of the month, through the opening of the sluices and the flooding of the coastal area.   At Ypres the crisis came later and was repeated, October 31 and November 11 marking the turning points of the struggle.   That the Allied line, though battered and terribly strained, was in the end unbroken was due to the dogged resistance of the British and the timely arrival of French reënforcements.

This defense of Ypres is in a dual sense the supreme memorial to the British Regular Army, for here its officers and men showed the inestimable value of the disciplined morale and unique standard of musketry which were the fruit of long training, and here was their tombstone.   "From failing hands they threw the torch" to the national armies rising in England to the call of country.   With the Continental Powers the merging of conventional armies into national armies was a hardly perceptible process, because of their system of universal service. But with Britain it was clearly stamped as revolution, not evolution. While the little professional army sacrificed itself as the advanced guard of the nation, the truth of the new warfare of peoples was beginning to come home to the civilian population. Lord Kitchener with a supreme flash of vision had grasped, in contrast to governments and general staffs alike, the probable duration of the struggle. The people of Britain responded to his call to arms, and like an ever-rising flood the "New Armies" came into being. By the end of the year nearly 1,000,000 men had enlisted, and the British Empire had altogether some 2,000,000 under arms.

Perhaps Kitchener was wrong in not basing this expansion, from a professional to a national scale, on the existing Territorial foundation — although it must be remembered that the Territorial Force was enlisted for home defense and that, initially, its members' acceptance of a wider rôle was voluntary. Perhaps, also, he was tardy in recognizing their military value. The duplication of forces and of organization was undoubtedly a source of delay and waste of effort. Kitchener has also been reproached for his reluctance to replace the voluntary system by conscription, but this criticism overlooks how deeply rooted was the voluntary system in British institutions, and the slowness with which lasting changes can be effected in them. If Kitchener's method was characteristic of the man, it was characteristic of England. If it was unmethodical, it was calculated to impress most vividly on the British people the gulf between their "gladiatorial" wars of the past and the national war to which they were committed. It took even longer to impress the British military mind, as represented by General Headquarters in France. Henry Wilson wrote that Kitchener's "ridiculous and preposterous army of twenty-five corps is the laughingstock of every soldier in Europe. . . . Under no circumstances could these mobs take the field for two years. Then what is the use of them?" For by his calculation the British army was almost due to arrive in Berlin.

While a psychological landmark, the battle of Ypres is also a military landmark. For, with the repulse of the German

attempt to break through, the trench barrier was consolidated
from the Swiss frontier to the sea. The power of modern
defense had triumphed over attack, and stalemate ensued.
The military history of the Franco-British Alliance during the
next four years is a story of the attempts to upset this deadlock, either by forcing the barrier or by haphazardly finding
a way round.

On the eastern front, however, the greater distances and
the greater differences between the equipment of the armies
ensured a fluidity which was lacking in the west. Trench lines
might form, but they were no more than a hard crust covering
a liquid expanse. To break the crust was not difficult, and,
once it was broken, mobile operations of the old style became
possible. This freedom of action was denied to the Western
Powers, but Germany, because of her central position, had an
alternative choice, and from November 1914 onwards Falkenhayn adopted, although temporarily and half-heartedly, a
defensive in France while seeking to cripple the power of
Russia.

The Russian Front. The opening encounters in the east had
been marked by rapid changes of fortune rather than by any
decisive advantage. The Austrian Command had detached
part of their strength in an abortive attempt to crush Serbia.
And their plan for an initial offensive to cut off the Polish
"tongue" was further crippled by the fact that the German
part of the pincers did not operate. It was indeed being
menaced by a Russian pair of pincers instead, for the Russian
Commander-in-Chief, the Grand Duke Nicholas, had urged his
First and Second Armies to invade East Prussia without waiting to complete their concentration, in order to ease the pressure
on his French Allies. As the Russians had more than a two-
to-one superiority, a combined attack had every chance of
crushing the Germans between the two armies. On August 17,
Rennenkampf's First Army (six and a half divisions and five
cavalry divisions) crossed the East Prussian frontier, and on
August 19–20 met and threw back the bulk (seven divisions
and one cavalry division) of Prittwitz's Eighth Army at
Gumbinnen. On August 21 Prittwitz heard that the Russian

Second Army (ten divisions and three cavalry divisions) under Samsonov had crossed the southern frontier of East Prussia, in his rear, which was guarded by only three divisions. In panic Prittwitz momentarily spoke on the telephone of falling back behind the Vistula, whereupon Moltke superseded him by a retired general, Hindenburg, to whom was appointed, as Chief of Staff, Ludendorff, the hero of the Liége attack.

Developing a plan which, with the necessary movements, had been already initiated by Colonel Hoffmann of the Eighth Army Staff, Ludendorff concentrated some six divisions against Samsonov's left wing. This force, inferior in strength to the Russians, could not have been decisive; but, finding that Rennenkampf was still near Gumbinnen, Ludendorff took the calculated risk of withdrawing the rest of the German troops, except the cavalry screen, from that front, and bringing them back against Samsonov's right wing. This daring move was aided by the absence of communication between the two Russian commanders and the ease with which the Germans deciphered Samsonov's wireless orders to his corps. Under the converging pressure Samsonov's flanks collapsed, his centre was surrounded, and his army almost destroyed. If the opportunity was presented rather than created, this brief campaign and its sequel, afterwards christened the battle of Tannenberg, is a significant example of the use of what are technically called "interior lines" — more simply, a central position.

Then, receiving his two fresh army corps from the French front, the German Commander turned on the slow advancing Rennenkampf, and drove him out of East Prussia. As a result of these battles Russia had lost a quarter of a million men and, what she could afford still less, much war material. But the invasion of East Prussia had at least, by causing the dispatch of two corps from the west, helped to make possible the French recovery on the Marne. And, with peculiar irony, these corps had arrived too late to be of service at Tannenberg.

But the effect of Tannenberg was diminished because, away on the southern front, in Galicia, the scales had tilted against the Central Powers. The offensive of the Austrian First and Fourth Armies into Poland had at first made progress, but this was nullified by the onslaught of the Russian Third and Eighth Armies upon the weaker Second and Third Armies which were guarding the Austrian right flank.   These armies were heavily defeated (August 26–30), and driven back through Lemberg. The advance of the Russian left wing thus threatened the rear of the victorious Austrian left wing.   Conrad tried to swing part of his left round, in turn, against the Russian flank, but this blow was parried.   And then, caught, with his forces disorganized, by the renewed advance of the Russian right wing, he was forced on September 11 to extricate himself by a general retreat, falling back almost to Cracow by the end of September. Austria's plight compelled the Germans to send aid, and the bulk of the force in East Prussia was formed into a new Ninth Army and switched south to the southwest corner of Poland, whence it advanced on Warsaw in combination with a renewed Austrian offensive.   But the Russians were now approaching the full tide of their mobilized strength; regrouping their forces and counter-attacking, they drove back the advance and followed it up by a powerful effort to invade Silesia.

The Grand Duke Nicholas formed a huge phalanx of seven armies — three in the van and two protecting either flank.   A further army, the Tenth, had invaded the eastern corner of East Prussia and was engaging the weak German forces there. Allied hopes rose high as the much-heralded Russian "steam-roller" began its ponderous advance.   To counter it the German eastern front was placed under Hindenburg, for whom Ludendorff and Hoffmann devised a master-stroke, based on the system of lateral railways inside the German frontier.   The Ninth Army, retreating before the advancing Russians, slowed them down by a systematic destruction of the scanty communications in Poland.   On reaching its own frontier unpressed, it was first switched northwards to the Posen-Thorn area, and then thrust southeast, on November 11 — with its left flank on the Vistula — against the joint between the two armies guarding the Russian right flank.

The wedge, driven in by Ludendorff's mallet, sundered the two armies, forced the First back on Warsaw, and almost effected another Tannenberg against the Second, which was nearly surrounded at Lodz, when the Fifth Army from the van turned back to its rescue. As a result, part of the German enveloping force almost suffered the fate planned for the Russians, but managed to cut its way through to the main body. If the Germans were baulked of decisive tactical success, this manœuvre had been a classic example of how a relatively small force, by using its mobility to strike at a vital point, can paralyze the advance of an enemy several times its strength. The Russian "steam-roller" was thrown out of gear, and never again did it threaten German soil.

Within a week, four new German army corps arrived from the western front, where the Ypres attack had now ended in failure; and, although too late to clinch the missed chance of a decisive victory, Ludendorff was able to use them in pressing the Russians back by December 15 to the Bzura-Ravka river line in front of Warsaw. This setback and the drying up of his munition supplies decided the Grand Duke Nicholas to break off the seesaw fighting still in progress near Cracow, and fall back on winter trench lines along the Nida and Dunajec rivers, leaving the end of the Polish "tongue" in the hands of the enemy. Thus, on the east as on the west, the trench stalemate had settled in, but the crust was less firm, and the Russians had drained their stock of munitions to an extent that their poorly industrialized country could not make good.

The Grip on the Seas. We deal thirdly with the operations at sea, which actually occurred first in chronological order. The reason is that sea-power only came to exert a dominant, eventually the dominant, influence on the war after the initial plans on land had miscarried. If the quick decision expected by the military leaders had been reached, it is questionable whether sea-power could have affected the issue. How narrowly Germany missed decisive victory, and by what a combination of hardly conceivable blunders, is in the light of history now clear. While it is possible that Britain could, and would, have carried on the war unaided, we need to remember that in August 1914 the condition was still that of a professional war with popular backing rather than a truly national war; that British intervention was still regarded as a chivalrous effort to succor violated Belgium and challenged France rather than as a life-and-death struggle for Britain's existence. And when a friend lies prone in a tiger's claws it is mistaken friendship to engage in a tug-of-war for the fragments if there is any chance of enticing the tiger from his prey.

But fortunately, in 1914, the tiger was held at bay, and with this breathing space gained Britain had the opportunity to exert her traditional weapon — sea-power. Its effect on the war was akin not to a lightning flash, striking down an opponent suddenly, but to a steady radiation of heat, invigorating to those it was used in aid of, and drying up the resources of the enemy.

But if its effect was extended and cumulative, its application was instantaneous, comparable almost to turning on an electric switch. This simple act, yet perhaps the most decisive of the war, took place before the actual outbreak — on July 29, when at seven o'clock in the morning that greater Armada, the British Grand Fleet, sailed from Portland for its war station at Scapa Flow. Few eyes saw its passage, fewer minds knew its destination in those northerly Orkney Isles controlling the passage between North Britain and Norway, but from that moment Germany's arteries were subjected to an invisible pressure which never relaxed until on November 21, 1918, the German fleet arrived in those same northern waters to hand itself into the custody of a force of whom it had seen no more than a few fleeting glimpses during four and a half years of intangible struggle.

The fundamental cause of this unprecedented type of conflict lay in the recent development of new weapons, the mine and the submarine, which reproduced in naval warfare that same predominance of defensive over offensive power which was the key factor on land. The immediate cause, however, was the strategy adopted by Germany's Naval Command, partly through a miscalculation of Britain's probable strategy. Appreciating their own inferiority to the British fleet, as well as the impossibility of a surprise blow in face of its preparedness, and believing that their enemy was obsessed with the Nelsonian tradition of seeking battle, the German Command adopted a Fabian strategy. They aimed to refuse conflict until their mine-layers and submarines had weakened the strength of the British navy, until the strain of a close blockade had begun to tell on the superior fleet, and perhaps provided the chance of a surprise stroke, and until the conquest of Britain's Allies on land had made her position more difficult.

The plan had at least a sound geographical basis, for the nature and configuration of the German coast lent itself to this strategy. The short North Sea coastline was heavily indented, the estuaries a maze of difficult channels, and screened by a fringe of islands — of which Heligoland formed a strongly fortified shield to the naval bases at Wilhelmshaven, Bremerhaven, and Cuxhaven. Best of all, from the estuary of the Elbe there was a back door into the Baltic Sea, the Kiel Canal. By this the naval forces in the Baltic could be rapidly reënforced, while an enemy advance into that landlocked sea was not only hampered by the neutral possession of its approaches, but could be imperiled by submarine and destroyer attack while passing through the narrow channels between the Danish islands. The natural defensive power of Germany's sea frontiers made attack almost impossible, and conversely gave her an excellent base for raiding operations — save for the geographical handicap that the coastline of Great Britain, like a vast breakwater, narrowed the exit for operations on the outer seas.

The one obvious defect of this Fabian strategy was that it involved the immediate abandonment of Germany's foreign trade and reduced the possibility of her interference with the sea-borne supplies of Britain and her Allies. Moreover, the German plan of progressive attrition was vitiated by the strategy adopted by the British Admiralty, which abandoned the direct doctrine of seeking out the enemy for the indirect doctrine of "the fleet in being." Realizing how the mine and submarine, combined with Germany's natural advantages, had made a close blockade hazardous, the Admiralty adopted a strategy of distant surveillance, keeping the battle fleet in a position which commanded the North Sea and in instant readiness for action if the enemy appeared, and using the light

craft for closer, but not close, observation.   This strategy was
not as passive as it seemed to a critical public, eagerly expecting
a new Trafalgar.   It appreciated that Britain's general command of the sea was the pivot of the Allied cause, and that to
hazard it by exposure to uncompensated losses was the negation
of this supreme requirement.   Therefore, while desiring battle
and being ready for it, the Admiralty quietly set about its
primary duties of maintaining the security of the ocean routes,
dealing with the sporadic threats to those routes, and, thirdly,
ensuring the safe passage to France of the British Expeditionary
Force.

The idea of economic pressure exercised by sea-power was
still in embryo.   Not until a later phase did it crystallize into
a formal doctrine, and the term "blockade" assume a new and
wider definition.   The attack on sea-borne commerce was
deep-rooted in the traditions of the British navy, and thus the
transition to an indirect attack on the life of the enemy nation
— her supplies of food and raw material — was an almost imperceptible progress.   When this pressure was exercised against
herself in a novel form and by a new weapon — the submarine
— it was human, if illogical, that she should decry it as an
atrocity.   It was not easy for a conservative mind to realize
that with the transition from a war of government policies
into a war of peoples, the indefinite code of military chivalry
must be submerged by the primitive instincts let loose by a
struggle for existence.   But in 1914 this "absolute" war was
still only a latent conception, and had no influence on the opening operations, great as was to be their influence on it.

The history of the naval struggle must be dated from July
26, 1914, when the Admiralty, in view of the clouded international situation, sent orders to the fleet assembled for review
at Portland not to disperse.   If the review was a happy chance,
the use made of it was one of the decisive acts and wisest judgments of the war, for, while free from any of the provocation
of an army mobilization, it placed Britain in automatic control
of the situation at sea.   It was followed, on July 29, by the
unnoticed sailing of the fleet for its war stations in the North
Sea, and warning telegrams to all squadrons abroad.   To

students of war and politics the lesson should not be lost, for, whatever its other limitations, a professional force has this power of unprovocative readiness which a national force inevitably lacks. "Mobilization" is a threat, creating an atmosphere in which peaceful argument withers and dies. Between negotiations and mobilization there is a gulf, between mobilization and war an imperceptible seam, and the act of any irresponsible man can draw a nation across it.

Admiral Jellicoe, the new commander of the Grand Fleet, had one initial weakness to contend with: his base at Scapa was without defenses against torpedo attack, and the fortified base being prepared at Rosyth was still incomplete. The historic concentration of British sea-power had been on the Channel coast, where lay the best prepared and defended harbors, and the Government had been slow to provide funds for bases on the North Sea to accompany the change in the concentration areas.

The danger compelled him to take his fleet west of the Orkneys, although it came down as far as the Forth during the transport to France of the Expeditionary Force — which was directly protected by the older battleships of the Channel Fleet, and by a layered system of patrols in the southern waters of the North Sea. The safe passage of the Expeditionary Force was the first direct achievement of the navy. The next followed on August 29 when Beatty's battle-cruiser squadron and Tyrwhitt's destroyer flotillas made a swoop into the Bight of Heligoland, sank several German light cruisers, and achieved the much greater indirect effect of confirming the Germans in their strictly defensive strategy — not an unmixed blessing, for it led them to concentrate on the development of submarine attack. Apart from this engagement the story of 1914 in the North Sea is a record of unceasing vigilance on the one side, of minor submarine and mine-laying successes and losses on the other.

The war in the Mediterranean opened with a mistake that was to have far-reaching political consequences. Two of Germany's fastest ships were there, the battle-cruiser *Goeben* and the light cruiser *Breslau*, and received orders from Berlin to steer for Constantinople. They evaded the British efforts made to cut them off, partly owing to inelasticity in applying the Admiralty instructions.

On the high seas the chase was more prolonged. Germany had not been allowed time to send out commerce-destroyers from home waters, but for some months her few cruisers on foreign service were a thorn in the side of the British navy. It was not easy to reconcile the needs of the North Sea concentration with the duty of patrolling and protecting the tremendous length of sea-routes along which supplies as well as troops were flowing from India and the Dominions to the support of the Mother Country. By the destruction of the *Emden* on November 9, the Indian Ocean was finally cleared, but this success was offset by disaster in the Pacific, where Admiral Cradock's cruiser squadron was crushed by the heavier metal of Admiral von Spee's armored cruisers, *Scharnhorst* and *Gneisenau*. This setback was, however, promptly redeemed by the Admiralty, who dispatched Admiral Sturdee with two battle-cruisers, *Inflexible* and *Invincible*, on a lightning dash to the south Atlantic, while another battle-cruiser, *Australia*, swept down from Fiji on Admiral von Spee's rear. Trapped on December 8 at the Falkland Isles, by this finely conceived surprise, Spee was sunk, and with him the last instrument of German naval power upon the oceans.

From this time onward, the ocean communications of Britain and her Allies were secured for trade, for supplies, and for the conveyance of troops. But as to all ocean routes there must be a land terminus, the development of the submarine made this security gradually less effective than it seemed on the morrow of Sturdee's victory.

The nature of the war at sea began to undergo definite changes early in 1915. During the first phase Britain had been too busy in clearing the seas and maintaining the security of the sea-routes to devote much attention to the use of her sea command as an economic weapon against Germany. In any case her naval power was fettered by the artificial restrictions on blockade embodied in the Declaration of London of 1909, which the British Government with singular blindness announced on the outbreak of war that it would accept as the basis of maritime practice. Their release from these self-imposed fetters was aided by Germany's action.

On November 2, 1914, a German battle-cruiser squadron made a raid on the Norfolk coast, as a reconnaissance to test the scope of Britain's naval defense. Another followed on December 16 against the Yorkshire coast, Scarborough, Whitby, and the Hartlepools being bombarded. Each time the Germans slipped away safely, but when they attempted a third, on January 24, the English battle-cruiser squadron, under Beatty, trapped them off the Dogger Bank, sank the *Blücher* and badly damaged the *Derrfflinger* and *Seydlitz*. Although the stroke missed full success, it convinced the Germans of the futility of their attrition strategy, and Ingenohl, the Commander of their High Seas Fleet, was replaced by Pohl, who proposed to Falkenhayn an offensive submarine campaign, which for success must be unlimited.

As a result, on February 18, Germany proclaimed the waters round the British Isles a war zone where all ships, enemy or neutral, would be sunk at sight. This gave Britain a lever to loosen the Declaration of London, and she replied by claiming the right to intercept all ships suspected of carrying goods to Germany, and bring them into British ports for search. This tightening of the blockade caused serious difficulties with neutrals, America especially, but Germany eased the friction by torpedoing the great liner *Lusitania*, May 7, 1915. The drowning of 1100 people, including some Americans, was a spectacular brutality which shocked the conscience of the world, and appealed more forcibly to American opinion than even the desolation of Belgium. This act, succeeded by others, paved the way for the entry of the United States into the war, though it was to be later than seemed likely on the morrow of the tragedy.

One result of Britain's early established command of the sea was that it gave her the opportunity to sweep up Germany's oversea colonies with little hindrance or expenditure of force. Their seizure was valuable in that it gave the Allies important assets to bargain with in case of an unfavorable or negative issue to the war. In August a New Zealand expedition took possession of New Guinea and Samoa, and the Australian navy cleared several important German wireless stations in the Pacific Isles. Japan, entering the war on Britain's side, sent a division with a naval squadron to besiege the German fortress of Tsing-tao on the coast of China. The first landing took place on September 2, and a tiny British contingent arrived on the twenty-third, but the defenses were modern, the land approach narrow, and the actual siege was not begun until October 31. Seven days' bombardment was followed by an assault, which led to the capitulation of the garrison, after a rather feeble resistance.

In Africa, Togoland was occupied in August; the equatorial forest of the Cameroons was a sterner obstacle, and not until the beginning of 1916 were the German forces conquered by joint British and French forces after a prolonged but economically conducted campaign. General Botha, the South African Premier, once in arms against England, now for her, organized a force which conquered German Southwest Africa. Almost concurrently Botha rendered a still greater service to the British cause by putting down the rebellion of a section of disaffected Boers, which, save for the Irish rising of Easter, 1916, was the only revolt within the borders of the Empire during these four trying years.

Only German East Africa, the largest and richest of Germany's colonies, remained, and that, owing to the difficulties of the country and the skill of General von Lettow-Vorbeck, the German Commander, was not to be completely subdued until the end of 1917. An Expeditionary Force was sent thither in November to support the local British East African forces, and was repulsed at Tanga. Not until late in 1915 could the British Government, occupied with greater problems, spare either the time or the force to deal with this hornet's nest.

The year 1915 witnessed the dawn of another new form of war which helped to drive home the new reality that the war of armies had become the war of peoples. From January onwards, Zeppelin raids began on the English coast and reached their peak in the late summer of 1916, to be succeeded by aeroplane raids. The difficulty of distinguishing from the air between military and civil objectives smoothed the path for a development which, beginning with excuses, ended in a frank avowal that in a war for existence the will of the enemy nation, not merely the bodies of their soldiers, is the inevitable target.

The first psychological symptom of the World War, as it seemed to many, was an immeasurable sigh of relief. Had the peoples of Europe sat on the safety-valve too long? The war-weary mind of to-day cannot reconstruct the tension and anxiety, the strain and stress of hope and fear of the long years of the peace that was no peace and yet was not war. It may be read as a revolt of the spirit against the monotony and triviality of the everyday round, the completion of a psychological cycle when the memories of past wars have faded, and paved the way for the emergence and revival of the primordial "hunting" instinct in man.

This first phase of enthusiasm was succeeded by one of passion, the natural ferocity of war accentuated by a form of mob spirit which is developed by a "nation in arms." The British army was relatively immune because of its professional character, whereas in the German army, the most essentially "citizen," it gained scope because of the cold-blooded logic of the general staff theory of war. With the coming of the autumn a third phase became manifest, more particularly among the combatants. This was a momentary growth of a spirit of tolerance, symbolized by the fraternization which took place on Christmas Day, but this in turn was to wane as the strain of the war became felt and the reality of the struggle for existence came home to the warring sides.

1914 — THE CLINCH

Scene I

THE BATTLE THAT WAS NOT, YET TURNED THE TIDE — THE MARNE

No battle has caused more controversy, produced so large a literature in so short a time, or given rise to more popular interest and legend, than that of the Marne. But then, this crisis of September 1914 wrought the downfall of the German war plan and thereby changed the course of history. For if it be true, as it certainly is in part, that Germany lost the war when she lost this battle, it is natural that claimants to the distinction of having won it should be many.

The first legend to arise was that Foch had won it by driving the German centre into the marshes of St. Gond, and even to-day, in total disregard of the facts and times of the battle, this is still given currency by reputable historians outside France.

But while, like a pebble dropped in water, the ripples of this story were still spreading, knowledgeable opinion in France was violently arguing whether the credit was due to Joffre, the Commander-in-Chief, or Galliéni, his quondam superior and then subordinate, who had delivered from Paris the blow at the German flank, exposed by Kluck's wheel inwards before Paris. One school contended that Joffre had conceived the idea of the counter-offensive, and at most admitted under pressure of facts that Galliéni's initiative in seeing the opportunity had given an impulse to Joffre's decision to seize it. The other school argued that Joffre, after the failure of his first attempt to stage a counter-offensive on the line of the Somme, had given up all idea of a fresh attempt at an early date, and that but for Galliéni's fiery determination and persuasion the retreat would have continued. A dispassionate judgment is now possible, and if we recognize that on Joffre fell the grave responsibility of taking the decision, the weight of evidence shows that Galliéni's inspiration dictated both the site and the promptness of the thrust. Furthermore, it rebuts the alternative case of Joffre's advocates that Galliéni marred the prospect by precipitating the blow, for we know that twenty-four hours' delay would have enabled the Germans to complete the protective redistribution which Galliéni interrupted.

On the German side a similar controversy has raged as to whether the order to retreat was a mistake, and whether Kluck of the First Army, Bülow of the Second, or the envoy of the Supreme Command, Colonel Hentsch, was responsible for the fatal decision.

The multiple controversy has at least served to show that the Marne was a psychological rather than a physical victory. So, also, have been most of the immortal victories of history, with the actual fighting a secondary influence. For the profoundest truth of war is that the issue of battles is usually decided in the minds of the opposing commanders, not in the bodies of their men. The best history would be a register of their thoughts and emotions, with a mere background of events to throw them into relief. But the delusion to the contrary has been fostered by the typical military history, filled with details of the fighting and assessing the cause of a victory by statistical computations of the number engaged.

The Marne was so clearly a psychological issue that the minds of the commanders have received due analysis. But even so, the "combat complex" has tended to narrow the analysis of minds to the area where the clash of bodies took place. Thereby certain suggestive evidence has escaped comment. This evidence may be expressed in a startling question. Was the victory primarily due to the heated imagination of an English railway porter and to a party of temporary visitors to Ostend? Or, at the least, did these humble worthies constitute with Galliéni the mainspring of victory?

The suggestion is not so fantastic as it seems when we study the mental atmosphere of the German commanders. Before and during the crisis they were constantly looking backward apprehensively over their right shoulders, fearful of an Allied stroke against their ever-lengthening communications in Belgium and Northern France. Unfortunately for the Allies, there was small warrant for this nervousness. The belated plea for landing the B.E.F. on the Belgium coast had been overruled by the Wilsonian pledge and policy of tying it as an appendix to the French left wing. Yet the Belgian Field Army, if under German guard at Antwerp, had at least caused a serious detachment of German strength to its guard and, more, was a chronic irritation to German nerves.

The fertile brain of Mr. Churchill was also at work. Resources were scanty, but he dispatched a brigade of marines under Brigadier-General Aston to Ostend, with orders to give their presence the fullest publicity. They landed on August 26, and stayed ashore several days.

Now to turn to the "other side of the hill." On September 5, the day when the French troops were moving forward to strike at Kluck, Colonel Hentsch, the representative of the Supreme Command, came to the threatened army with this ominous and despairing warning: "The news is bad. The VII and VI Armies are blocked. The IV and V are meeting with strong resistance. . . . The English are disembarking fresh troops continuously on the Belgian coast. There are reports of a Russian expeditionary force in the same parts. A withdrawal is becoming inevitable." We know from other sources that the 3000 marines had grown in the German Command's imagination to 40,000, and that the Russians were said to be 80,000.

Thus the German flank army was left to face its ordeal with the belief that their rear was seriously menaced, and that, in any case, the Supreme Command was contemplating a withdrawal. At the least such knowledge must have been insidiously enervating during a period of strain. If the Supreme Command came to have doubts of the Belgian news, it also became imbued with the idea of a retirement, and when Hentsch came again on September 9 with full powers to coordinate it, "should rearward movements have begun," not only had these begun, but they also coincided with fresh disturbing news from Belgium. For if the Belgian sortie from Antwerp that day was short-lived, it had all the incalculable psychological effect of menacing news at a moment of crisis. The German retreat gathered momentum and spread. With it turned the tide of the war.

History should do justice to Mr. Churchill's happy inspiration and General Aston's handful of "Marine promenaders." But equally helpful was that amazing "Russian" myth which originated and spread so mysteriously. Mr. Churchill, we know, had actually proposed to bring a Russian expeditionary force in such a way. Did the proposal perhaps leak out and become exaggerated into realization in the process? General opinion, however, has long ascribed the legend to the heated imagination of a railway porter working on the simple fact of the night passage of troop trains with Gaelic-speaking occupants. If so, a statue in Whitehall " to the Unknown Porter " is overdue.

Keeping this external factor on the circumference of our thought, let us turn to trace the sequence of events in the actual battle zone. The immediate chain of causation begins with the escape by retreat of the French and British armies from the frontier trap into which Joffre's plan had led them. The first, highly colored, reports from the army commands in the battles of the frontiers had given the German Supreme Command the impression of a decisive victory. It was under this hallucination that Moltke, on August 25, cheerfully and needlessly dispatched four divisions to the Russian front, — to the detriment of his right wing punch, already weakened by seven divisions left for the investment of derelict fortresses, — truly a bad investment. Then the comparatively small totals of prisoners raised doubts in Moltke's mind and led him to a more sober estimate of the situation. The Kaiser's easy optimism now irritated him — "He has already a shout-hurrah mood that I hate like death." The new pessimism of Moltke combined with the renewed optimism of his army commanders to produce a fresh change of plan, which contained the seeds of disaster.

While Kluck's army, on the German extreme right or outer flank, was pressing on the heels of the British, — so close that

the "outside" British corps (Smith-Dorrien) was forced to halt
and give battle, — Kluck's neighbor on the inside, Bülow,
was following up Lanrezac's French Fifth Army. When, on
August 26, the British left wing fell back southwards badly
mauled from Le Cateau, Kluck had turned southwestwards
again. If this direction was partly due to misconception of
the line of retreat taken by the British, — the idea that they
were retreating to the Channel ports, — it was also in accordance with his original rôle of a wide-circling sweep. And by
carrying him into the Amiens-Péronne area, where the first
parts of the newly formed French Sixth Army were just detraining after their "switch" from Alsace, it had the effect of
dislocating Joffre's design for an early return to the offensive
— by compelling the Sixth Army to fall back hurriedly towards
the shelter of the Paris defenses.

But Kluck had hardly swung out to the southwest before
he was induced to swing in again. For, in order to ease the
pressure on the British, Joffre had ordered Lanrezac to halt
and strike back against the pursuing Germans, and Bülow,
shaken by the threat, called on Kluck for aid. Lanrezac's
attack, on August 29, was stopped before Bülow needed this
help, but he asked Kluck to wheel in nevertheless, in order to
cut off Lanrezac's retreat. Before acceding, Kluck referred to
Moltke. The request came at a moment when Moltke was
becoming perturbed in general over the way the French were
slipping away from his embrace and, in particular, over a gap
which had opened between his Second (Bülow) and Third
(Hausen) Armies through the latter having already turned
south, from southwest, to help the Fourth Army, its neighbor on the other flank. Hence Moltke approved Kluck's
change of direction — which meant the inevitable abandonment of the original wide sweep round the far side of Paris.
Now the flank of the wheeling German line would pass the
near side of Paris and across the face of the Paris defenses. By
this contraction of his frontage for the sake of security, Moltke
sacrificed the wider prospects inherent in the wide-circling
sweep of the original plan. And, as it proved, instead of con-
tracting the risk, he exposed himself to a fatal counter-stroke.

The decision to abandon the original plan was definitely taken on September 4, and in place of it Moltke substituted a narrower envelopment, of the French centre and right. His own centre (Fourth and Fifth Armies) was to press southeast while his left (Sixth and Seventh Armies), striking southwestwards, sought to break through the fortified barrier between Toul and Epinal, the jaws thus closing inwards on either side of Verdun. Meantime his right (First and Second Armies) was to turn outwards and, facing west, hold off any countermove which the French might attempt from the neighborhood of Paris. Moltke's order ignored the fact that Kluck was ahead of Bülow in the race southward and had already crossed the Marne. For it not only told Kluck to "remain facing the east side of Paris" (that is, facing west), but to remain north of the Marne while Bülow wheeled into line, facing west, between the Marne and the Seine. Thus, to fulfill the order, Kluck had not merely to halt, while Bülow caught up and passed him, but to perform a sort of backward somersault. Such gymnastics are somewhat upsetting to the equilibrium of a large army. And in this case the French counter-move which Moltke wished to guard against had already begun before his new plan could take effect. Moreover, Kluck, reluctant to be thus deprived of the chance of being the agent of decisive victory, continued his advance south towards the Seine on the fifth, saying that "the movement to face west might be made at leisure." For the moment he merely left a weak detachment of three brigades and a few cavalry to guard his flank. Next morning it was struck by the French Sixth Army moving out from Paris.

During these days the Franco-British retreat had continued. On August 30, Joffre — yielding to the pressure of a government alarmed at seeing him abandon the capital by his direction of retreat — detached Maunoury's Sixth Army to reënforce the Paris garrison. Parting with it signified his parting with any early hope of a counter-stroke, for this was the force he had assembled for its execution. On September 1, Joffre issued an order for the retreat of the Allied armies to be continued to a line south of the Seine, Aube, and Ornain rivers.

Not only was the effect to take the armies away from and far to the southeast of Paris, but a commander who is contemplating an early counter-offensive does not place the obstacle of a river barrier between himself and the enemy. And a further note to the several army commanders next day added that it was Joffre's intention to "organize and fortify" this line, whence he planned to deliver not an immediate but an eventual counter-offensive. That same day he replied to a suggestion of a stand on the Marne, made by Sir John French and communicated through the Minister of War: —

I do not believe it possible to envisage a general action on the Marne with the whole of our forces. But I consider that the coöperation of the English army in the defense of Paris is the only course that can give an advantageous result.

To the Minister of War and to Galliéni he repeated the same verdict. When Joffre's advocates assert that the idea of a counter-offensive was at the *back* of Joffre's mind, the historian can agree. This array of evidence is more than sufficient to dispel the legend that Joffre had any intention of giving battle on the Marne or that he planned the counter-stroke which tilted the balance so dramatically.

The definite nature of his reply was the more significant because, on September 1, a staff officer with Lanrezac's army had found the German order for a change of direction in the wallet of a dead officer, and this was sent to Joffre's headquarters early next day. And on the morning of the third, the changed direction, to the southeast, of Kluck's marching columns had been noticed and reported by British aviators. In the afternoon they added that these columns were crossing the Marne and in the evening Maunoury reported that there were no German troops left in the area west of the line Paris–Senlis. All this was reported to Joffre without making any impression on his plans — save that on the night of the second he altered the limit of his retirement to a line still further south!

But from Galliéni, the new military governor of Paris, even a fragment of information gained on the third had drawn an instant response. He ordered Maunoury to carry out further

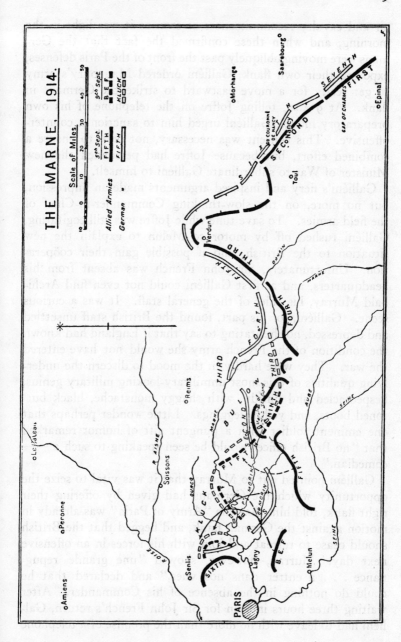

air and cavalry reconnaissances as soon as it was light in the morning, and when these confirmed the fact that the Germans were moving obliquely past the front of the Paris defenses, exposing their own flank, Galliéni ordered Maunoury's army to get ready for a move eastward to strike the Germans in flank. At 9 A.M., telling Joffre on the telephone of his own preparatory moves, Galliéni urged him to sanction a counter-offensive. This consent was necessary, not only to ensure a combined effort, but because Joffre had persuaded the new Minister of War to subordinate Galliéni to himself.

Galliéni's fiery and inspired arguments made an impression, but no more, on the slow-thinking Commander-in-Chief of the field armies. To save time while Joffre was still cogitating, Galliéni rushed off by motor to Melun to explain the new situation to the British, and if possible gain their coöperation. Unfortunately, Sir John French was absent from his headquarters, and at first Galliéni could not even find Archibald Murray, his chief of the general staff. It was a curious scene. Galliéni, for his part, found the British staff unsettled and depressed, not hesitating to say that if England had known the condition of the French army she would not have entered the war. They were hardly in the mood to discern the underlying qualities of this most unmilitary-looking military genius, bespectacled and untidy, with shaggy moustache, black buttoned boots, and yellow leggings. Little wonder perhaps that one eminent soldier with a pungent gift of humor remarked that "no British officer would be seen speaking to such a —— comedian."

Galliéni pointed out to Murray that it was vital to seize the opportunity which the Germans had given by offering their right flank, told him that the "Army of Paris" was already in motion against the German flank, and begged that the British should cease to retreat and join with his forces in an offensive next day. Murray, however, showed "une grande repugnance . . . à entrer dans nos vues," and declared that he could do nothing in the absence of his Commander. After waiting three hours in vain for Sir John French's return, Galliéni had to leave with no more than the promise of a telephone message later. This brought no satisfaction, for its purport was that the British would continue their retreat next day. Their decision had been confirmed by receiving a letter, written that morning, from Joffre, who said: "My intention, in the present situation, is to pursue the execution of the plan that I have had the honor to communicate to you — that of retiring behind the Seine — and only to engage on the selected line with all forces united." The meagre influence which the news of Kluck's change of direction had achieved was shown by a subsequent paragraph which said: "In the case of the German armies continuing their movement towards the S.S.E. . . . perhaps you will agree that your action can be most effectively applied on the right bank of this river, between the Marne and Seine." This casual qualification to the definite opening statement gave the British little encouragement to fall in with Galliéni's audacious suggestion. There is a dramatic contrast between the sluggish working of Joffre's mind, gradually but all too slowly veering round, and Galliéni's swift *coup d'œil* and instantaneous reaction.

After Galliéni's morning message, Joffre had been moved so far as to send a telegram, timed 12.45 P.M., to Franchet d'Esperey (who had superseded Lanrezac in command of the Fifth Army), saying, "Please inform me if you judge that your army is in a state to make it [an attack] with chance of success" — an inquiry which hardly suggests a sense of vital opportunity or an urge to action. This reached Franchet d'Esperey while Henry Wilson, of French's staff, was with him, and, after discussion, he sent a reply, at 4 P.M., which said that "the battle cannot take place before the day after to-morrow," and that he would continue his retreat on the morrow, attacking on the sixth. At 4.45 P.M., he sent a qualifying note, even less encouraging: "In order that the operation may be successful the necessary conditions are: (1) The close and absolute coöperation of the Sixth Army debouching on the left bank of the Ourcq on the morning of the sixth. It must reach the Ourcq to-morrow . . . or the British won't budge. (2) My army can fight on the sixth, but its situation is not brilliant. No reliance can be placed on the Reserve divisions."

What was likely to be the effect on a Joffre of such a discouraging reply to his tentative inquiry? To harden his hesitation.

The next link in the chain of causation fits in with a click — the click of a telephone switch putting a call through. For if Galliéni's *coup d'œil* gained the opportunity, it was, as he himself said, "*coups de téléphone* which gained the Battle of the Marne." On returning to his headquarters in Paris he had found a belated message from Joffre which was favorable to his proposal for a counter-stroke, but preferred it to be delivered south of the Marne — where it would have lost the greater effect given by a blow against the enemy's flanks and rear.

Galliéni seized the telephone, got through to Joffre, and by the fervor and force of his arguments at last won his sanction for the "Army of Paris" to strike north of the Marne as part of a general counter-offensive by the left-wing armies. Joffre promised to obtain the coöperation of the British. Galliéni promptly issued orders (10.30 P.M.) to Maunoury's army, which he reënforced, and a few hours later Joffre's telegraphic orders (sent out shortly after midnight) for the general offensive arrived, fixing the date for September 6 — it was too late now for the fifth, and too late to be generally effective even for the sixth. The delay had far-reaching consequences — not all ill.

On the morning of the fifth, while Maunoury's troops were moving east towards the enemy, the British, as well as Franchet d'Esperey's troops, were marching leisurely south, — away from the enemy, — in accordance with their original orders. When they turned about next day, they had much ground to recover, and were not as quick in retracing their steps as the situation demanded. This "disappearance" of the British not only enabled but encouraged Kluck — who had been taken completely unawares — to pull back half his main body (II and IV Corps) from the sector where the British had been, to reënforce the hard-pressed flank guard which was trying to hold off Maunoury's menacing advance against the German rear. The arrival of these fresh forces began to check Maunoury's advance on the seventh, and Galliéni pushed forward every possible reserve he could scrape up in order to strengthen Maunoury.

Here occurred the famous if legend-crusted episode of the Paris taxicabs. A fresh division had just detrained near Paris, but it was forty miles from the battle front. If it marched thither it would be too late, and there was only sufficient rail transport to take half the division. That afternoon, the police held up taxicabs in the streets, bundling the passengers out in some cases, and after collecting 600 cabs sent them to the suburb of Gagny, where they filled up with soldiers. Galliéni came to see the performance and, with mingled gratification and amusement, exclaimed: "Well, at least it's not commonplace!" During the night this forerunner of the future motorized column swept, as only Paris taxicabs can sweep, through the outlying villages and past their amazed inhabitants, making two journeys, with 3000 soldiers at a time. Unfortunately these taxicabs maintained their traditional preference for speed over reliability and, passing and repassing, became so mixed that on the morning of the eighth several hours were spent in sorting out their passengers before the division could attack.

The pressure on the Germans gained extra force from the fact that it was directed against their rear flank. If Galliéni had received the two further army corps for which he had asked days before and which were only just arriving piecemeal, the German forces south of the Marne might have been cut off and the battle been as decisive tactically as it was strategically. Even in the actual situation, the menace was such that at 10 P.M. on the sixth, Kluck called back his two remaining army corps, so creating a thirty-mile-wide gap between himself and the neighboring army of Bülow. Only two weak cavalry corps, with a few *Jäger* battalions, were left to fill it, and Kluck failed to arrange that this thin screen should be put under a single command. The consequences were fatal. Although he was able to hold and even press back Maunoury's troops, the gap he had left in the southern front uncovered Bülow's flank. Although still untouched by Franchet d'Esperey's slow advance on the seventh, Bülow, sensitive to his raw side, drew back his right to the north bank of the Petit Morin. And when

news came that the British were advancing into the centre of
the gap, it proved the signal for the German retreat, which
began on September 9. If the continuance of the British withdrawal on September 5 had marred the chance of a crushing
victory, it was a pleasant irony of fate that their very withdrawal made possible the "victory" as actually achieved.

It is necessary, however, to take account of the situation on
other parts of the battle front, for unless the German intentions elsewhere had been frustrated, Joffre's victory would
have been impossible and defeat probable. To the frustration
of their left-wing attack in the east, or Lorraine sector, the
Germans themselves were the chief contributors. For by
pressing the French back on their own fortress line they had
already made their task of breaking through it almost impossible. And yet another of the many "accidents of the Marne"
made their repulse certain. For when Dubail's and de Castelnau's armies, after their defeat in the battle of Sarrebourg–
Morhange, ended their hasty retreat, their line sagged inwards.
And into this reëntrant, formed quite unintentionally, the
main German attack was launched, pushing towards that
very "gap of Charmes" which the French in earlier years had
prepared for their reception.

Thus the French were given an opportunity to strike back
effectively at the German flanks, and thereby they temporarily paralyzed the original German advance, which came to
a halt on August 27. This not only gave the French breathing space to strengthen their position, but enabled Joffre,
with safety, to transfer part of the force from the right wing
to the more critical left wing. News of this transfer inspired
Moltke to frame his new plan of September 5, and lured him
into another vain attack on the French fortified barrier, despite
protest from the Crown Prince Rupprecht of Bavaria, commanding the Sixth Army. The new attack was launched
frontally against the Grand Couronné de Nancy, the ridge
which formed a flank buttress for the gap of Charmes. And
the Kaiser arrived with his white cuirassiers, like an actor
waiting his call, to make a triumphal entry into Nancy. But
successive assaults, inadequately prepared, collapsed under

the well-knit and superior fire of the French artillery, and on September 8, Moltke ordered Rupprecht to stop the offensive and the vain loss of life. Rupprecht had been urged into it against his own judgment by the excessive confidence of the artillery expert, Major Bauer, that his super-heavy howitzers would have the same effect as on the obsolete Belgian fortresses. Yet, curiously, he now only gave up the attack under protest — so Micawberish was the judgment of the military leaders of 1914–1918.

The German centre (Fifth and Fourth Armies), west of Verdun, was no better able to fulfill its rôle as the right arm of the pincer-like squeeze ordained in Moltke's modified plan. In the Verdun area Sarrail had replaced Ruffey as commander of the French Third Army, and the first instructions he received indicated not only a continued retreat but the abandonment of Verdun. Sarrail thought differently, however, and determined to cling on to the Verdun pivot as long as possible, without losing touch with the Fourth Army to the west. It was a happy piece of initiative, and the brake thus placed on the southeastward advance of the enemy's Fifth Army (under the German Crown Prince) was an essential factor in upsetting Moltke's plan. The stout resistance of Sarrail's troops, and still more the deadly fire of their artillery, not only held up but paralyzed the Crown Prince's advance. And a belated attempt on the ninth to break the deadlock by a night attack ended in a suicidal fiasco, with the Germans firing on each other. Sarrail, however, asked in vain for reënforcements which might have enabled him to convert his resistance into a dangerous counter-stroke from Verdun westwards against the German flank — for by holding on to Verdun he had formed one side of a sack into which the German armies between him and Maunoury, on the other side, had pushed.

The German Third Army (Hausen) formed a link between the German centre and right wing, and was assigned the indefinite rôle of being ready to support either. This rôle was perhaps in part the reflection of the fact that, being composed of Saxons, the Prussians tended to discount its value. In the event it was virtually divided. Its left was used to help the

Fourth Army in the abortive attack on the French Fourth Army (de Langle de Cary); an attack which, after perhaps the severest fighting of the whole battle, was driven to ground by the French artillery. Its right joined with Bülow's left in an attack on Foch, who had taken over command of a new Ninth Army, in the French centre, formed by simple subtraction from de Langle de Cary's army.

Among all the legends of the Marne, that which has grown up round Foch's part is the most comprehensive and has the least substance. The first claim, still widely believed, is that Foch decided the issue of the whole battle by a counter-stroke which threw the Prussian Guard "into the marshes of St. Gond." In fact, however, the Germans took their leave without interference — after the issue had been decided farther west. The second, and more modest claim, is that Foch made the victory possible by preventing a German break-through in the French centre. Even this is inaccurate — because the Germans were not trying to break through here. Bülow was merely carrying out his new protective task of wheeling his line to face west. And, in the course of this wheel, his left wing naturally bumped against Foch's front.

A further paradox is that although Foch was ordered to join in the general counter-offensive, and certainly issued repeated orders for attacks, his troops in reality were merely, and barely, holding on in defense.

At 1.30 A.M. on September 6, Foch had received Joffre's famous order for the general "about turn." Unlike the other armies, he received it in time to act on his share of it, which was to cover the flank of Franchet d'Esperey's attack by holding the southern exits of the marshes of St. Gond. His troops were tired and much reduced by the hard retreat. But the Germans on arrival at the northern side were surprised to find that they could only cross by the narrow causeways, and in consequence their fumbling attacks and belated attempt to side-step lost time without compensation. And, on the seventh, their attack east of the marshes broke down under the fire of the French artillery. As the only way of evading it, a bayonet attack in the half light before dawn was arranged. This caught

Foch's right by surprise and it gave way rapidly. Fortunately the Germans did not follow up as rapidly and so captured few of the tormenting guns. Even so, the situation was serious and Foch called for help; Franchet d'Esperey lent a corps to support his left and Joffre sent another to fill the gap now yawning on his right. On the ninth the continued German attack against Foch's right made fresh progress and met little resistance — until, shortly before 2 P.M., it was stopped by receiving Bülow's now notorious order for a general retirement. The Germans drew off undisturbed and even unobserved. To meet the earlier emergency Foch had taken the 42nd Division from his intact left wing and switched it across to his right; but it only arrived in time to fire its guns in the twilight after the vanished foe — contrary to the popular legend of its decisive counter-stroke against the flank of the German break-through. Throughout this "battle" in the centre both sides had been staggering with the blindness and unsteadiness of drunken men.

In our survey of the battle front we have now traveled back to the decisive western flank. Let us focus our eyes on the various headquarters behind the German front and examine the wavering gusts of opinion which culminated in the German retirement. The Supreme Command was back at Luxembourg, whither it had moved from Coblenz, on August 30, and depended for communication with the armies on wireless, supplemented by occasional visits by staff officers in motor cars. No regular motor or motorcycle dispatch service had been organized, and wireless communication suffered not only from the time lost in enciphering and deciphering, but from interference from the Eiffel Tower in Paris. As the army commanders, faithful to the tradition of 1870, were jealous of control, information was as sparse as it was slow except when they had successes to report — and exaggerate. Throughout the crisis of the battle, from September 7–9, no single report of any value came back from the front, and as late as the twelfth, Moltke had no knowledge of what had happened to Kluck's army, or where it was. Perhaps this ignorance made little difference, for on the fifth, Falkenhayn, then at Luxembourg in his capacity of Minister of War, noted in his diary: "Only one thing is certain: our General Staff has completely lost its head. Schlieffen's notes do not help any further, and so Moltke's wits come to an end."

Moreover, Moltke had already reconciled himself to defeat. For the gloom at Luxembourg is well shown by the fact that when, on September 8, Lieutenant-Colonel Hentsch left, as his emissary, to visit in turn the five armies west of Verdun, he was given full powers to coördinate the retreat, "should rearward movements have been initiated." He found none had occurred, if he found little confidence, at the headquarters of the Fifth, Fourth, and Third Armies. Passing on, he spent the night of the eighth with Bülow, and there found such an intensification of gloom that when he left in the morning he could at least feel confidence on one point — that orders for a retreat would soon be given. And at 9 A.M. on the ninth air reports told Bülow that six enemy columns (five British and one of French cavalry) were approaching the Marne — and so entering the mouth of the gap. By 11 A.M. he had issued orders for the retreat of his army to begin at 1 P.M., sending word to Kluck of his action.

Hentsch, delayed by blocks and panics on the road, did not reach Kluck's headquarters till past noon. There, according to his evidence, he found that orders for a retirement had already gone out, and in confirming them merely added the direction of the retreat — northeastward. But Kluck's Chief of Staff, Kuhl, asserts that these orders were only the mistake of a subordinate and that he had merely ordered a swing-back of his left in view of the fact that the British were almost behind it. He further says that Hentsch, in view of Bülow's situation, gave him orders to retreat. And Hentsch is not alive to contradict him. But the facts that the withdrawal began at 2 P.M., that the roads behind had been cleared, and that neither Kuhl nor Kluck troubled to ask for a written order, go far to support Hentsch — by showing their eagerness to be off. Kuhl, indeed, has admitted that the imminent break-through of the British and Franchet d'Esperey made the retreat inevitable. And, owing to the British penetration, Kluck's army had to retreat northward, thus leaving the gap still open.

The most curious of all the many accidents of the Marne is its accidental reproduction of the perfect-pattern Napoleonic battle — the pattern which Napoleon several times fulfilled and which General Camon and other students believe was normally in his mind. Its characteristics were that while the enemy was gripped in front, a manœuvre was directed against one of his flanks, a manœuvre which was intended not to be decisive in itself, but to create the opportunity for a decisive stroke. For the threat of envelopment caused a stretching of the enemy's line to ward it off and so created a weak joint on which the decisive stroke then fell. On the Marne Galliéni caused this stretching and the British pierced the joint. The pattern was executed perfectly, yet quite unconsciously.

Hence we see clearly that the continued retreat of the British on the fifth and their slow advance on the sixth and seventh were strategically invaluable, holding back unintentionally as Napoleon would have done purposely. If their "decisive" thrust had been disclosed earlier, the joint would hardly have been weakened by the removal of Kluck's last two corps — the departure of which, even as it was, Bülow delayed until early on the eighth. And the fact that Maunoury's stroke was definitely checked while these two corps were still on the march towards him is sufficient evidence that his stroke in itself could not have caused a decision.

But the continued slowness of the British on the eighth, ninth, and tenth was the negation of the Napoleonic pattern. And it proved fatal to the chance of converting the German retreat into a disaster. Thereby it paved the way for the four long years of trench warfare. In part it was due to the obstacle provided by successive rivers. But in still greater part it was due to want of impulsion, and misguided direction. Sir John French seems to have had little faith in the prospect, and still less in his Allies' efforts. In consequence he trod on the brake rather than the accelerator, besides keeping most of his cavalry on his right flank, and even in rear of it, as a link with his French neighbor instead of a spearhead of the pursuit. Indeed, not until the eleventh was the cavalry really launched in

pursuit. If Franchet d'Esperey's advance was still slower, he
at least had Bülow and not a gap in front of his centre and right
— although his left had a completely open path.

A further cause of delay, however, was the tactical method
employed in the advance. The old idea of keeping an even
alignment still ruled, as it did until 1918, so that if one corps
or division was checked its neighbors tended to halt. Thus
frequent opportunities were missed for pushing on past the
flanks of a temporary resistance and maintaining the momentum of the advance. And because the British and French
missed this opportunity it was to be left for 1918 to see and
the Germans to apply the method of Nature — for thus does
any current or stream take the line of least resistance, finding
a way past an obstacle and then flowing on, while the back
eddies wash away the now isolated obstacle.

Perchance also the victory might have been more decisive
— to the shortening of the war — if its creator had not been removed from control at the beginning of it. Having already
limited the power of Galliéni's blow, Joffre seized the first chance
to deprive him of his powers of directing it. Would that he
had been as quick in exploiting the weakness of the rival army!
For, on September 4, Joffre informed Galliéni that he would
resume direct control of Maunoury's army, leaving Galliéni
to fret his soul within the confines of Paris while watching the
fruits of victory slipping from the grasp of his slow-thinking
superior. Throughout the battle Galliéni's governing idea
had been to direct all reserves to the north, — towards the
enemy's rear, — although several times frustrated by Joffre.
With Galliéni's disappearance the advance became purely
frontal, giving the Germans the breathing space to reorganize
and stand firm on the line of the Aisne. Not until then,
September 17, did Joffre's mind awake to the idea of concentrating by rail a fresh mass of manœuvre behind the German
flank. As a result, in the so-called "Race to the Sea," the
French were always "an army corps too few and twenty-four
hours too late," until the trench front stretched to the sea.

But his was not the sole failure to take advantage of the
temporary state of disorder and indecision behind the Ger-

man line. It is the sober verdict of General Edmonds, the British official historian, that "had some of the 14 British Territorial Force Divisions and 14 mounted brigades, with the 6th Division still in England, been landed at the Channel coast ports to fall on the German communications and rear, a decisive tactical result might have been obtained and the war finished."

The question has often been posed whether the trench stalemate would have come to pass if France had possessed a Napoleon. Although the unappreciated defensive power of modern weapons and the unwieldy masses of 1914 weighted the scales against the mobility and decisiveness of warfare, the Galliéni interlude raises a doubt. For not only did Galliéni afford the one instance of "Napoleonic *coup d'œil*" witnessed on the western front in 1914–1918, but his intuition, his boldness of manœuvre, and his swift decision were so vivid in contrast to the other leaders, French, British, and German, as to suggest that it was possible to snatch a decision by manœuvre from the jaws of trench warfare — before the artisan swallowed the artist.

The hypothesis is strengthened by the fact that Galliéni's influence was exercised under the most shackling conditions. The command of a fortress was governed by rules and limitations which ordained a strictly defensive rôle, even gave the governor power to refuse assistance to the field armies, and discouraged him from any wider horizon than that of his immediate responsibility for the defense of the fortress. It was the irony of fortune that the Commander-in-Chief in the field should have led the way to universal siege-warfare; that the commander of a fortress should have conceived and launched the most decisive manœuvre of the war. Yet war is a game where the "joker" counts, and when Joffre withheld the trump Galliéni played the "joker." As he remarked later, half humorously, half bitterly, "There has not been a Battle of the Marne. Joffre's instructions ordained a retreat on the Seine and the evacuation of Verdun and of Nancy. Sarrail did not obey: he saved Verdun; Castelnau held on to the Grand Couronné: he saved Nancy. I have taken the offensive. As for asserting now that it is the Commander-in-Chief — who had gone back far to the rear while I advanced — who conducted, foresaw, and arranged it all, it is hard to believe !"

The truest phrase of all was his first, "There has not been a Battle of the Marne." Nor had there been a "battle" of Sedan in 1870. The folly of MacMahon in face of the first Moltke was paralleled, and even excelled, by the folly of the second Moltke in face of shadows.

Scene II

THE FIELD OF LEGEND — TANNENBERG

LIKE that of the Marne, the popular story of the great German victory of Tannenberg is a monument of monumental error. For it consists, actually, of a figure of wood, on a pedestal of clay, varnished with legend.

The first and most popular of these legends provided a romantic picture of an old general who, as the hobby of his years of retirement, spent his time in devising a gigantic trap for a future Russian invasion, exploring paths through and sounding the bottom of the marshes in which the Russian hordes were to be engulfed — and then, when war came, carrying his dream to fulfillment. The next legend, which rose as the shadow of Ludendorff rose behind the figure of Hindenburg, was of a masterly plan for a second Cannæ conceived and dictated in the train that was carrying Ludendorff to pick up his nominal master *en route* to East Prussia. History, alas, must dissipate both.

For the Germans, essentially a people of combination, found their Galliéni in a conjunction between the brain of a young staff officer and the drive of an old corps commander. And they, in turn, were much helped because Russian leadership was able to combine the faults of a Moltke and a Joffre. Indeed, the military history of modern Russia is epitomized in the brief record of the invasion of East Prussia.

The man who was, in large measure, responsible for the blundering execution was also responsible for that disastrous invasion being made, and being made before the Russian forces were ready. This was General Jilinsky, who had been Chief of the General Staff until 1913. For he had made the military convention with France whereby Russia was pledged to put

800,000 men in the field on the fifteenth day of mobilization. This arrangement put a strain on the cumbrous Russian war machine which caused numerous cracks and local failures when it began moving. And it also put a strain on the Russian Headquarters Staff which led them to make decisions in a state of nervous flurry. But the arrangement did not end with this promise, for the new plan envisaged an offensive against the Germans simultaneously with the main thrust against the Austrians.

To increase the drawbacks the plan was to be carried out by a man who had not worked it out; who had even been deprived deliberately of any influence upon it by General Sukomlinov, the Minister of War. Sukomlinov, indeed, was scheming to get command himself. But he was not the only one who had a belief in his own divine fitness for command. And his rival claimed divine right. For when the war came the Tsar proposed to take command himself — to the alarm of his Ministers. Under pressure from them the Tsar regretfully appointed the Grand Duke Nicholas, who was at least a trained soldier, but handicapped him by nominating his two principal assistants. One of these, Yanushkevich, was a courtier general, unpopular with the working army. The second, Danilov, was an able but orthodox soldier, and really directed the Russian strategy.

From the earliest days of August the Grand Duke was incessantly pressed by the French, through the Russian Foreign Office, to do something to relieve the German pressure on the French, and to do it quickly. Thereby, although the Russian invasion of East Prussia did not begin before the promised time, it began before it was ready.

East Prussia formed a long tongue of land pointing across the Niemen River to the heart of Russia, and flanked on the north by the Baltic and on the south by Russian Poland. Along the land frontier two armies had been assembled, the First or Vilna Army under Rennenkampf and the Second or Warsaw Army under Samsonov. The two formed a group under the higher control of Jilinsky. His plan was that Rennenkampf should advance against the eastern tip of East Prussia, drawing upon himself the German defending forces;

then, two days later, Samsonov was to cross the southern frontier and bestride the Germans' rear, cutting them off from the Vistula. The fault of this plan lay not in the conception but in the execution. Its potential value was well proved by the alarm — indeed, the dislocation of mind — caused in the German headquarters when the menace was disclosed. But it suffered two natural handicaps, apart from faulty leadership and military unreadiness. The first was that the two armies were separated by the fifty-mile chain of the Masurian Lakes; these also, in conjunction with the fortified Königsberg area on the west, narrowed Rennenkampf's line of advance to a gap only about forty miles wide. Secondly, the Russians' own invasion from the south was now to be handicapped by the fact that they had left the border country a desert, with poor railways and worse roads, as a barrier against a German invasion.

On August 17, Rennenkampf crossed the eastern frontier with six and a half divisions and five cavalry divisions. The problem of meeting such a double thrust had long been studied, and Schlieffen's solution had been that of utilizing the obstacles of the country, especially the Masurian Lakes, to strike hard and with full strength at whichever Russian army first came within reach, and then to turn against the other. But Prittwitz, the commander in East Prussia, was akin to his superior, Moltke, in his fear of taking calculated risks. Unwilling to rely on Landwehr and garrison troops to supplement natural obstacles in delaying Samsonov, he also left the two divisions of the XX Corps (Scholtz) on the southern front. The remainder of his Eighth Army, seven divisions and one cavalry division, concentrated to oppose Rennenkampf. And, to handicap himself further in gaining quick and decisive results, he launched a frontal attack on the invaders — owing to a mistaken idea of their position.

This attack was delivered near Gumbinnen on August 20. The German centre corps, the XVII (Mackensen), had to deliver the most straightforward attack and suffered a heavy repulse, which offset — at least psychologically — the success of the corps on either wing. Even so, Rennenkampf was on the point of ordering a retreat to save his own centre from encirclement when, next morning, he found that the Germans were retreating instead.

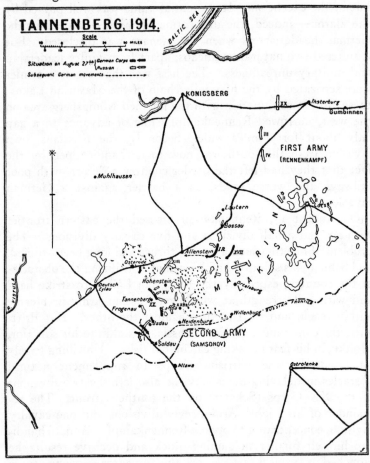

For on the day of Gumbinnen Samsonov had reached the frontier, so hurried on by Jilinsky that his troops were tired and hungry, their transport incomplete, and the supply services in chaos. He had with him eight divisions and three cavalry divisions, while two more divisions were following on.

His appearance was reported by the XX Corps to Prittwitz,

and his force was rather under- than over-estimated. Prittwitz was unnerved by the news, although the XX Corps was
not. That evening two of his staff General Grünert and
Lieutenant-Colonel Max Hoffmann, were talking outside their
office in the headquarters at Neidenburg — uncomfortably
close to the southern frontier — when Prittwitz appeared and
called them into his office. There also was his Chief of Staff,
Count Waldersee, another wavering bearer of a famous name.
With anxiety writ on his face, Prittwitz said, "I suppose,
gentlemen, you also have received this fresh news from the
southern front? The army is breaking off the battle and
retiring behind the Vistula."

Both the junior staff officers protested, urging that the
Gumbinnen thrust should first be driven home, that there was
adequate time, and that, in any case, a precipitate retreat
without fighting would give Samsonov, who was much nearer
the Vistula, the chance to cut off the main German forces.
Prittwitz, however, curtly told them that the decision rested
with him and not with them. He then left the office, leaving them to continue the argument with Waldersee — and,
eventually, to persuade him to take bolder measures. It was
decided that, to gain time, and room, an attack should be
launched against Samsonov's left or western flank. And for
this purpose three divisions should be railed back from the
Gumbinnen area to reënforce the XX Corps, while the remainder of the force there (I Reserve and XVII Corps) were to
retreat westwards by road. Here was the foundation of the
Tannenberg manœuvre.

On returning to the office, Prittwitz agreed to their moves,
and spoke no more of retiring behind the Vistula. Next day
he grew quite cheerful when word came that his forces had been
disengaged safely from Rennenkampf's front, and that Samsonov had almost come to a standstill. But on the twenty-
second, when the headquarters had been moved north to
Mühlhausen, a bombshell was exploded by a telegram which
announced that a special train was on its way with a new Commander-in-Chief and a new Chief of Staff on board — the first
being General von Hindenburg and the second General Luden-

dorff.   Half an hour after came the delayed telegram which told
Prittwitz and Waldersee that they had been superseded.

Not until later did the astonished staff discover the clue to
this dramatic upset.   It lay in the fact that while Prittwitz was
out of the office, during the discussion on the twentieth, he had
not only telephoned to Mackensen and to the Lines of Communication authorities, to tell them that he was going to retire
behind the Vistula, but had telephoned also to the Supreme
Command — then at Coblenz on the Rhine.   He had even
told Moltke that he could only hold the Vistula line if he
received reënforcements.   To crown his nerve-broken folly,
he forgot to tell his staff of this telephone talk when he came
back, and so prevented them from informing Moltke of his
change of plan.   And Moltke, whose own loss of nerve and
lapse into pessimism were still to come, though imminent, was
remarkably quick to penalize such a manifestation in a subordinate.

He looked round at once for a man of decision and found
him in Ludendorff, who had just wrenched victory from defeat
at Liége.   Then, as an after-thought, he chose a nominal
superior for Ludendorff, who was summoned to Coblenz.
Arriving there on the twenty-second, he had the situation in
East Prussia explained to him, dispatched his initial orders
direct to the unfortunate Prittwitz's corps commanders,
caught the train for his new "command," and picked up his
"commander," Hindenburg, at Hanover.

Let us pause to contemplate this delightful and amusing
picture of the German system of command.   The staff officer
chosen first and alone consulted, while the figurehead waits
unclaimed in the "lost property office" at Hanover.   The staff
officer telegraphing *his* orders, and then collecting his "bag-
gage" on the way.   But the supreme jest was that the plan had
already been framed and the necessary movements made by
a still more junior staff officer, Hoffmann, who was to remain
under Ludendorff in his post as head of the Operations branch.

The calculated daring of the plan, moreover, owed much
to an earlier experience of Hoffmann's.   For Schlieffen, with
discerning insight, had picked this impishly brilliant young

captain, whom many deemed merely a witty flaneur, to go as observer with the Japanese forces in the war against Russia. There he learned much about the Russian army, and not least a story that two Generals, Rennenkampf and Samsonov, had boxed each other's ears on the railway platform at Mukden. Thus, in his judgment, Rennenkampf would be in no hurry to aid Samsonov by pressing on from Gumbinnen. He had also learned in Manchuria the incredible carelessness of Russian methods, and this knowledge led him in August 1914 to accept the intercepted Russian wireless orders, sent out "in clear," as authentic, whereas his seniors were distrustfully inclined to regard them as an artful deception.

Paradoxically, the fulfillment of Hoffmann's plan and its development by Ludendorff — the plan on which Ludendorff was to rise to world fame — were hindered by Ludendorff's initial orders. For, in order to amputate Prittwitz's control, Ludendorff had telephoned from Coblenz to the several army corps, telling them to act independently until he arrived. The I Reserve and XVII Corps on Rennenkampf's front utilized this order to take a day's rest in their retreat westwards. Another check on rapidity was that the whole of the Eighth Army headquarters had to move back to Marienburg to meet the new commanders.

On arrival there on the twenty-third, Ludendorff was pleasantly surprised to find that the movements already in progress fitted in with his own half-formed plan, and he confirmed Hoffmann's arrangements. Next day it became clear that Rennenkampf was not moving forward in pursuit, and Ludendorff enlarged the plan by accelerating the retirement of the I Reserve Corps (Below), so that it could strike Samsonov's right flank. Then, on the twenty-fifth, intercepted wireless messages showed him the slowness of Rennenkampf's movements, and he began to think that he could use the XVII Corps (Mackensen) also, leaving only the cavalry to watch and hoodwink Rennenkampf. Thereby he might strike hard at not one but both of Samsonov's flanks, and bring off a decisive double envelopment. Unfortunately for his now matured plan, even forced marches could not overtake the lost day of rest.

Samsonov meantime had been staggering forward, driven on by telegraphic lashes from Jilinsky, who had jumped to the conclusion that the Germans were doing what Prittwitz had contemplated — retreating to the Vistula. And in driving Samsonov on to cut them off, Jilinsky not only neglected to hasten Rennenkampf, but even diverted his energy by orders to invest Königsberg. Meantime Samsonov's army was spread out over a front of nearly sixty miles, and his right, centre, and left were widely separated. If they had been linked by mobility, this width might have been an advantage, but with sluggish troops and bad roads it became a danger. And an attempt to side-step further west as he advanced led through self-dislocation to self-destruction.

Scholtz's XX Corps had been slowly giving way, and wheeling back westwards, before the advance of the Russian centre (XIII and XV Corps) towards the line Allenstein-Osterode. Fearing both the strain and the effect of a further retirement, Ludendorff ordered François's I Corps to attack on the twenty-sixth and break through the Russian left wing (I Corps and two cavalry divisions) near Usdau. Francois protested that part of his troops, three-quarters of his field guns, all his heavy guns, and his ammunition columns had not yet arrived; he also urged that instead of making a frontal attack he should get round the Russian flank. Ludendorff summarily overrode these objections. His sense of time was perhaps greater than his sense of tactical reality. But François, who had no wish to repeat Mackensen's experience at Gumbinnen, avoided the Russians' active resistance by passive resistance to Ludendorff's orders, and contented himself with the capture of an outlying ridge. And any danger to Scholtz's XX Corps was avoided by the inactivity of Samsonov's exhausted troops — one corps, for example, had marched more than 150 miles in twelve days over roads that were merely deep sand.

But the twenty-sixth did not pass without hard fighting. For away on the other flank the Russian right wing (VI Corps and cavalry division), separated by two days' march from the rest of the army, had encountered near Lautern the two German corps that were marching back from the east front. The

Russian right wing was thrown back in confusion, but the attacks of Below and Mackensen were badly coördinated, their troops were tired by the forced marches, and they did not press the pursuit. Thus the Russian right wing, although disorganized, was able to retire safely. Part of one division, however, had been hemmed in with their backs to the Bössau Lake, and in the panic a number were drowned. From this small incident arose the legend that Hindenburg had driven Samsonov's army into the lakes and marshes, drowning thousands.

The real crisis of the battle, as a whole, came on the twenty-seventh. For that morning François, now amply supplied with shells, opened a fierce bombardment on the position of the Russian left wing near Usdau. The Russian troops could not stand high explosive on top of an empty stomach, and they broke in flight without waiting for the German infantry. François ordered the pursuit to be made towards Neidenburg, to get across the rear of the Russian centre, but a Russian counter-attack against his outer flank caused him to wheel south towards Soldau. At daybreak on the twenty-eighth, however, he discovered that the beaten Russian left wing had retired precipitately from Soldau across the frontier, and he once more turned his forces eastwards to Neidenburg.

The time that he had lost on the twenty-seventh was compensated for by the fact that the Russians had engulfed themselves still further — to their doom. For although Samsonov knew the night before that his right had been beaten and his left was menaced, he had ordered his centre to strike northward again. As he can be acquitted of undue optimism, there are two possible explanations — that he was too rigidly loyal to his orders in trying to carry out his mission, or that he was unwilling to retreat when Rennenkampf, his old enemy, was advancing. His attack probably saved the Germans a repulse, for Scholtz had been ordered by Ludendorff to chime in after François's attack. As it was, the Russian centre made several cracks in Scholtz's front, although at the price of further exhaustion to itself. These cracks seem to have momentarily cracked Ludendorff's nerve, for he ordered François both to send back assistance and, with the rest of his corps, to march northeast towards Lahna, against the immediate rear of the Russian centre. This direction, which traversed thick forest country, would have given François less time and chance to bar the Russian line of retreat. Fortunately, he again disregarded his orders, and continued towards Neidenburg. Soon after midday Ludendorff discovered that the Russians were not attempting to deepen the cracks, but rather were showing signs of retreat. So he sent François fresh orders to move not only on Neidenburg but, through it, eastward on Willenberg. And by the night of the twenty-ninth, François's troops held the road from Neidenburg to Willenburg, with a chain of entrenched posts between, forming a barricade across the line of retreat of the Russians, who were now flowing back and becoming inextricably mixed in the forest maze which François had avoided. With its rear closed and its roads congested, the Russian centre (XIII, XV, and half the XXIII Corps) dissolved into a mob of hungry and exhausted men, who beat feebly against the ring of fire and then let themselves be rounded up in thousands.

The crowning scene of the tragedy was enacted by Samsonov himself, who had moved up from Neidenburg on the twenty-seventh to control the battle, only to find himself caught up in the swirling eddies of the retreat. Unable to do anything, he turned and rode south again on the twenty-eighth, only to get lost in the depths of the forest. In the darkness he turned aside, and his absence was unnoticed by his staff until a solitary shot rang out — he had taken his own life rather than survive the disaster.

But when he died the disaster was not so complete as his despair, nor so certain. If the Russian centre had only been able to reorganize itself for an aimed attempt to break out, it might well have succeeded. For François's barricade was thin and was itself menaced from the outside. The source of the menace was Artamanov's I Corps, which, after its defeat at Usdau and retreat over the frontier, had been reënforced, and now returned to the rescue. Air reports warned François of the danger on the twenty-ninth, but he stoutly refused to give up his "blockade," although he dispatched such force as he could possibly spare to check the advancing Russians at Neidenburg. Even so, the town was lost on the thirtieth, but Lundendorff was already sending reënforcements, and Artamanov, having made little attempt to press his advantage, retreated south once more on the thirty-first.

The cause of François's weakness, however, and the escape of part of Samsonov's army was due to the failure of Mackensen and Below from the east to join up with François. Thus the barricade was neither as firm nor as complete as it might have been. Owing to faulty coöperation between Mackensen and Below, and lack of clear guidance from above, their corps abandoned the pursuit of the Russian right wing and turned northwards towards Allenstein — marching, in good German style, "to the sound of the guns" instead of weaving a net round the enemy's rear in Hannibalic style. Ludendorff, divided between fear of Rennenkampf's advance and his desire to annihilate Samsonov, issued a contradictory series of orders which did not help to sort out the tangle into which Mackensen and Below had got their forces. In the outcome, he thereby risked more and gained less. For he took longer to close up his battle accounts and left a gap in the southeast through which part of the Russian XIII Corps actually escaped, and most of it might have escaped if Mackensen, on his own initiative, had not turned southward again in an effort to close the gap and the Russians had not been blinded by panic.

Nevertheless, 92,000 prisoners were taken, two and a half army corps annihilated, and the other half of Samsonov's army severely shaken, especially in morale. Making due allowance for the fog of war and the difficulties of this wild region, the victory of Tannenberg was a great achievement, as it was a unique one in the history of the war. But Ludendorff was not the designer of victory, and still less Hindenburg. To Hoffmann is due the chief credit of the design, if Prittwitz and Ludendorff have some share for accepting it in turn, and Ludendorff also for certain additions of detail. Nor was Ludendorff even the agent of victory, for François's share was the most essential. And against Ludendorff's share must be

offset the fact that his original telegram from Coblenz was the
original and echoing cause of the failure to complete Samsonov's encirclement. For the battle of Tannenberg was not
a second Cannæ, deliberately planned, as it has so often been
acclaimed. The aim was to break the force of the Russian
invasion, and not to surround the Russian army, and the idea
of the double envelopment only an afterthought, which became
possible of fulfillment when Rennenkampf continued to remain
passive. As much an afterthought as the very name given to
the victory. For Ludendorff's order for the pursuit on the
twenty-eighth had been headed "Frögeneau," when Hoffmann
suggested that he might aptly wipe out a stain on German
annals by using instead the name of the town in front of them,
Tannenberg, where in 1410 the Teutonic knights had suffered
a historic rout.

IV

1915 — THE DEADLOCK

BEFORE the end of 1914 the state of deadlock on the western front was realized, if in varying degree, by the governments and general staffs of the warring countries, and each was seeking a solution. The reaction varied in form and in nature, according to the mental power and predisposition of the different authorities. With the Germanic Powers the opinion of Falkenhayn was the decisive factor, and the impression derived not merely from his critics, but from his own account, is that neither the opinion nor the direction was really clear as to its object.

On his appointment after the Marne reverse, he still adhered to the Schlieffen plan of seeking a decision in the west, but he did not follow the Schlieffen method of weakening his left wing in order to mass on the vital right wing. The autumn attack at Ypres was made largely with raw formations, while war-experienced troops lay almost idle between the Aisne and the Vosges. Colonel Gröner, Chief of the Field Railways, even went so far as to submit a detailed plan to Falkenhayn for transferring six army corps to the right wing, but it was rejected. When we remember how close to breaking-point came the British front at Ypres, it can only be said that for a second time the German Supreme Command saved the Allies. At this juncture, too, Ludendorff was pleading for reënforcements to make his wedge-blow at the Russian flank near Lodz decisive, but Falkenhayn missed the chance by delaying until the Ypres failure had passed from assurance to fact.

Reluctantly dissuaded from a fresh attempt to break the trench-barrier in the west, Falkenhayn seems to have been vague as to any alternative object. His feeling that the war must ultimately be decided in France led him to distrust the value, as he doubted the possibility, of a decision against

Russia. Hence while he realized that the eastern front was the only practicable theatre for operations in the near future, he withheld the necessary reënforcements until forced to send them by the threatening situation of the Austro-Hungarian front. And even then he doled out reserves reluctantly and meagrely; enough to secure success, but never in sufficient quantity or in time for decisive victory.

It is to his credit, however, that he realized a long war was now inevitable, and consequently set to work to develop Germany's resources for such a warfare of attrition. The technique of field entrenchment was carried to a higher pitch than with any other army; the military railways were expanded for the lateral movement of reserves; the supply of munitions and of the raw material for their manufacture was tackled so energetically and comprehensively that an ample flow was ensured from the spring of 1915 onwards — a time when the British were only awakening to the problem. Here was laid the foundation of that economic organization and utilization of resources which were to be the secret of Germany's resisting power to the pressure of the British blockade. For the scientific grasp of the economic sphere in war Germany owed much to Dr. Walter Rathenau, a great captain of industry. She was also a pioneer in the psychological sphere, for, as early as the autumn of 1914, she launched a vast scheme of propaganda in Asia to undermine British prestige and the loyalty of Britain's Mahomedan subjects. The defect of her propaganda, its crudeness, was less apparent when directed to primitive peoples than when applied to the civilized peoples of Europe and America.

The same period witnessed also the one great success for German diplomacy, the entry of Turkey into the war, although this was fundamentally due to a combination of pre-war causes with military events. Since 1909 the country had been under the control of the Young Turk party, to whom traditions, including that of friendship with Britain, were abhorrent. Germany, filled with her own dream of a Germanic Middle East, — of which the Baghdad railway was the symbol, — had skillfully exploited the opportunity to gain a dominating influence over the new rulers of Turkey. Their leader, Enver Pasha, had been military attaché in Berlin; German instructors permeated the Turkish army; and a definite understanding existed between Germany and the Young Turk leaders as to common military action — urged by the common bond of necessary safeguard against danger from Russia. The arrival of the *Goeben* and *Breslau* reënforced the moral pressure of Wangenheim, the German ambassador, and eventually, on October 29, the Turks committed definite acts of war — at Odessa against Russia, and in Sinai against Britain.

Falkenhayn has shown "the decisive importance of Turkey's joining in the struggle" — first as a barrier across the channel of munition supply to Russia, and secondly as a distraction to the military strength of Britain and Russia. Under German dictation, Turkey struck as early as mid-December against the Russians in the Caucasus, but Enver's over-ambitious plan ended in disaster at the battle of Sarikamish. Turkey was no more fortunate in her next venture — to cut Britain's Suez Canal artery with the East. The Sinai Desert was a check on an invasion in strength, and the two small detachments which got across were easily repulsed, at Ismailia and El Kantara, although allowed to make good their retreat. But if both these offensives were tactical failures, they were of great strategic value to Germany by pinning down large Russian and British forces.

As an offset to Turkey's joining the Central Powers, Italy definitely threw over the artificial ties of the Old Triple Alliance and joined the Entente. On May 24 she declared war on Austria, — her hereditary enemy, — although avoiding an open breach with Germany. If her main object was to seize the chance of redeeming her kinsmen in Trieste and the Trentino from Austrian rule, there was also a spiritual desire to reassert her historic traditions. Militarily, however, her aid could not have an early or far-reaching effect on the situation, for her army was unready to deliver a prompt blow, and the Austrian frontier was a mountainous obstacle of great natural strength.

On the Entente side the reality of the trench deadlock pro-

duced different and diverse reactions. If the desire to hold
on to territorial gains swayed German strategy, the desire to
recover their lost territory dominated the strategy of the
French. It is true that their mental and material concentration on the western front, where lay the main armed force of
the enemy, was justified by military tenets, but without any
key to unlock the barrier they were merely knocking themselves to pieces. Winter attacks in Artois, on the Aisne, in
Champagne and the Woevre, afforded costly proof that against
the Germans' skill in trench fighting, Joffre's "nibbling" was
usually attrition on the wrong side of the balance sheet.
As for any new key, the French were singularly lacking in
fertility of idea.

Britain's trouble was rather an excess of fertility, or rather
an absence of decision in choosing and bringing to fruition
these mental seeds. Yet in great measure this failing was due
to the obscurantism of professional opinion, whose attitude
was that of blank opposition rather than expert guidance.

British-inspired solutions to the deadlock crystallized into
two main groups, one tactical, the other strategical. The
first was to unlock the trench barrier by producing a machine
invulnerable to machine-guns and capable of crossing trenches,
which would restore the tactical balance upset by the new
preponderance of defensive over offensive power. The idea of
a machine for this definite purpose was conceived by Colonel
Swinton in October 1914, was nourished and tended in infancy
by Mr. Winston Churchill, then First Lord of the Admiralty,
and ultimately, after months of experiment hampered by official
opposition, came to maturity in the tank of 1916.

The strategical solution was to go round the trench barrier.
Its advocates — who became known as the "eastern" in contrast to the "western" school — argued that the enemy alliance
should be viewed as a whole, and that modern developments
had so changed conceptions of distance and powers of mobility that a blow in some other theatre of war would corre-
spond to the historic attack on an enemy's strategic flank.
Further, such an operation would be in accordance with the
traditional amphibious strategy of Britain, and would enable

it to exploit the advantage of sea-power which had hitherto been neglected. In October 1914, Lord Fisher, recalled to the office of First Sea Lord, had urged a plan for landing on the German coast. In January 1915, Lord Kitchener advocated another, for severing Turkey's main line of eastward communication by a landing in the Gulf of Alexandretta. The post-war comments of Hindenburg and Enver show how this would have paralyzed Turkey. It could hardly, however, have exercised a wider influence, and it was anticipated by another project — partly the result of Churchill's strategic insight and partly due to the pressure of circumstances.

This was the Dardanelles Expedition, about which controversy has raged so hotly that the term just applied to Churchill may be disputed by some critics. This is answered by the verdict of Falkenhayn himself: "If the straits between the Mediterranean and the Black Sea were not permanently closed to Entente traffic, all hopes of a successful course of the war would be very considerably diminished. Russia would have been freed from her significant isolation . . . which offered a safer guarantee than military successes . . . that sooner or later a crippling of the forces of this Titan must take place . . . automatically." The fault was not in the conception, but in the execution. If the British had used at the outset even a fair proportion of the forces they ultimately expended in driblets, it is clear from Turkish accounts that victory would have crowned their undertaking.

The cause of this piecemeal application of force and dissipation of opportunity lay in the opposition of Joffre and the French General Staff, supported by Sir John French. Despite the evidence of the sequel to the Marne, of the German failure at Ypres, and subsequently of his own still more ineffectual attacks in December, Joffre remained confident of his power to achieve an early and decisive victory in France. His plan was that of converging blows from Artois and Champagne upon the great salient formed by the entrenched German front, to be followed by an offensive in Lorraine against the rear of the enemy armies. The idea was similar to that of Foch in 1918, but the vital difference lay in the conditions existing and the methods employed. A study of the documents conveys the impression that there has rarely been such a trinity of optimists in whom faith was divorced from reason as Joffre, Foch, his deputy in Flanders, and French — albeit the latter's outlook oscillated violently. In contrast, the British Government considered that the trench-front in France was impregnable to frontal attacks, had strong objection to wasting the man-power of the new armies in a vain effort, and at the same time felt increasing concern over the danger of a Russian collapse. These views were common alike to Churchill, Lloyd George, and Kitchener, who on January 2, 1915, wrote to Sir John French, "The German lines in France may be looked upon as a fortress that cannot be carried by assault and also that cannot be completely invested, with the result that the lines may be held by an investing force while operations proceed elsewhere."

Lloyd George advocated the transfer of the bulk of the British forces to the Balkans, both to succor Serbia and to develop an attack on the rear of the hostile alliance. This view was shared by a section of French opinion, and, in particular, by Galliéni, who proposed a landing at Salonika as a starting point for a march on Constantinople with an army strong enough to encourage Greece and Bulgaria to combine with the Entente. The capture of Constantinople was to be followed by an advance up the Danube into Austria-Hungary in conjunction with the Rumanians. But the commanders on the western front, obsessed with the dream of an early breakthrough, argued vehemently against any alternative strategy, stressing the difficulties of transport and supply and insisting on the ease with which Germany could switch troops to meet the threat. If there was force in their contention, it tended to ignore the experience of military history, that " the longest way round is often the shortest way there," and that the acceptance of topographical difficulties has constantly proved preferable to that of a direct attack on an opponent firmly posted and prepared to meet it.

The weight of military opinion bore down all these counter-proposals, and the Balkan projects were relinquished in favor of a concentration of effort on the western front. But misgivings were not silenced, and at this juncture a situation arose which revived the Near Eastern scheme in a new if attenuated form.

The Dardanelles. On January 2, 1915, Kitchener received an appeal from the Grand Duke Nicholas for a diversion which would relieve the Turkish pressure on Russia's army in the Caucasus. Kitchener felt unable to provide troops and suggested a naval demonstration against the Dardanelles, which Churchill, appreciating the wider strategic and economic issues, proposed to convert into an attempt to force the passage. His naval advisers, if not enthusiastic, did not oppose the proposal, and in response to a telegram the Admiral on the spot, Carden, submitted a plan for a methodical reduction of the forts and clearance of the mine-fields. A naval force, mainly of obsolete vessels, was got together with French aid, and after a preliminary bombardment entered the straits on March 18. Drift mines, however, caused the sinking of several ships, and the attempt was abandoned.

It is a moot point whether a prompt renewal of the advance would not have succeeded, for the Turkish ammunition was exhausted, and in such conditions the mine obstacle might have been overcome. But the new naval commander, Admiral de Robeck, decided against it, unless military aid was forthcoming. Already, a month before, the War Council had determined on a joint attack, and began the dispatch of a military force under Sir Ian Hamilton. But as the authorities had drifted into the new scheme, so were they tardy in releasing the necessary troops, and even when sent, in inadequate numbers, several more weeks' delay had to be incurred — at Alexandria — in order to redistribute the force in its transports suitably for tactical action. Worst of all, this fumbling policy had thrown away the chance of surprise, which was vital for a landing on an almost impregnable shore. When the preliminary bombardment took place in February, only two Turkish divisions were at the straits; this was increased to four by the date of the naval attack, to six when Ian Hamilton was at last able to attempt his landing. For this he had only four British divisions and one French division — actually inferior in strength to the enemy in a situation where the inherent preponderance of defensive over offensive power was multiplied by the natural difficulties of the terrain. His weakness of numbers and his mission of aiding the passage of the fleet compelled him to choose a landing on the Gallipoli peninsula in preference to one on the mainland or on the Asiatic shore; and the rocky coast-line limited his possible landing places.

On April 25, he made his spring, at the southern tip of the peninsula, near Cape Helles, and — with Australian and New Zealand troops — near Gaba Tepe, some fifteen miles up the Ægean coast; the French, as a diversion, made a temporary landing at Kum Kale on the Asiatic shore. Owing to the Turks' uncertainty, the British were able to gain a lodgment on several beaches, strewn with barbed wire and swept by machine-guns. But the momentary asset of tactical surprise was forfeited, and the difficulties of supply were immense, while the Turks held the commanding heights and were able to bring up their reserves. The invaders managed to hold on to their two precarious footholds, but they could not expand them appreciably, and the stagnation of trench-warfare set in. They could not go on, and national prestige forbade them to go back.

Ultimately, in July, the British Government decided to send a further five divisions to reënforce the seven now on the peninsula. By the time they arrived the Turkish strength in the region had also risen, to fifteen divisions. Ian Hamilton decided on a double stroke — a reënforced blow from Gaba Tepe and a new landing at Suvla Bay, a few miles north — to sever the middle of the peninsula and secure the heights commanding the Narrows. He deceived the Turkish Command and achieved surprise on August 6, but the first blow failed and the second lost a splendid chance by the inexperience of the troops and, still more, by the inertia and fumbling of the local commanders. For over thirty-six hours, before reserves arrived, only one and a half Turkish battalions barred the path. Energetic new commanders, for whom Ian Hamilton had previously asked, were sent out when the opportunity had passed. The British were once more condemned to hang on to tenuous footholds, and, with the autumn rains setting in, their trials were increased. The government had lost faith and were anxious to withdraw, but fear of the moral effect delayed their decision. Ian Hamilton was asked for his opinion, however, and when he pronounced in favor of continuing — in which course he still had confidence — he was replaced by Sir Charles Monro, who immediately declared for evacuation.

It was a remarkable example of prompt decision. While Monro visited Anzac, Suvla, and Helles during a single morning, without going further than the beach, his Chief of Staff sat on board ship drafting the recommendation for evacuation. Well may Churchill say, "He came, he saw, he capitulated." Kitchener at first refused to sanction the withdrawal and himself hurried out to investigate. The government was most relieved to see him go because they hoped to utilize his absence to relieve him of his post. Most of the Coalition Cabinet were united in dissatisfaction with his secretiveness and his administration, although disunited over the question of evacuating Gallipoli. Mr. Bonar Law, the leader of the Conservative Party, took a strong line on both questions. The Prime Minister, however, feared a public outcry over Kitchener's removal only less than he feared Mr. Bonar Law's resignation, and so temporized by giving way to Bonar Law's demand for evacuation, and by excluding Churchill from the War Committee of the Cabinet. Evacuation, therefore, was virtually decided upon before Kitchener reached Gallipoli. The fresh wave of opinion at home undoubtedly had an effect on his mind, and after his revived proposal for a fresh landing near Alexandretta had been vetoed by the War Committee, he reluctantly veered round and consented to evacuation.

Ironically, in the last phase it was the navy that tried to avert this. For de Robeck, who had passively resisted since March all promptings to a further naval attack, was now relieved by Admiral Wemyss, who not only opposed evacuation but, basing himself on a plan devised by Commodore Keyes, offered "to force the straits and control them for an indefinite period." The proposal came too late. The forces of opposition at home were now too strong, and in obedience to orders a withdrawal of the troops was carried out from Suvla and Anzac on the night of December 18, and from Helles on that of January 8. If the bloodless evacuation was an example of masterly organization and coöperation, it was also a proof of the greater ease of such operations in modern warfare. And as a final touch of irony Monro and his Chief of Staff, who had nothing to do with its skillful execution, received high decorations in reward. Thus the curtain rang down on a sound and farsighted conception, marred by a chain of errors in execution almost unrivaled even in British history.

The German Campaign. While the British were striving to unlock the back door to Russia, the Germanic Powers were hammering the Russians, whose resistance was collapsing in large measure from a lack of munitions which could only be made good by foreign supplies through that locked entrance, the Dardanelles. This fact and its effect were acutely appreciated by Russia's most formidable opponent. In the autumn of 1915, Hoffmann emphatically declared that the success of Germany's efforts against Russia depended on keeping "the Dardanelles firmly closed." For if "the Russians saw that there was no means of exporting their wheat, or importing war material, there would be a gradual collapse in that country."

On the eastern front, the campaign of 1914 had shown that a German force could count on defeating any larger Russian force, but that when Russians and Austrians met on an equality victory rested with the Russians. Falkenhayn was forced, reluctantly, to dispatch German reënforcements as a stiffening to the Austrians, and thus was dragged into an offensive in the east, rather than adopting it as a clearly defined plan. Ludendorff, in contrast, had his eyes firmly fixed on the ultimate object, and from now on advocated unceasingly a wholehearted effort to break Russia. Ludendorff's was a strategy of decision, Falkenhayn's a strategy of attrition.

In the conflict of wills between these two men lies the clue to the resultant strategy of Germany — highly effective, yet not decisive. This tug of wills was marked by the "offensive" use of the telegraph and by the unceasing pull of wires, with the Kaiser as the chief puppet.   While Falkenhayn was constantly trying to nullify a potential supplanter by denuding Hindenburg of the power to strike the enemy effectively, Ludendorff countered by screwing Hindenburg up to threats of resignation. Well might Hoffmann, watching the intrigues, note in his diary, "When one gets a close view of influential people, — their bad relations with each other, their conflicting ambitions, — one must always bear in mind that it is certainly much worse on the other side among the French, English, and Russians, or one might well be nervous." His intuition was correct. "The race for power and personal position seems to destroy all men's characters. I believe that the only creature who can keep his honor is a man living on his own estate; he has no need to intrigue and struggle — for it is no use intriguing for fine weather."

The Russian plan for 1915 embodied some of the lessons of experience and was soundly conceived, but the means were lacking and the instrument defective. The Grand Duke Nicholas aimed to secure both his flanks solidly before attempting a fresh blow towards Silesia. From January until April, under bitter winter conditions, the Russian forces on the southern flank of the Polish salient strove to gain possession of the Carpathians and the gateways into the Hungarian plain. But the Austrians, with a German infusion, parried their efforts, and the loss was disproportionate to the small gains. The long-besieged fortress of Przemysl, however, at last fell into Russian hands on March 22. In Northern Poland the Russians were preparing to strike upwards at East Prussia, when they were forestalled by a fresh Ludendorff stroke eastwards towards the frontier of Russia proper. The blow was launched on February 7, over snow-buried roads and frozen swamps, and was distinguished by the envelopment and capture of four Russian divisions in the Augustovo forests — near the Masurian Lakes. Moreover, it extracted the sting from the Russian attack further west.

These moves were, however, merely a "curtain-raiser" to

the real drama of 1915.   But before turning to this it is necessary to glance at events on the western front, the importance
of which is partly as a signpost to the future and partly because
of their reaction on the eastern front.

While a way round the trench barrier was being sought in
Gallipoli and experiments with a novel key were being carried
out in England, the Allied Commands in France were trying
more orthodox solutions.   The most significant was the British
attack at Neuve-Chapelle on March 10.   Save as a pure
experiment, the attempt stood self-condemned.   For it was an
isolated attempt on a small front with inadequate resources.
The arrival in France of several new regular divisions — made
up from foreign garrisons, of the Indian Corps, and of the
1st Canadian Division — had brought the British strength up
to thirteen divisions and five cavalry divisions, besides a
number of selected territorial battalions.   This increase
enabled French to divide his forces into two armies, and
gradually to extend his share of the front.   But Joffre was
insistent that General French should relieve the French of the
Ypres salient, which they had taken over in November, and he
made the intended French attack contingent on this relief.
Sir John French considered that he had not sufficient troops for
both purposes, and so decided to carry out the attack single-
handed.   An additional motive was his resentment of the
constant French criticisms that the British were not "pulling
their weight."

In design, however, the attack, entrusted to Haig's First
Army, was both original and well thought out.   After an intense
bombardment of thirty-five minutes' duration on a two thousand yards frontage, the artillery lengthened their range and
dropped a curtain of fire to prevent reënforcements reaching
the enemy's battered trenches, which were rapidly overrun
by the British infantry.

Complete surprise was attained and most of the first positions
captured, but when, in the second phase, the frontage was
extended, the artillery support proved inadequate.   Further,
owing to scanty information and to the two corps commanders
waiting upon each other, a long pause occurred which gave the

Germans five clear hours to organize fresh resistance. Then, too late and mistakenly, Haig ordered the attack to be pressed "regardless of loss." And loss proved the only result. An underlying factor was that the narrowness of the attack sector made the breach more easy for the defenders to close, although this defect was unavoidable owing to the general shortage of munitions, especially heavy guns and high-explosive shell for them.

The British had been slower than the Germans to awaken to the scale of munition supply required for this new warfare. Even so, deliveries fell far behind contract, owing largely to the handicap imposed by trade-union rules on the dilution of skilled labor. These could only be modified after long negotiation, and the shortage of shells became so obvious in the spring of 1915 as to lead to a public outcry initiated by Colonel Repington, the military correspondent of the *Times*, after consultation with Sir John French. Lord Northcliffe, with fearless disregard of the odium, threw the full weight of his newspaper into the campaign, which culminated in the establishment of a Ministry of Munitions, under Lloyd George, to coördinate and develop both the supply and the manufacture of raw materials. Although this press campaign failed to recognize some of the major causes of the shortage, as well as the fact that the need was for more heavy guns and not merely for more shells, its general effect was of incalculable value. Nothing else could have so roused the people or cleared away obstructions. Apart from shells, the crudeness and inferiority of all the British trench-warfare weapons, compared with the German, made such a radical reorganization overdue, and its urgency was emphasized by the near approach of the time when Britain's new national armies would take the field. If the task was undertaken late, it was carried out with energy and thoroughness, although improvisation was long in overtaking the evil consequences of earlier neglect. Apart from labor difficulties the immediate fault lay largely with military short-sightedness, which manifested itself in a constant tendency to underestimate needs and underrate novelties. Even when the machine-gun had obviously gained a dominance of the battle-

field, General Headquarters in France resisted its growth from
the puny pre-war scale of two in each battalion.   One army
commander, Haig, declared that it was "a much overrated
weapon" and that this scale was "more than sufficient."   Even
Kitchener laid down that four were a maximum and any in
excess a luxury — until the Ministry of Munitions came to the
rescue of the machine-gun advocates and boldly multiplied
the scale by sixteen.   It was due also to Mr. Lloyd George that
the Stokes Gun, a quick-firing light mortar, had the chance to
surmount the official barrier and develop into the outstanding
and ubiquitous trench weapon of the war.   And later, the
Ministry of Munitions succored the tank when it was repeatedly
threatened by the suffocating embrace of the War Office.

Nevertheless the ultimate responsibility for the munition
failure lay with the British people and their representatives
in Parliament.   Although before the war came the new Committee of Imperial Defense had done much preparatory spade
work, a strict limit was set to its efforts by the passivity as well
as parsimony of Parliament and people in face of the growing
danger of war.   Preparedness crawled forward to meet the
onrushing menace.   Most fundamental of all faults was the
neglect to organize the industrial resources of the country for
conversion and expansion in case of war.   While an increase
in the fighting forces may, by its air of threat, accelerate the
danger of war, readiness for industrial mobilization is unprovocative and, if war comes, a more essential foundation for
the power to wage it.

This pre-war neglect is a far graver charge against the
government which declared war on August 4, 1914, than any
failure to increase the army estimates or to introduce conscription.   Yet in making that declaration, the government,
however conscious of the political and moral issues, appears
to have been unconscious that it was dooming the manhood
of the nation to a terrible drain of life through want of weapons.
It is a moral question how far, in such circumstances, any
government is justified in taking the decision for war and in
retaining office.   The only excuse lies in the sanction of public
indifference to such needs.   And, unhappily, experience has

shown the practical difficulties suffered by a democratic government which tries to outstrip public opinion. Thus the ultimate responsibility falls on the British people. Even the military conservatism which obstructed improvements and reorganization during the war may be charged to lack of public concern with the training and selection of officers in peace. In the light of 1914–1918 the whole people bear the stigma of infanticide.

No belated wartime spurt could overtake the consequences of pre-war neglect until many thousands of lives had been wasted vainly. Even the Somme offensive was to be hampered by a limited supply of ammunition, while of this much was wasted because of the failure of hastily produced fuses. Not until the end of 1916 did the flow of munitions reach a volume, still expanding, which finally removed any material handicap on the strategy of the British leaders.

The tactical sequel of Neuve-Chapelle was less fortunate. It was clear that the small-scale experiment had only missed success by a narrow margin, and that there was scope for its development. But the Entente Commands missed the true lesson, which was the surprise attainable by a short bombardment that compensated its brevity by its intensity. And only partially did they appreciate the fact that the sector attacked must be sufficiently wide to prevent the defender's artillery commanding, or his reserves closing, the breach. Instead, they drew the superficial deduction that mere volume of shell-fire was the key to success. Not until 1917 did they revert to the Neuve-Chapelle method. It was left to the Germans to profit by the experience against the Russians in May.

But before that occurred, the western front was destined to increase the tally of military blunders. In the first, it was the Germans' turn to find and misuse a new key to the trench deadlock. This was the introduction of gas, and, unlike the British introduction of tanks later, the chance, once forfeited, did not return, owing to the relative ease of providing an antidote. On October 27, 1914, in the Neuve-Chapelle sector, the Germans fired three thousand shrapnel shells containing

a nose and eye irritant as well as bullets. This was the first
battlefield experiment, but the effect was so weak that the
fact was not even known until revealed by the Germans after
the war. Then, in a local attack in Poland on January 31, 1915,
the Germans tried the use of improved lachrymatory gas-
shell, but the experiment was a failure owing to the nullifying
effect of the intense cold. At the next attempt the gas was
lethal and was discharged from cylinders owing to the failure
of the authorities to provide the inventor, Haber, with adequate
facilities for the manufacture of shells. Further, the initial
disappointment led the German Command to place little
trust in its value. In consequence, when gas was discharged
against the French trenches at Ypres on April 22, there were
no reserves at hand to pour through the wide breach it created.
A strange green vapor, a surging mass of agonized fugitives,
a four-mile gap without a living defender — such was the
sequence of events. But the resistance of the Canadians on
the flank of the breach and the prompt arrival of English and
Indian reënforcements saved the situation in the absence of
German reserves.

The chlorine gas originally used was undeniably cruel, but
no worse than the frequent effect of shell or bayonet, and
when it was succeeded by improved forms of gas both experience and statistics proved it the least inhumane of modern
weapons. But it was novel and therefore labeled an atrocity
by a world which condones abuses but detests innovations.
Thus Germany incurred the moral odium which inevitably
accompanies the use of a novel weapon without any com-
pensating advantage.

On the Entente side, wisdom would have counseled a period
of waiting until their munition supply had grown and the new
British armies were ready, but the desire to regain lost territory
and the duty of relieving the pressure on Russia combined with
ill-founded optimism to spur Joffre to premature offensives.
The German losses were exaggerated, their skill and power in
defense underrated, and a series of diffused and unconnected
attacks was made. The chief was by the French between Lens
and Arras, under Foch's direction, when the earlier experience

of failure to make an effective breach in the trench barrier was repeated. The attack was launched on May 9 by d'Urbal's army (of eighteen divisions) on a four-mile frontage. It was quickly checked with murderous losses except on the front of Pétain's corps, which, thanks to meticulous preparation, broke through to a depth of two miles. But the penetration was too narrow, reserves were late and inadequate, and the gap closed. Foch, however, persevered with vain attacks which gained a few acres of ground at excessive loss. Meantime Haig's First Army had attacked towards Aubers Ridge simultaneously with the larger French attempt. The plan was to penetrate at two points north and south of Neuve-Chapelle, four miles apart, — the total frontage of the two being two and a quarter miles, — and then to converge in exploiting the double penetration. But the Germans, profiting also from the experimental value of Neuve-Chapelle, had developed their defenses. Thus the attack died away quickly from a surfeit of German machine-guns and an insufficiency of British shells. Under pressure from Joffre the attack was renewed on May 15 on the Festubert sector south of Neuve-Chapelle, and continued by small bites until May 27. The larger French offensive between Lens and Arras was not abandoned until June 18, when the French had lost 102,500 men — rather more than double the defenders' loss.

The effect of these attacks was, moreover, to convince even the dubious Falkenhayn of the strength of his western line, and of the remoteness of any real menace from the Franco-British forces. His offensive on the eastern front had already opened. Tactically unlimited, its strategic object was at first only the limited one of relieving the pressure on the Austrian front, and, concurrently, of reducing Russia's offensive power. Conrad proposed and Falkenhayn accepted a plan to break through the Russian centre as the best means to this end. In this plan the Dunajec sector between the upper Vistula and the Carpathians was selected as offering the fewest obstacles to an advance and best protection to the flanks of a penetration. The break-through was entrusted to Mackensen, whose Chief of Staff and guiding brain was Seeckt, the man who was to rebuild the German army after the war. Mackensen's force comprised the newly formed German Eleventh Army — strengthened by divisions from the west — and the Fourth Austro-Hungarian Army. The Ypres gas attack and a large cavalry raid from East Prussia were initiated to cloak the concentration on the Dunajec of fourteen divisions and one thousand five hundred guns against a front held by only six Russian divisions and lacking rear lines of trenches.

On May 2, after a four hours' intense bombardment had flattened the Russian trenches, the attack was launched behind a gas cloud and swept through with little opposition. The surprise was complete, the exploitation rapid, and, despite a gallant stand on the Wisloka River, the whole Russian line along the Carpathians was rolled up, until on May 14 the Austro-German advance reached the San, eighty miles from its starting point. Russian defeat almost turned into disaster when the San was forced at Jaroslav, but the impetus of the advance had momentarily spent itself and reserves were lacking. A new factor was introduced by Italy's declaration of war against Austria, but Falkenhayn persuaded the Austrian Command, with some difficulty, not to move troops from the Russian front, and to maintain a strict defensive on their Italian frontier, which was secured by the mountain barrier. He realized that he had committed himself too far in Galicia to draw back, and that only by bringing more troops from France could he hope to fulfill his object of transferring troops back there. For this could only be possible when Russia's offensive power was crippled and her menace to Austria removed. Strengthened by these reënforcements, Mackensen attacked again in coöperation with the Austrians, retook Przemysl on June 3, and captured Lemberg on June 22, cutting the Russian front into two separated portions.

But the Russians, from their vast man-power resources, had almost made good the loss of 400,000 prisoners, so that Falkenhayn's anxiety about the stability of his Austrian allies led him to yield to Seeckt's insistence and to continue the offensive, although still with limited objects and with one eye on the situation in France. Mackensen's direction was changed, however, from eastwards to northwards, up the

EASTERN FRONT.

Scale of Miles.

50   0   50   100

Line at outset of German Offensive, May, 1915
"   "   " 2nd Phase, July, 1915
"   " close of main offensive, early in Sept., 1915 (before Ludendorff's Vilna manœuvre).
Direction of main German thrusts

GULF OF RIGA

RIGA

LIBAU

BALTIC SEA

DVINA

Dvinsk

NIEMEN

Kovno

Vilna

Lake Narocz

Königsberg

Gumbinnen

EAST PRUSSIA

DANZIG

Marienburg

Lautern

Allenstein

Masurian Lakes

Augustovo

Hohenstein

Tennenberg

Minsk

NAREW

Bialystok

Thorn

VISTULA

Bug

NIEMEN

WARSAW

BZURA

Pinsk

PRIPET MARSHES

POLAND

Lodz

Brest Litovsk

VISTULA

Lublin

STOCHOD

Korel

Luck

SILESIA

WEST

VISTULA

Cracow   Tarnow   Jaroslav

Gorlice

Przemysl

GALICIA

Brody

Lemberg

Tarnopol

DNIESTER

CARPATHIANS

Stanislau

DNIESTER

Czernowitz

BUKOVINA

HUNGARY

BUDAPEST

ROMANIA

R U S S I A

ROMANIA

wide corridor between the Bug and Vistula, where lay the main Russian forces. In conjunction, Hindenburg was ordered to strike southeast from East Prussia, across the Narew and towards the Bug. Ludendorff disliked the plan as being too much of a frontal attack; the Russians might be squeezed by the closing in of the two wings, but their retreat would not be cut off. He urged once more his spring scheme for a wide enveloping manœuvre through Kovno on Vilna and Minsk, but Falkenhayn rejected it, fearing that it would mean more troops and a deeper commitment. The result justified Ludendorff's expectation — the Grand Duke extricated his troops from the Warsaw salient before the German shears could close on him. Falkenhayn, on the other hand, considered that Ludendorff had not put his full weight into the attack.

Nevertheless, by the middle of August 750,000 prisoners had been taken, Poland had been occupied, and Falkenhayn decided to break off large-scale operations on the eastern front. Bulgaria's entry into the war was now arranged and he wished to support the combined attack of Austria and Bulgaria against Serbia, as well as to transfer troops back to meet the French offensive expected in September. Mackensen was sent to the Serbian front and Ludendorff was given a belated permission to carry out his Vilna scheme, with such resources as he had, but as an independent operation.

It began on September 9, Below's Army of the Niemen and Eichhorn's Tenth Army forming two great horns which gored their way into the Russian front, the one east towards Dvinsk and the other southeast towards Vilna. The Russians were driven back in divergent directions and the German cavalry, advancing between the horns, far overlapped Vilna and drew near the Minsk railway. But the German strength was slender, the Russians free to concentrate against this isolated menace, and in face of the stiffening resistance Ludendorff took the wise course of suspending operations. The crux of the situation was that the Russian armies had been allowed to draw back almost out of the net before the long-delayed Vilna manœuvre was attempted; the degree of success attained with such weak forces was confirmation of its practicability and of Ludendorff's claim that a powerful blow delivered while the Russians were deeply enmeshed in the Polish salient might have annihilated the armed force of Russia. She had been badly lamed, but not destroyed, and although never again a direct menace to Germany, she was able to delay the full concentration of German strength in the west for two years, until 1918. Falkenhayn's cautious strategy was to prove the most hazardous in the long run, and indeed to pave the way for Germany's bankruptcy.

Thus, at the end of September, the Russian retreat, after a nerve-racking series of escapes from the salients which the Germans systematically created and then sought to cut off, came to a definite halt on a straightened line, stretching from Riga on the Baltic to Czernowitz on the Rumanian frontier. But the Russian armies had gained this respite at a ruinous price, and their western allies had effected little in repayment of Russia's sacrifice on their behalf in 1914.

For the Franco-British relief offensive of September 25 had been no more fruitful than its predecessors. The main blow was launched by the French in Champagne, in conjunction with a Franco-British attack in Artois, on either side of Lens. One fault was that the sectors were too far apart to have a reaction on each other, but a worse was that the Command tried to reconcile two irreconcilable factors — they aimed at a break-through, but preceded it with a prolonged bombardment which gave away any chance of surprise. Joffre's plan was that the break-through in these two sectors was to be followed by a general offensive on the whole Franco-British front which would "compel the Germans to retreat beyond the Meuse and possibly end the war." The unquenchable optimist! Both in Champagne and in Artois the attacks penetrated the German forward positions without difficulty, but subsequent delay in bringing reserves forward allowed the German reserves to close the gaps, a task simplified by the narrowness of the frontage of attack. The slight gains of ground in no way compensated for the heavy price paid for them — the Allied loss was approximately 242,000 against 141,000 Germans. And if the Allied Commands had gained more experience, so had the Germans, in the art of defense. The British share in this offensive is, however,

notable as marking the appearance in strength of the New
Armies; at Loos they were "blooded," and if inexperience
detracted from their effectiveness, their courage and driving
force were an omen of Britain's power to improvise a national
effort comparable with the long-created military machines of
the Continent.

The direction of this effort inspired less confidence, and Sir
John French gave place to Sir Douglas Haig as Commander-
in-Chief, just as already in September the Russian Command
had been transferred from the Grand Duke Nicholas, nominally
to the Tsar, as a moral symbol, but actually to General
Alexeiev, the new Chief of Staff. Simultaneously, French's
Chief of Staff, William Robertson, who had been long slighted
by him owing to Henry Wilson's stronger influence, went home
to become Chief of the Imperial General Staff, in order to give
a stronger direction to the general strategy of Britain — if also
to give it a western-front bias. Somewhat curiously, Haig
chose as his own Chief of Staff an old friend, Kiggell, who had
not hitherto seen any service in France.

Italy's First Campaign. Italy's military contribution to the
Allied balance-sheet of 1915 was handicapped not only by her
unreadiness, but by the awkward strategic position of her
frontier, difficult for initiating an offensive and hardly more
favorable for a secure defensive. The Italian frontier province
of Venetia formed a salient pointing to Austria and flanked on
the north by the Austrian Trentino, on the south by the Adriatic. Bordering on the Adriatic was a stretch of relatively low
ground on the Isonzo sector, but the frontier then followed the
Julian and Carnic Alps in a wide sweep round to the northwest.
Any advance eastwards inevitably suffered the potential menace
of an Austrian descent from the Trentino upon its rear.

Nevertheless the eastern front, though difficult enough,
seemed to offer more prospect of success — besides threatening
a vital part of Austria — than an advance northward into the
Alps. When Italy was preparing to enter the war, General
Cadorna, who assumed command, drew up his plan on this
basis of an offensive eastwards and a defensive attitude in the
north. The overhanging menace of the Trentino was miti-

gated by the expectation of simultaneous pressure upon Austria from Russia and Serbia. But on the eve of Italy's declaration of war this hope faded, the Russian armies falling back under Mackensen's blows, while the Serbs, despite requests from the Allies, failed to make even a demonstration. This lack of pressure enabled the Austrians to dispatch five divisions to the Isonzo from the Serbian front, these being relieved by three newly formed German divisions. Even so there were only some eight divisions in all available to oppose the Italians, who had a numerical superiority of more than three to one.

In order to secure good covering positions on the north a limited advance was made into the Trentino, with success, but another into the northeast corner of the frontier salient was forestalled. This local failure was to have unfortunate results later, — in 1917, — for it left the Austrians with a good strategic sally port into the Tagliamento Valley.

Meantime the main Italian advance, by the Second and Third Armies, had begun at the end of May, but out of their total of twenty-four divisions only seven were ready. Bad weather increased the handicap, the Isonzo coming down in flood, and the initial advance soon came to a standstill. The Isonzo front crystallized, like the others, into trench warfare. The Italian mobilization, however, was not complete, and Cadorna mounted a deliberate attack, which opened on June 23. This first battle of the Isonzo continued until July 7 with little gain to show. A fresh series of efforts after a ten days' pause were hardly more effective, and the front then relapsed into the spasmodic bickering characteristic of trench warfare, while Cadorna made preparations for a new and larger effort in the autumn. When it was launched in October he had a two-to-one superiority in numbers, but was weak in artillery. This defect, coupled with the superior experience of the defender, rendered the new offensive as barren as its predecessors. It was sustained too obstinately, and when finally broken off in December the Italian loss in the six months' campaign totaled some 280,000 — nearly twice that of the defenders, who had shown on this front a fierce resolution which was often lacking when they faced the Russians.

The Conquest of Serbia. While stalemate, although with marked changes beneath the surface, had once more settled in on both the Russian and the French front, the later months of 1915 witnessed fluid operations elsewhere which were to have an unforeseen influence on the war.

Austria had proved capable of holding the Italians on the Isonzo, and once the Russian danger began to fade under the pressure of the summer offensive, her Command was anxious to deal conclusively with Serbia. Austria's attempted invasions in August and September, and again in November, 1914, had been brusquely repulsed by Serbian counter-strokes, and it was not pleasant for a great power, especially one with so many Slav subjects, to swallow such military rebuffs. Her impatience coincided with Falkenhayn's desire to gain direct railway communication with Turkey, hard-pressed at the Dardanelles. Throughout the summer the rival coalitions had been bidding for Bulgaria's support, and in this bargaining the Entente suffered the moral handicap of military failure and the material handicap caused by Serbia's unwillingness to give up any part of Macedonia — of which she had despoiled Bulgaria in 1913. As Austria had no objection to offering territory that belonged to her enemy, Bulgaria accepted her bid. This accession of strength enhanced the chance of a decision against Serbia, and in August Falkenhayn decided to reënforce Kövess's Austrian Third Army with Gallwitz's Eleventh Army from the Russian front. In addition two Bulgarian armies were available. Mackensen was sent to direct the operations. To meet this new threat Serbia, apart from her own relatively small forces, had only a treaty guarantee of Greek aid and promises from the Entente Powers. The first disappeared with the fall of Venizelos, the pro-Ally Greek Premier, and the second, as usual, was too late.

On October 6, 1915, the Austro-German armies attacked southwards across the Danube, with a flanking movement across the Drina on the right. The sturdy resistance of the Serbs in delaying actions and the natural difficulty of the mountainous country checked the advance, but before Franco-British reënforcements could arrive, the Bulgarian armies struck westwards into southern Serbia across the rear of the main Serbian armies. This drove a deep wedge between the Serbs and their Allies, moving up from Salonika, and automatically loosened the resistance in the north. With their line bent at both ends until it resembled a vast bow, threatened with a double development, and with their retreat to the south cut off, the Serbian armies decided to retire west through the Albanian Mountains. Those who survived the hardships of this midwinter retreat were conveyed to the island of Corfu, and after being reëquipped and reorganized, joined the Entente force at Salonika in the spring of 1916. The conquest of Serbia — though not, as it proved, of Serbian military power — relieved Austria of danger on her southern frontier and gave Germany free communication and control over a huge central belt from the North Sea to the Tigris. For the Entente this campaign dug a military sump-pit which for three years was to drain their military resources, there to lie idle and ineffective. Yet ultimately that sump-pit was to overflow and wash away one of the props of the Central Alliance.

The Salonika Expedition. When, at the beginning of October, the Entente Governments had awakened to Serbia's danger, British and French divisions had been dispatched hurriedly from Gallipoli to Salonika, which was the only channel of aid to Serbia — by the railway to Uskub. The advanced guard of this relieving force — which was under the command of General Sarrail — pressed up the Vardar and over the Serbian frontier, only to find that the Bulgarian wedge had cut it off from the Serbians, and it was forced to fall back on Salonika, pursued by the Bulgarians. On military grounds an evacuation of Salonika was vigorously urged by the British General Staff, but political reasons induced the Allies to remain. The Dardanelles failure had already diminished their prestige, and by convincing the Balkan States of German invincibility had induced Bulgaria to enter the war and Greece to break her treaty with Serbia. To evacuate Salonika would be a further loss of prestige, whereas by holding on the Allies could check German influence over Greece and maintain a base of operations from which to aid Rumania, if, as expected, she entered the war on their side. To this end the Salonika force was augmented with fresh British and French divisions, as well as contingents from Italy and Russia, and there also the rebuilt Serbian army was brought. But apart from the capture of Monastir in November 1916, and an abortive attack in April 1917, the Entente forces made no serious offensive until the autumn of 1918. Its feeble effect was due partly to the natural difficulties of the country in the form of mountain ridges guarding the approach to the Balkans, partly to the feeling of the Allied Governments that it was a bad debt, and partly to the personality of Sarrail, whose conduct and reputation for political intrigues failed to command the confidence and coöperation essential if such a mixed force was to "pull its weight." On their side the Germans were content to leave it in passivity, under guard of the Bulgarians, while they steadily withdrew their own forces for use elsewhere. With gentle sarcasm they termed Salonika their "largest internment camp," and with half a million Allied troops locked up their jibe had some justification — until 1918.

Mesopotamia. Nor was Salonika the only "drain" opened in 1915. Mesopotamia was the site of a fresh diversion of force from the centre of military gravity, and one which could only be excused on purely political grounds. It was not, like the Dardanelles and Salonika, undertaken to relieve a hard-pressed ally, nor had it the justification of the Dardanelles expedition of being directed at the vital point of one of the enemy states. The occupation of Mesopotamia might raise British prestige, and it might annoy Turkey, but it could not endanger her power of resistance. Although its origin was sound, its development was another example of "drift" due to the inherent faultiness of Britain's machinery for the conduct of war.

The oilfields near the Persian Gulf were of essential importance to Britain's oil supply, and thus when war with Turkey was imminent a small Indian force of one division was dispatched to safeguard them. To fulfill this mission effectively it was necessary to occupy the Basra vilayet at the head of the Persian Gulf, in order to command the possible lines of approach.

On November 21, 1914, Basra was captured, but the rising

stream of Turkish reënforcements compelled the Indian Government to add a second division. The Turkish attacks in the spring of 1915 were repulsed, and the British commander, General Nixon, judged it wise to expand his footing, for greater

security. Townshend's division was pushed up the Tigris to Amara, gaining a brilliant little victory, and the other division up the Euphrates to Nasiriya. Southern Mesopotamia was a vast alluvial plain, roadless and railless, in which these two great rivers formed the only channels of communication. Thus a hold on Amara and Nasiriya covered the oilfields; but Nixon and the Indian Government, inspired by these successes, decided to push forward to Kut-el-Amara. This move led the British one hundred and eighty miles further into the interior, but had a partial military justification in the fact that at Kut the Shatt-el-Hai, issuing from the Tigris, formed a link with the Euphrates by which Turkish reserves might be transferred from one river line to the other.

Townshend was sent forward in August; he defeated the Turks near Kut, and his cavalry carried the pursuit to Aziziya, halfway to Baghdad. Enthusiasm spread to the Home Government, anxious for a moral counterpoise to their other failures, and Nixon received permission for Townshend to press on to Baghdad. But after an indecisive battle at Ctesiphon, the growing superiority of the Turkish strength compelled Townshend to retreat to Kut. Here, isolated far from help, he was urged to remain, as several fresh divisions were being sent to Mesopotamia. Kut was invested by the Turks on December 8, 1915, and the relieving forces battered in vain against the Turkish lines covering the approach on either bank of the Tigris. The conditions were bad, the communications worse, the generalship faulty, and at last, on April 29, 1916, Kut was forced to surrender. However unsound the strategy which dispatched Townshend on this adventure, it is just to emphasize the actual achievements of his small force in face of superior numbers. With inadequate equipment and primitive communications, and utterly isolated in the heart of an enemy country, it wrote a glorious page of military history. When these handicaps are compared with the four-to-one superiority in number and highly organized supply system of the force which ultimately took Baghdad, the comparison explains the awe in which Townshend and his men were held by the Turks.

The Home Front, 1915. Perhaps one of the most significant landmarks in the transition of the struggle from a "military" to a "national" war was the formation of a National Ministry in Britain, which occurred in May 1915. For the prototype of Parliaments to abandon the deep-rooted party system and pool the direction of the war was proof of the psychological upheaval of traditions. The Liberal Prime Minister, Asquith, remained, but the Conservative element acquired a preponderant voice in the Cabinet, although the dynamic personality of Lloyd George began to gain such a hold on public opinion that the real leadership slipped into his hands. Churchill, whose vision had saved the menace to the Channel ports and made possible the future key to the deadlock, was shelved, as already had been Haldane, the creator of the Expeditionary Force.

Political changes were general in all countries, and were symptomatic of a readjustment of popular outlook. The early fervor had disappeared, and been replaced by a dogged determination which, if natural to the British, was in strange contradiction to popular, if superficial, conceptions of the French temperament.

Economically, the strain had yet to be felt severely by any country. Finance had shown an unexpected power of accommodation, and neither the blockade nor the submarine campaign had seriously affected food supply. If Germany was beginning to suffer some shortage, her people had more tangible omens of success to fortify their resolution than had their enemies. In 1916, however, the strain on them was to be intensified by the failure of the 1915 harvest — the worst for forty years. Fortunately for Germany's powers of endurance the danger was to be relieved, and the British blockade partly nullified, by the inexpensive capture of a wheat-growing country on the eastern front. Ironically, the enemy were to throw Germany this lifebuoy, by encouraging Rumania to enter the war, after Falkenhayn had almost drowned the war-will of the German people in a bath of blood and tears by his renewed offensive on the western front.

1915 — THE DEADLOCK

Scene I

THE BIRTH OF A "PLAN" — THE DARDANELLES

A GIANT, three ships, and the fear of a rape were the main factors in bringing Turkey into the war against her traditional ally, Britain. The giant was Baron Marschall von Bieberstein, who for fifteen years, until 1912, was German ambassador at Constantinople. To a race whose sole criterion of conduct and admiration was might, whose "chivalry" was only extended to the mighty, Marschall von Bieberstein's huge frame, scarred face, and trampling manner formed a living picture of the growing power of Germany. Perhaps one man alone could have counteracted the impression with that of Britain's more mature and quieter strength. This man was Kitchener, who, curiously, seems to have felt an ungratified desire for the post. Instead, the British ambassador during the critical years was one from whose personality the requisite prestige and strength were absent — and who, during the critical weeks, was even absent on leave.

The ships were the new German battle-cruiser *Goeben* and the British-built battleships *Sultan Osman* and *Reschadieh*. As a shrewd step to enhance German prestige and weaken the one remaining foothold of British influence — that of the naval mission — the *Goeben* was sent out early in 1914 to Constantinople and for long lay anchored near the entrance to the Golden Horn. Then, in the war-charged atmosphere of late July, the ever-present Turkish fear of Russian lust for the Dardanelles developed almost to panic point. It was none the less powerful because mingled with Turkish lust for wider dominion. Certain of war between Germany and Russia, uncertain of Britain's entry, and egged on by the Germanophile Enver Pasha, the Turkish Grand Vizier responded to previous German over-

tures by asking the German ambassador, on July 27, for a
secret alliance against Russia. Next day the proposal was
accepted, and on August 2 the treaty was signed — unknown
to most of the Turkish Cabinet. On the morrow the first
mines were laid in the Dardanelles; and Enver had already
mobilized the Turkish forces on his own initiative. But the
news of Britain's entry into the war was a shock which nearly
burst the new treaty like a paper balloon. Indeed, so much
"hot air" was generated during the next few days that it even
sufficed to blow out another *ballon d'essai* — the astonishing
offer to Russia of a Turkish Alliance. But this offer did not
suit Russia's ambition, even though it promised her the one
chance of having a channel through which she could receive
munitions from her Western allies. She preferred isolation to
the sacrifice of her dream of annexation, and did not even
report the offer to her allies.

But Turkey's sudden reversal of attitude, and the predominance of her fear of British power over the fear of Russian
ambition, were short-lived. And the revival of confidence was
greatly helped by annoyance. Turkey, smarting under her
wounds of the Balkan War, had been awaiting the delivery of
her first two modern battleships with an eagerness and pride
all the more general because the money had been raised by
collections among the people. On August 3, however, the
British Government informed Turkey that it was taking over
the ships — and the announcement caused an explosion of
indignation. Every man who had contributed his mite felt an
injury akin to a personal betrayal. This popular outcry was
at its height when, on August 10, the *Goeben*, accompanied by
the cruiser *Breslau*, appeared at the entrance to the Dardanelles, having slipped past the British fleet near Sicily.

An officer of the German Military Mission, Lieutenant-
Colonel von Kress, brought the news to the War Minister,
Enver Pasha, and told him that the forts were asking instruc-
tions as to whether they should allow the warships to enter.
Then a vital interchange took place. Enver: "I can't decide
that now. I must first consult the Grand Vizier." Kress:
"But we must wire immediately." A moment of inward

turmoil. Then: "They are to allow them to enter." A further and guileful question from Kress: "If the English warships follow the Germans, are they to be fired on if they also attempt an entrance?" "The matter must be left to the decision of the Cabinet." "Excellency, we cannot leave our subordinates in such a position without issuing immediately clear and definite instructions. Are the English to be fired on or not?" Another pause. "Yes." As General Kannengiesser, a German witness of this eventful discussion, says, "We heard the clanking of the portcullis descending before the Dardanelles."

International law was evaded, British objections frustrated, Turkish pride satisfied, and Enver's dubious colleagues calmed by arranging the fictitious sale to Turkey of these warships. Turkey was not yet ready for nor agreed upon war, and Britain had every motive to avoid it.

Thus, during the weeks that followed, the Turks were successively enabled and emboldened to advance along the path to war by the passivity of Britain in face of growing provocation. The German crews were kept, the German Admiral appointed to command the Turkish navy, the British Naval Mission removed from control, and then forced to withdraw; British ships were detained, their wireless dismantled; German soldiers and sailors filtered into Constantinople, and the straits were closed. Meantime Turkish ministers, ever ready with glib assurances, congratulated themselves on the gullibility of the British, whose restraint was rather due to an acute sense of vulnerability, as a power with millions of Moslem subjects. Conciliation was pressed to the point of folly, however, when the British Admiralty's intention to appoint Admiral Limpus, ex-chief of the Naval Mission to Turkey, to command the British Dardanelles Squadron was abandoned for fear of giving offense to the Turks! And when the need for conciliation had passed, a misplaced chivalry seems to have taken its place in preventing the use of the one man who knew the Turks and the Dardanelles intimately.

Even the Germans began to be worried when a series of raids on the Egyptian frontier could not goad Britain to war. So

the German Admiral, with Enver's connivance, led the Turkish
fleet on a raid into the Black Sea against Britain's more
sensitive ally, shelling Odessa and other Russian ports. The
story of this provocation, as related to and recorded by Lord
d'Abernon after the war, is illuminating. The official sanction
came to the German Embassy in a sealed envelope addressed to
the Admiral. An official took the initiative and precaution to
open it and send on merely a copy. The first report that
reached Constantinople was that the *Goeben* had been sunk,
and so, thinking that the order had sunk with her, the Grand
Vizier conciliatingly replied to Russian protests by denying
that any such order had been given. Thereupon the German
Embassy sent to him, saying : " The order of which you deny
the existence, because you think it was sunk with the *Goeben*,
is in a safe place . . . at the German Embassy. . . . Pray
cease to deny that the Turkish Government has given the order
to attack Russia." Thus the war-fearing Grand Vizier was
compelled to stand aside helplessly while German cunning
removed any excuse to the Triple Entente for avoiding war —
at the end of October.

The best chance for both Britain and Russia was now in
making war, instantly. The defenses of the Dardanelles were
obsolete and still incomplete. The only two munition factories in Turkey lay on the shore close to Constantinople and
open to easy destruction by any warships which penetrated
thither. The misuse of the opportunity is a tale of almost
incredible haphazardness on the part of Britain, of equal short-
sightedness on the part of Russia.

On November 3 the Allied fleet carried out a short bombardment of the outer forts at the Dardanelles, the only use of
which was to help the German authorities in trying to overcome Turkish inertia over the defenses. They had sunk back
into lethargy again when, six weeks later, a British submarine
gave a fresh alarm and gained its commander a V.C. by diving
under the mines and sinking a ship near the Narrows. But the
effect of these warnings has been overrated. Turkish lethargy
was almost as boundless as British folly. Not until the end of
February did the Turks post more than one division on the

Gallipoli Peninsula, and not until March did the improvements in the defenses of the straits approach completion. In part, this state of weakness seems to have been due to a feeling that it was waste of energy to try to prevent a passage which could not be prevented, against any serious attempt. If the few well-informed experts, German or Turk, were dubious of their power to stop a purely naval attack, they were still less confident of resisting a combined attack. And the Turkish Staff history frankly says: "Up to February 25, it would have been possible to effect a landing successfully at any point on the peninsula, and the capture of the Straits by land troops would have been comparatively easy."

At one time the Entente might have found such troops, in quantity, without touching their own resources. For in mid-August the Greek Prime Minister, Venizelos, had formally and unreservedly placed all his country's forces at the disposal of the Entente. The offer was not accepted, owing mainly to Sir Edward Grey's desire to avoid antagonizing Turkey, whose hatred for Greece was stronger than for any other of her adversaries of 1912. But the hope, if not the desire, soon began to fade, and before the end of the month Russia asked Greece whether she would send an expedition to help in forcing the Dardanelles. King Constantine agreed, but made the proviso that Bulgaria's neutrality must be assured, to avoid the danger of a stab in the back. The Greek plan, a thorough one, was that 60,000 men should land near the outer tip of the peninsula to take in rear the forts guarding the straits, while another 30,000 landed near Bulair to seize and hold the isthmus. But by the time Turkey entered the war, Constantine had withdrawn his reluctant consent, believing that Bulgaria was already pledged to Germany.

In England, the only leader who showed a consistent appreciation of the importance of opening the Dardanelles was Churchill. From August onwards he frequently tried to arouse the interest of the War Office — which, for several years, had not made even a perfunctory review of the question. Three weeks after Turkey had entered the war, he raised it again at the first meeting of the new War Council, but all eyes were still focused on the French front, and he got no support from Kitchener. The Turks were granted a fresh lease of repose. But during December the blankness of the prospect on the western front was realized by many in England, and a few in France. Simultaneously the growth of the new armies evoked a natural question as to their use. The two factors combined to freshen, if not to clear, the atmosphere. Suggestions for a new strategic line of approach came from several quarters.

The most definite and practical was contained in a paper of December 29, written by the Secretary of the War Council, Lieutenant-Colonel Maurice Hankey, who emphasized the deadlock in France, and, while urging the development of new mechanical and armored devices to force a passage through the wire entanglements and trenches, suggested that Germany could be struck most easily through her allies, especially Turkey. He advocated the use of the first three new army corps for an attack on Constantinople, if possible in coöperation with Greece and Bulgaria, as a means not only to overthrow Turkey and bring the weight of the Balkans into the Entente scale, but to open communication with Russia. Further advantages would be to bring down the price of wheat and release 350,000 tons of shipping. The argument revealed a grasp of grand strategy, whereas the horizon of most soldiers, especially the highest, was narrowly bounded by tactics.

Sir John French, of course, objected to any effort outside his own command in France, but at this juncture an appeal came from the Grand Duke Nicholas for a British demonstration to relieve the pressure on his forces in the Caucasus. Ironically, this danger had almost passed before his appeal was received. Still more ironically, the emergency had been due to his own objection to spare troops from the main front.

Kitchener's response was to suggest the Dardanelles as the best place for such a demonstration, and also that "reports could be spread at the same time that Constantinople was threatened." Fisher now chimed in, to suggest not a demonstration but a combined attack on a large scale, in conjunction with which old warships should be used to "force the Dardanelles." He concluded characteristically and prophetically, "But as the great Napoleon said, 'Celerity — without it Failure.'" Churchill knew how little hope there was of obtaining troops for a large-scale attack, but eagerly caught hold of the naval possibility. Later in the day, January 3, he telegraphed, with Fisher's agreement, to the Admiral on the spot, Carden: "Do you consider the forcing of the straits by ships alone a practicable operation?" Back came Carden's answer: "I do not consider Dardanelles can be rushed. They might be forced by extended operations with large numbers of ships."

Carden's detailed plan was submitted to the War Council on January 13. The fatal decision was to be taken in a fateful atmosphere. Strategy, instead of being the servant of policy, had become the master, a blind and brutal master. From many sides there was an urgent call upon policy. Russia was faltering before she had even got into her stride; Serbia had barely escaped a fall; Greece and Rumania were leaning back the more that Bulgaria seemed to be leaning forward to grasp Germany's outstretched hand; Italy was sitting on the fence. The one front where troops were available was in France; and there ammunition was not — for the scale of ammunition that would suffice in other theatres would not even make a dent in the trench barrier in France. But strategy, as embodied in Sir John French, baulked the desires of policy, and as he was loyally rather than logically supported by Kitchener, the rest of the Cabinet was persuaded by a sense of numb, though not dumb, despair, aggravated by their amateur status. Hence they clutched too desperately at a straw of professional opinion which offered the chance of making bricks without men. And the words in which the decision was formulated was an epitome of their confused thought — "to prepare for a naval expedition in February, to bombard and take the Gallipoli Peninsula, with Constantinople as its objective." The suggestion that ships were to "take" a part of the land is delightfully naïve.

A few days later Churchill made an attempt to strengthen his plan by suggesting to the Grand Duke Nicholas that the Russians should coöperate by a simultaneous land and sea

attack on the Bosphorus. Strategically, his suggestion was
the best possible. Paradoxically, it proved void because the
political aspect here dominated the mind of the Russian
strategists! Strong as was their desire to possess Constantinople, they had no wish to coöperate with their Allies in gaining
it. The corner-stone of Russian policy was the annexation of
both Constantinople and the Dardanelles. Sazonov, the
Foreign Minister, had tried to make this claim more palatable
to his allies by suggesting the internationalization of Constantinople in return for Russian control of the straits, but the
weight of military opinion had overborne this partial concession. Thus it is not surprising that military Russia viewed
with jealousy and suspicion any move of her Allies towards her
own goal, and withheld her assistance. Even Sazonov records:
"I intensely disliked the thought that the Straits and Constantinople might be taken by our Allies and not by the Russian
forces . . . when the Gallipoli expedition was finally decided
upon by our Allies. . . . I had difficulty in concealing from
them how painfully the news had affected me." Russia would
not help even in helping to clear her own windpipe. She preferred to choke rather than disgorge a morsel of her ambition.
And in the end she was choked — the verdict should be *felo-
de-se*.

In England, too, fresh complications arose. Churchill's
quarrel with the plan was that the scale was too petty; Fisher's,
that it might become too large — and so obstruct his Baltic
project. And from this divergence a quarrel developed between the two — the political and the professional heads of
the Admiralty. At the next War Council meeting Fisher
rose to tender his resignation, but Kitchener intervened
and, drawing him aside, persuaded him to fall in with the
general opinion of the meeting. Thus the compromise plan
was a compromise even in its acceptance. Most apt is the
verdict of General Aspinall-Oglander in his official history —
that operations on the western front were a gamble with pounds
for a possible gain of pence, whereas in the east "pence were
to be wagered in the none too sanguine hope of winning pounds."
The naval attack began with the bombardment of the outer

forts on February 19 — curiously, the anniversary of Admiral Duckworth's successful attempt to pass through the straits, in 1807. Five days of bad weather then intervened, and when the bombardment was renewed on the twenty-fifth, the forts were outranged and the Turks retired from them. Next day the fleet began the second phase, the crushing of the intermediate defenses — more difficult because these, being inside the mouth of the straits, were more difficult targets to observe. Although results were disappointing, the chance was taken to land demolition parties, on the tip of the peninsula, which destroyed the guns in the abandoned outer forts. Thereby history, at least, gained a dramatic comparison. For on the same spot where this handful of marines moved about freely on February 26, thousands of men fell two months later. Further landings were made next day, and again on March 3, but on the fourth they met opposition, and were reëmbarked.

Meantime, the bombardment continued in rather desultory fashion — due in part, but not wholly, to the bad weather — and trawlers made a few rather feeble attempts to sweep the first mine-field. Lack of aircraft to observe and correct the shooting was, however, a great handicap, and on the ninth Carden reported that he could do no more until his air service was reënforced, and would meanwhile concentrate on clearing the mine-field.

But the weeks were slipping away, and the Admiralty could not help feeling that Carden's caution was disproportionate to the importance of his task — and of speed in his task. Hence, on March 11 a telegram was sent to urge him to decisive action, and to free him from any fear of being held responsible if serious loss ensued. Carden responded at once and arranged a general fleet attack, under cover of which the mines were to be cleared. And the principle governing the attack was to be that the battleships should only move in, and fire from, waters clear of mines. At this point Carden fell sick and was succeeded by his Second in Command, de Robeck.

The attack was begun on March 18 and was foiled not by resistance but by inadvertence. For, evading the British destroyer patrols, a little Turkish steamer had laid a new line

of mines well outside the main mine-field, dropping them
parallel to the shore in Eren Keui Bay, where the Allied fleet
had taken up its position in earlier bombardments. This new
line of mines lay undiscovered and unsuspected while the fleet
advanced past it to engage the forts. By 1.45 P.M. the forts
had been practically silenced, with little damage to the battleships, and the mine-sweepers were now sent forward to clear
the main mine-field, while the French Battle Squadron, in the
van, was temporarily withdrawn. As this squadron was
retiring through Eren Keui Bay, a tremendous explosion was
heard, and a dense cloud of smoke seen, in the *Bouvet*, and in
less than two minutes she had heeled over and sunk with nearly
all her crew. But the relieving line of battleships continued
the attack from closer ranges and the fire from the forts,
momentarily renewed, became more and more flickering as
guns were buried in rubble and telephone wires cut. Suddenly,
however, about 4 P.M. the *Inflexible* and the *Irresistible* were
seen almost simultaneously to have a heavy list. Mystery
accentuated the moral effect.

No one suspected the presence of the new line of mines, and
guesses as to the cause ranged from that of a shoal of floating
mines, turned loose to drift down with the current, to that of
torpedoes fired from some hidden point on shore. Fear of the
unknown prompted Admiral de Robeck's decision to order
a general retirement forthwith, and even as this was in progress
the *Ocean*, sent to the *Irresistible's* aid, struck the same line of
mines, and both foundered during the night. Although the
whole British fleet lost only sixty-one men in casualties, the
loss in material was large, for out of the eighteen Allied battleships three had sunk and three more were badly damaged.
But a far worse loss was that of nerve and of imagination —
to see the enemy's side — among the naval authorities. Actually, the enemy were suffering greater depression, and
with more reason. More than half their ammunition had been
expended and they had no reserve of mines. Many of the
gun-crews were demoralized, and the widespread opinion
among both Turkish and German officers was that they had
little hope of opposing a renewal of the attack.

But that attack, contrary to their expectation, was never renewed. When he came out of action de Robeck had the full intention of renewing it, and so had the Admiralty, which informed him that five more battleships were being sent out to replace his losses, and added that it was "important not to let the forts be repaired, or to encourage the enemy by an apparent suspension of the operations." But on the twenty-third he sent a telegram which not only revealed his reversal of view but reversed the opinion of the Admiralty — except Churchill, who had to bow to the weight of professional opinion. For de Robeck's new opinion was that the fleet could not get through without the help of the army, and that any further effort must be postponed until this was ready. And, in practice, this opinion meant that the navy was to hand over the whole offensive burden to the army, and to stand by, watching, while the army spent itself in vain assaults unaided by any fresh naval attack. Perhaps the underlying factor was that service tendency of mind which sentimentally values things more than lives, a tendency which may have its foundation in totemism, but is also accentuated by the peace-time shortage of material and the penalties attached to any loss of it. The artilleryman's love of his guns, and readiness to sacrifice his life to avert the disgrace of losing them, is paralleled by the sailor's adoration of his ship, even an old and obsolete ship such as these at the Dardanelles. It hinders him from adopting the common-sense view that a ship, like a shell, is merely a weapon to be expended profitably. Perhaps, also, a powerful auxiliary factor in the sailors' decision was now the presence of soldiers and their willingness to assume the burden.

For, coincidently with the preparations for a naval attack, the British Government had drifted independently towards a land attack. It had its origin, not in a wider consideration of the Dardanelles problem, but in a separate consideration of where the new armies could be used as an alternative to France. The committee reported in favor of Salonika, as an immediate aid to Serbia and an ultimate stab in the back to the Central Powers — up the Danube. The opinion won favor at the meeting of the War Council on February 9, being reënforced by the news that Bulgaria had contracted a loan with Germany and by the desire of encouraging Greece to support Serbia. And Kitchener, who had declared that he could find no troops for the Dardanelles plan, now announced that he would send the Regular 29th Division to Salonika, in conjunction with a French division. The promise of two divisions, however, was naturally not enough to allay Greek misgivings; Greece was unwilling to accept the offer unless Rumania was persuaded to join, and Rumania was held back by the sight of Russia's misadventures.

But the fact remained, and could no longer be hidden from the Cabinet by Kitchener's veil of mystery and authority, that the 29th Division was available. Nor did he for the moment seek to withhold it. In consequence, the War Council, on February 16, decided that it should be dispatched to the centrally placed harbor of Mudros in the Ægean "at the earliest possible moment, together with troops from Egypt," with the idea that "all the forces [were] to be available in case of necessity to support the naval attack on the Dardanelles." No one, however, suggested that the naval attack should be postponed to obtain surprise and the greater effect of a combined operation. The troops were merely to mount guard over what the navy gained.

But the 29th Division immediately became the rope in a tug-of-war between the "Eastern" and "Western" schools of thought, and on to the western end were pulling not only the British headquarters in France, but Joffre. Joffre's foresight was always, and only, quick when his own preserves were threatened, and he saw in the dispatch east instead of west of the newly assembled 29th Division a disquieting omen of the destination of the new army divisions. Kitchener could easily have hardened his heart against French, but he could not against the French. Just as his loyalty to France was an earlier instinct than his love of the East, so it now proved stronger than his belief in the eastern theatre. At the next meeting of the War Council, only three days later, he turned about face and asserted that the 29th Division could not be spared. In its place he suggested the dispatch of raw Australian and New Zealand troops, two divisions from Egypt. And he even notified the Admiralty behind Churchill's back that the 29th was not to go, thereby interrupting the collection of the transports required to carry it.

That same day the naval attack had opened — and the bombardment echoed throughout the Near East. When the news came that the outer forts had fallen the Turkish Government made ready to flee into the interior of Asia Minor. The Germans expected not only the appearance of the Allied fleet off Constantinople but that its appearance would be the signal for a revolt against Enver, and the consequent signature of peace by Turkey. For the Turks, in any case, could not have carried on the war once Constantinople, their only munition source, was abandoned. Italy and Greece began to incline more strongly towards war, and Bulgaria away from it. On March 1 Venizelos proposed to land three Greek divisions on the Gallipoli peninsula — but here Russia fatally intervened by notifying Athens that "in no circumstances can we allow Greek forces to participate in the Allied attack on Constantinople."

Only the neutral part of these favorable echoes reached the War Council in London, but it was sufficient to encourage the believers and win over the doubters. The original idea that the naval attack was only tentative, to be abandoned if found difficult, now faded, and all save one were agreed that the attack must be carried through, if necessary with land forces. The one dissenting voice was that of Lloyd George, who objected to the army having "to pull the navy's chestnuts out of the fire." Curiously, he alone sounded the warning truth of history that the renewal along the same line of an attack that has failed is rarely justified, and that it is better to switch the effort in a fresh direction. If his just objection was not immediately justified it was because of the Turks' lethargy in profiting by their warning.

In contrast, Kitchener laid down emphatically that, "having entered on the project of forcing the straits, there can be no idea of abandoning the scheme." But not until March 10 did he make up his mind to release the 29th Division, and,

perhaps worse, not until the twelfth did he nominate a commander for the expedition.   Yet the French, despite Joffre's
refusal to contribute from the field armies, had scraped together a division from the interior and had begun to embark
it as early as the third.   At the War Office in London not a
single preparatory step had been taken.   One result was
that when Ian Hamilton departed on the thirteenth none of
his administrative staff were available, and he had to leave
without them.   Further, the sum of his information comprised
a 1912 handbook of the Turkish army, a pre-war report on the
Dardanelles forts, and an inaccurate map!   To compensate
for this deficiency some of his staff had scoured the booksellers
for guidebooks to Constantinople.

   The one swift action in this halting period was Ian Hamilton's passage out to the Dardanelles.   A chain of special
trains and fast cruisers whisked him thither faster than he
could have traveled in peace time by the Orient Express, and
he reached the fleet on March 17 — the eve of its attack.   His
first discovery was the unsuitability of Lemnos as a base, owing
to lack of water, as well as lack of piers and shelter in Mudros
harbor.   His second was that the troops already present were
so ill-distributed in their transports that they would have to be
disembarked and redistributed before they could land on an
open and hostile shore.   Hence his first step on the eighteenth
had to be the unfortunate one of changing his base to Alexandria and directing all transports there.   So ill-conceived and
chaotic had been the original loading that battalions were
separated from their first line transport, wagons from their
horses, guns from their ammunition — and even shells from
their fuses.   One infantry battalion of the 29th Division had
actually been split up among four ships.   Even with the ample
wharfs and camps of Alexandria, unloading and reloading was
a slow business, not accelerated by the delayed arrival of the
administrative staff.

   On March 22, after the naval attack and before sailing for
Alexandria, Ian Hamilton with his chief assistants met de
Robeck in conference.   "The moment we sat down de Robeck
told us he was now clear he could not get through without

the help of all my troops." Soldiers could not argue with a naval verdict, even had they any wish to do so, and so without discussion the army was committed to the task. And the task was committed to the army. For although Ian Hamilton politely suggested to the Admiral that he should "push on systematically" with the attack on the forts, and Churchill made similar representations, the admirals both at the Admiralty and at the Dardanelles were as rigid as rock in passive resistance, and henceforth the fleet was dedicated to what Churchill has aptly termed the "No" principle — an "unsurmountable mental barrier." Sired by strategic confusion and dammed by naval negation, the landing on Gallipoli was born — and marred in delivery by muddled military midwifery. From this welter only one clear note emerged, in a memorandum drawn up for the Prime Minister by Maurice Hankey on March 16. In it he emphasized that "combined operations require more careful preparation than any other class of military enterprise. All through our history such attacks have failed when the preparations have been inadequate, and the successes are in nearly every case due to the most careful preparation beforehand. It would appear to be the business of the War Council to assure themselves, in the present instance, that these preparations have been thoroughly thought out." He pointed out that surprise had already been forfeited and in consequence the task had become far more formidable. Hence he enumerated a comprehensive list of practical points upon which the War Council should cross-examine the naval and military authorities, saying, in conclusion, "Unless details such as these . . . are fully thought out before the landing takes place . . . a serious disaster may occur." It may occur to the historian that Hankey was the only expert adviser of the British Government who had thought out the foundations of strategy. For when the Prime Minister, loth to question Kitchener's omniscience, tentatively asked if any scheme had been worked out, Kitchener replied that "that must be left to the commanders on the spot," and thereby shut down all discussion. No heed was given to the wider aspects of the plan — its immediate and potential needs in men, guns, ammunition, and supplies. In consequence, the expedition was to live from hand to mouth, nourishment being always too small and too late, yet in sum far exceeding what would originally have sufficed for success.

SCENE II

THE SLIP 'TWIXT LIP AND CUP — THE LANDING ON GALLIPOLI

APRIL 25, 1915

DESPITE the chain of folly which preceded it, was there still a chance of success when the belated land attack on the Dardanelles was launched? The verdict of history is affirmative. Part, if not all, of the opportunity forfeited by the British was redeemed for them by the Turks.

The panic caused by the opening of the naval attack, and the feeling that the passage of the Dardanelles could not be prevented, led the Turks to order new military dispositions which, in the words of Liman von Sanders, head of the German Military Mission, "did away with any defense of the exterior coast of the Gallipoli peninsula with its dominating heights; it did away with the defense of the Asiatic coast at the mouth of the Dardanelles. It was the feeblest imaginable defensive measure." That it was not put into operation may have been due to Liman von Sanders's protests — with which, however, Enver replied that he did not concur — but was more probably due to pure inertia.

The absence of renewed naval attacks after the failure of March 18 was rightly taken as a sign that a land attack was being prepared, and this assurance was confirmed by abundant reports from various Mediterranean ports, especially Alexandria and Port Said. This was the less surprising in that public reviews of the troops were held at Alexandria and Cairo, while at least one member of Ian Hamilton's staff received official letters from home through the ordinary post, addressed "Constantinople Field Force." Any chance of secrecy had indeed disappeared with the necessity of disembarking the force in Egypt.

Thus, on March 25, Enver was led to form a separate army for the defense of the Dardanelles, and to place it under the command of Liman von Sanders. After a hurried survey Liman exclaimed to his subordinate, Hans Kannengiesser: "If the English will only leave me alone for eight days!" They left him for four weeks. This month of grace, he records, "was just sufficient to complete the most indispensable arrangements and to bring the 3rd Division under Colonel Nicolai from Constantinople." Its arrival brought his strength up to six divisions — six times the strength present on Gallipoli before the naval attack began.

But he found them dispersed "as coast-guards," and his first step was to concentrate them. To do this effectively he had to decide where to expect a landing. The Asiatic coast, where movement and an approach to his rear were easy, he deemed the point of greatest danger. And so he placed two divisions near Besika Bay to cover the line of forts on this side. On the European side he most feared a landing at the neck of the peninsula, near Bulair, where the waters of the Gulf of Saros were separated by a mere three and a half mile strip from the waters of the Sea of Marmora. A landing here would cut off the defenders of the peninsula from Thrace and Constantinople, although if they did not lose their nerve they might be able to maintain themselves by drawing supplies from the Asiatic side, across the Narrows. This, however, was only a possibility. Near Bulair, therefore, Liman von Sanders posted two more divisions. The two other and lesser danger points were near Gaba Tepe at the six-mile waist — a low waist — of the peninsula, where a wide valley ran across to Maidos at the Narrows; and near Cape Helles, at the southern end, where the gradual ascent up the slopes of Achi Baba might be swept by the fire of the British fleet. Liman von Sanders distributed one division to guard the whole of the southern part of the peninsula, while his remaining division, under Lieutenant-Colonel Mustapha Kemal, was posted near the waist as a general reserve. The scheme of defense was essentially based on mobility, and to obtain the utmost value from his dispositions, as well as to offset the British ease of sea movement, he concentrated his energy on increasing and improving the roads.

Liman von Sanders's dispositions are the best justification for Ian Hamilton's plan. In this the governing factors were the small size of the British force and its mission. The force comprised only five divisions, 75,000 men to the Turks' 84,000. The object was to open a path for the fleet through the Narrows, not to engage independently in a campaign for big strategic prizes. Kitchener's bare instructions "strongly deprecated," although without explanation, an advance on the Asiatic side; and there the guns of the fleet could give no support beyond the initial landing. The Gulf of Saros was obviously the most vulnerable strategic point, but as Liman von Sanders himself has pointed out, "it afforded no direct artillery effect against" the defenses of the straits. Moreover, the beaches near Bulair were seen to be strongly prepared for defense, while a landing on the west side of the Gulf would be uncomfortably close to the Bulgarian frontier, and with difficult country to traverse. In either case, a small force would be in danger of being itself attacked in flank and rear from the mainland of Thrace, and so being caught between two devils and the deep sea.

Weighing up these conditions, and his handicaps, Ian Hamilton decided on a dual blow in the southern half of the peninsula. The 29th Division was to land on four beaches at the toe and seize Achi Baba, while the French waited in support, meanwhile sending a regiment to land at Kum Kale on the Asiatic side as a feint and distraction. The two divisions of the Australian and New Zealand Army Corps — whose initials were to enrich both dictionary and history with the word "Anzac" — were to land north of Gaba Tepe, while the Royal Naval Division made a feint near Bulair.

If the idea of security seems to have dictated the landing at the toe, surprise was to be its effect. And surprise was assiduously sought in manifold ways. Commander Unwin was inspired by the proximity of Troy to make the apt suggestion of reproducing the immortal wooden horse — in this case to be a sea-horse. A collier, the *River Clyde*, was to be run ashore at V Beach and to disgorge troops through large openings

cut in its sides.   Ian Hamilton himself added another stratagem
— which had some parallel to Wolfe's at Quebec — whereby
a detachment of two battalions was to be landed further up

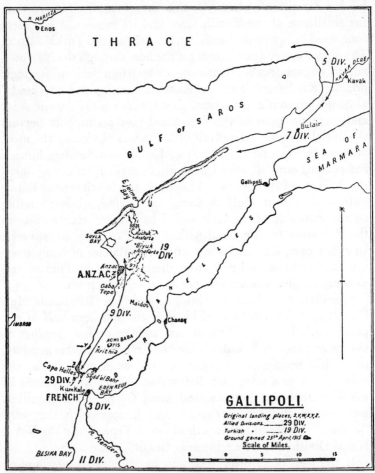

the coast at a spot apparently inaccessible, and so unlikely to
be defended, whence it could menace the rear of the Turks
defending the southern beaches.   This spot was christened
Y Beach.   Further, the French transports were to make a
pretense of landing troops at Besika Bay.   Ian Hamilton also
wished to increase the chance of local surprise, and decrease

the risk of loss, by landing at night, even though it meant foregoing the support of the guns of the fleet. But Hunter-Weston, commanding the 29th Division, preferred a daylight landing, to avoid the risk of confusion. He gained his way through the support of naval opinion, which was based on the difficulties of the current. For the Anzac landing, the corps commander, Birdwood, wisely preferred any risk to that of the obvious, and if his landing was to suffer in effect through confusion — which was due more to lack of training than to initial loss of direction in the dark — it escaped the heavy losses of the 29th Division.

By April 20 the preparations for the venture were complete and the troops assembled at Mudros on their transports. The weather, almost continuously unfavorable for several weeks, was both the determining and the most uncertain factor. Not until the twenty-third did it allow the scheme to be set in motion. For the mechanism, like an alarm clock, required, and was timed to strike, thirty-six hours from the start of the movement.

On the evening of the twenty-fourth, eleven transports of the Royal Naval Division sailed for the Gulf of Saros, escorted by warships which opened a slow bombardment at daybreak on the Bulair lines. Towards evening, boats were ostentatiously swung out, filled with troops, and began pulling for the shore — to return to the ships as soon as darkness cloaked them. During the night an officer, Lieutenant-Commander B. C. Freyberg, swam ashore from a boat two miles out and lit flares along the beach. His feat, and its effect, were an outstanding proof that in war it is the man, and not men, who count — that one man can be more useful than a thousand.

For the Gaba Tepe landing, 1500 men of the covering force were carried in three battleships to the rendezvous five miles offshore. They clambered down into the boats at 1.30 A.M. just as the moon was sinking. Then, towed by the battleships and followed by seven destroyers with the rest of the covering force, they moved silently inshore until the distance was halved. Here the twelve "tows," each with a steam picket boat at the head, cast loose and continued the approach. But darkness and the strong current caused the tows to arrive off the beach a mile north of the intended point, and so on a more rugged part of the coast, skirted by precipitous cliffs, seamed with steep gullies and covered with scrub. Day was just breaking when at 4.25 A.M., under a scattered and erratic fire from a few small and stupefied posts, the forty-eight boats were rowed across the last fifty yards until they touched bottom. Then, in a headlong rush and scramble, the Australians swept inland. Hardly a man had fallen, but units were badly mixed, and soon became worse. The next contingent, landed from the destroyers, suffered rather more, at least on the left, but carried the advance over a mile inland. One small party even penetrated far enough to see the glistening straits beyond and beneath.

The Helles landing was less fortunate, although the opponents were little more numerous. Only two Turkish battalions were present in the whole area south of Achi Baba, and only two of the five selected landing places were covered by wire entanglements and machine guns. These were the central beaches W and V on either side of Cape Helles itself. The British covering force comprised the four battalions of Hare's 86th Brigade, which with an extra half battalion were to land at V, W, and X Beaches; one battalion at S Beach; and two battalions at Y Beach for the threat to the enemy's rear. Thus seven and a half battalions were to be thrown ashore initially, followed by five more of the main body, and ultimately by the French Division. At 5 A.M., under cover of a heavy fleet bombardment, the tows crept towards the shore. The first mischance was the slow progress, against the current, of the tows making for S Beach, on the east flank, which caused those destined for the three main beaches to be held back until nearly 6 A.M. Nevertheless, the tows for X Beach, round the western tip of the peninsula, landed without a casualty beneath a low cliff, where their arrival was unexpected by the Turks and opposed only by a piquet of twelve men. But at W, the next beach eastwards, the landing parties ran into a well-prepared death trap. Not a shot was fired as the boats rowed in, but as they grounded they were

swept by bullets, and the men, jumping overboard, were entangled in submerged wire.   Despite heavy loss they struggled
forward, drove off the defenders, and gained a lodgment on
the cliffs.   But Hare, too gallantly exposing himself, was
wounded, and the effort subsided.

The landing at V Beach, beside the old fort of Sedd el Bahr,
fared still worse.   Here the invaders ran, like gladiators,
into a gently sloping arena designed by nature and arranged
by the Turks — themselves ensconced in surrounding seats —
for a butchery.   The tows, checked by the current, were caught
up by the *River Clyde*, and as it grounded hell yawned.   In the
incoming boats oars dropped like the wings of scorched moths,
while the boats drifted helplessly with their load of dead and
wounded.   Many men jumped overboard only to be drowned
in water stained with their own blood.   A few gained the
beach and found shelter beneath a low bank — which was
to mark the limit of the day's advance.   Those who tried to
emerge from the *River Clyde*, and reach the shore across a
bridge of lighters, were no more fortunate, and fell in heaps.
The few survivors on the beach and the thousand left in the
River Clyde could only wait for nightfall to release them.   Two
companies of Turks, distributed between V and W Beaches,
had checked the main British landing.

But S Beach, at the other side of Morto Bay, was, like X,
an unlikely spot and so guarded by only a platoon of Turks.
The landing battalion got safely ashore and then, having had
preliminary instructions to await the advance from the other
beaches, fulfilled them to the letter.   Its inertness, however,
was approved by Hunter-Weston, owing apparently to an
exaggerated estimate of the Turkish strength.   Actually the
two intact battalions ashore at the two flank beaches, S and
X, totaled four times the strength of the Turkish defenders
of V and W Beaches, and by an advance inwards could have
taken them in rear.

Soon, also, that superiority was increased — but not the
pressure.   Two battalions of the 87th Brigade (the other two
had been used for the original landings at S and Y) were put
ashore safely on X Beach by 9 A.M., but they had been ear-

marked as divisional reserve, and the Brigadier did not feel justified in using them, except to dig in, unless and until he received instructions from Hunter-Weston. These never came, so the force at X Beach remained passive.

Meantime, after another vain attempt to land at V Beach — in which the Commander of the 88th Brigade was killed — the remaining two and a half battalions of the main body were disembarked at W Beach. "But," as the official history gently says, "in contrast to the gallant exploits of the morning a certain inertia seems to have overtaken the troops on this part of the front, who now amounted to at least 2000 men. . . . Faced with a definite task — the capture of the beaches — the 29th Division had put an indelible mark on history. But once that task was done, platoon, company, and even battalion commanders, each in their own sphere, were awaiting fresh and definite orders, and on their own initiative did little to exploit the morning's success or to keep in touch with the enemy." Instead, they allowed themselves to be paralyzed by an enemy "whom they had already driven from his trenches and whom, though unaware of the fact, they outnumbered by at least six to one."

But a still greater opportunity was missed at Y Beach, three miles up the coast, where " 2000 men were safely disembarked without a hitch and without any opposition. For eleven hours they were left undisturbed by the enemy, and throughout that period they alone were equal in numbers to all the Turkish forces south of Achi Baba. Yet throughout the twenty-fifth the initial success remained unexploited. During the ensuing night the troops gallantly repulsed a succession of fierce attacks on their line. But the whole enterprise was suddenly abandoned next morning, and the men reëmbarked, at the very moment when the enemy himself was in full retreat."

The one man who realized the opportunity was Ian Hamilton himself, out at sea, but he had delegated the execution of the landing to the commander of the 29th Division, and had kept no reserve. Somewhat naturally, he was loth to interfere except by suggestion. But he was far quicker than the man on the spot to appreciate the check in the south, and as early as 9.21 A.M. he signaled to Hunter-Weston: "Would you like to get some more men ashore at Y Beach? If so, trawlers are available." But Hunter-Weston's attention was glued to the bloody beaches where the enemy was better prepared, and there he preferred to concentrate his efforts.

At Y Beach itself the landing had been made without a shot being fired or a Turk being discovered. But the commander, Colonel Matthews, was content to await further orders. "Crowds of troops were . . . sitting about the edge of the cliff," and not until late in the afternoon did they even attempt to entrench. Towards dark one Turkish battalion was brought up and launched a series of counter-attacks against the two British battalions. Repeatedly beaten off, the Turks finally fled in disorder soon after 7 A.M. But their night assaults caused such loss and confusion among the defenders that panic spread. A string of alarmist messages were signaled to the ships and many stragglers poured down to the beach, swarming into the boats sent for the wounded. This state continued even after the disappearance of the Turks, and Matthews, who saw no response to his urgent appeal for reënforcements, reluctantly decided to follow the example set by his stragglers. By 11.30 A.M. the whole force had reëmbarked. Some hours later a naval party under Lieutenant-Commander Keyes went ashore and made a prolonged search for wounded without being fired on.

But if anything can justify Matthews's action, and previous inaction, it is his utter neglect by his superior, Hunter-Weston. Throughout the twenty-nine hours on land "no word of any kind reached him from divisional headquarters." No officer was sent to visit him, no reply was sent to his urgent appeals. And when, early in the morning of the twenty-sixth, Ian Hamilton once more intervened with the offer of a French brigade (six battalions), Hunter-Weston had no thought but to land them on W Beach — in the enemy's face. The measured verdict of the official history upon Y Beach is that "in deciding to throw a force ashore at that point Sir Ian Hamilton would seem to have hit upon the key of the whole situation. . . . It is as certain as anything can be in war that a bold advance from Y on the morning of April 25 must have freed the southern beaches that morning, and ensured a decisive victory for the 29th Division."

At Anzac, too, a great opportunity went begging, although here the initiative of one opponent, the then unknown Mustapha Kemal, contributed to its unfulfillment. The surprise landing had placed 4000 men before 5 A.M., and another 4000 before 8 A.M., on a shore guarded by only one Turkish company. The next company was more than a mile to the south, two battalions and a battery in local reserve were four miles inland, and still further away lay the general reserve of eight battalions and three batteries, commanded by Mustapha Kemal. He was out watching a regiment at training, when suddenly a number of gendarmes, bareheaded and weaponless, came running frantically towards him crying, "They come, they come!" "Who comes?" "Inglis, Inglis." He turned to ask, "Have we ball cartridges?" "Yes." "All right. Forward." Leading a company himself, and leaving the rest of the regiment to follow, he raced to the great dividing ridge of Chunuk Bair in time (about 10 A.M.) to cross the crest and check the leading Australians as they were climbing up the steeper slopes on the west. Until now barely 500 Turks had been available to hold up 8000 Australians, but henceforth the defenders were to be augmented steadily until by nightfall six battalions (perhaps 5000 men) had been brought up, and from 4 P.M. onwards launched in a series of counter-attacks which forced back, but failed to break, the ragged Australian line. Both sides had suffered about 2000 casualties, the Turks far more heavily in proportion, but the raw Australians were in unknown country, under fire for the first time, and the moral effect of the shrapnel from the enemy's handful of guns was made worse by the absence of their own. Although 15,000 men were ashore by 6 P.M., the front was but a thin and much intermixed line, and the beach was crowded with leaderless men who had drifted back — many because they had lost themselves rather than lost their nerve. But the sight naturally confirmed the fears of the commanders, themselves in rear, and so gloomy was their report to Birdwood, when he landed at 10 P.M., that he sent a message to Ian Hamilton saying, "Both my divisional commanders and brigadiers have represented to me that they fear their men are thoroughly demoralized by shrapnel fire. . . . If troops are to be subjected to shell fire again to-morrow morning there is likely to be a fiasco . . . if we are to reëmbark it must be at once." All available boats were ordered to be sent to the beach.

Only by a fluke did the message ever reach the Commander-in-Chief, for in the hurry it was not addressed to anyone. But, being thrust into the hands of the beach-master, who was going out to the flagship, he handed it when there to Admiral Thursby. After reading it, Thursby decided to go ashore to discuss the reëmbarkation with Birdwood, but at that moment the *Queen Elizabeth*, with Ian Hamilton on board, unexpectedly arrived from Helles, so that Thursby went instead to report to him. Thus by a chain of happy mishaps Birdwood's grave message reached Ian Hamilton in time.

Insight must have guided him in an extraordinarily difficult decision, for no other guidance, or comfort, was available, and no time to obtain it. The reply which he wrote was epitomized in its postscript: "You have got through the difficult business. Now you have only to dig, dig, dig, until you are safe."

Like a fresh breeze this definite and confident order dispersed the rumor-laden and gloomy atmosphere on the beach. The rear ceased to talk about evacuation and the front did not know that the rear had been talking about it. When morning broke there was also a respite from the real enemy, for Mustapha Kemal had no further reserves with which to renew his counter-attack, and the shrapnel from his few guns was no longer a terror to troops now safely dug in. Indeed, it was the Turk who suffered demoralization — from the guns of the fleet, and especially the huge 15-inch shells of the *Queen Elizabeth*.

Could the lost opportunity still have been regained? History answers, "Yes." And the reason lies in the profound impression made, by Ian Hamilton's original plan, on the

mind of the enemy Commander-in-Chief.   Liman von Sanders
records of the first day, April 25, that "from the many pale
faces among the officers reporting in the early morning it was
apparent that, although a hostile landing had been expected
with certainty, a landing at so many points surprised and dis-
quieted them."   "We could not discern at the time where
the enemy was actually seeking a decision."   The last sentence
is a euphemism, for Liman von Sanders actually thought
that the place where the British were merely making a bluff
was the place where they were seeking a decision.   If he kept
his head he lost his sense of direction.

His first act was to order his 7th Division to march from
the town of Gallipoli to Bulair.   His next, to gallop thither
himself. - And there he stayed while the critical struggle was
in progress at the other end of the peninsula.   Not until
evening would he spare even five battalions, out of his two
divisions around Bulair, to go to the real battle zone, and not
until over forty-eight hours after the British landing did he
release the remainder.

But the extension of the opportunity was of no avail to the
British.   Partly for want of fresh troops — when so many, in
comparison, were locked up in the western front safe-deposit.
But partly, also, for want of effort from those who had landed.
Ian Hamilton's optimism, although justified, was not shared
by his subordinate commanders on the morning of the twenty-
sixth.   It was not merely the Anzac force which remained
passive.   At Helles, Hunter-Weston, appreciating the tiredness
of his troops but not the weakness of the enemy, gave up
any idea of advancing until French reënforcements arrived.
Expecting a Turkish onslaught, and fearing the result, he
issued the order, "Every man will die at his post rather than
retire."   So far from attacking, the Turks went back to a
new line in front of Krithia.   Well they might, for their total
strength here up to the twenty-seventh was only five battalions, and casualties had reduced them to a real strength
scarcely more than the original two.   Not until the twenty-
eighth was a new attack attempted, and by then the Franco-
British force had almost lost its advantage of numbers, and

suffered the disadvantages of ignorance of the ground, thirst, increased tiredness, besides complicating its task by combining the attack with a right wheel. The small gains were lost to Turkish counter-attacks, and near the coast the line wavered and broke. The danger here was averted by a single shell from the *Queen Elizabeth*. It burst its 24,000 shrapnel bullets right in the midst of the onrushing mass of Turks, and when the dust cleared not a Turk was to be seen. But by nightfall the whole 29th Division was back at its starting point. Meantime the troops at Anzac were reorganizing and making their front secure. But so also were the Turks, and thus the Anzac force was locked in a tiny cell only one and a half miles long and half a mile deep, while the Turk looked down from the "roof" upon the arrested trespassers.

The almost blank credit side of the Allied balance sheet was now relieved by a Turkish contribution. Urged on by Enver's peremptory order "to drive the invaders into the sea," Liman von Sanders launched massed bayonet attacks on the nights of May 1 and 3. Several thousand dead were heaped as a sacrifice before the Allied front, which was only, and momentarily, endangered in the French sector.

The Turks' forfeit was soon redeemed — by the British. Two brigades were brought from Anzac, and a new brigade, of Territorials, came from Egypt. Even so, the Allied force at Helles could only bring a fighting strength of 25,000 against a Turkish strength now raised to nearly 20,000. And, in the issue, it did not even test their strength. The Allied attack arranged for May 6 suffered every possible disadvantage. It was purely frontal, on a narrow three-mile front, against unlocated positions, with an extreme shortage of shells, and a shortage of aircraft to observe the fire, at the shortest notice — Hunter-Weston's orders were not issued to brigades until 4 A.M. for an attack to begin at 11 A.M. Once more the control of the battle and the last remaining reserves were handed over to Hunter-Weston by Ian Hamilton — "all that was left to him," as the official history says, "of the high office of Commander-in-Chief was its load of responsibility."

Fatigue rather than resistance foiled the attack. The troops,

worn out by strain and lack of sleep, had not even the energy
to press on to the slaughter, and they did not even push back
the Turks' advanced posts. As the best remedy for lack of
rest Hunter-Weston ordered a fresh effort next morning.
This was no more effective, except in draining the ammunition almost to zero. So a third attack was ordered for the
third morning. In this the loss at least was confined to a
smaller circle, by launching four weak battalions of New
Zealanders, in daylight, against a position held by nine Turkish
battalions. Then Ian Hamilton, finding that three brigades
were still in reserve, himself intervened. The whole Allied
line was to "fix bayonets, slope arms, and move on Krithia
precisely at 5.30 P.M." This produced heavy casualties, if
nothing else. The attacking force had lost a third of its
strength in the three days. Thereafter the front of the two
small footholds gained by the Allies inevitably relapsed into
stagnation, which soon froze solidly as the Turks converted
their hasty defenses into an organized trench system.

Now, at last, Ian Hamilton was driven to ask for reënforcements, and to awake the Government to his serious need and
situation. Hitherto, although conscious of the inadequacy of
his force, he had been too loyal to Kitchener, and perhaps too
aware of his old chief's arbitrary methods, to worry him by
importunate demands. Before leaving England he had been
told that 75,000 men would and must suffice, that even the
29th Division was but a temporary loan, and the fact that
Kitchener had warned Maxwell, the commander in Egypt,
to help him with additional troops was not communicated
to him by Maxwell despite Kitchener's explicit instructions.
Lack of ammunition was another handicap, and when he
called attention to it the War Office reply merely told him
that it was "important to push on." Yet, almost simultaneously with his vain three days' attack, May 6 to 8, in which
he could use only 18,500 shells, Haig was expending 80,000 on
Aubers Ridge in one day — for less result, a far less object, and
twice the loss of life. Up to a point, the astonishing feature of
Gallipoli was how near Ian Hamilton came to success with
his inferior forces and resources.

His oft-criticized choice of landing place could hardly have been improved on if, by supernatural power, he had been able to know the enemy's mind and dispositions. By avoiding the natural line of expectation, the pitfall of commonplace generalship, and by distracting the enemy's attention to that line, he ensured his own troops an immense superiority of force at the actual landing places — although his total force was less than that of the Turks. The enemy commander let his attention be so fixed on Bulair that for forty-eight hours after the British were ashore their immediate opponents were denied adequate reënforcements. This fact is the best answer to the common criticism that Ian Hamilton should have struck at Bulair, a point so obvious to everyone at home that, curiously, it was also obvious to the enemy. Another popular criticism is that Ian Hamilton dispersed his force at too many points and should have concentrated his effort on one small sector. This is answered not only by the "pale faces" of which Liman von Sanders tells, but by the next three years' experience of this abortive method on the western front — experience which was purchased at an infinitely greater cost.

Perhaps, as an alternative landing place, also in the least defended area, Suvla Bay might have offered the advantages of Ian Hamilton's choice with fewer disadvantages. But in April, accurate information was lacking and exaggerated faith placed in the effect of the naval guns at Helles.

Another reasonable criticism is that the British power of rapid sea movement might have been utilized more fully — to withdraw troops where checked before they were deeply committed and switch them to reënforce the unopposed landings or to fresh points. Thereby the lack of reserves might have been partly compensated through the power to create fresh ones by "switching." This, indeed, had been suggested to Braithwaite, the Chief of Staff, on the day before the landing by Captain Aspinwall, an officer of the General Staff. He urged that the plan should be adapted to meet the contingency that either or both the landings at Anzac and Helles might fail. An equal or greater fault in the plan was that it failed to provide for partial success, the most probable case in war, and left no "floating" reserve in the hands of the Commander-in-Chief ready for prompt application at the most promising point ashore. Unhappily, both the plan and the execution suffered from lack of the elasticity which is an essential axiom in war. And the partial success of both landings in the first phase tended to harden the design — until it became hard and stuck fast.

For years controversy has centred round the incubation period of the Dardanelles project, and the plan which was evolved. More depressing is the later revelation of the opportunities thrown away after the force had landed — lost opportunities hitherto obscured by a halo of romance.

1915 — THE DEADLOCK

Scene III

THE GAS CLOUD AT YPRES — APRIL 22, 1915

The sun was sinking behind Ypres. Its spring radiance had breathed life that day into the dead town and the mouldering trench lines which guarded it. A month hence the town would be a shell with all the eerie moonlit grandeur of a greater Colosseum. Three years hence it would be merely a vast ant heap of tumbled ruins. But on that day of April 22, 1915, it had merely the dreariness of incomplete abandonment, momentarily relieved by the fragrance of a spring day's sunshine.

As that fragrance faded with the waning sun, the guns even became silent, and an evening hush spread over the scene as if in awed awaiting of a benediction. The hush was false; purely a prelude to the devil's malediction, with organ pealing, censers swinging. At five o'clock a fearful din of guns broke out and heavy shells struck with reverberating crash on Ypres and many villages rarely or never touched before. And to the nostrils of men nearer the front came the smell of a devilish incense. Those nearer still to the trenches north of Ypres saw two curious wraiths of greenish-yellow fog creep forward, spread until they became one, and then, moving forward, change to a blue-white mist. It hung, as it had come, over the front of the two French Divisions, one Algerian, one Territorial, which joined up with the British and held the left of the salient. Soon, officers behind the British front and near the canal bridges were startled to see a torrent of terrified humanity pouring backward. The Africans, nearest the British, were coughing and pointing to their throats as they fled; mingled with them soon came horse-teams and wagons. The French guns were still firing, but at 7 P.M. these suddenly and ominously became silent.

The fugitives left behind them a gap in the front over four miles wide, filled only by the dead and by those who lay suffocating in agony from chlorine gas-poisoning. Otherwise the two French Divisions had almost completely disappeared. With the aid of gas the Germans had removed the defenders on the north flank of the salient as deftly as if extracting the back teeth from one side of a jaw. The remaining teeth in front and on the south flank of the salient were formed by the Canadian Division (Alderson), nearest the gap, the 28th Division (Bulfin), and the 27th Division (Snow), which together comprised Plumer's 5th Corps. The Germans had only to push south for four miles to reach Ypres, and loosen all these teeth by pressure from the rear. That evening they walked forward two miles and then, curiously, stopped. The space of four and a half miles between the raw edge of the Canadian front and the canal which formed the chord of the salient was only filled by a few small posts, taken up hastily by packets of French and Canadians hitherto in reserve, and between these posts there were three untenanted gaps of two thousand yards, one thousand yards, and three thousand yards, respectively. Yet on May 1 the Germans had only advanced a few hundred yards further. And when the fighting at last died down, at the end of May, the only outward change was that the nose of the salient had been flattened — mainly by a voluntary British withdrawal. But, in curious contrast to normal experience, it was the defenders who had lost most heavily. The British loss was fifty-nine thousand — nearly double that suffered by the Germans who attacked them.

Why did the gas come as so complete a surprise? Why did the Germans fail to exploit such a surprise? Why did the British escape disaster when taken unawares by the French collapse and yet suffer so disproportionately when the Germans had forfeited their advantage? These are the three crucial questions of "Second Ypres."

Towards the end of March, prisoners taken on the south of the salient, then held by the French, gave full details of the way that gas cylinders had been stored in the trenches, and of its method of discharge. Perhaps because they were about to

be relieved, the French commanders took no action in regard
to this warning, although, curiously, the details appear in the
Bulletin of the French Tenth Army, away down in Picardy, for
March 30. A more complete and localized warning came on

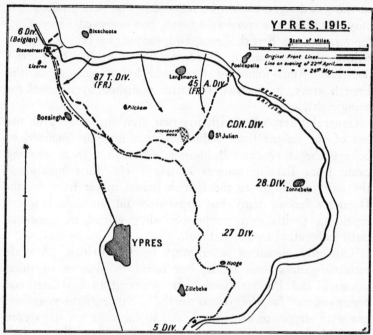

April 13, when a German deserter gave himself up near Langemarck to the French 11th Division, then holding the sector,
and related that "tubes with asphyxiating gas [had been]
placed in batteries of twenty tubes for every forty metres along
the front." A crude respirator, issued as a safeguard to the
attackers, was even found on him. The French Divisional
commander, General Ferry, gravely impressed, warned the
French Division on his left, the British 28th Division on his
right, and the Canadian Division — which took over part of
his front two days later while the Algerian Division took over
the rest. More significant still, Ferry warned his corps commander, Balfourier, and the liaison officer from Joffre's headquarters, who came to visit him.

How did these two key-men react? Balfourier deemed Ferry a credulous fool and ignored his suggestions that the German trenches should be shelled in order to destroy the cylinders, and that the number of men in the front line, exposed to the gas danger, should be reduced. The liaison officer not only dismissed the story as a myth, but reproved Ferry, first, for warning the British direct, and, second, for taking steps to reduce the garrison of the·front line contrary to Joffre's doctrine. And, following the usual happy custom of the French army, Ferry was thereafter punished by removal for being right.

General Putz, who, with his two divisions, took over the left of the salient from Balfourier, was no more inclined to believe the story than Balfourier, although a fresh warning came from Belgian sources on April 16. Putz mentioned the story scoffingly to the British liaison officer from Smith-Dorrien's Second Army, but apparently did not think it worth repeating to his own troops. So they waited in ignorance until suffocation overtook them.

The only measures taken were by the British. Aircraft reconnaissances were made, but failed to observe anything unusual, and Plumer passed the warning to his divisional commanders "for what it was worth." No precautions against gas were suggested or ordered, and in the next few days even the fact of the warning was forgotten — perhaps all the easier because it sounded such an "ungentlemanly" novelty. Yet acquaintance with the German practice of getting in the first verbal blow might well have made the British Command suspect the sinister significance of the German wireless communiqué of April 17: "Yesterday, east of Ypres, the British employed shells and bombs with asphyxiating gas."

But one factor which undoubtedly lulled suspicion of an attack was the lack of any sign that the Germans were concentrating reserves for it. This lack of signs was due, not to special precautions, but to the lack of such reserves. And thereby the Germans lost the opportunity created by the most complete surprise of the war.

As scientifically hidebound as its opponents, the German

Supreme Command had little faith in the new weapon. So little that for want of facilities the inventor, Haber, had to use cylinders mainly for projection instead of shells. A discharge of gas from cylinders must be dependent on a favorable wind, and as a westerly or southwesterly wind was the most frequent in Flanders, the Germans thus offered a hostage to fortune. Disclosing their new weapon prematurely and for a paltry prize, they gave their opponents the advantage in retaliation until sufficient gas-shell was produced to replace gas-cylinders.

However weak their faith, it is incredible — but for the result — that the Germans should have neglected to be ready for a possible success. Yet, actually, Falkenhayn allotted no fresh reserves for the attack, and even refused the request for extra ammunition. Falkenhayn's idea was merely to try the gas as an experimental aid to an attack which itself was merely a cloak to his projected blow against the Russians. If the Ypres salient could be erased, so much the better, but he did not take any longer view.

Originally the attack was to be launched by the XV Corps against the southern side of the salient, and the gas-cylinders were in position by March 10. But the attack had to be postponed repeatedly for want of a favorable wind, and towards the end of March an alternative attack was prepared on the north side of the salient. Intended for April 15, this in turn was delayed a week. It was then launched by the two divisions of the XXVI Reserve Corps, with one division of the XXIII Reserve Corps attacking on their right. As an aid to the main thrust the other division of the XXIII Reserve Corps was to strike at Steenstraat, which was both the hinge of the salient and the junction between the French and the Belgians. Unaided by gas, this subsidiary attack made little progress. Only one division was available in army reserve, and this was not released until next day, and was then given to the XXIII Reserve Corps, not to the XXVI, which had an open gap before it.

But if lack of reserves was the fundamental cause of the Germans' failure, the immediate cause was the troops' fear of their own gas. They had only been issued with the crudest form of respirator, which many of them did not even wear; no special tactics had been thought out; and after passing through the gasping and agonized men who littered the French trenches, they were only too willing to comply with the letter of their limited orders, and dig in as soon as they reached the short-distance objective that had been assigned. The failing light, too, prevented them discovering the extent of their success and the weakness of the few stout-hearted knots of Canadians who were strung across their path. And during the succeeding days they were equally content to act as camp followers to their artillery, merely taking a short step forward to occupy and consolidate such fresh patches of ground as the guns and gas had swept practically clear of defenders. However shortsighted during the first days when opportunity lay open to their embrace, this pure siege-warfare method was good sense later. It foreshadowed the Verdun method of a year later, and, thanks to Foch, the Allies helped to make it most profitable to the Germans.

Foch was then, as Joffre's deputy, in higher control of the French troops in Flanders, and charged with the duty of co-ordinating the efforts of the French, British, and Belgians. On hearing the news of the German break-through, he ordered Putz to make sure of holding his ground, now the line of the canal, and to organize a counter-attack to regain the ground he had lost. But the French had lost their artillery and all they could do was to fulfill the first point. Fortunately, the Belgians baffled the German efforts to break the hinge. Putz, however, told the British that he would be counter-attacking, and to aid him two Canadian battalions made a midnight counter-attack. They penetrated the new German line, and captured Kitchener's Wood, but as no French attack developed they had to withdraw from it later. Next day, the British, scraping together a few handfuls of reserves, attempted further petty counter-attacks which naturally failed at heavy cost, as they were delivered in daylight and with negligible support from the French and from artillery. By evening on the twenty-third, however, the broad way to Ypres and the British rear was almost filled, although by only twenty-one and a half sorely weakened British battalions (twelve of them Canadian), who faced forty-two German battalions — and a five to one superiority in guns.

Sir John French ordered a continuation of these vain efforts on the twenty-fourth — but the Germans anticipated him. At 3 A.M. they attacked the Belgian "hinge" and were badly discomfited; henceforth they were unable either to widen or deepen their small foothold across the canal. At 4 A.M. they launched a heavy blow, with gas, against the jagged corner of the Canadians' front. No respirators were yet available and the only protection was handkerchiefs, towels, and cotton bandoliers, wetted with the liquid most readily available in the trenches and placed over the mouth. Many men were overcome, and although there was only a small break in the line at the first onset, this gradually spread. For a time good artillery shooting prevented the Germans probing the breach, but in the afternoon they surged forward to and beyond St. Julien. The situation looked critical, but a counter-attack by two Yorkshire Territorial battalions, helped by Canadian batteries firing over open sights, rolled the leading Germans back to St. Julien. This slight taste of repulse sufficed to quench the Germans' thirst for further advance that day. But their irresolution was hidden from the eyes of the British commanders by the general confusion. In the patchwork line across the Germans' path, Canadians, British Regulars, Territorials, even Zouaves, of various divisions and brigades, were intermingled, clinging on wherever they had been pushed, like dabs of cement into a crumbling wall. The salient had now been compressed by German pressure into a narrow tongue of land, barely three miles across, although nearly six miles deep. Thus, in attempting to hold it, the defenders were now so crowded that they provided an easy harvest for the German guns.

Yet Sir John French, beguiled by the optimism of Foch and Putz, and the assurance that two fresh French divisions were coming up to retake the lost ground, was unwilling to sanction any withdrawal. Early on the twenty-fifth, the day

of the Gallipoli landing, a fresh Regular Brigade was brought
up and thrown blindly into an attack near St. Julien, there to
be "mown down like corn, by machine-guns in enfilade." With
appalling swiftness two thousand four hundred men were
scythed — more loss than Ian Hamilton's army paid for the
capture of the Gallipoli beaches. And that evening the bulk
of the Canadian Division was withdrawn into reserve, having
lost some five thousand men in its gallant efforts to battle
against gas and heavy guns with their rifles, supplemented
meagrely by guns that the official history terms "the ancient
and obsolete weapons of the South African War." Nor did the
burden of this hopeless struggle cease with the relief of the
Canadians; it was merely shifted more fully to other shoulders. For another month operations were to continue, methodical German attacks answered by unmethodical British attacks.
Lest I be thought to emphasize the futility unduly, let me
quote the sober and sombre words of the official history : —

> The governing idea was that the French should restore the line lost by
> them, and that the British should assist. . . .   General Foch ordered immedi-
> ate counter-attacks which General Putz was not in a position to execute;
> whilst the British whole-hearted attempts to carry out their share by means
> of offensive action, which was as a rule neither a true counter-attack nor a
> deliberately prepared attack, led to heavy losses without restoring the
> situation. . . . It seemed to the British officers at the front, that they were
> being sacrificed to gain time until the French were ready for a big spectacular
> effort; but this, even if ever intended, did not materialize.

To study the cause of the tragedy we must shift our gaze
from the front to the rear. After expending the Indian Lahore
Division and the Northumberland Territorial Brigade in
another vain attack on the twenty-sixth, with a loss of another
four thousand men, Smith-Dorrien realized the futility of such
efforts and the improbability of French coöperation. Hence
on the twenty-seventh he wrote to Robertson, the Chief of the
General Staff, asking him to put the real situation before French,
and saying: "I am doubtful if it is worth losing any more men
to regain this French ground, unless the French do something
really big." He further suggested that it would be wise to
prepare for a withdrawal to a less acutely bent line nearer to

Ypres. All that he got in reply was a telephone message from Robertson: "Chief does not regard situation nearly so unfavorable as your letter represents." In fact, however, Smith-Dorrien's letter was far more optimistic than the grim conditions justified. Yet this "comforting" message from the comfortable and peacefully remote General Headquarters was followed by a still worse rebuff — a telegram, sent through unciphered, telling Smith-Dorrien to hand over command of all the troops engaged at Ypres to General Plumer, and also to send the latter his Chief of Staff, General Milne. Relations between French and Smith-Dorrien had become very strained ever since Smith-Dorrien had saved French's situation against his own orders at Le Cateau in August 1914. Now French, true to a habit of his namesakes, seized the chance to punish Smith-Dorrien for making a true diagnosis, and administered a public rebuff which left Smith-Dorrien no option but to send a hint that he would resign if desired. French instantly embraced it and ordered him to hand over his shrunken command and go home.

Nevertheless, Plumer's first instructions from French were to prepare the very withdrawal that Smith-Dorrien had tentatively proposed. Then French went off to see Foch at Cassel and came back with a different outlook. Foch argued vehemently against a withdrawal, said that the lost ground could be retaken by the troops already available, urged that a retirement "should be forbidden," and begged French "to support the French *offensive to retake the Langemarck region at all costs*, beginning at noon on the twenty-ninth." The days that followed were a comedy behind the front, a tragedy for the troops in front. Day after day, French heard from his fighting subordinates of the sufferings of the men and of the continued absence of the ever-promised French offensive. Thereupon he would incline towards a withdrawal, only to be swung the other way by Foch's buoyant assurances and flattering entreaties.

Once more let us quote the official history : —

For ill now, although for weal in the last year of the war, General Foch was the very spirit of the offensive. . . . Sir John French, though at first he had whole-heartedly complied with General Foch's wishes, appreciated the small result of the French efforts — or, rather, the smallness of the first efforts — and the heavy losses of his own troops crowded together in the small place d'armes of the narrowed salient. . . . Sir John French then became convinced that he must withdraw his troops, and passed from optimism to pessimism. It was naturally most difficult for his subordinates to follow his moods, particularly when his mind was on the border line between one phase of thought and the next, and when, at the entreaty of General Foch, he more than once agreed to wait a little longer before withdrawing his men — and to order one more counter-attack.

However, he clutched at a straw in the wind when, late on May 1, Foch confessed that Joffre, so far from sending reën-forcements, was calling for troops to be sent from Ypres to strengthen his forthcoming offensive near Arras. French forthwith sanctioned the long-planned withdrawal, by nightly stages, although only to a line some three miles short of Ypres, so that the front still formed a salient, if a flatter one. This was more inconvenient for defense and control than the original salient, the head being exposed to pounding from all sides while Ypres itself formed a dangerously narrow throat of supply and communication. The political and sentimental objection to yielding ground, especially Belgian ground, and the military desire to facilitate the task of any belated French effort, led Sir John French to overrule the fighting commanders' wish to withdraw to the natural straight line of defense formed by the ramparts of Ypres and the canal. So they stayed in the reduced salient, "one huge artillery target," there to be pounded and gassed incessantly, with their scanty ammunition running out, until relief came at last, in the fourth week of May, through the Germans exhausting their own comparative superfluity of shells. For the Germans had at least the good sense to cease attacks when they came to the choice between economizing infantry lives and economizing artillery ammunition. All that the French had done in the interval was to clear the west bank of the canal, on May 15, while the continued British bayonet attacks east of Ypres did not even succeed in preventing the Germans switching troops from the British sector to check the eventual small French attack — truly a mountain that was long in labor and brought forth a mouse. And having forfeited sixty thousand men for the privilege of acting as midwife, the British were then left to hold the most uncomfortably cramped new salient, or target, at continued expense for over two years.

To throw good money after bad is foolish. But to throw away men's lives where there is no reasonable chance of advantage is criminal. In the heat of battle, mistakes in the command are inevitable and amply excusable. But the real indictment of leadership arises when attacks that are inherently vain are ordered merely because if they could succeed they would be useful. For such "manslaughter," whether it springs from ignorance, a false conception of war, or a want of moral courage, commanders should be held accountable to the nation.

1915 — THE DEADLOCK

SCENE IV

THE UNWANTED BATTLE — LOOS (SEPTEMBER 15, 1915)

IN early September the "back of the front" in France was seething with rumors of a great Franco-British offensive which was to shatter the German front. And if the atmosphere among the fighting troops was tense, it had also an exhilarating breath of confidence in the result. For the first time the New Armies and Territorials were to take a prominent part, and few seemed to doubt that the joint hammer-blows of British and French together could fail at least to dissolve the static trench warfare that had persisted for nearly a year. But there was one extreme contrast to this air of confidence — and that was in the headquarters of the British higher commanders.

For the ill-fated Loos offensive was undertaken directly against the opinion of Haig — the man who, as Commander of the First Army, had to carry it out. Haig argued that the supply of heavy artillery and of shells was still inadequate, that its adequacy was the governing factor of the situation, and that until this weakness was remedied, it was of little use to make plans for offensives. For in June the British army still had only seventy-one heavy guns to one thousand four hundred and six field guns, and the factories in England were turning out no more than twenty-two thousand shells a day, compared to one hundred thousand by the French, and two hundred and fifty thousand by the Germans and Austrians — according to report.

Haig's view was by no means an isolated one. Robertson, Chief of the General Staff of the British Expeditionary Force, fully endorsed it, but his influence with his own Chief had been undermined by Sir Henry Wilson, who was a devout believer in the infallibility of French military judgment, and

Robertson had even been excluded from Sir John French's personal mess. Meantime, Wilson, the friend and confidant of French, was proposing to Kitchener that the British army should be divided into two groups, one to be located away in Lorraine, so as to ensure that French should be unable to take an independent attitude towards the French!

Equally emphatic, and pessimistic, was Sir Henry Rawlinson, who, under Haig, would have the main task with his army corps. He noted in his diary: "My new front is as flat as the palm of my hand. Hardly any cover anywhere. . . . D.H. tells me that we are to attack 'au fond,' that the French are doing likewise and making a supreme effort. It will cost us dearly, and we shall not get very far." He, however, was left no choice but to do that his men might die. For, in face of all these warnings, only too truly founded, the better judgment of the British commanders was overborne by Joffre's pressure.

The next revelation is that the instrument of this pressure was not the eternally vacillating Commander-in-Chief, Sir John French, but Lord Kitchener. It is a curious sidelight on one who had been among the first of British leaders to appreciate the state of deadlock in the west and to throw his influence into the scale against the stubborn folly of seeking to pass the impassable.

How was this strange chain of causation forged? Joffre, spiritual twin of his subordinate Foch, in the sense of being an unquenchable optimist, was undeterred by his hard experiences of the spring from the repetition of them in the autumn. In his plan, two great convergent blows were to be delivered from the widely separated sectors of Artois (Arras–Lens) and Champagne (Reims–the Argonne), the former being originally intended as the main blow. Note this point, for it had a vital influence and suffered a vital alteration.

A successful break-through both in Champagne and Artois was to be the signal for a general offensive of all the French and British armies on the western front. This, Joffre confidently declared, would "compel the Germans to retreat beyond the Meuse and possibly end the war."

Yet in the event one and a third German divisions sufficed to break the back of the attack of the six British divisions north of Lens, and south of Lens the French attack by fourteen divisions was hardly even developed in face of five German divisions. What a superb conception was this plan of Joffre's, and how utterly unrelated to the material conditions of modern warfare! Is it possible after this ever again to make disparaging comparisons between professional and "amateur" strategy?

When Joffre's draft plan was sent on June 4 to Sir John French, the British Commander-in-Chief expressed his general agreement. Then a strong gust of common sense came from his subordinate, Haig, and the military weathervane swung the other way.

Haig had made a personal reconnaissance of the area south of the La Bassée canal (La Bassée–Lens) and as a result declared definitely that it was "not a favorable one for an attack." His verdict was to prove most accurate. In his view, the German defenses were so strong that until a great increase of heavy artillery was provided they could only be taken by siege methods. "The ground, for the most part bare and open, would be so swept by machine-gun and rifle fire both from the German front trenches and from the numerous fortified villages immediately behind them, that a rapid advance would be impossible." He suggested that if an offensive on the left of the French was imperative, subsidiary attacks only should be made south of the canal, and the main one delivered astride and north of it. But he concluded with the cold douche already mentioned.

Joffre, however, would not accept arguments for a postponement of the offensive or a change of site. He even remarked with that magisterial infallibility which is so delightful in retrospect (but in retrospect only) that "your attack will find particularly favorable ground between Loos and La Bassée"! It was certainly both a simple and a magisterial way of brushing aside the adverse evidence of Haig, who had seen the ground.

Meantime the Germans, in full expectation of an attack, were working with feverish energy to strengthen their defenses and to create a second system in rear of the front. This was nearing completion by the end of July and knowledge of it accentuated Sir John French's doubts — under Haig's reiteration of his opinion. Hence a conference was arranged at Frévent on July 27 with Foch, who, however, maintained that it was essential that, regardless of the ground and the strength of the enemy's defenses, Haig's army should make its main attack just north of Lens in close connection with the French Tenth Army south of Lens, pinching out this maze-like mining town.

The tug-of-war between Haig and French, and Joffre and Foch, continued, with Sir John French seeking a way out through a project of coöperating with artillery fire alone. This was quashed and the tug-of-war decided by the intervention of Kitchener. Visiting Sir John French in August, he told him that "we must act with all energy and do our utmost to help France in this offensive, even though by so doing we may suffer very heavy losses."

In this reversal of his own previous attitude, he was apparently influenced by the disasters then occurring on the Russian front, and his feeling of the urgent need to succor our Russian Allies, as well, perhaps, as by his reaction from the disappointment at the Dardanelles. But two blacks do not make a white, and as he had long since declared his view that the western front was impassable, it is difficult to see how he could feel that a hopeless offensive there could bring fresh hope to the Russians.

As General Edmonds says in the official history : —

Under pressure from Lord Kitchener at home, due to the general position of the Allies, and from Generals Joffre and Foch in France, due to the local situation in France, the British Commander-in-Chief was therefore compelled to undertake operations before he was ready, over ground that was most unfavorable, against the better judgment of himself and of General Haig, and with no more than a quarter of the troops, nine divisions, instead of thirty-six, that he considered necessary for a successful attack.

French was himself, as we shall see, to extinguish its last hope of success. The last but one had been extinguished by a final alteration of the French plan. This was Joffre's decision to make the Champagne attack, and not the Artois, his main attack, for the reason that the ground in Champagne had fewer obstacles or villages in the way of the attackers. The sudden preference for tactical over strategical considerations is in curious contrast to his view where the British attack was concerned.

This change, again, had a damaging influence on the British attack, for both the British and French official accounts make it clear that the French Artois attack south of Lens by seventeen divisions on a twelve-mile frontage — supported by four hundred and twenty heavy guns — was not seriously pressed once the strength of the defense was realized. Yet the French had nearly twice as many heavy guns to the mile as the British (one hundred and seventeen in all). In Champagne twenty-seven French divisions, with eight hundred and fifty heavy guns, were assembled for the attack — on an eighteen-mile frontage. Thus the proportionate artillery support here was still higher.

When the decision to attack at Loos was definitely taken, Haig's first intention, to curtail his commitment and probable loss, was to attack at first with only two divisions. But a too successful demonstration of the possibilities of chlorine gas projected in a "wave" from cylinders led him to modify his views, and to believe that if the wind was favorable the gas discharge might even procure "decisive results" and justify him in attacking on the wider frontage of six divisions — Rawlinson's IV Corps (47th, 15th, and 1st Divisions) on the right, or south, and Gough's I Corps (7th, 9th, and 2nd Divisions) on the left.

With sound judgment of the chances, Haig urged that "under no circumstances should our forthcoming attack be launched without the aid of gas," but he was overruled by French and Foch. He then obtained permission to reserve his decision until the last possible moment and to let the choice — between the large or limited attack — depend on the weather conditions. By the irony of fortune, the wind was most favorable for the use of gas on September 15, the day originally fixed by Foch for the attack, and this fact encouraged Haig's hopes. But the retention of a dual plan led to a distribution of the artillery on the whole army front instead of a concentration on one-third.

Over five thousand cylinders of gas, containing nearly one hundred and fifty tons, were carried up to the front trenches and safely installed in special recesses, without one being hit by enemy fire. Even so, there was barely half the volume of gas necessary to maintain a continuous flow for the forty minutes that, in turn, were considered necessary to outlast the protective power of the oxygen apparatus used by the enemy machine-gunners. Hence the cylinders had to be turned on and off intermittently. Smoke candles were used in the intervals to simulate gas, and, at the end, to form the first smoke screen of the war.

The artillery bombardment began on September 21, the ammunition being eked out by limiting each heavy gun to ninety rounds, and each field gun to one hundred and fifty in the twenty-four hours. The results were not encouraging, so far as effect could be discovered, and led the commanders to study the wind all the more attentively.

The last night was a time of tense anxiety. Repeatedly Haig studied fresh charts sent in by a chain of meteorological observers. At 6 P.M. the forecast was that the wind would be "on the border line between favorable and unfavorable with a slight bias towards favorable." At 9 P.M. the forecast was better, indicating a probable change to a southwesterly or even westerly wind, which would carry the gas over the German trenches. Thereupon Haig unhesitatingly ordered the full-scale offensive with gas, although as a precaution staff officers of each corps had been ordered to stand by their telephones. At 3 A.M., after a further report not quite so encouraging, he fixed sunrise (5.50 A.M.) as the hour for releasing the gas. During the hours of darkness the wind changed as predicted, but only as far as southwest, and, worse still, was so slight as to be almost a calm. About 5 A.M., as soon as it was light, Haig went out. He could feel only the faintest breath of air, and he asked his senior A.D.C. to light a cigarette. The smoke drifted in puffs to the northeast.

Did it justify the venture? Would the gas merely hang in the British trenches? A slight increase of wind was felt and at 5.15 A.M. Haig gave the decisive order to "carry on" and climbed his wooden lookout tower. But the improvement was delusive, and a few minutes later one of his staff telephoned to the 1 Corps, to ask whether it was possible to stop the discharge and the attack. For this emergency the gas officers had made ample arrangements. But Gough replied that it was too late. If it would certainly have been a close shave, one may suspect, especially in view of Gough's record, that with this ardent fighter the wish was at least the midwife, if not the father, of the thought.

When the gas was actually turned on at 5.50 A.M. it carried fairly well over the German trenches on the right, if too slow and slight for full effect, but on the left was a failure, in some places drifting back and upsetting the attack. In Horne's 2nd Division, the officer in charge of the gas on the 6th Brigade front declined to assume the responsibility of turning on the cylinders. But when this was reported to divisional headquarters, Horne replied with an order that "the programme must be carried out whatever the conditions. . . ." As a result of this stupidity many of the infantry were poisoned by their own gas. Those who were able to advance were soon stopped, and slaughtered by the ungassed German machine-gunners. Nevertheless, Horne ordered a fresh assault, which was only abandoned after his brigade commanders had protested against the "useless sacrifice of life."

The general infantry assault had been launched at 6.30 A.M., and into it was thrown the entire strength of the First Army, except for local reserves. Neither Haig nor the commanders of his two attacking corps kept any reserve, as they understood that the Commander-in-Chief expected a breakthrough and would use his general reserve to back them up promptly.

On the extreme right the 47th Division nearly carried out its task of throwing forward a defensive flank, but the "not quite" had an important bearing on the surprisingly successful initial rush of its neighbor, the 15th Division, contributing

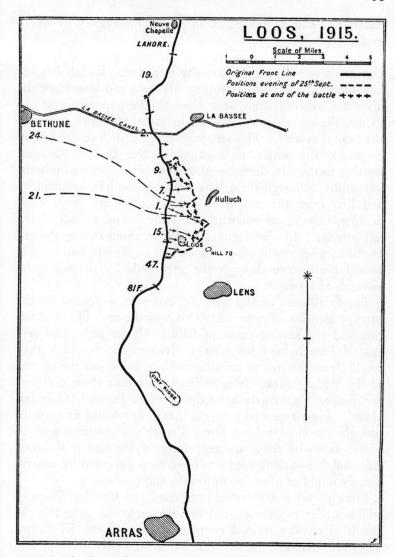

LOOS, 1915.

Scale of Miles.

Original Front Line
Positions evening of 25th Sept.
Positions at end of the battle

Neuve Chapelle
LAHORE.
19.
LA BASSEE CANAL
LA BASSEE
BETHUNE
24.
9.
7.
1.
Hulluch
21.
15.
LOOS
HILL 70
47.
81 F.
LENS
VIMY RIDGE
ARRAS

towards the loss of direction which nullified its near approach to a break-through, beyond Hill 70. So swift and deep was the advance of these Scotsmen of "K's" army that the German Command made hurried preparations to evacuate the whole area, and as far back as Douai "there were endless convoys of wagons formed up in double lines ready to march away."

Another ill effect was due to the long delay in the 1st Division's advance, only partially retrieved. Its left brigade had suffered similarly to Horne's division, and instead of the divisional reserve being sent through the gap made on the flanks, the morning was wasted in futile attempts to renew the frontal assault. This stoppage in the British centre tended to check the whole momentum of the British advance. Further to the left, the 7th and 9th Divisions obtained promising results, although the 9th had suffered, both in opportunity and life, from the misguided insistence of the corps commander, Gough, on renewing the vain frontal assault of the left brigade. In wise contrast, Capper, commanding the 7th Division, when confronted with a check on his left, had quickly passed his reserve through the gap made by the successful advance of his right.

The fulfillment of any promise, however, depended on the prompt infusion of reserves. This was the crux of the situation and the sealing cause of failure. Even Joffre had said that if French kept his reserve divisions too far back they would "run the risk of arriving too late to exploit the success of the leading ones. It is indispensable that these divisions are put, before the attack, at the absolute disposal of General Haig." Haig repeatedly urged that they should at least be brought up close behind him. French's assurances were so vague as to be simultaneously unsatisfying and misleading. As usual, his outlook seems to have been governed by contradictory impulses of undue optimism and pessimism.

French's general reserves comprised the Cavalry Corps — which, under modern conditions, did not count except in the minds of cavalry-trained commanders — and the XI Corps. The last included the Guards Division, newly formed, and the 21st and 24th Divisions, newly arrived in France. With curious judgment, French left seasoned divisions lying idle on the quiet Somme front, and chose to use these two raw divisions for the critical phase of the battle. Moreover, he had given Haig to understand that they would be immediately at hand for Haig's use, whereas he placed them sixteen miles in rear. And in his subsequent dispatch he untruthfully stated that they were put at Haig's disposal at 9.30 A.M. on the twenty-fifth. Actually, Haig did not hear until 1.20 P.M., and then in-directly. Haig bitterly remarked, "If there had been even one division in reserve close up we could have walked right through. General headquarters refuses to recognize the teaching of the war as regards the control of reserves." His confidence was probably exaggerated, at least as to the effect of such a nar-row breach, and he was himself to err somewhat similarly in the following July. But his natural disgust, accentuated by French's untruthful dispatch, led first to an acrimonious inter-change of letters and then to an irreconcilable quarrel. He seems, also, to have been galled, and not for the first time, at the way his own sound advice had been overruled by Foch's influence with French. French in retort charged Haig with the folly of trying to push reserves through a far too narrow gap. The sequel was that Haig wrote personally to Kitchener and spoke to Haldane about French's failure and incompetence, and thereby helped to precipitate French's downfall and his own succession.

As for the long and slow march up of those divisions, bad traffic arrangements were more responsible than their own inexperience for accentuating the evil caused by the Com-mander-in-Chief's dispositions. As General Edmonds causti-cally says, "It was like trying to push the Lord Mayor's pro-cession through the streets of London, without clearing the route and holding up the traffic." Folly was capped by farce when, on the outskirts of Béthune, a military policeman stopped the 72nd Brigade because the Brigade commander had no pass to enter the area.

Never, surely, were "novice" divisions thrown into a vital stroke in a more difficult or absurd manner, and in an atmos-phere of greater misconception of the situation in all quarters. This amply explains their subsequent failure when their belated attack was at last launched at 11 A.M. on the twenty-sixth, and redresses the hasty judgments which were spread at the time — a stigma that was slow to fade. That in courage they

were not lacking is clear, and equally that its fruits were
reduced by their rawness, by that of their staff still more.

The handicap of inexperience in these and the other New
Army divisions engaged can be overemphasized. It does not
appear that, as a whole, apart from certain battalions in them,
the regular divisions were more effective or even as effective
in the battle. "Battlecraft" is a rare quality, the product of
gifted and original leadership, and in its absence mere dash is
often more effective than so-called experience.

The ineffectiveness of the larger French attack south of the
Lens also affected the British opportunity. For the French
did not advance until six and a quarter hours after their Allies,
and even then made little progress where they did not make
merely a demonstration. The bitter experiences of the spring
and summer seem to have led the fighting commanders to discount Foch's faith in a break-through, and to annul his vehement order by gentle evasion in places. Joffre also put a
brake on him from above, for on the second morning he telephoned him to "go cautiously," and followed this by the warning: "Stop the attacks of the Tenth Army, taking care to
avoid giving the British the impression that we are leaving
them to attack alone." His reason was apparently that he
now pinned his hopes to the attack in Champagne, which on
the first day gave a delusive promise of a real break-through.

It is worth while to note that the partial opening success of
the attack in Champagne, and also in Artois, was largely due
to the obstinate self-delusion of Falkenhayn, who had disregarded ample warnings from many sources, and requests
for reserves. Only two hours before the attack began he
assured the Kaiser that the local army commanders "see things
too black," and that the French were not in a condition to
attack.

Early reports on the twenty-fifth had also led Haig to over-
estimate his initial success, and as early as 10.30 A.M. he ordered
the 3rd Cavalry Division forward. The Commander soon
discovered Haig's mistake, but Haig, believing that the cavalry
had gone on, hurried the 21st and 24th Divisions forward as
soon as he could get hold of them. But before they came up

the known situation had changed, and the two leading brigades were taken to strengthen the line gained by the original attack. Haig still hoped to break the intact German second line of defenses, and to this end the rest (four brigades) of these divisions continued their march across country, and unknown country, in the dark and rain. Tired, hungry, and as confused as their commanders, they were launched to the attack next morning without effective artillery support, and against defenses now stronger and more strongly manned than the original first line. For the Germans had not only been reënforced, but had covered themselves with a thick wire entanglement during the night. The attack broke down at or before this uncut obstacle, and the survivors turned and flowed backwards. Their disappearance left a hole in the ragged British front between Loos and Hulluch, which the Guards Division came up to fill. Meantime German counter-attacks were multiplying dangerously, especially on the flanks. At last, on the twenty-eighth, Foch came to the relief, not only by taking over the British flank sector near Loos, but with a local success on Vimy Ridge, which drew off most of the newly arrived German Guard Corps to check it. And in concert with Sir John French he arranged to make a renewed general offensive on October 2. The same course was adopted in Champagne, where the French for three days had vainly hurled themselves at the German second position, suffering fearful loss, which would have been worse if Pétain (Second Army) had not stopped his attack in disregard of higher orders.

But as the pause was to be followed by a renewal at the same point, it merely gave the Germans time to strengthen it and accumulate resources in the rear. Local upsets due to German counter-attacks, and the exhaustion of the troops, caused further delay, and the renewed offensive was repeatedly postponed. Eventually all three attacks were delivered on different dates, the British last on October 13. And, in the words of the official history, it "had not improved the general situation in any way and had brought nothing but useless slaughter of infantry." Curiously, Haig's sense of realism waned in this last phase, or, perhaps more truly, it was subdued by his bulldog tenacity. For although Joffre had abandoned the effort, Haig was working up a new general attack for November 7, an operation whose inevitable cost does not seem to have had any adequate excuse. Happily, Generals Winter and Weather intervened. But the British casualties already amounted to 50,380, — or 60,392 if the subsidiary attacks by Haig's army be included, — whereas the German loss was barely 20,000, despite their costly counter-attacks. The French in Champagne and Artois had lost 191,797 officers and men, and inflicted 120,000 casualties — a proportion which suggests that the actual handling of these attacks was better than that of the British, if helped by more powerful artillery. Both Allies had gained in experience, if not in wisdom, but they had afforded the Germans still better experience in the way to frustrate such attacks. And in 1916 it was the Germans who profited heavily both by the offensive and the defensive lesson.

1916 — THE "DOG-FALL"

In 1914 the centre of gravity of the World War had been on the western front; in 1915 it shifted to the eastern front; in 1916 it once more moved back to France. Although the Entente had dissipated some of their strength in Salonika and Mesopotamia, the rising tide of England's new armies and of her munition supplies promised the power for an effort far larger in scale than before to break the trench deadlock. Measures had also been taken to keep these new divisions up to strength. By the end of 1915 the British force in France had risen to thirty-six divisions through the entry into the field of "Kitchener's Army," as well as of the Territorial divisions. Although the principle of voluntary enlistment had not yet been abandoned, the method was systematized and based on a national register. This scheme, launched in October 1915, under the ægis of Lord Derby, aimed to reconcile the demands of the army with the needs of industry, calling up men by groups as they were wanted, and taking single men first. But the response among the latter was not adequate to preserve this graduated principle, and in January 1916, by the Military Service Act, the voluntary system — system is hardly the correct term — was replaced by conscription.

At the close of 1915, the first serious effort to obtain unity of action between the Allies was made, and a conference of the leaders of the French, British, Belgian, and Italian armies, with representatives present from the Russian and Japanese, was held at Joffre's headquarters on December 5. As a result they adopted the principle of a simultaneous general offensive in 1916 by France, Britain, Russia, and Italy. In view of the rawness of the British troops, it was recognized that time must be allowed for training, and Russia also needed time for reëquipment, so that the offensive could not begin before the summer of 1916, although it was hoped to carry out preliminary attacks to wear down the enemy's strength. But in January both Joffre and Foch gave Haig a clear intimation that it was for him to carry out this preparatory task, and that they did not intend to take the offensive until he had done so.

German action was to dislocate this scheme, and only the British share came fully into operation, and not even that into full effect. By a grim jest, however, it forced the French to carry out the wearing down process — in an indirect form. For Falkenhayn was about to fulfill his long-cherished plan for a western offensive, but with characteristic limitations. Always a believer in the strategy of attrition, he now carried this ruling idea into tactics, and produced the new form of attack by methodical stages, each with a limited objective. In an appreciation made at Christmas, 1915, he argued that England was the staple of the enemy Alliance. "The history of the English wars against the Netherlands, Spain, France and Napoleon is being repeated. Germany can expect no mercy from this enemy, so long as he still retains the slightest hope of achieving his object." Save by submarine warfare, however, England and her army were out of reach, for their sector of the front did not lend itself to offensive operations. "In view of our feelings for our arch-enemy in the war that is certainly distressing, but it can be endured if we realize that for England the campaign on the Continent . . . is at bottom a side-show. Her real weapons here are the French, Russian and Italian armies." He regarded Russia as already paralyzed, and Italy's military achievements as unlikely to affect the situation. "Only France remains." "France has almost arrived at the end of her military effort. If her people can be made to understand clearly that in a military sense they have nothing more to hope for, breaking-point would be reached, and England's best sword knocked out of her hand." He added that a breakthrough in mass was unnecessary, and that instead the Germans should aim to bleed France to death by choosing a point of attack "for the retention of which the French command would be compelled to throw in every man they have." Such objectives were either Belfort or Verdun, and Verdun was chosen, because it was a menace to the main German communications, because it offered a salient and so cramped the defender, and because of the moral effect if so renowned a place were lost to France. It has also been suggested that the choice was influenced by a peculiarly German moral, or unmoral, consideration. For Verdun was the ancient gate of the west through which the German hordes had passed to attack the Gauls. Similarly the Germans were fond of christening their trench positions after the heroes of the Nibelungen — Siegfried, Brünnhilde, and so on. The vein of superstition is still more clearly suggested in the Kaiser's choice of a second Moltke to guide his armies, and in the original location of their headquarters in the same hotel and same town, Coblenz, as they had occupied in 1870.

The keynote of the tactical plan at Verdun was a continuous series of limited advances, which by their menace should draw the French reserves into the mincing-machine of the German artillery. And each of these advances was itself to be secured from loss by a short but intense artillery bombardment. By this means the objective would be taken and consolidated before the enemy could move up his reserves for counter-attack. Although the Intelligence branch at French General Headquarters gave early warning of the German preparations, the Operations branch were so full of their own offensive schemes that the warning fell on deaf ears. Further, the easy fall of the Belgian and Russian fortresses had led to a commonly held view that fortresses were obsolete, and Joffre, persuading the French Government to "declass" Verdun as a fortress, had denuded it of guns and troops. The forts were only used as shelters, and the trench lines which took their place were inadequate and in poor repair.

At 7.15 A.M. on February 21, the German bombardment began, on a front of fifteen miles, and at 4.45 P.M. the infantry advanced, although the first day only on a four and a half miles front. From then until February 24 the defenders' line east of the Meuse was crumbled away as by the erosion of the tide.

Joffre was now aroused so far as to entrust the defense to Pétain, for whose use reserves were assembled. On March 6 the Germans extended the attack to the west bank of the Meuse. But the defense was now stiffening, the numbers balanced, and the immediate threat to Verdun was checked.

A slight lull followed, and during it the Allies of France made efforts to relieve the pressure on her. The British took over the Arras front from the French Tenth Army, their front becoming now continuous from the Yser to the Somme; the Italians made their fifth attack, though in vain, on the Isonzo front; and the Russians hurled untrained masses on the German front at Lake Narocz, near Vilna, where the slight gains were soon lost through a counter-stroke. These efforts did not prevent Falkenhayn pursuing his attrition offensive at Verdun. The advances were slight, but they were cumulative in effect, and the balance of loss turned definitely against the defenders. On June 7 Fort Vaux fell, and the German tide crept ever closer to Verdun. And in the Asiago region, Conrad had launched his offensive against Italy's Trentino flank.

Again Russia came to the rescue. In the spring of 1916 she had one hundred and thirty divisions, but was still woefully short of equipment, facing forty-six German and forty Austrian divisions. The preparation and reorganization for her intended share in the year's Allied offensive were cut short by the emergency at Verdun, and in relief of her French Allies she had launched the costly and obstinately prolonged attack at Lake Narocz in March. When at last it was broken off, the preparations for the main offensive were resumed. This was to begin in July, coincidently with the Somme offensive, and Brusilov, commanding the southwestern front, was ordered to prepare such attacks as he could stage from his own resources as a distraction of the enemy's attention from the main offensive. But the distraction was released prematurely, on June 4, in response to Italy's appeal to Russia to prevent the Austrians reënforcing their Trentino attack. Without warning, because without any special concentration of troops, Brusilov's troops advanced against the Austrian

Fourth Army near Luck, and the Austrian Seventh Army in the Bukovina, whose resistance collapsed at the first shock. In three days Brusilov took 200,000 prisoners.

This last vital effort of the Russian army in the war had important consequences. It stopped the Austrian attack on Italy, already impaired by an Italian riposte. It compelled Falkenhayn to withdraw troops from the western front, and so abandon his plan for a counter-stroke against the British offensive preparing on the Somme, as well as the hope of nourishing his Verdun attrition process. It led Rumania to take her fateful decision to enter the war on the Entente side, and caused the supersession of Falkenhayn in the supreme command, and his replacement by Hindenburg — with Ludendorff, officially styled First Quartermaster-General, as the directing brain. Although Rumania's entry was the immediate reason, the underlying one was the fact that Falkenhayn's "limited" strategy in 1915 had made possible the Russian recovery which stultified his strategy of 1916. Falkenhayn was history's latest example of the folly of half measures; the ablest and most scientific general — "penny wise, pound foolish" — who ever ruined his country by a refusal to take calculated risks. In 1916 he had turned back westwards to pursue his long-cherished goal, and his strategy had faithfully fulfilled the canons of military orthodoxy by taking for its objective the enemy's strongest army and the strongest point of that army's position. It certainly achieved the object of compelling the French to pour their reserves into the Verdun "blood-bath," but it did not achieve any decisive strategic result.

Falkenhayn had rejected Conrad's proposal for a concentration against Italy such as had previously overthrown Serbia. Conrad's reasons had been that such a blow against the "hereditary enemy" would act as a tonic to the Austro-Hungarian forces, and that the theatre of war lent itself to decisive results by a thrust southwards from the Trentino against the rear of the Italian armies engaged on the Isonzo. The success attained by the relatively light blow of 1917 — Caporetto — lends historical support to his contention. But

Falkenhayn was dubious both of the feasibility and value of the plan, and was unwilling even to lend the nine German divisions which Conrad asked for to relieve Austrian divisions in Galicia. In default of this aid Conrad persisted in attempting his design single-handed, taking some of his best divisions from Galicia, and thereby exposing their front to Brusilov's advance without obtaining adequate force to achieve his Italian plan. Falkenhayn's smouldering resentment at this disregard of his views was fanned into flame by the Galician disaster, and he intervened in Vienna to procure the deposition of Conrad. With retributive irony his own fall followed close on that of Conrad.

Brusilov's offensive continued for three months with fair success, but reserves were not at hand for immediate exploitation, and before they could be moved down from the north the Germans were patching up the holes. His later efforts were never so dangerous, but they absorbed all the available Russian reserves, and his ultimate loss of 1,000,000 casualties completed the virtual ruin of Russia's military power.

Great as was the influence of Brusilov's offensive on German strategy, its effect on the Verdun situation was less immediate. But the long-planned offensive on the Somme came to the rescue, and for want of nourishment the Verdun offensive faded away. Nevertheless, although the Germans at Verdun had fallen short of their object, moral and material, they had so drained the French army that it could play but a slender part in the Allied plan for 1916. The British had now to take up the main burden of the struggle, and the consequence was to limit both the scope and effect of the Entente strategy.

On July 1, after a week's prolonged bombardment, the British Fourth Army (recently created and placed under Rawlinson) attacked with thirteen divisions on a front of fifteen miles, north of the Somme, and the French with five divisions on a front of eight miles, mainly south of the river, where the German defense system was less highly developed. The unconcealed preparations and the long bombardment had given away any chance of surprise, and in face of the

German resistance, weak in numbers but strong in organization, the attack failed along most of the British front. Owing to the dense and rigid "wave" formations that were adopted the losses were appallingly heavy. Only on the south of the British front, near Fricourt and Montauban, did the attack gain a real footing in the German defenses. The French, with slighter opposition, and being less expected, made larger gains.

This set-back negatived the original idea of a fairly rapid penetration to Bapaume and Cambrai, and Haig soon fell back on the attrition method — of limited advances aimed to wear down the German strength. Rejecting Joffre's desire that he should again throw his troops frontally on the Thiepval defenses, Haig at first resumed the attack with his right wing alone, and on July 14 the penetration of the Germans' second position offered a chance of exploitation, which was not taken. From now onward a methodical but costly advance continued, and although little ground was gained the German resistance was seriously strained when the early onset of winter rains suspended operations in November. The effect, however, can be exaggerated, for it did not prevent the Germans withdrawing troops from the west for the attack on Rumania.

But in one respect the Somme shed a significant light on the future, for on September 15 the first tanks appeared. Their early employment before large numbers were ready was a mistake; losing the chance of a great strategic surprise, and owing also to tactical mishandling and minor technical defects, they had only a limited success. Although the higher military authorities lost faith in them, and some urged their abandonment, more discerning eyes realized that here was a key which, when properly used, might unlock the trench barrier.

The Somme offensive had a further indirect effect, for its relief to the Verdun pressure enabled the French to prepare counter-strokes, carried out by Mangin's corps on October 24 and December 15, which regained most of the lost ground with small casualties. These economical successes were due to a partial revival of surprise, to a more elastic use of the limited objective method, and to a high concentration of artillery, with a minimum of infantry to occupy the defenses crushed by the guns. But the French success was greatly helped by Hindenburg's misguided insistence, for the sake of prestige, on maintaining the earlier gains instead of withdrawing the tired troops to a more secure line somewhat in rear. He at least profited by the lesson, to the Allies' detriment, in the spring of 1917.

Rumania, sympathetic to the Entente cause, had been waiting a favorable opportunity to enter the war on their side, and Brusilov's success encouraged her to take the plunge. Her command hoped that this, combined with the Allied pressure on the Somme and at Salonika, would fix the German reserves. But Rumania's situation had many inherent defects. The strategical position of her territory was bad, the main section, Wallachia, sandwiched between Austro-Hungary and Bulgaria. Her army, though externally of a modern pattern, had grave weaknesses beneath the surface. Of her Allies, only Russia could give her direct aid, and they failed her. And, with all these handicaps, she launched an offensive into Transylvania, which bared her flank to Bulgaria.

While the Entente fumbled, the Germans acted. The plan was initiated by Falkenhayn and developed by Hindenburg-Ludendorff when they took over the Supreme Command on August 28. While one force concentrated in Transylvania for a counter-stroke, a Bulgarian army with German stiffening — under Mackensen — was to strike through Rumania's "backdoor" and invade the Dobruja. This automatically halted the Rumanian offensive in Transylvania, and drew away its reserves; at the end of September the Rumanians were thrown back by the Austro-German counter-offensive, of which Falkenhayn was given executive command. They succeeded in holding the passes of Rumania's mountain border in the west until mid-November, but Falkenhayn just broke through before the snows blocked the passes. Mackensen switched his main forces westwards, and crossed the Danube close to Bucharest, on which both armies now converged. It fell on

December 6, and, despite belated Russian aid, the Rumanian forces were driven north into Moldavia. The brilliantly coördinated German strategy had crippled their new foe, gained possession of the bulk of Rumania, with its oil and wheat, and given the Russians another three hundred miles of front to hold. Sarrail, at Salonika, had not succeeded in fixing the Bulgarian reserves.

The only territorial success that the Entente could show for their year's campaign (and, even so, it did not reveal itself fully until the New Year) was away in Mesopotamia — the capture of Baghdad. This moral token was seized on with an enthusiasm which, militarily, it hardly warranted. The bitter experience of the past had damped the ardor of the British Government, and Sir William Robertson, the new Chief of the Imperial General Staff, was opposed to any further commitments which drained the strength available for the western front. But Maude, the new commander on the spot, by subtle if unconscious steps succeeded in changing this defensive policy into one of a fresh offensive. After thorough reorganization of the Mesopotamian force and its communications, he began on December 12, 1916, a progressive right wheel and extension of his front on the west bank of the Tigris above and below Kut. These methodical trench-warfare operations had placed him ready for a spring across the Tigris at the Turks' line of retreat, which was thus parallel to his front. But despite his four-to-one superiority of force, the failure of his right to pin down the enemy, and of his cavalry to cut off their retreat, prevented a decisive success. But it led to permission for an advance on Baghdad, and he entered the Mesopotamian capital on March 11, 1917. A series of skillfully conducted operations then drove the Turks into divergent lines of retreat and secured the British hold on the province.

Ever since the abortive Turkish attempt to invade Egypt early in 1915, the British had kept a fairly large force there, even when the Dardanelles expedition was crying out for troops. When Gallipoli was evacuated, the release of the Turkish forces threatened a fresh move on Egypt. To anticipate this by gaining command of the Sinai desert, Sir Archibald Murray advanced in the spring of 1916, defeating the Turkish forces, freshly arrived, at Romani, Magdhaba, and Rafa. The rate of advance was governed by the time taken in extending a railway and pipe-line (for water) across the desert. This new "exodus" inspired the British Government to carry out an invasion of Palestine, at as cheap a cost in troops as possible. The towns of Gaza, on the coast, and Beersheba, twenty-five miles inland, guarded the approach to Palestine. Murray attacked Gaza on March 26, but the attempt fell short when on the brink of success. By nightfall Gaza was practically surrounded, but the victorious position was given up bit by bit, not under enemy pressure, but on the orders of the executive British commanders, through faulty information, misunderstandings, and overanxiety. Nor did the harm end there, for Murray reported the action to the Government in terms of a victory, and without hint of the subsequent withdrawal, so that he was encouraged to attempt, without adequate reconnaissance or fire support, a further attack on April 17–19, which proved a costlier failure against defenses now strengthened.

The Austrian offensive in the Trentino had interrupted Cadorna's plans for a renewed effort on the Isonzo, but when the former was halted, Cadorna switched his reserves back to the Isonzo. In preparation for this offensive the whole sector from Monte Sabotino to the sea was entrusted to the Duke of Aosta's Third Army, under which sixteen divisions were concentrated against six Austrian divisions. Following a preliminary feint near the sea on August 4, the attack opened well two days later. North of Gorizia, Capello's corps swept over the long impregnable Monte Sabotino, which guarded the approach to the river, and, crossing the river on the night of August 8, occupied the town. This compelled an Austrian retreat in the Carso sector to the south, but attempts to exploit the success eastward failed against fresh positions of resistance. Three more efforts were made in the autumn, and if they imposed a wearing strain on the Austrians, they caused greater loss to the attackers. During the year Italians had suffered some 483,000 casualties, and inflicted 260,000.

The War at Sea, 1915–1916. Germany's first submarine campaign — associated by Allied opinion with the name of Admiral von Tirpitz, the exponent of ruthlessness — had been a signal failure, both in its meagre results and the disproportionate ethical damage it did to Germany's cause. A series of notes exchanged between the American and German Governments culminated in April 1916 in a virtual ultimatum from President Wilson, and Germany abandoned her unrestricted campaign. The deprivation of this weapon spurred the German navy to its first, and last, attempt to carry out the initial plan on which it had begun the war. Late on May 30, 1916, the British Grand Fleet left its bases on one of its periodical sweeps through the North Sea, but with reason to expect a possible encounter. On May 31, early in the morning, the German High Seas Fleet also put to sea, in the hope of destroying some isolated portion of the British fleet.

For such an encounter the British Admiral, Jellicoe, had formulated an outline plan in the early months of the war. Its basis was the cardinal necessity of maintaining the unimpaired supremacy of the Grand Fleet, which he viewed as an instrument, not merely of battle, but of grand strategy, the pivot of the Allies' action in all spheres, economic, moral, and military. Hence, while desirous of bringing the German fleet to battle under his own conditions, he was determined not to be lured into mine and submarine infested waters.

Early in the afternoon of May 31, Beatty, with his battle-cruisers and a squadron of battleships, after a sweep to the south, was turning north to rejoin Jellicoe, when he sighted the German battle-cruisers, five in number. In the initial engagement two of Beatty's six battle-cruisers were hit in vital parts and sunk; when thus weakened he came upon the main German fleet under Admiral Scheer. He turned north to lure them into reach of Jellicoe, fifty miles distant, who raced to support him. Mist and failing light put an end to an indecisive action, which, however, left the British fleet between the German and its bases. During the night Scheer broke through the destroyer guard, and although sighted was not reported. Thus he slipped safely through a net which Jellicoe dared not draw too close in view of his guiding principle, and of the danger of torpedo attack.

If the battle of Jutland could be counted a tactical advantage to the Germans, it had no effect on their strategic position. The grip of Britain's blockade was unrelaxed. Once more Germany fell back on submarine warfare, and the first development was an extension of range. In July one of her large submarine-cruisers appeared off the American coast and sank several neutral ships.

In the narrow seas the Mediterranean was the scene of active operations, but the immediate pressure on Britain was relaxed during the summer. For Scheer, in a fit of pique at the German Government's surrender to President Wilson's threat, refused to let his submarines operate under the code of visit and search. Hence the burden of the restricted campaign fell on the Flanders flotillas, and, fortunately for Britain, the German naval chiefs had been obtusely slow to realize and exploit the advantages of the Belgian coast as a base. The six months lost originally through neglect to organize a base were never fully redeemed, and the scale of the forces here was never in proportion to the possibilities of menacing Britain from this close-range post. On October 6 Scheer was overruled by an order to reënforce the effort with his flotillas. This veiled renewal of the general submarine campaign was inspired mainly by Admiral von Holtzendorf, the Chief of the Naval Staff, and Captain von Bartenbach, the Chief of the Flanders flotillas. The indirect result was to deprive Scheer automatically of the submarines which he required to safeguard his own sorties and lay traps for the British fleet.

Thus the paralysis of the German fleet henceforth was the result of the Germans' own alternative plan, and not of Jutland. And it did not even leave the British Grand Fleet in possession of the North Sea. For the moral effect of a submarine ambush which marked the German sortie of August 19 was so great, even though it miscarried, that henceforth the Grand Fleet was almost as confined as an old-time debtor in the Fleet Prison, and was definitely debarred from the southern half of the North Sea. Jellicoe and the Admiralty were agreed upon the necessity for this self-imprisonment. The "command of the sea" became almost a burlesque when the danger of a German invasion of Denmark loomed up that autumn and, after examination by the Admiralty and War Office, the verdict was that "for naval reasons it would be almost impossible to support the Danes at all." The shadow of the submarine was longer than the shadow of Nelson's column. With illuminating candor the British official naval history says, "The Grand Fleet could only put to sea with an escort of nearly one hundred destroyers, no capital ship could leave its base without an escort of small craft, and the German U-boats had hampered our squadrons to an extent which the most expert and far-sighted naval officer had never foreseen." Yet, with curious inconsistency, the voices of naval officers have been heard ever since the war proclaiming the sovereignty of the battleship, the ineffectiveness of the submarine.

The Grand Fleet in the autumn of 1916 was all the more heavily fettered because its warders were reduced, owing to the call for light craft to combat the new "veiled" submarine campaign against commerce. Despite all counter-measures this was so successful that the monthly loss of shipping rose steadily from 109,000 tons during June, to 368,000 tons in January 1917 — approximately half being British. During the "veiled" campaign the Mediterranean was both an ill-favored and, by the Germans, too well-favored area, for besides simplifying the submarine's task of finding targets it simplified the problem of evading the undertakings given to America — in the Mediterranean there was little risk of injuring American ships or interests by mischance. One U-boat alone in five weeks' cruise sank 65,000 tons of shipping.

Counter-measures proved utterly unable to stem the rising tide of sinking ships, even when more destroyers and other small craft became available. During one week of September 1916, thirty ships were sunk by two, or at the most three, submarines in an area patrolled by ninety-seven destroyers and sixty-eight auxiliary craft. Among the remedies tried were those of secret routes, of hoisting false colors, and of decoy ships. This last ruse was carried out by what were known as

Q-ships, equipped with torpedo-tubes, depth charges, and guns concealed behind collapsible bulwarks, while disguised as merchant ships. The disguise was enhanced by the acting of the crews, who coolly simulated panic under conditions where most men would not have needed to do so, and thereby lured the molesting submarine to the surface within close range. Although these Q-ships provided the most romantic phase of the naval war, and sank eleven U-boats, their effect was almost exhausted by the end of 1916, save that it made the enemy more wary — and naturally less inclined to merciful discrimination between armed and apparently unarmed ships. This Q-ship risk to the U-boat was accentuated by the British arming of ordinary merchant ships, which placed the slow, fragile, and half-blind U-boat in a perilous dilemma. The more merciful the U-boat the greater danger it ran; the less heed it paid to the nature of its target and the rescue of those on board the more its safety and success were assured. Hence the outcry in Germany for a policy of sinking at sight was naturally strengthened.

Moreover, if Britain was feeling the strain of economic pressure, so also was Germany, and her leaders feared that the race between decisive success on land and economic collapse would end against her. The naval authorities declared that a renewal of the "unlimited" submarine campaign, which with her increased numbers could now be far more intense, would bring the Entente to their knees. Accepting this opinion, Ludendorff agreed to a step which he had hitherto opposed; the combined weight of naval and military opinion overbore the protests of the Imperial Chancellor. A proposal of peace discussions, and its foreseen rejection by the Entente powers, was made the moral justification for openly abandoning the restrictions of visit and search, and for withdrawing the promise given to President Wilson. On February 1, 1917, the "unrestricted" policy — of sinking all ships, passenger or cargo, without warning — was proclaimed, with the full realization that it involved the weight of America being thrown into the scales against Germany. Doubts of its wisdom in Germany were stifled by the plea of necessity, the

promise of certain victory, and the argument of inevitability
— that America was bound to come to the help of the Allies
in order to ensure their ability to pay their debts to her. But
the Germans reckoned on victory before America's weight could
count in the scales.

1916 — THE "DOG-FALL"

Scene I

THE MINCING MACHINE — VERDUN

It is a truism that the war of 1914–1918 revolutionized all ideas of time, in a military sense, and especially in the duration of its battles. For several thousand years of warfare, a battle, however great the scale, had been a matter of hours. This remained the general case down to the beginning of this century, though a few battles from the Napoleonic wars onwards increased the span to days — for example, Leipzig, Gettysburg. The real change was inaugurated with the Russo-Japanese campaign, when battles at last had to be reckoned in weeks. With the World War the standard became months — because the battles had usually become sieges, without being recognized or scientifically treated as such. The change, it is to be hoped, is a transitory one, for quantity does not imply quality, and duration does imply immobility and indecisiveness — which are perforce the negation of generalship. So that whether from the standpoint of military science or from that of the drain of human life, long battles are bad battles.

The prolongation, too, has complicated the task of the military historian, for unless he desires to fill massive tomes with profuse detail, it is difficult to pick out salient features where there are either none, or else so many that they tend to merge into a formless mass. And of all the so-called "battles" of the war, Verdun holds the duration record, extending from February 21 to December 15, 1916. Even if the suspension of the German offensive be taken as the last date, and the French counter-offensive considered as distinct, the duration is seven months.

This difficulty of singling out any one date is unfortunate, for no battle of the whole war was more heroic or more dramatic in its course, or made so vivid an appeal to the sympathies of the watching nations. It was France's supreme sacrifice and her supreme triumph, and to the splendor of her achievement all the world paid homage.

From February 25 onwards, there was a series of crises until June 23, and many French authorities select the former date as the chief. Yet who should know better than the Germans the moment when the tide really turned against them? So distinguished a critic as General von Zwehl considers that the real turning-point was on March 9, when the Germans failed to capture the Côte de Poivre. It was on March 4 that the Crown Prince called on his army group for a supreme effort to take Verdun, "the heart of France." On March 6, after a two days' bombardment, the new blow fell, and by the ninth was definitely frustrated.

The determination of such a datum point is affected also by the question as to the object of the German Supreme Command in launching the attack on Verdun. General von Falkenhayn, the Chief of the Great General Staff and the responsible officer, has stated categorically that it was to bleed France white by choosing a point of attack for which, sooner than let go, the French Command would have to fight to the last man. He has also quoted from a paper prepared at Christmas 1915, to show that he argued that a break-through in mass was not necessary for this purpose.

Yet, despite his post-war statements, there is still a just doubt as to the initial object. A distinguished German critic, Colonel Foerster, has pointed out how difficult it is to reconcile Falkenhayn's statement with the manner in which the attack was carried out, and declares that the initial operation was obviously an accelerated attack for the purpose of breaking through. He has adduced extracts from Falkenhayn's own order of January 27, 1916, and the latter's vehement marginal criticisms on the explanation of failure rendered by the Crown Prince's Headquarters on March 31. These show that Falkenhayn called for an unchecked and continuous advance.

There is cause to suspect that the real idea underlying the plan was that of a revival of the "Sedan" double envelopment which had been attempted in September 1914. It could now be launched with more favorable chances, for the salient was more acute than at the time of the Marne battle, owing to the St. Mihiel wedge that had been driven into its eastern flank. And the fact that the salient lay astride a river, the Meuse, would hamper the defenders in holding back the German pincers. Moreover, this hypothesis provides a logical explanation for what outwardly seems the unaccountable German mistake in launching their first attack only on the east bank of the river. But if a Sedan was the Germans' object, they might expect that their attack on the east bank would draw the French reserves thither so that the later attack on the west bank, when released, would be able to sweep across the rear of the French, using the river as their prison wall. Thereby, not only would part of the French army be cut off, but the rest be cut in two, while the vast breach would ensure the collapse of the whole trench front in France.

If steady attrition was the object at Verdun, then no particular day can be regarded as decisive, but if a successive left and right hand break-through was intended the German emphasis on March 6–9 is justified.

The German offensive was to be based on fire-power rather than on man-power, and its main agent was to be an intense artillery bombardment, making up for its relatively short duration by the number of batteries and their rapidity of fire, and so seeking to regain the supreme advantage of surprise which was inevitably lost by an artillery preparation of several days, or even a week — as the Allied method had been at Loos, in Champagne, and was still to be on the Somme. To increase their chance of surprise the Germans constructed none of the customary "jumping off" trenches close to the enemy lines, confident that their tremendous artillery bombardment would enable their infantry to cross the wide No Man's Land, in places half a mile across, without meeting effective resistance. With their rear preparations they were less successful. But although the Intelligence branch at French General

Headquarters was thus able to deduce the German intentions, the Operations branch disregarded the warning. On February 1 a driblet of two Territorial divisions was sent, but only at the last moment were adequate reënforcements — two army corps — ordered there. Even when the first of these arrived there were only three divisions on the right bank of the Meuse, two on the left, and three south of the fortress facing east — with no reserves at hand. It is not difficult to guess what would have happened if the German attack had come on the thirteenth, as intended, before this first corps arrived. Bad weather saved the defenders in a double sense, for it also hampered the moving forward of the Germans' heavy guns.

There is, however, another important aspect of this preliminary phase which is comparatively little known. A hasty generalization from the easy fall of the Belgian and Russian fortresses may have caused much of the subsequent critical position at Verdun. Originally the French fortresses were not under the control of the field army, but Joffre used the examples of Liége and Namur as an excuse to persuade the French Government to "declass" Verdun as a fortress, and, having got control in August 1915, from then on he drained it of its men and armament. This removal of guns continued even until January 30, 1916, and the casemates were simply used as shelters for troops. Instead of an all-round defense a single trench position was taken up beyond the forts, and in rear only one subsidiary trench line was usable.

For this continuous front, the commander, General Herr, had not enough men or material — to garrison it or keep it in an efficient state of defense. Its wire was incomplete, and it had scarcely any shell-proof cover. Little wonder that when the blow fell the trench position was blotted out. In contrast was the extraordinary imperviousness of the forts. Forts Douaumont and Vaux fell into German hands, and when they were recaptured in October, the French found that months of tremendous bombardment had made scarcely an impression. The underground cover remained intact, not one field-gun turret was destroyed, and hardly any of the casemates rendered unoccupiable. It was a grim jest of fate that the

French should have thrown away their shield for a target, through a hasty assumption that fortresses were valueless.

The original Governor, General Coutanceau, had not shared this view, but when, before a Parliamentary delegation, he dared to express his opinion, in contradiction to the Army Group commander, General Dubail, he was not only rebuked but dismissed. For some time, rumors had percolated through to Paris about the inadequate state of the Verdun defenses, and in December Galliéni, as Minister of War, had written to Joffre asking for information and an assurance that they should be developed. Joffre's reply might well be framed and hung up in all the bureaus of officialdom the world over — to serve as the mummy at the feast. Rebutting the suggestions, he added: "But since these apprehensions are founded on reports which allege defects in the state of the defenses, I request you to . . . specify their authors. I cannot be a party to soldiers under my command bringing before the Government, by channels other than the hierarchic channel, complaints or protests concerning the execution of my orders. . . . It is calculated to disturb profoundly the spirit of discipline in the Army." The enemy was soon to dispel his doctrine of infallibility, as the mutinies of 1917 were to show that the incapacity of generals and their waste of human life are the most potent factors in disturbing the spirit of discipline. But retribution is slow. Colonel Driant, Deputy for Nancy and a well-known military writer, who had given the warning, was one of the first victims of its neglect, while Joffre for a time gained fresh popular laurels from the heroic sacrifice of Driant and his fellows.

At 7.15 on the morning of February 21, a cold, dry day, the German bombardment began on both banks of the Meuse and on a front of fifteen miles. Steadily the trenches and wire were flattened out or upheaved in a chaos of tumbled earth. "The craters made by the huge shells gave to all the countryside an appearance like the surface of the moon." Familiar as it was to be later, in February 1916, so violent a bombardment was new, and therefore the more appalling. So it went on — until at 4 P.M. the fury of the shell-storm reached its

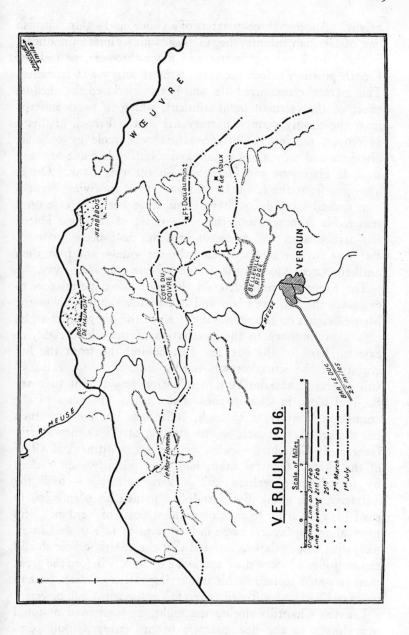

VERDUN, 1916.

Scale of Miles

	Original Line on 21st Feb
	Line on evening 21st Feb
	25th
	7th March
	1st July

BAR LE DUC 25 miles

height.   Another three-quarters of an hour, and a thin skirmish line of German infantry began to advance almost unnoticed, followed by bombing parties and flame-throwers, to feel the French position before the rest of the infantry was launched. This method economized life, and it also disclosed the unequal effect of the German bombardment, which in parts suffered from the deadly counter-battery fire of the French artillery. Moreover, the initial German attack was made by only six divisions and only along a four and a half mile front between Bois de Haumont and Herbebois on the east bank.   On so narrow a front the few scattered packets of surviving Frenchmen caused more delay than should have been the case on a reasonable frontage, and the early onset of darkness halted the attack after the foremost trenches had been occupied. But next day the attack developed more widely, and from then until the twenty-fourth the defenders' line crumbled away.

The French commanders on the spot asked permission to evacuate the Woevre plain and draw back the line on to the Meuse heights on the right bank.   Even this they felt must be only a preliminary to the evacuation of the whole right, or eastern, bank of the Meuse.   But behind the front the full gravity of the situation was hardly realized.   "Operations" still asserted that the Verdun offensive was a feint to cover the real blow, in Champagne.   Even when the news of the crumbling front came through, Joffre was not moved, much less disturbed.   At last, on the evening of the twenty-fourth, General de Castelnau — who, since his appointment as Chief of the French General Staff, had been adroitly side-tracked by Joffre's ever zealous, and jealous, *entourage* — took the initiative and, going direct to Joffre, gained his permission to send Pétain's army to take over the defense of Verdun.   Still more alarming reports came in later, and at 11 P.M. de Castelnau, with unique daring, insisted that the orderly officer should rap on Joffre's locked door and wake him up.   Before the great man returned to resume his unvarying ration of sleep, he had given de Castelnau authority to go to Verdun with "full powers."

Leaving Chantilly during the night, de Castelnau motored post haste to the headquarters of the Army Group com-

mander, de Langle de Cary.   Joffre meanwhile had telegraphed
that the front north of Verdun must be held at all costs:
"Every commander who . . . gives an order for retreat will
be tried by court-martial."   He left it to de Langle de Cary to
decide whether to swing back his right on to the Meuse
heights, and the latter acted on this permission.

De Castelnau's first day at Verdun was not auspicious.
For on the twenty-fifth occurred the strange incident of Fort
Douaumont, and with it the first crisis of the long battle.
Like most of the other forts it had no garrison, except for a
crew of twenty-three gunners who manned one turret.   When,
however, the German tide approached the fort, General
Chrétien, commanding the right sector, dictated an order
that the line of the forts was to be made the principal line of
resistance.   This was shortly before midnight on the twenty-
fourth.   Unfortunately his staff waited for the preparation
of some sketches to attach to the order, and so delayed its
issue until 9.45 A.M. on the twenty-fifth.   Meantime a patrol
of Brandenburgers, finding the drawbridge down and no sign
of any defenders (the gunners had fallen asleep dead-beat),
walked in and took possession without firing a shot.   A triumphal German communiqué announced the capture of Douaumont "by assault" in the presence of the Kaiser.   This piece
of official bombast, however, was to be outclassed and out-
farced when, owing to a misunderstood telephone message,
the communiqué of March 9 announced the capture of Fort
Vaux — three months too early.   But the cream of the jest
was that both the divisional commander who made the report
and the officer who had *not* taken the fort received from the
Kaiser the highest Prussian order, *Pour le Mérite!*   A bad
telephone is not without compensations.

On February 25 Pétain took over command at Verdun,
and the nucleus of a reserve army was assembling in rear.
His first problem was not so much defense as supply.   The
German heavy guns had closed all avenues except one light
railway and the Bar-le-Duc to Verdun road — which later
became immortal as "the Sacred Way."   To push up troops
was no use unless they could be fed and supplied with ammuni-

tion.   The road was already cracking under the strain of the
incessant transport, and so gangs of territorial troops were
brought up to keep it in repair and to double it by parallel
tracks.   Henceforward the flow of traffic rose to as many as
six thousand lorries in the twenty-four hours.   Up in front
Pétain was organizing the front into sectors, each with its own
heavy artillery, and throwing in repeated counter-attacks.
If these gained little ground, they disconcerted and checked
the attacking Germans.   Another assisting factor was that
the further they advanced on the east bank the more did they
expose themselves to flanking fire from the French artillery
across the river.   The advance lost its momentum, slowed
down, and already on the German side "a grievous pessimism
had set in," so Zwehl tells us.

The German Command now sought belatedly — even if it
was according to plan — to widen the front of attack.   On
March 6, after two days' bombardment, the Crown Prince
attacked on the west bank of the Meuse, and on the eighth the
troops on the east bank joined in this supreme effort.   The
gains did not repay the losses, and against Mort Homme on
the west and the Poivre height on the east the attack beat in
vain.   Any hope of a break-through faded, for the defense was
now consolidated and the numbers had been balanced.   Whatever we think of his foresight, there can be no question that
Joffre's imperturbable temperament was a great asset in calm-
ing the anxiety of those days, and in Pétain he made the right
choice for the emergency.   It is proverbial that fortune favors
the brave, and two great pieces of luck befell the French —
the fortunate destruction of all the German 17-inch howitzers
by the French long-range guns, and the blowing up of the great
German artillery park near Spincourt, which held 450,000
heavy shell, unwisely kept fused.   One authority, indeed,
General Palat, gives it as his opinion that these two factors
saved Verdun.

From March 9 onwards, there can be no question that the
German policy was primarily attrition, and that so far as Verdun was aimed at it was as a moral objective.   Publicity
had given it a symbolical value definitely superior to its mili-

tary value. It must be confessed that the strategy nearly succeeded. The advances were slight, but they were cumulative in effect, and worse still, the balance of loss turned against the defenders — nearly three to the Germans' two. Pétain did his best to mitigate the strain by a rapid rotation of reliefs, which kept each division under fire for the shortest possible time. But, as a result, a great part of the French army was drawn through the "mincing machine," and the drain on the French reserves almost bankrupted their share in the forthcoming Somme offensive. Up to July 1 the French had used sixty-six divisions — 50 per cent more than the Germans. On June 7, after a heroic resistance, Fort Vaux really fell — by another German telephone mistake the wrong officer again received the credit — and with it a large stretch of ground was submerged by the German tide, that now seemed to the anxious watchers to resemble the forces of nature rather than of men. On June 11 Pétain was forced to ask Joffre to hasten the relief offensive on the Somme. On June 23 came the last crisis, an advance that brought the Germans almost to the Belleville height, the last outwork of Verdun. Mangin's incessant counter-attacks could do no more than put a brake on the advance, and Pétain made all ready for the evacuation of the east bank, though to his troops he showed no signs of anxiety and ever repeated the now immortal phrase, "On les aura!"

But strategically the defenders had now gained their goal, for Falkenhayn stopped the flow of ammunition to Verdun next day — when the British bombardment began on the Somme, preparatory to the long-arranged attack which was delivered on July 1. From that day on the Germans at Verdun received no fresh divisions, and their advance died out from pure inanition. The way was thus paved for the brilliant French counter-offensives of the autumn, which retook by bites what had been lost by nibbles. It is no disparagement of the sterling defenses to recognize, as we must, that the Somme saved Verdun, and, second, that the Germans, after throwing away their best chance by too narrow an attack frontage, came desperately close to their goal four months later.

1916 — THE "DOG–FALL"

SCENE II

THE BRUSILOV OFFENSIVE

ON June 5, 1916, began an offensive on the eastern front which was to prove the last really effective military effort of Russia. Popularly known as Brusilov's offensive, it had such an astonishing initial success as to revive enthusiastic dreams of the irresistible Russian "steam-roller," which was perhaps the greatest and most dangerous myth of the war. Instead, its ultimate achievement was to sound Russia's death knell. Paradoxical in its consequences, it was still more so in its course — an epitome of the delusive objectives, of the blunders leading to success, and the successes leading to downfall, which marked perhaps the most erratic war in history. In 1915, the Entente had pinned their hopes on Russia, only for the year's campaign to close with the Russian armies, battered and exhausted, barely escaping complete disaster by a seemingly endless retreat. When Falkenhayn turned in 1916 to inaugurate the Verdun attack he left Russia lamed but not crippled, and her surprisingly rapid, if perhaps superficial recovery, enabled her to dislocate the German plans for 1916. As early as March she attacked at Lake Narocz, on the Baltic flank, in gallant sacrificial attempt to relieve the pressure on France. Her command then prepared, for July, a main offensive, also in the northern sector. But before this was ready the needs of her Allies once more led her into a premature move. While the strain at Verdun was growing ever more serious, the Austrians took the opportunity to launch an attack in the Trentino, against the Italians, who appealed to their Russian Ally to prevent the Austrians releasing further forces from the eastern front to reënforce the Trentino menace.

Brusilov, commanding the group of four armies on the

Russian left or southern wing, had already been ordered to stage diversionary attacks in aid of the main blow planned in the north near Molodeczno.   The appeal of Russia's Ally hastened his action.   His strength was no more than equal to that of the opposing force — thirty-eight against thirty-seven divisions — and no special concentration was made.   Thus a decisive exploitation was impossible.   On the other hand, the absence of any concentration gave the Austrians no warning of the impending move, and when, on June 5, the Russian Eighth Army, under Kaledin, advanced near Luck for what was little more than a reconnaissance in force, they took the Austrians by surprise.   The front broke like a crust of pastry at the first touch, and almost unresisted the Russians pushed between the Austrian Fourth and Second Armies.   And, although the Russian Eleventh Army (Sakharov) failed near Tarnopol, the other two armies further south gained as rapid success as that at Luck.   The Seventh Army (Shcherbacher) drove the Austrians back across the Strypa, and the Ninth Army (Lechitski), breaking through in the Bukovina, captured Czernowitz — the southernmost position of the Austrian front.

Never has a mere demonstration had so amazing a success since the walls of Jericho fell at Joshua's trumpet blasts. With both flanks collapsed, the Austro-German armies in the south were in danger of a greater Tannenberg, if only the Russians could exploit their chance.   But all the reserves were massed in the north for the intended main offensive, and although this was promptly abandoned, the poor lateral communications prevented them reaching Brusilov before the Germans could hurry reënforcements to stem the tide. The German Command showed its usual cleverness, using the first reënforcements for a counter-stroke by Linsingen against the northern edge of the Luck break-through, and this at least checked the Russian progress at the most critical point.   To the south, in the Bukovina, the Russian advance continued until it came to a natural halt against the barrier of the Carpathian Mountains.

Late in July the Russian attack was renewed, first in the centre towards Brody and Lemberg by Sakharov, then further north towards the Stokhod River and Kovel by the Russian Guard Army, long prepared for a supreme effort. But the opportunity had passed, and although the attacks still dragged on throughout August, the gains in no way compensated for their heavy cost, and an effort which opened in a blaze of sunshine faded out in autumn gloom.

Its indirect were, however, greater than its direct effects, although not unmixed in benefit. It had compelled Falkenhayn to withdraw troops from the western front, and so abandon his plan for a riposte against the British Somme offensive, as well as the hope of nourishing his attrition process at Verdun. It led Rumania to take her fateful decision to enter the war on the Entente side — to her undoing. And it wrought the downfall of Falkenhayn, who had "spoiled the ship for a ha'porth of tar."

But these indirect effects, not all good, were purchased at too heavy a price. Brusilov had captured the Bukovina and much of Eastern Galicia; he had captured 350,000 prisoners — but he had lost over 1,000,000 men, and so undermined morally, even more than materially, the fighting power of Russia. The imminent sequel was to be revolution and collapse. For the last time Russia had sacrificed herself for her Allies, and it is not just that subsequent events should obscure the debt.

1916 — "THE DOG-FALL"

Scene III

THE SOMME OFFENSIVE

THE series of "battles" — or, to be strategically accurate, the series of limited actions — which opened on July 1 constituted the offensive campaign of the Franco-British armies in 1916. Into it was thrown the entire British effort of the year on the western front, and such part of the French effort as was available after the exhausting strain of the long defensive "battle" at Verdun. And it proved both the glory and the graveyard of "Kitchener's Army" — those citizen volunteers who, instantly answering the call in 1914, had formed the first national army of Britain.

The Somme offensive had its genesis at the Chantilly Conference of the Allied commanders on December 5, 1915. Joffre, in his appreciation of the situation, claimed that the autumn offensives in Champagne and Artois (including Loos) had brought "brilliant tactical results," and ascribed the failure to develop these into a strategical success partly to bad weather and partly to a temporary shortage of ammunition. The essential for the next effort was that "the Higher Command must have no anxiety as regards ammunition," and for this reason it could not be undertaken in less than three months. By early February he had realized that the date must be later still, if, as was essential, the Russians were to attack simultaneously and the British were to take an adequate share with their newly raised armies. At a meeting with Haig he emphasized the view that a broad frontage of attack was the method of success, and to this end desired a combined offensive by the French and British "bras dessus bras dessous," with the attacking line of one Ally prolonging that of the other Ally. Joffre envisaged the French attacking with forty divisions on a

twenty-five miles front from Lassigny to the Somme, and the
British attacking thence to Hébuterne, fourteen miles, with
twenty-five divisions, or as near that number as possible.

While there was unanimity on the main scheme, a certain
divergence of view became manifest in regard to the method.
In these discussions Joffre constantly pressed for the British
to make preparatory attacks north of the Somme and in
conjunction with the French and Belgians between Ypres and
the Belgian coast — to draw in and fix the enemy's reserves,
so easing the way for the Franco-British main blow. Haig
preferred to trust in one great stroke, with all the forces available and when they were fully prepared. Although Haig's
attitude was justified by the incompleteness of his resources
and by the barrenness of such preparatory attacks the previous
autumn, the critic is compelled to recognize that Joffre had the
experience of history on his side, and that the experience of
the war was to show that decisive offensives were vain until the
enemy's reserves had been attracted elsewhere. But if Haig
acceded only reluctantly and in a modified form to the French
pressure, he was unquestionably right in maintaining that any
such preparatory offensive to fulfill its object should only
precede the general offensive by ten days or a fortnight.

The result of the postponement of the Allied offensive,
whether inevitable or not, was to yield the initiative to the
Germans, and their attack at Verdun, from February 21
onwards, impaired the whole of the Allied plan and campaign
in 1916.

On February 22 Joffre urged anew that the British should
launch the preparatory attacks without delay, and also take
over more line. Haig did not see his way to comply with the
first request, and in the outcome no such moves preceded the
July assault. To meet the second request, hitherto evaded,
he hastened the relief of the French Tenth Army, round Arras,
which was sandwiched between his own First and Third Armies.
Allenby's Third Army sideslipped northwards, and the newly
formed Fourth Army, under Rawlinson, took over its front
between Maricourt and Hébuterne. The British now held a
continuous front from Ypres almost to the Somme.

As the French were drained of their strength at Verdun, so did their share of the Somme plan evaporate. Ultimately their front of attack shrank from twenty-five miles to eight,

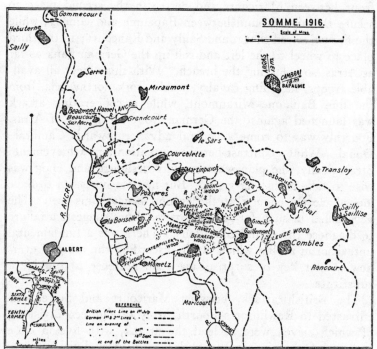

and their force from forty divisions to sixteen, of which only five attacked on July 1. From now onwards the British were to take up the main burden of the western front campaign, and because of this fact alone July 1, 1916, is a landmark in the history of the war.

It is a question how far Haig's real aims were reduced in proportion to the shrinkage of resources. His orders no longer ordained the unlimited objectives of Loos and Champagne, nor foresaw so rapid a break-through as had then proved a mirage. And he framed an alternative plan, to switch his Reserve Army north to Ypres, in case of complete failure. But he does not seem to have foreseen the case of mixed success and failure — always the greater probability in war. And for

this want of elasticity his plan suffered in execution. Realism
was perhaps equally lacking. The hopeful intention of the
British Command was, in the first place, to break the German
front between Maricourt and Serre; in the second place to
secure the high ground between Bapaume and Ginchy, while
the French seized that round Sailly and Rancourt; in the third
place to wheel to the left and roll up the German flank as far
as Arras, so enlarging the breach. With this object all available troops, including cavalry, would work northwards, from
the line Bapaume–Miraumont, while a coöperating attack
was launched against the German front southwest of Arras.
Fourthly was to come a general advance towards Cambrai–
Douai. What a contrast between intention and achievement!
Strategically, the plan was shrewdly designed, and Haig was
wise to take such long views. But he does not seem to have
looked clearly enough at the ground beneath his feet. The
very belief in such far-reaching possibilities suggests a failure
to diagnose the actual conditions. There was a fundamental
unrealism in a plan which, while discarding the old and ever-
new master key of surprise, made no pretense to provide a
substitute.

The British attack, between Maricourt and Serre, was
entrusted to Rawlinson's Fourth Army of eighteen divisions,
of which eleven were to lead the attack, with five in close
reserve. Only two, together with three cavalry divisions, were
in army reserve. In addition a corps of three divisions and
the headquarters of a reserve army — under Gough — were
located in the battle area in the hands of the Commander-
in-Chief. Two divisions of the Third Army were to make a
subsidiary attack round Gommecourt. The artillery concentration totaled one thousand five hundred guns, averaging one
gun to every twenty yards of front, a record at that time,
although far eclipsed by later concentrations. The gun
strength was the same as that of the Germans for their great
Dunajec break-through, but the defenses on the Russian front
a year before could not be compared with the network of wire
and trenches on the Somme front. Another significant contrast was that, whereas the French had nine hundred heavy

guns, the British had less than half this number for a far wider front.

In subsequent years it has been claimed that Haig did not aim at a break-through. Undoubtedly as the hour approached he became less hopeful, in view of the shrinkage of French aid and aims, and some weeks before the attack he gave the Cabinet a warning that a decision might not be possible, and that his purpose was to wear down the Germans in readiness for a final blow in 1917. But caution in dealing with one's employers is natural. And on such questions personal evidence is usually a truer guide than the discreet ambiguity of official documents. Rawlinson, according to his diary, was against an attempt to break through "the whole of the enemy's lines of defense . . . in one attack." And on April 30 he records: "The attack is to go for the big thing. I still think we would do better to proceed by shorter steps; but I have told D.H. (Douglas Haig) I will carry out his plan with as much enthusiasm as if it were my own." But the slow and long-drawn-out bombardment which he advocated had been adopted instead of a six hours' hurricane bombardment. General Seely, then in command of one of the cavalry brigades, has also stated that his orders for July 1 were "to gallop right through to Cambrai, encircle it, and cut the railway lines to the east."

To understand both the problem and the course of the battle a brief description of the ground is necessary, for in few battles on the western front did topography have so important an influence or make so deep an impression on the minds of the combatants. From Péronne, where the Somme makes a right-angled turn south, a range of hills runs northwest, forming the watershed between the Somme and the basins of the Scarpe and the Scheldt. This ridge, intersected by the narrow valley of the little river Ancre, had been in German possession since the "race to the sea" of October 1914, and it gave the enemy command and observation over the Allied lines and the land behind them. For the first year this disadvantage mattered little, for when British troops relieved the French here in July 1915 the front had an air and a condition of peacefulness astonishing to men accustomed to the incessant "bickering" of Ypres or La Bassée. Report said that in some places the troops of our Ally went back for *déjeuner* to villages hardly touched, close to the line, leaving only sentries in the trenches; that in another hamlet which stood in No Man's Land the sleeping accommodation was nightly shared between the opposing sides by tacit consent. I can vouch for the fact that in the first months after the British had taken over this front it was possible for battalions to drill undisturbed on fields in full view of the German lines — whereas six months later billets several miles further back were harassed by gunfire. The campaign policy of the French, except when engaged in active operations, was "live and let live," and in retrospect there seems little doubt that it was wiser than the British policy of continual "strafing." For when the Germans held the dominating positions, as well as a superiority in ammunition and equipment, these worrying tactics wore down the British troops more than the enemy — attrition on the wrong side of the balance-sheet. Further, they stirred the Germans to strengthen their trench defenses, to develop by art the advantages of nature, so that the offensive came against an almost impregnable fortress instead of against the relatively weak defense system which existed in the autumn of 1915. Masefield, in his book, *The Old Front Line*, expressed the situation aptly: "Almost in every part of this old front our men had to go up hill to attack. . . . The enemy had the lookout posts, with the fine views over France, and the sense of domination. Our men were down below, with no view of anything but of stronghold after stronghold, just up above, being made stronger daily." To-day the tumbled desolation that was the Somme battlefield has passed. Though he underestimated the time, Masefield's instinct was correct that "when the trenches are filled in and the plough has gone over them the ground will not keep the look of war. One summer with its flowers will cover most of the ruin that man can make, and then these places, from which the driving back of the enemy began, will be hard indeed to trace, even with maps." "Centre Way, Peel Trench, Munster Alley, and these other paths to glory will be deep under the corn, and gleaners will sing at Dead Mule Corner." Yet, while even memory finds it difficult to recapture the war-time aspect, a tranquil visit impresses the mind with the steepness of the ascent and the command from the ridge, even more than in days when progress was reckoned in yards and the contour was seen from the eye-level of trenches and shell-holes. From an artillery point of view there were advantages in attacking uphill, because the German trenches were more clearly displayed, but in other ways it was a physical and psychological handicap — not only to the attacking infantry.

Surprise, difficult in face of such commanding positions, was the more difficult because the art of concealing preparations, and of camouflage, had yet to be relearned. The construction of new hutments on both sides of the Ancre provided the Germans with the first clue, in February, and thenceforward signs continually multiplied. Falkenhayn contemplated an attempt to dislocate the British offensive, but found that he could not spare the necessary troops. If the vast preparations had not given it away, a bombardment of a week's duration would in any case have announced the coming assault. Even earlier, an incautiously worded speech of appeal to the munition workers by the British Minister of Labor, Mr. Arthur Henderson, on June 2, had given the German Command a hint of its early delivery. The one redeeming factor was that, despite accurate predictions and warnings of the attack both from the immediate army command (the Second) and from agents abroad, Falkenhayn continued to believe that it was only a preliminary to the real blow further north, apparently feeling that British preparations were too blatant to be true. In consequence he withheld reënforcements, and not until July 5 was he convinced that the Somme was Haig's chosen battleground. In the meantime he dismissed the Chief of Staff of the Second Army for having been right and "asking for more."

The bombardment began on June 24; the attack was intended for June 29, but was later postponed until July 1, owing to a momentary break in the weather. This postponement, made at French request, involved not only the spreading out of the ammunition over a longer period, and a consequent loss of intensity, but a greater strain on the assaulting troops, who, after being keyed up for the effort, had to remain another forty-eight hours in cramped trenches under the exhausting noise of their own gunfire and the enemy's retaliation — conditions made worse by torrential rain which flooded the trenches.

July 1 dawned a day of broiling heat, and at 7 A.M. the bombardment rose to its height. Half an hour later the infantry advanced from their trenches — and thousands fell, strewing No Man's Land with their bodies, before the German front trench was even reached. For their opponents were the Germans of 1916, most stubborn and skillful fighters; while the shells flattened their trenches, they sheltered in dugouts or shell-holes, and then as the barrage lifted dragged out their machine-guns, to pour an unslackening hail of lead into the unduly dense waves of the attackers — for 1916 marked the nadir of infantry attacks, the revival of formations that were akin to the eighteenth century in their formalism and lack of manœuvring power. Battalions attacked in four or eight waves, not more than a hundred yards apart, the men in each almost shoulder to shoulder, in a symmetrical well-dressed alignment, and taught to advance steadily upright at a slow walk with their rifles held aslant in front of them, bayonets upwards — so as to catch the eye of the observant enemy. An excellent imitation of Frederick's infantry *automata*, with the difference that they were no longer advancing against muskets of an effective range of barely a hundred yards. It is hardly remarkable that by nightfall on July 1 many battalions were barely a hundred strong. Haig, indeed, had laid down that the Verdun method of the Germans should be adopted, strong patrols feeling their way forward to test the result of the bombardment before the mass of the infantry were committed. But his Chief of Staff, Kiggell, nevertheless ordered "waves." Only as the upstanding waves were broken up by the fire did advance become possible. For then human nature and primitive cunning reasserted themselves against authorized tactics; the more enterprising and still uncowed survivors formed little groups, usually under some natural leader, and worked their way by short rushes, and crawling from shell-hole to shell-hole, stalking the opposing machine-guns, and often progressing to a considerable depth with little further loss. But in many places packets of the enemy and nests of machine-guns were left in their wake, to take heavy toll of the supports.

Thus, save in the south, the force of the tide slackened and later ebbed. Fricourt, on the right centre, formed a turning point both in the front and in the fortune of the day. The French, south of the Somme and north of it as far as Maricourt, gained all their objectives with slight loss. This success they owed partly to their more flexible tactics and heavier artillery concentration, partly to the lesser strength of the German defenses, and to the fact that the attack here came as a tactical surprise to the Germans, who had expected an attack only on the British front. Between Maricourt and Fricourt the British XIII Corps (30th and 18th Divisions) reached its objectives, though with greater loss, capturing Montauban. On its left the XV Corps partially achieved its task of pinching out the bastion of Fricourt village and wood. The 7th Division turned one flank by capturing Mametz, and on the other flank the 21st Division penetrated some half a mile into the German lines, holding on to a narrow tongue of captured land with both its own flanks in the air until Fricourt fell next day.

But the 21st Division marked the boundary of success, and all to the north was failure — with the heaviest British loss of any day's fighting in the war. One significant factor was the greater width of No Man's Land. Of the III Corps the 34th Division pushed past La Boisselle to Contalmaison, but it was forced to fall back, its flank enfiladed by Ovillers, against which the waves of the 8th Division beat practically in vain. Northward, again, the X Corps (32nd and 36th Divisions) penetrated some distance into the German lines, portions of the 36th Ulster Division even to Grandcourt, but the supports could not get forward, the advanced parties were cut off, and at nightfall only small fractions of the German front trenches near Thiepval remained in British hands. The attack of the VIII Corps (29th, 4th, and 31st Divisions) on the left flank was shattered more abruptly, though here again a few isolated parties pressed through to Beaumont Hamel and Serre.

The tally of prisoners who passed through the corps cages that day is in some degree an index of the comparative initial success: XIII Corps (Congreve), 934; XV Corps (Horne), 517; III Corps (Pulteney), 32; X Corps (Morland), 478; VIII Corps (Hunter-Weston), 22. It reveals that in the north the X Corps made a deep penetration, although the Ulstermen were forced to relinquish the ground later because of the repulse of the troops on their flanks. For the French, who had taken 6000 prisoners at little cost, July 1 may be counted a victory. But the major attack was that of the British, and here the Germans could justly claim success, for with only six divisions available, and roughly a regiment holding each British division's sector of attack, they had only yielded 1983 prisoners and a small tract of ground to the assault of thirteen British divisions. The high hopes built up beforehand had fallen to the ground, and the months of preparation and sowing had only garnered a bitter fruit. Yet, although a military failure, July 1 was an epic of heroism, and, better still, the proof of the moral quality of the new armies of Britain, who, in making their supreme sacrifice of the war, passed through the most fiery and bloody of ordeals with their courage unshaken and their fortitude established.

All along the attacking line these quondam civilians bore a percentage of losses such as no professional army of past wars had ever been deemed capable of suffering — without being broken as an effective instrument. And they carried on the struggle, equally bitter, for another five months. Experience would improve their tactical action, still more their handling by the Higher Command, but no subsequent feats could surpass the moral standard of July 1, "a day of an intense blue summer beauty, full of roaring violence, and confusion of death, agony, and triumph, and from dawn till dark. All through that day little rushes of the men of our race went towards that No Man's Land from the bloody shelter of our trenches. Some hardly left our trenches, many never crossed the green space, many died in the enemy wire, many had to fall back. Others won across, and went further and drove the enemy back from line to line till the Battle of the Somme ended in the falling back of the enemy." That falling back, however, was long postponed, and when it came was so timed as to discomfort the attackers far more than it advantaged them.

Late on July 2, Haig, confronted with a difficult situation, decided to press the attack where success had been gained, instead of making a fresh frontal assault on the intact defenses from Ovillers northwards. The tactical experience of the later years — and earlier history — confirms his wisdom, and the only question is why the exploitation of the success in the south was not more prompt. Part of the dense infantry strength which had been used to strew No Man's Land with dead might better have been kept to swell the reserve for such a purpose. Even as it was, the Germans were badly shaken, and if British reserve divisions were few, theirs were less, as their delay in counter-attacking showed. But the Fourth Army made no attempt to push reserves through at the sectors of least resistance, and at 10 P.M. on July 1 merely ordered its corps to "continue the attack" evenly along the whole front. Fortunately the two left wing corps commanders pointed out the hopelessness of a fresh attack without adequate preparation, and the plan was then modified on Haig's intervention. Less fortunately, this intervention was somewhat belated. All that he did on July 1 was to place the two left corps (X and VIII) under Gough — but without removing them from the control of the Fourth Army. As they were not in a state to attack unbroken defenses again, nothing happened on July 2. Meantime the XIII Corps, which had made a real penetration on the extreme right, was held back. This passivity was the more regrettable because, in conjunction with the French, it had already shattered a ragged and fumbling right counter-attack by a German division hurried up from Cambrai — the one enemy reserve immediately available.

Opportunity receded further when, for July 3, Rawlinson merely ordered a renewed attack by the left wing in conjunction with his centre. This plan Haig approved, but modified — with not altogether happy results. He was now turning his eyes to the right, and he reduced the morrow's attack to thrusts by small packets against Thiepval and

Ovillers. The rearrangement accentuated the defects due to divided control, so that the attacks became not only petty in scale but disjointed in delivery — and proved void of any effect except further casualties. Meantime, troops of the XIII Corps on the right walked into Bernafay Wood almost without opposition, but were restrained from going further. The French XX Corps next to it was, as a corollary, also constrained to inactivity, but south of the Somme the French captured the German second line and the high ground overlooking Péronne.

Haig was now convinced of the advisability of concentrating his effort on the right. But he met a French stumblingblock. Both Joffre and Foch — who was in direct charge of the French share of the offensive — insisted that Haig should capture the ridge from Pozières to Thiepval in the centre as a preliminary to any attack on the right, or Longueval, sector. Haig's contention that he had not enough ammunition to cover effectively a renewed attack on the whole front, and that the Longueval ridge defenses were weaker than at Thiepval, made no impression, and Joffre declared that if the British attacked Longueval they would be beaten. Indeed, he went so far as to give Haig a direct order to attack in the centre, whereupon Haig retorted that he was responsible to the British Government, and that, although he was ready to follow Joffre's strategy, in matters of tactics he would take his own line. This settled the question.

A long interval followed, however, before the Fourth Army was ready for the attack on the enemy's second line. The interval was the longer because Haig considered it necessary to clear away all the enemy's outlying footholds before attempting the main stroke, and sought to seize these by a series of nibbling attacks. At the same time the X and VIII Corps on the left were definitely transferred from Rawlinson's Fourth Army to Gough's Reserve Army, later to become the Fifth, and the available reserves and guns were concentrated on the reduced Fourth Army front.

Thus, during the days immediately following July 1, when the German defense was seriously shaken in the southern sector, — Montauban–La Boisselle, — the renewed attacks were slight in strength and spasmodic. The resistance had breathing space to reorganize and harden, to strengthen its hold on the commanding ridge, Ginchy–Pozières, where ran the German second line. The British progress became very slow, and a special obstacle was offered by Mametz Wood. The three days' abortive attacks — by the 38th (Welsh) Division — and consequent delay here were to prejudice the main stroke. But as great a handicap was imposed from above.

If the British Higher Command had been overambitious and unduly optimistic before July 1, it perhaps now tended to the other extreme. Rawlinson, however, had been brought to realize that bold and rapid measures were essential if he was to forestall the German reënforcements and labor which were rebuilding, in rear, the fortified front faster than the British could force a way through it. If the British waited until their front line had been carried near enough to the German second line (Braune Stellung) for a close assault, they might well be confronted with a barrier as firm as the original of July 1. Rawlinson framed a plan to attack and break the German defenses on a four-mile front between Delville Wood on the right, and Bazentin-le-Petit Wood on the left. His right was fully three-quarters of a mile distant from this second line, with the vital tactical feature of Trônes Wood between still in German hands. Thence towards his left No Man's Land gradually narrowed, until in front of Mametz Wood it was only about three hundred yards wide; but Trônes Wood enfiladed a large part of the line of advance. If the obvious course was adopted, and an attack delivered only on the left, the prospects were barren. For the experience of 1915 had shown that an attack on a narrow frontage against an enemy with ample guns might gain an initial success, only to be blown out of the captured fragment by the concentration of hostile gunfire thus facilitated.

Instead of the obvious, Rawlinson took a course which for all its risks — calculated risks — was more truly secure and economical of force. The troops were to cross the exposed area by an advance under cover of darkness, followed by a dawn attack, preceded by a hurricane bombardment of only a few minutes' duration. This plan revived the use of surprise, which lay rusting throughout the greater part of the war, until, in fact, the last year from Cambrai onwards.

In 1916 the ideas of a night advance and of such a brief bombardment were alike so fresh in revival as to be a shock and appear a gamble to orthodox opinion. That he should attempt the manœuvre with New Army troops, men who had been civilians less than two years before, made his plan seem yet more rash. The Commander-in-Chief was strongly opposed to it, preferring a more limited alternative, but Rawlinson persevered, his own confidence reënforced by the confidence of the actual troop-leaders in their ability to carry out the night operation. For once Horne, whose capacity for agreeing with the Commander-in-Chief was as consistent as his own rise, agreed instead with his immediate superior, and this fact may have helped to tilt the scales. Rawlinson gained his way, but instead of the already delayed attack being launched on July 13, as he intended, the reluctance of the Higher Command caused it to be postponed until July 14 — a day's delay that was to have grave consequences. Another drawback was the lack of French coöperation, owing to lack of faith in the prospects of the attack.

The attacking troops were composed of the 9th and 3rd Divisions of the XIII Corps on the right (W. T. Furse and J. A. L. Haldane), and the 7th and 21st Divisions of the XV Corps on the left (H. E. Watts and D. G. M. Campbell), while on the extreme right flank Maxse's 18th Division had the task of clearing Trônes Wood. On the extreme left the III Corps formed a defensive flank between Bazentin-le-Petit Wood and Contalmaison. Cavalry divisions were brought up close and placed under the orders of the two attacking corps.

The German front was held by only six battalions of mixed divisions in General Stein's group, with the 7th Division in reserve south of Bapaume. The trenches of the Braune Stellung ran just in front of Delville Wood, Longueval, Bazentin-le-Grand and Bazentin-le-Petit Woods, with High Wood, "like a dark cloud on the skyline" behind, dominating the whole area of approach. From it the Germans could see several miles behind the old British front line of July 1.

On the right, markers went out some hours after darkness had fallen on July 13 and placed white tapes to guide the troops along their 1000 yards approach; then further tapes at right angles to mark the forward line on which the troops were to form up, so that they should start parallel with their objective. The hazardous and difficult task was carried through successfully, and soon after midnight the battalions assembled in the shelter of Caterpillar Valley, moving up in long worm-like lines of companies or platoons in single file. At 3.20 A.M. the barrage fell on the German trenches, and five minutes later the whole line moved forward to the assault. The vision which had dared to attempt such a surprise stroke, and had supported imagination with good staff work, was justified. The whole of the German second line was rapidly overrun, and the attacking troops passed beyond. From left to right, the 21st Division pressed through Bazentin-le-Petit Wood to the village, the 7th Division cleared Bazentin-le-Grand Wood and pushed up the slopes towards High Wood, the 3rd Division captured Bazentin-le-Grand, and the 9th Division fought their way, albeit with difficulty, through Longueval to the outskirts of Delville Wood.

On this right flank every yard of advance was bitterly opposed, and in the depths of Delville Wood, during the ensuing days, the South Africans made their supreme sacrifice of the war — where to-day a white stone colonnade of peaceful beauty commemorates, and contrasts with, the bloodiest battle-hell of 1916.

But on the left flank opportunity — and open country — stretched out its arms. Soon after midday the German resistance was clearly disintegrating on the front of the 7th Division, and an effort was made to exploit the chance, although some hours were lost. The 7th Division moved forward soon after 6 P.M. with two squadrons of cavalry working on their flank — the first mounted cavalry seen on a British battlefield since 1914. Roseate expectations pictured open warfare on the skyline, but once more it proved a mirage in the military desert. The troops of the illustrious 7th Division were a shade battle-weary; their depleted ranks had been filled with many untried drafts. Whatever the cause, the advance tended to lack vigor, and although most of the wood was cleared that evening, the northern corner of the flanking trenches remained in the Germans' grip. Worst of all, twenty-four hours' postponement had enabled fresh reserves to come up, and, as their strength steadily swelled, the German hold tightened, the British relaxed. Late on July 15 the wood was evacuated under pressure of counter-attacks, and two months were to pass before possession was regained. The surprise storm of the Somme "Bastille" on July 14 brought the British to the verge of a strategic decision; thereafter their effort degenerated into a battle of attrition.

After the disappointing end of the July 14 stroke, Haig played for smaller stakes. His overdrawn supplies of ammunition were causing concern, and he had in mind no effective substitute for gun-pounding as an "opener" for the enemy's sealed front. Early in June he had contemplated the step of transferring his main offensive to the Messines sector in Flanders if the German reserves held him up on the Somme. And the Anzac Corps began to move thither in readiness. But by July 7 he had decided instead to pour his own reserves down to the Somme — now, for the enemy, the line of expectation — and to throw all his weight into the direct offensive there.

He ordered, however, a number of local attacks in the north as a means to fix the enemy's attention and keep his reserves there, and away from the Somme. The method reveals a most curious military delusion, for while simulated preparations for a large-scale offensive would cause the enemy natural apprehension, the actual delivery of a narrow-fronted local attack would merely disclose the bluff. One consequence was the shattering of the 5th Australian Division in an absurdly advertised attack at Fromelles, an attack which was the final link of an almost incredibly muddled chain of causation.

The rest of the Anzac Corps had been moved to the Somme, where Haig's aim was now to enlarge his lodgment on the main ridge. He had favored the idea of trying to carry out his original third phase, — of rolling up the German front northwards, — although the original conditions had not been fulfilled. But he had not sufficient elbow-room to deploy an adequate force for it. And it would have diverged from the line of coöperation with the French. Hence he decided to continue his main pressure with his right, eastward towards the French line of convergence, while on his left Gough sought to gain the Pozières-Thiepval end of the ridge, and so widen the British holding upon it.

To this end Gough was given the Anzac Corps (Birdwood), and on July 23 he launched part of it against Pozières in conjunction with a renewed assault by the three corps of the Fourth Army along the whole of its narrow front, from Guillemont to Bazentin-le-Petit. This failed completely; on the left the 1st Australian Division gained a footing in Pozières. Haig reverted to the method of nibbling, now to be exalted as a definite and masterly strategy of attrition, and to be defended by optimistic miscalculations of the German losses.

Nearly two months of bitter fighting followed, during which the British made little progress at much cost, and the infantry of both sides served as compressed cannon-fodder for artillery consumption. On the left flank the Anzac Corps was the main agent of the new plan of "methodical progress." The effect is best described in the measured words of the Australian official history : —

Doubtless to the Commander-in-Chief, and possibly to the Cabinet, the use of terms implying leisurely progress brought some comfortable assurance of economy of life as well as of munitions; but to the front line the method merely appeared to be that of applying a battering-ram ten or fifteen times against the same part of the enemy's battle-front with the intention of penetrating for a mile, or possibly two, into the midst of his organized defenses. . . .

Even if the need for maintaining pressure be granted, the student will have difficulty in reconciling his intelligence to the actual tactics. To throw the several parts of an army corps, brigade after brigade . . . twenty times in succession against one of the strongest points in the enemy's defense may certainly be described as "methodical," but the claim that it was economic is entirely unjustified.

Twenty-three thousand men were expended in these efforts for the ultimate gain, after six weeks, of a tiny tongue

of ground just over a mile deep.   And what of the moral
effect?

Although most Australian soldiers were optimists, and many were opposed
on principle to voicing — or even harboring — grievances, it is not surprising
if the effect on some intelligent men was a bitter conviction that they were
being uselessly sacrificed.   "For Christ's sake, write a book on the life of an
infantryman (said one of them . . .), and by doing so you will quickly
prevent these shocking tragedies."   That an officer who had fought so nobly
as Lieutenant J. A. Raws should, in the last letter before his death, speak of
the "murder" of many of his friends "through the incompetence, callousness,
and personal vanity of those high in authority," is evidence not indeed of the
literal truth of his words, but of something much amiss in the higher leadership. . . .   "We have just come out of a place so terrible (wrote ——, one
of the most level-headed officers in the force) that . . . a raving lunatic
could never imagine the horror of the last thirteen days."

The history indicates that Birdwood lost much of his Gallipoli popularity through his failure to interpose against Gough's
impetuous desire for quick results and his lack of thought.
Perhaps this was a factor in leading the Australian troops to
reject Birdwood's personal appeal when they voted against
the conscription of other men to share the horrors that they
had experienced.

But Pozières was matched on the other flank by Guillemont — now a peaceful hamlet amid cornfields, then a shambles
of blended horror and mystery.   From Trônes Wood it is
down one slope, up another, only a few hundred yards of farm
road now, yet, in July and August 1916, an infinite distance.
Division after division essayed to cross it, felt the petty prize
within their fingers, and then slipped back, unable to maintain
their hold.   And when it was at last secured on September 3,
Ginchy, a few hundred yards further up the slope, was a similar
obstruction until September 9.   Save Thiepval, still defiant,
no hamlets have exacted a heavier price for their possession.

Now at last the British line was straightened on a seven-
mile front running northwest from Leuze Wood, overlooking
Combles, where it joined up with the French.   They had just
extended further south the attack south of the Somme, storm-
ing three miles of the old German front line near Chaulnes and
taking 7000 prisoners.   On August 30 Rawlinson had recorded

in his diary, "The Chief is anxious to have a gamble with all the available troops about September 15, with the object of breaking down German resistance and getting through to Bapaume." And he added, somewhat illogically, "We shall have no reserves in hand, save tired troops, but success at this time . . . might bring the Boches to terms." Despite his professed faith in attrition, Haig was now reduced to gambling on a break-through.

The attack was to pivot on the left wing — Gough's army. The primary object of the main blow, by Rawlinson, was to break through what had originally been the Germans' last line between Morval and Le Sars, in coöperation with a French thrust to the south between Combles and the Somme — thus pinching out Combles. If the opening success warranted the attempt the British attack was to be extended northward to seize Courcellette and Martinpuich. Eight divisions were deployed for the original attack, and two detailed for the "extension." A special feature was the employment for the first time of tanks, the armored cross-country machines which had been invented as an antidote to the defensive obstacle of machine-guns and barbed wire. In disregard of the opinions of the tank's progenitors, and of their own expressed agreement with these opinions, the British Higher Command had decided to utilize such machines as were available, as a stake to redeem the fading prospects of the Somme offensive. When this decision was taken, only sixty of the initial one hundred and fifty machines had been transported to France. Forty-nine were actually employed, to work in tiny detachments of two or three machines — another breach of the principles laid down by Colonel Swinton. The scant and hasty preparation combined with the mechanical defects of this early model to reduce the total, so that only thirty-two reached the starting point. Of these, nine pushed ahead with the infantry, nine failed to catch the infantry but helped in clearing the captured ground, nine broke down, and five were "ditched" in the craters of the battlefield. The first nine rendered useful aid, especially in capturing Flers, but the greater prize — of a great surprise stroke — was a heavy forfeit to pay for redeeming in a limited degree the failure of the Somme offensive.

The attack was launched at dawn on the fifteenth in a slight mist, and the XV Corps in the centre made early and good progress; by 10 A.M. its left division was beyond Flers. But on the right the XIV Corps lost heavily and was held up long before it could reach Morval and Lesbœufs. The III Corps, on the left, also fell short of its objectives, although its 47th Division finally cleared the long-sought High Wood. On the extreme left the projected extension of the attack was carried out, and both Martinpuich and Courcellette were taken. As a result of the day the crest of the ridge had been gained, except on the right, and with it the commanding observation which the Germans had so long enjoyed.

The failure on the right was redressed on September 25 by another big attack which, in conjunction with the French, compelled the Germans to evacuate Combles. Next day Thiepval at last fell to Gough's army. Haig still called for pressure "without intermission," and, as a result of further small gains, by the first week of October the Germans were back in their last completed line of defenses, which ran from Sally-Saillisel, on the right, past Le Transloy and in front of Bapaume; they were busily constructing fresh lines in rear, but these were not yet complete. On the other hand, these days had proved the continued strength of the German resistance, and the limited success held but little hope of a real break-through or its exploitation. The early onset of the autumn rains made this hope more slender daily. The rains combined with the bombardments to make the ground a morass in which guns and transport were bogged, while even lightly equipped infantry could barely and slowly struggle forward. Attacks under such conditions were terribly handicapped; that most of them failed was inevitable, and if a trench was taken the difficulties of consolidating it liquidated the gain.

By October 12 Haig seems to have been at last convinced that he could not pierce the German defenses that year. But Joffre and Foch continued to urge him on, and in partial response Haig continued to call for fresh attacks through the mud towards Le Transloy, until a strong protest was made by

Lord Cavan, commanding the XIV Corps, who desired to know whether it was deliberately intended to sacrifice the British right in order to help the French left, and pointedly added, "No one who has not visited the front can really know the state of exhaustion to which the men are reduced." But other corps commanders had less moral courage, and Rawlinson, although sympathetic, seems to have yielded against his better judgment to his Chief's determination. Hence the III and Anzac Corps continued a hopeless series of petty attacks until November 16. Their ineffectiveness was redeemed, as their ineptitude was obscured, by a welcome, last-hour success of Gough's army. Even this had an offset, for by redeeming Gough's reputation it paved the way for fresh sacrifices at Ypres the next year.

The wedge that had been slowly driven eastwards between the Ancre and the Somme had turned the original German defenses north of the Ancre into a pronounced salient. For some time Gough's army had been preparing an attack against this, and a temporary improvement in the weather allowed it to be launched on November 13, by seven divisions. Beaumont-Hamel and Beaucourt-sur-Ancre were captured, with 7000 prisoners, but on the left Serre once more proved impregnable. Haig was pleased — because it would "strengthen the hands of the British representatives" at the forthcoming Allied Military Conference at Chantilly. So the Somme offensive could at last be suspended with honor satisfied.

The folly of the last phase, from September 25 onwards, was that, the crest of the ridge and its commanding observation having at last been won, the advantage was thrown away by fighting a way down into the valley beyond. Thereby the troops were doomed to spend the winter in flooded trenches. "Somme mud" was soon to be notorious.

Thus the miscalled Battles of the Somme closed in an atmosphere of disappointment, and with such a drain on the British forces that the coincident strain on the enemy was obscured. This strain was largely due to the rigidity of the German higher commanders, especially General Von Below of the First Army, who issued an order that any officer who gave up an inch of trench would be court-martialed, and that every yard of lost trench must be retaken by counter-attack. If German mistakes do not condone British mistakes, they at least caused a vain loss of life, and still more of morale, which helped to balance the British loss — until on August 23 Below was compelled to swallow his own orders and modify his method of resistance, in accord with that of the new Hindenburg-Ludendorff régime.

1916 — THE "DOG–FALL"

Scene IV

THE GROWING PAINS OF THE TANK

On September 15, 1916, a new instrument of war received its baptism of fire, and helped to make the British attack on that day one of the landmarks of the Somme offensive. It was one of the few attacks which did not require the use of a large-scale map and a magnifying glass to detect its progress. But, far more significant, it cast its shadow over the whole future of the war. And as it thus becomes a greater landmark in the history of the war than in the history of the Somme, so it is likely to become a still greater landmark in the history of war.

For this new instrument — the tank — changed the face of war by substituting motor-power for a man's legs as a means of movement on the battlefield and by reviving the use of armor as a substitute for his skin or for earth-scrapings as a means of protection. Hitherto he could not fire if he wished to move, and could not move if he wished for cover. But September 15, 1916, saw the simultaneous combination in one agent of fire-power, movement, and protection — an advantage until then enjoyed in modern warfare only by those who fought on the sea.

But although sea warfare on land may be the ultimate consequence of the tank, and was foreshadowed in its first name of "landship," the original intention was more limited and more immediately practical — to provide an antidote to the machine-gun, which, in alliance with barbed wire, had reduced warfare to stagnation and generalship to attrition.

The cure was a British production, the most significant achievement of British brains during the World War. Yet it has an essential transatlantic link, symbolical in view of the association on the battlefield that was soon to follow. For the source of both the evil and the antidote was American. The trench deadlock was due above all to the invention of an American, Hiram Maxim. His name is more deeply engraved on the real history of the World War than that of any other man. Emperors, statesmen, and generals had the power to make war, but not to end it. Having created it, they found themselves helpless puppets in the grip of Hiram Maxim, who, by his machine-gun, had paralyzed the power of attack. All efforts to break the defensive grip of the machine-gun were vain; they could only raise tombstones and not triumphal arches. When at last a key to the deadlock was produced, it was forged from the invention of another American, Benjamin Holt. From his agricultural tractor was evolved the tank — an ironic reversal of the proverbial custom of "beating swords into ploughshares."

The eventual effect of the tank is best appreciated by study-ing the evidence of those who had to face it. Was it not Ludendorff himself who spoke of the great tank surprise of August 8, 1918, as the "black day of the German army in the history of the war," and added, "Mass attacks by tanks . . . remained hereafter our most dangerous enemies"? More emphatic still is the comment of General von Zwehl: "It was not the genius of Marshal Foch that beat us, but 'General Tank.'" Nor can it be suggested that these were afterthoughts put forward in mitigation of defeat, for the most striking evidence of all, red-hot from the forge of battle, is to be found in the momentous report submitted, on October 2, 1918, by the representatives of the German Military Head-quarters to the leaders of the Reichstag: "The Chief Army Command has been compelled to take a terribly grave decision and declare that according to human possibilities there is no longer any prospect of forcing peace on the enemy. Above all, two facts have been decisive for this issue; first, the tanks. . . ." The confession thus made gains force from comparison with the earlier disparagement of the tanks by the German Command.

For history the first question is how the tank came to be introduced, and the second, why its decisive effect was delayed until 1918. The first question is befogged rather than guided by the popular question, so widely raised during and after the war: "Who invented the tank?" So many claimed the honor, many with some show of reason, and still more without, that the public became confused. And the Government did not help to establish the actual chain of causation, perhaps influenced by the instinct of the Treasury to avoid the recognition of financial obligations. Thus it did not become clear until the evidence in an action brought against the Crown in 1925 was available to supplement that given in 1919 before the Royal Commission on Awards to Inventors. In order to defeat this unjustified claim to reward, the Treasury had to provide an opportunity for evaluating the genuine claims to honor.

The historical evolution of the tank has been confused also by the lack of any clear definition of the tank and its purpose, and this vagueness owes something to the fact that prior to the time when the camouflage name "tank" was invented the machine was known as a "landship" or "land-cruiser." Such a title, due to its being mothered in infancy by the Admiralty, however prophetic of its still distant future, is far from applicable to its past, in the war. Regarded as a landship, or even as an armored battle-car, the origin of the tank is lost in the mists of antiquity. Among its forebears might be included the ancient war-chariot, the Hussite war-carts which formed their famous *Wagenburg*, even, with some show of reason, the battle elephants of Pyrrhus, or the mediæval knight in armor.

If the search be limited to self-moving as distinct from men- or animal-moved machines, its origin might be traced to Valturio's wind-propelled war chariot of 1472, or to the proposals made by that many-sided genius, Leonardo da Vinci, to his patron Ludovico Sforza. In 1599 Simon Stevin constructed for the Prince of Orange two actual landships, wheel-borne and sail-propelled. As far back as 1634, David Ramsey took out the earliest patent for a self-moving car capable of use in war. So, through an endless chain of experiments, the origin might be traced. The caterpillar track itself — perhaps, in general opinion, the distinctive feature of the tank — goes back to the early nineteenth century, or even to Richard Edgeworth's device of 1770.

If the definition be drawn still closer to mean a petrol-driven tracked machine for military use, the Hornsby tractor, used at Aldershot in 1908, takes precedence of the American Holt tractor in the ancestry of the tank. If the use of "tank-like" machines as weapons be the test, then Mr. H. G. Wells deserves the credit popularly accorded him for priority of conception, although his prophetic story of 1903 in the *Strand Magazine* was itself twenty years behind the writings and drawings of M. Albert Robeida in *La Caricature;* if similarity of design, then one recalls Mr. L. E. de Mole's model, superior to the 1916 tank, which was pigeonholed in the War Office in 1912. To these add also the story of the Nottingham plumber whose hobby it was to make toy machines of this nature, and whose design, submitted to the War Office in 1911, and duly pigeonholed, was unearthed after the war, the file bearing the terse official comment, "The man's mad."

The chief result of this historical survey, however, is to show the futility of trying to determine the credit for the origination of this decisive weapon of the World War without a clear understanding and definition of its particular purpose. Leonardo da Vinci and the Nottingham plumber alike may claim to be among the fathers of mechanical warfare, but for the parentage of the actual tank of the World War we must look closer. The test of its origin is tactical rather than technical. It was a specific antidote for a specific disease which first broke out virulently in the World War. This disease was the complete paralysis of the offensive brought about by the defensive power of serried machine-guns, and aggravated by wire entanglements. This disease doomed the manhood of the nation to a slow and lingering end, prolonged only by the capacity to produce fresh victims for the futile sacrifice. Wycherley's phrase, "Necessity, mother of invention," has never had a truer example, and it provides the real test to determine the immediate origin of the World War tank.

The first military physician who diagnosed the disease and

conceived the antidote was Colonel Ernest Swinton, whose pen-name of "Ole-Luk-Oie" had become well-known through *The Green Curve* and *Duffer's Drift* — studies of war in fiction-form, wherein the pill of knowledge was delightfully coated with jam. A term of hard labor on the British official history of the Russo-Japanese War gave him the opportunity to analyze its tendencies and to deduce the potential domination of the machine-gun. Later, he took an interest in the Holt tractor experiments. These two impressions soon fitted together like the two segments of a circle. For when, soon after the outbreak of war, he was sent to France as official "Eye-witness" at General Headquarters, he was both well placed and well prepared to recognize the first symptoms of stalemate, and to suggest a remedy. On October 20, visiting London, he saw Colonel Maurice Hankey, the Secretary of the Committee of Imperial Defense, and, after describing the situation, — the domination of the machine-gun-based defense, — outlined his proposals for an antidote. These were, in brief, to develop such a machine as the Holt tractor into a bullet-proof trench-crossing machine-gun destroyer, armed with one or more small quick-firing guns. In Hankey he found an acute and receptive mind, and a further discussion the next day led to an understanding that Hankey would take up the matter at home and Swinton in France. On October 23 Swinton took up the question at General Headquarters, but the suggestion came up against a blank wall.

Meanwhile Hankey put the idea before Lord Kitchener, with equally barren result. But he also submitted to the Prime Minister (Mr. Asquith) a memorandum on various ways, strategic and technical, of overcoming the deadlock, which embodied, among others, Swinton's suggestion. This reached Mr. Churchill. His mind was already active with the problem of enabling armored cars to cross broken ground and trenches, because of his concern with the armored-car detachments of the Royal Naval Air Service operating on the Belgian coast. On January 5, 1915, Churchill wrote a letter to the Prime Minister supporting and amplifying the suggestion in Hankey's memorandum for the use of armored cater-

pillar tractors to overrun trenches. This letter was sent by
Asquith to Kitchener. By a coincidence Swinton had called
at the War Office on January 4 to press anew his proposals,
now extended owing to the continued experience of conditions
in France.

The seed thus planted at the War Office by two sowers
fell on stony soil, and after some attention finally withered,
owing largely to the freezing verdict of Sir Capel Holden,
Director of Mechanical Transport. Fortunately, the general
idea was kept alive on other soil, for Churchill, in February,
formed a committee at the Admiralty, which later became
known as the Landships Committee. But this committee,
though investigating many lines of thought and experiment,
did not make much practical headway, its energies being
diverted for a time in the direction of a landship with giant
wheels. A worse blow was the removal of Churchill's vision
and driving force, though even when he left the Admiralty it
was his influence which kept the experiments alive. By this
time also, fortunately, the committee — under the guidance
of Mr. Tennyson d'Eyncourt, the Director of Naval Construction — had got on to the right line, that of the caterpillar. Even so, concrete results seem to have been hindered,
and energy leaking, through lack of any exact specification
of the military requirements of such a machine, for in the
scheme of scientific war the tactical takes precedence of the
technical.

This essential, but hitherto missing, link came in a memorandum forwarded from General Headquarters, and, once
this was available, progress became rapid and practical. The
memorandum was compiled by Swinton, who had surmounted
the barrier of unbelief and convention by an appeal direct
to the Commander-in-Chief. It formulated the performance
required of the machine, and on this specification the newly
framed joint committee of War Office and Admiralty went
to work.

On July 19 Swinton returned to England as acting Secretary to the War Committee of the Cabinet, and got in touch
with the Joint Committee later, on the Prime Minister's

authorization, calling an Inter-Departmental Conference to coördinate the work on the new machines. On September 19 an inspection was held at Lincoln of a provisional machine, "Little Willie," but this was rejected by Swinton as failing to conform to requirements. He was then shown a full-size wooden model, or mock-up, of a larger machine, which had been specially designed by Mr. Tritton and Lieutenant Wilson to meet the latest army specification. This was accepted, as it looked capable of complying with the two main conditions, — to climb a vertical face of five feet and cross a ditch eight feet wide, — and it was decided to concentrate on the production of a sample machine of this type.

Finally, on February 2, 1916, at Hatfield was held the official trial of this machine — christened "Mother" or "Big Willie," and as a result forty of these machines were ordered, a number subsequently increased to one hundred and fifty. The French, now, had independently begun similar experiments through the initiative of Colonel Estienne, whose project was sanctioned by Joffre on December 12. Although both idea and machine were later in maturing than the British, it is a significant contrast that the first French order was for four hundred; and that order was soon doubled.

During the summer of 1916 the crews for the new machines were being trained in a vast secret enclosure, surrounded by armed guards, near Thetford in Norfolk. They formed a unit that was christened the Heavy Section, Machine-Gun Corps. For secrecy's sake also a new name had been chosen for the machines. The need was to find a name sufficiently mystifying and yet plausible to any outside observer who might see the tarpaulined machines in transit on the railway, and after discussing the merits of "tank," "cistern," and "reservoir," the choice fell on the first.

Through the secrecy so well maintained, surprise was obtained when the "tanks" made their début on the battlefield. Unhappily the fruits of the surprise were forfeited. Herein lay the tragedy of September 15, 1916. For the official guardians disregarded the entreaties of the parents and insisted on putting the tank to work before it was mechanically mature and before its numbers were adequate. Thus they not only endangered its future usefulness, but threw away the chance of surprising the enemy while he was unprepared with any counter-measures. The consequence was to prolong the hardships and toll of the war.

The reply normally made to this charge is to point out the mechanical defects which the early tanks suffered, the numbers that were "ditched," and to argue that a weapon must be tested under battlefield conditions before mass-production is begun. The contention is plausible, but unconvincing in view of the facts. The tank first used in the shell-mangled chaos of the Somme, and against the deep and intricate trench systems of 1916, was built to a specification laid down in the summer of 1915, when trench lines were far less developed and artillery bombardments were not so heavy as to turn the ground into a morass — as in 1916 and 1917.

Moreover, the apologists gloss over the fact that in September 1916 the tanks were hurried out to France and rushed into battle before their crews were fully trained and before the commanders in France had time to think, or had been given instructions, how to use them. Again, the very likelihood that the proportion of mechanical failures in this early model would be high was surely a logical reason for the production of a large number, so that sufficient might survive to reap the harvest of surprise. As the British nation was paying over several million pounds a day for the pleasure of watching and occasionally tapping on the locked gates of the German front, it would surely have been worth risking an extra day's expenditure in the purchase of a possible means of breaking the lock.

Let us probe a little further the mystery of the premature use of this immature instrument. In December 1915, Churchill drafted a paper on the use of the tank. Printed for the Committee of Imperial Defense, copies were given to the Commander-in-Chief in France. In February 1916, as soon as the design and armament of the machine had been settled sufficiently for accurate calculations, Swinton produced a more comprehensive and detailed memorandum. This emphasized that the vital factor was the secret production of tanks until masses could be launched in a great surprise stroke, and that on no account should they be used in driblets as they were manufactured. Haig expressed his full agreement with this memorandum in the spring. Yet in August he suddenly decided to use the mere sixty then available. At that time the offensive on the Somme had practically come to a standstill, and the reports of petty gain at heavy loss grated unpleasantly on the ear of the public.

Haig's decision came as a shock to the Cabinet at home, and Lloyd George, now War Minister, energetically protested, while Montagu, his successor at the Ministry of Munitions, went out to General Headquarters in a vain attempt to avert the premature use of the tanks. Haig was immovable, and the powerless parents had to submit to the sacrifice of their offspring's future.

Thus history is left to surmise that the tanks were "pawned for a song" — of the Somme. Pawned to pay for a resounding local success which might draw an encore from the public — and, incidentally, drown the growing volume of criticism. But the greater prize thus lost beyond recall was a heavy forfeit to pay for redeeming in a limited degree the ill-success of the Somme offensive. With Haig this act may have been prompted by a laudable if unwise desire to economize the lives of his infantry without giving up his offensive. He had certainly shown his eagerness to clutch at any new aid. But the attitude of some of his staff cannot be similarly excused.

For the breach of principle does not complete the tally of General Headquarters. Swinton's memorandum laid down a number of conditions which were disregarded in September 1916, only to be adopted after bitter experience had shown their necessity. The sector for tank attack was to be carefully chosen to comply with the powers and limitations of the tanks — this condition was neither considered nor fulfilled until the Cambrai offensive in November 1917. Their routes of approach were to be specially prepared, as well as suitable railway trucks or barges to bring them up — despite six months' warning these preparations were not begun until the

tanks arrived in August. The need for reserves of tanks was
stressed — but the lesson was not even learned by the time of
Cambrai, nor, indeed, until August 1918. The combined
tactics of tanks and infantry were expounded — also to be
overlooked until Cambrai. In addition to shell, the tank guns
were to fire case shot. It was designed, but its manufacture
was debarred until the commanders in France clamored for
it after the Somme. Some of the tanks were to be equipped
with wireless sets; these were designed and operators trained
— but General Headquarters would not allow the equipment
to be sent out, and it was dispersed. The attitude and mentality prevailing at General Headquarters are illustrated by a
story current at the time. A general on Haig's staff gave
instructions that the tanks were to be brought to the front by
a certain railway route. The technical expert in charge of
the movement pointed out that this was impossible because of
the loading gauge. The General retorted, "What the hell is a
loading gauge?" The officer explained, and pointed out that by
another route they could avoid the two tunnels that made this
route impossible. But the General, still refusing to recognize
the impossible, curtly said, "Then have the tunnels widened."

The trial of the tank on the Somme did not complete its
trials. A thousand of a new model had just been ordered by
the Ministry of Munitions in England. But their opponents
— by which one means not the Germans but the General
Staff in France — made haste to report so adversely that the
War Office canceled the order. Unfortunately for their intention, if fortunately for England, the officer in charge of
the construction of tanks was a temporary soldier, Major
Albert Stern, whose permanent position in the City enabled
him to bear with equanimity the frowns of his temporary
superiors. Disregarding the order, he went straight to the
War Minister, to find that the cancellation had been sent
without Lloyd George's knowledge. And, having satisfied
himself of Lloyd George's opposition to any such foolish
measure, Stern called on the Chief of the Imperial General
Staff, Sir William Robertson, to intimate that he was not
going to carry out the cancellation order.

Nevertheless, let it be said to the credit of those who, on the General Staff, opposed the tank that, if they had not the ingenuity to devise means of beating the Germans, they were fertile in devices to beat the sponsors of the tank. Swinton, as merely a soldier, was not a difficult adversary, and almost at once was ousted from his position in command of the whole tank unit in England. In July 1917, d'Eyncourt and Stern were neatly excluded from the meetings of the committee which now at the War Office controlled tank design and production — a committee whose three military members had not even seen a tank until a few weeks previously. The programme of building four thousand tanks for the next year's campaign was then cut down by two-thirds. And in October, under pressure from the generals, Stern was removed from his post at the Ministry of Munitions and replaced by an admiral who had not seen a tank at all. The General Staff would seem to have profited from contact with their French colleagues, and to have learned that the most important point when proved wrong is to get rid of the uncomfortable prophet who has proved right. Just as Swinton was sacrificed to balance for the General Staff's folly in launching the first model into the Somme battle, so Stern seems to have been chosen to expiate the folly of throwing the next model into the swamps of Passchendaele. Instead of losing faith in their own judgment, the General Staff again lost faith in the tank.

Happily, the younger regular soldiers who had taken charge of the tanks at the front had overcome their first doubts, and, realizing the stupidity of Passchendaele, fought for the chance to give the tanks a fair trial. They obtained it at Cambrai in November, a battle which at last fulfilled the pattern designed in February 1916. Although, for want of the resources wasted at Passchendaele, the victory itself was but a tinsel crown, it yielded the tanks a solid crown which none could any longer dispute. As 1917 was the year of vindication, so 1918 proved the year of triumph. Yet it is a sobering reflection that the price in lives might have been cheaper if tanks had been available in thousands instead of hundreds. The numbers manufactured under the reduced programme of 1917 sufficed to bring victory; but they could not bring back the dead. May the tank's hard childhood be an object-lesson for future generations, so that if war engulfs them they may learn by the experience of others and not at their own cost.

1916 — THE "DOG–FALL"

SCENE V

RUMANIA SWALLOWED

RUMANIA entered the war on August 27, 1916, and the fall of Bucharest on December 6, 1916, marked the virtual extinction of her war effort and of the misplaced exhilaration which had greeted her entry on the side of the Allies. Less known and less studied than almost any other campaign of the world struggle, it has a special interest, and deserves far more attention than it has received, because it epitomized the Allies' fundamental weakness and the Germans' strength — the evils inherent in a co-partnership system of conducting war as opposed to the concentration of effort and economy of force which spring from a single control.

Nor is this the sum of its lessons; there are others which have a more practical value, because more easily remedied. It revealed the fallacy of numbers, and the much-abused Napoleonic saying that God is on the side of the big battalions received yet another historical contradiction from the Alexandrine principle of quality rather than quantity. Once again the blend of superior hitting power with superior mobility played havoc with an army which pinned its faith to weight of human bodies.

During the preceding years of the war, public opinion in Rumania had gradually consolidated in favor of intervention on the Allies' side, and the friendly sentiments of Jonescu and Filipescu found a powerful lever in the people's desire to rescue their kinsmen in Transylvania from a foreign rule far more drastic than Alsace-Lorraine had suffered. At last, in the summer of 1916, the spectacular but, as we now know, superficial successes of the Russian advance under Brusilov encouraged Rumania to take the decisive step — into the abyss.

She might have fared better if she had declared war earlier, when Serbia was still an active force and Russia a real one. The two years of preparation had doubled the numbers of the Rumanian army, but in reality reduced its relative efficiency, for while her foes, under the pressure of hard experience, had developed their means of fire-power and equipment, Rumania's isolation and the incapacity of her military leadership had combined to prevent the transformation of her army from a militia of bayonetmen into a modern force.

Her infantry had no automatic rifles, gas equipment, trench mortars, and few machine-guns — in the ten active divisions only the usual pre-war proportion of two per battalion, and of the thirteen new divisions eight had none at all. Her artillery was inadequate, and her air force negligible. She had only six weeks' supply of ammunition at the start, — an explosion in the Bucharest arsenal had destroyed 9,000,000 rounds of small-arm ammunition, — and her Allies failed to maintain the daily supply of three hundred tons which they had promised. And the unwieldy size of her divisions, added to the indifferent quality of her corps of officers, was in itself a brake on mobile operations.

Her strategical situation was another source of weakness — her territory forming an "L" reversed, with the bottom section, Wallachia sandwiched between Transylvania and Bulgaria. Moreover, the length of her frontier was out of all proportion to the depth of the country, she suffered a shortage of lateral railways, and the capital was within thirty miles of the Bulgarian frontier. Further, she had in the Dobruja — on the other side of the Danube — a "back-yard" strip which offered an easy way of access.

These internal and geographical handicaps were accentuated by the divergent counsels of her Allies as to her action. While the British General Staff favored a southward advance against Bulgaria which might have crushed the latter between the Rumanians and the Salonika army, the Russians urged a westward advance which would, in theory, be in closer co-operation with their Bukovina advance. The political and moral advantages of a move into Transylvania led the

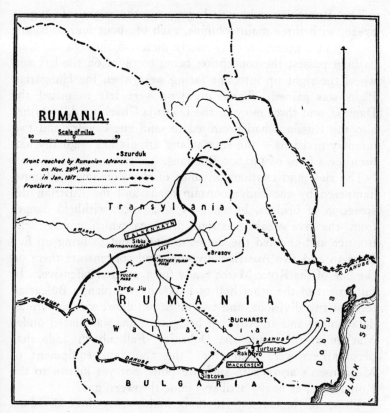

Rumanians to adopt the second course, and, bitter as the upshot was, their folly is not so certain as their critics have suggested. The Bulgarian territory offered many obstacles to an effective invasion by such a defective instrument as the Rumanian army proved, and they had ample ground to doubt the energy of Sarrail in pushing forward to meet them.

On the other hand, we now know that a more rapid invasion of Transylvania by the Rumanians would have put the Austro-Germans in a grave position, and that even with the breathing space they were unluckily given they were almost at their wits' end to scrape together forces for this new front. Rumania's fault was less in her choice of objective than in her incapacity to strike for it rapidly and forcefully.

The Rumanian advance began, on the night of August 27–28, with three main columns, each of about four divisions, moving in a general northwesterly direction through the Carpathian passes, the conception being to pivot on the left and wheel the right up into line facing west when the Hungarian Plain was gained. Three divisions were left to guard the Danube, and three more in the Dobruja "back-yard," whither also the Russians had promised to send one cavalry and two infantry divisions — the Rumanians' stipulation originally had been for a force of 150,000 Russians.

The slow and cautious advance of the Rumanian columns, hampered by the bad mountain roads and the Austrian destruction of bridges, but not by resistance, withheld danger from the five weak Austrian divisions which covered the frontier and enabled the Supreme Command to bring up five German and two Austrian divisions and concentrate them on the line of the River Maros ready for a counter-offensive. In fulfillment of the other half of Falkenhayn's plan, a Bulgarian force of two divisions, and two more to follow, with a German detachment and an Austrian bridging train, was placed under Mackensen to invade the Dobruja. Falkenhayn adds that preparations were made for "the abundant equipment of Mackensen's army with such weapons, not yet known to the Rumanians, as heavy artillery, mine-throwers, gas."

Thus, at the outset, Rumania had twenty-three divisions against seven, but within a week she would have sixteen against her, so that her chances of success turned on the rapidity of her action. While her columns were creeping westward into Transylvania, Mackensen stormed the Turtucaia bridgehead on September 5, destroying the three Rumanian divisions which covered the Danube front, and then, with his flank secure, pressed eastwards into the Dobruja. It was a shrewd moral blow, for the automatic strategic effect was to draw away the Rumanian reserves intended to support the Transylvanian offensive, and so check its progress for want of nourishment. And the dispersion left them weak everywhere. Thus on September 18, when Falkenhayn arrived to conduct the Austro-German offensive in Transylvania, he found the Rumanians' advance almost at a standstill, and their columns widely separated over a two-hundred-mile front. One must mention that Falkenhayn had now been replaced in the Supreme Command by Hindenburg (and Ludendorff), and given this executive command as a consolation.

Falkenhayn's decision was first to concentrate against the Rumanian southern column, which had crossed the Rother Turm Pass, while using smaller forces to hold off the other columns. Even allowing for his superior information, he took bold risks and suffered anxious moments before success, as so often in war, favored the brave. The Alpine Corps, by a fifty-mile march in three days over the mountains, turned the Rumanians' southern flank, and combined with the skillful manœuvre of the reserves in the direct attack to throw back the Rumanians from Sibiu (Hermannstadt) and force them to retreat through the mountains.

His next move was facilitated by the fact that the Rumanian Higher Command, like Napoleon's opponents, "saw too many things at once." They kept their Transylvanian armies inactive while diverting their reserves for an abortive attempt to force a crossing of the Danube at Rakhovo and take Mackensen in rear. This enabled Falkenhayn to concentrate against the Rumanian centre column at Brasov (Kronstadt), and by October 9 he had driven this back in turn, but he missed his greater goal of encircling and destroying it, which would have opened a clear passage into Rumania.

The mischance jeopardized the whole German plan and almost saved Rumania, for, with all the passes through the mountain barrier still in their hands, her troops sturdily repulsed the Austro-German efforts to press through on their heels, and compelled them to wait for reënforcements. A prompt attempt by Falkenhayn to swing further south and force a way by the Vulkan and Szurduk passes was also stopped, and the beginning of the winter snows was on the point of blocking operations when a concentrated last-minute effort at the same point, November 11–17, broke through to Targu Jiu. A rapid pursuit through the Wallachian Plain hustled the Rumanians back to the line of the Alt.

It was the signal for the next move in the ably coördinated plan. Mackensen, leaving only a fraction to hold the northerly part of the Dobruja, withdrew the bulk of his forces westwards to Sistovo, where, on November 23, he forced the crossing of the Danube and automatically turned the flank of the Rumanian line on the Alt. A prompt and well-planned Rumanian counter-stroke, inspired by General Presan, their new Chief of the General Staff, for a brief time threatened danger to Mackensen's force and almost enveloped its flank. But once the counter-stroke was parried, the converging pressure of Mackensen and Falkenhayn proved too great for the Rumanians' last desperate resistance on the line of the Argesu, and on December 6 the Austro-Germans entered Bucharest. The pursuit pressed the Rumanians and the Russians, whose action in the Dobruja had been ineffectual, rapidly back to the Sereth-Black Sea line. The greater part of Rumania, with its wheat and oil, lay under the heel of the invader, and the Rumanian army was crippled, while her Allies had suffered a moral setback greater than any material advantage for which they might have hoped from her intervention.

For military history this brief campaign furnished an object-lesson that men do not count more than machines, but, instead, that the better machine controlled by a better man — the commander — can discount the value of "big battalions." Weapons and training count far more than mere numbers.

1916 — THE "DOG–FALL"

Scene VI

THE CAPTURE OF BAGHDAD

THE entry of the British into Baghdad on March 11, 1917, was an event which impressed the imagination of the whole world, both because of the romantic appeal of the famed city of the Arabian Nights, and because it symbolized the first streaks of dawn coming to illumine the darkness which had lain like a pall over the Allied cause throughout 1916. If the historical data that are now available dim the radiance of popular impressions, revealing that the military achievement was less striking than it appeared at the time, the moral significance and value cannot be minimized. But, in justice to those who earlier fought and failed, it is well to realize the fallacy underlying this contemporary public view that the operations which led to the fall of Baghdad were as white as those which culminated in the surrender of Kut were black.

The strategy and organization of the campaign were infinitely more sound and more sure, but on the lower scale of tactical execution the record of the advance is spotted with missed opportunities, despite an overwhelming preponderance of force. While recognizing the difficulties of the country, the historian cannot but feel that a sledge-hammer was used to crush a flea — and the flea escaped being crushed. And if quality rather than quantity be the test of a feat of arms, comparison suggests that the advance and retreat of Townshend's original 6th Division, in face of superior numbers, with inadequate equipment, primitive communications, and utterly isolated in the heart of an enemy country, forged an intrinsically finer link in the chain of British military history.

Credit for the 1917 success is due, above all, to the strategical direction, and to the ability and energy of those who put the organization of supplies and transport on a sound and efficient basis. These assets, moreover, sufficed to attain the military goal, without any further uneconomic drain on the forces in the more vital theatres of war. The general direction was now transferred to Whitehall. After the surrender of Townshend at Kut, — despite the gallant but costly efforts to relieve him, — the Chief of the Imperial General Staff, Sir William Robertson, was emphatically in favor of a defensive strategy in Mesopotamia. He inclined to adopt a withdrawal to Amara as the simplest and cheapest way of safeguarding the oilfields and of commanding the two river arteries — the Tigris and Euphrates. But the new commander, Maude, who had been Robertson's own choice, maintained, after examination, that the advanced position at Kut was both militarily secure and politically wise. He was supported by Duff and Monro, the successive Commanders-in-Chief in India, and Robertson gave way, accepting the judgment of the man on the spot. There is profound psychological interest in studying how the strong personality of Maude, and the military results which, step by step, he obtained, combined to change this defensive policy, almost imperceptibly, into a fresh offensive policy. The mirage of Russian coöperation had also an influence, for, beginning as a mere supplementary aid to a Russian offensive, the advance became an all-British achievement.

The whole summer and autumn of 1916 were devoted to thorough reorganization and preparation, initiated by Lake, but greatly expanded and intensified by his successor, Maude. He strove to ameliorate the condition of the troops, to improve both their health and their training, to develop the precarious lines of communication, and to amass a large reserve of supplies and ammunition. Thus Maude ably established a secure base for his subsequent and sustained offensive, fulfilling Napoleon's maxim. The design of his plan of operations was equally admirable, blending boldness and circumspection. A study of his orders, both initial and during operations, shows that the lack of decisiveness cannot be charged to his want of energy. Where he tended to err was in excessive centralization and secrecy.   If the latter is usually a fault on the right side, it seems here to have been partly responsible for the pause at Aziziyah, on the advance to Baghdad.   For his Inspector-General of communications had to complain that even he had not been given warning that such a move was intended, and thus he had made no special preparations in readiness.

This "imperceptible" offensive began on December 12, 1916, the first step in a series of well-thought-out trench "nibbles," methodical and deliberate, on the west bank of the Tigris.   When it began, Maude faced the Turkish trenches at a right angle to the Tigris, and gradually brought his left shoulder up, pivoting on the river, and at the same time extending his front further and further upstream.   At last, by February 22, 1917, he had cleared the west bank, his extended line facing the main Turkish forces on the other bank, from Sannaiyat to the Shumran bend above Kut.   Thus the Turks had not merely to guard against a direct attack from the south upon their fortified position at Sannaiyat, but against a cross-river blow from the west, which might cut their communications.   The length of this patient siege-warfare process was not merely due to the intricacy of the defenses or the stubborn resistance of the weak Turkish detachments on the west bank. Robertson had no taste for further adventures, and his instructions from home were framed to prevent them.   The historian who studies the orders and operations gains the impression that Maude's operations were contrived, consciously or unconsciously, to undermine the stability, not merely of the Turkish position, but of Robertson's instructions.

The outcome of these deliberate and economical operations was that by the third week in February Maude was able, and admirably placed, to play for a bigger stake.   His plan was to pin the Turks' left at Sannaiyat while he sprang at their communications, by forcing the river crossing at the Shumran bend — where the right flank ended and their line of retreat prolonged their line of battle.   Wisely he realized that a mere feint at Sannaiyat was useless and that a real simultaneous menace to both extremities was essential if the Turkish force

was to be held while it was being cut off.   Unhappily his purpose was not fulfilled.   Splendid as was the gallantry of the
troops at the Shumran crossing, the difficulty of the task made
progress slow, and the Sannaiyat attack could not pin the
defenders long enough.

Even so, the Turks were placed in such peril that, as they
confess, "only the slowness of the enemy" saved them from
disaster.   The main cause was the tardy and feeble action of
the cavalry in pursuit — due partly to Maude's too strict control, partly to the cavalry commander's want of energy and
initiative, and partly to the inherent vulnerability of cavalry
under modern conditions.   On February 24, when there was
a splendid opportunity of turning retreat into rout, the cavalry
division broke off to go back to bivouac at 7 P.M., after a mere
twenty-three casualties.   And on subsequent days they were
no more effective.   The excuses offered are the need to water
and the obstacle of modern firearms, and their admission rather
accentuates than impairs the lesson as to the restricted modern value of cavalry — even in Asia.   Only the daring pursuit
of the naval flotilla disturbed the Turks' orderly retreat —
acting on the river as a few cross-country armored cars might
have done on land.

The strategic victory had at least won Maude sanction for
an attempt to gain Baghdad, and on March 5 his advance
from Aziziyah began.   When a check came at the line of the
Diyala, Maude switched the cavalry division and 7th Corps
to the west bank, for an outflanking move direct on Baghdad.
More mistakes enabled the Turks to hold up this menace, but
realizing their hopeless inferiority of strength and the inevitable end, against two powerful converging advances, they gave
up Baghdad on the night of March 10, and retired northward
up the river.   Next afternoon Maude entered the city, and
another name was added to the roll of Baghdad's innumerable
conquerors.   For the prestige of Britain and the morale of all
the Allies the capture was an invaluable stimulant worth the
immediate effort, if not the sum of the efforts which had gone
to fill the debit side of the victors' balance-sheet.

1916 — THE "DOG-FALL"

SCENE VII

THE BATTLE OF BLIND MAN'S BUFF — JUTLAND

ONLY once during over four years of war did the Grand Fleet of Britain and the High Seas Fleet of Germany meet. It would be more exact to say that they "hailed each other in passing" — with a hail that was awe-inspiring, but leaving an impression that was merely pen-inspiring. No battle in all history has spilled so much — ink. On the afternoon of May 31, 1916, the fleet that had been built to dispute the mastery of the sea stumbled into the fleet that had held it for centuries. In the early evening these two fleets, the greatest the world had seen, groped towards each other, touched, broke away, touched again and broke away again. Then darkness fell between them. And when the "glorious First of June" dawned a sorely puzzled Grand Fleet paraded on an empty sea.

A fundamental difference between the higher naval and military leadership in the World War was that the admirals would not intentionally give battle unless reasonably sure of an initial advantage, whereas the generals were usually ready to take the offensive whatever the disadvantages. In this attitude the admirals were true to their art, the generals were not. The sole reason for employing men who have made war their profession is the presumption that by training they have acquired a mastery of their art. Anyone with sufficient authority or inspiration can lead or push men to battle, especially if he is furnished with technically trained assistants who can help him to regulate the marshaling of the forces in movement and fire. For this shepherding of sheep to the slaughter, perhaps artful but essentially inartistic, a practised demagogue would have a definite superiority over the tongue-tied professional warrior. But the custom of employing a professional is based on the idea that through art he will be able to obtain more profit at less cost.

Only one consideration should override a commander's fidelity to the fundamental truths which govern his art, and that is national expediency. It is for the Government, and not for its employee, to decide whether the needs of policy compel a sacrifice of art and the consequent sacrifice of lives. Curiously, however, in the World War the generals were so full of the lust of battle that they voluntarily sacrificed art, and repeatedly sought battle at a disadvantage against the wishes of a Government reluctantly dragged in their wake. The admirals, in contrast, were so faithful to their art that they sometimes ignored or evaded the express wish of the Government for battle even without an assured advantage. If their sense of reality was refreshing, it tended to throw a heavier burden of expense on the armies, although it is fair to point out that this might not have occurred if the generals had not been so extravagantly eager to shoulder it.

Perhaps one explanation of the difference was that the admirals exercised their command in the forefront of the battle and the generals from headquarters far in rear. This does not imply that the difference was merely a matter of the physical courage required, for some generals were as ready to risk their own lives as their men's, while others undoubtedly gained moral courage through physical remoteness. But, undoubtedly, imagination and sense of reality are quickened by personal contact with the situation; a commander so placed is better able to appreciate where the advantage lies and when it fades; quicker, also, to recognize the impossible.

It would be natural to expect as a result of this difference that sailors would have a bias towards tactics, soldiers towards strategy. Actually, the reverse occurred. The explanation of the paradox would seem to lie in the different experience of peace training, wherein the soldier serves in small garrisons and exercises in cramped areas, while the sailor traverses the wide oceans and learns navigation as the staple of his craft. For him, geography precedes gunnery.

From the outbreak of war British naval strategy was gov-

erned, rightly, by the appreciation of the fact that maintenance of sea supremacy was even more vital than defeat of the
German fleet. Instantaneously, that sea supremacy had come
into force and upon it was based the whole war effort of Britain,
and her Allies, because upon it depended the very existence of
Britain. Churchill has epitomized the issue in a graphic
phrase, "Jellicoe was the only man on either side who could
lose the war in an afternoon." Hence the aim and desire to
defeat the German fleet was always subsidiary. If it could be
achieved it might do much to hasten the victory of the Allies.
It *might* even prevent their defeat. The collapse of Russia as
well as the near starvation of Britain by the U-boats may well
be traced to the inability of the British navy to crush the German fleet. But if, in trying to defeat the German fleet, the
British navy lost so heavily as to lose its strategic superiority,
national defeat *would* be certain.

The aim of German naval strategy, since August 1914, had
been to avoid the risk of a decisive action until the British
fleet was so weakened that the prospect of success veered from
gloomy to fair. Mines and torpedoes were the means on
which the Germans relied to achieve this preliminary weakening. And it was the fear of such under-water weapons, the
possibility that by trap or chance they might dramatically
alter the balance of strength, which infused an extra degree
of caution into the British strategy of precaution. In a letter
of prophetic foresight on October 14, 1914, Jellicoe had warned
the Admiralty that if a chance of battle came he would regard
the turning away of the German battle fleet as a sign that it
was trying to lure him into such a trap, where mines and submarines lay in wait; that he would refuse to be drawn into it
and, instead, would move quickly to a flank. In other words,
he would sidestep to avoid the chance of being surprised, and
so not only disarm the enemy of his best potential weapon, but
possibly throw him off his balance. The calculation is one
indication of how thoroughly Jellicoe had thought out his
theory of war.

Both the German and the British strategic keynotes were
well attuned to the reality of their respective conditions, and

the only question is whether more energy and subtlety could have been shown in executing them. The situation in May 1916, after nearly two years of war, was that the British fleet was still waiting for a favorable chance of battle and the German fleet was further away from the attainment of its preliminary aim of weakening the British. Despite a few losses due to mines and torpedoes, the British fleet was proportionately much stronger than at the beginning. In the coming clash it was to bring thirty-seven capital ships (battleships and battle-cruisers) of the Dreadnought type against the German twenty-three, and in gun power the margin was still greater: 168 guns of 13.5-15 inch calibre and 104 of 12 inch could be brought against 176 German guns of only 12 inch calibre. It is true that the German fleet also included six pre-Dreadnought battleships, but in a fleet action these would be little better than a target for the heavier guns of the British. Moreover, by their presence they reduced the already slower German fleet to a still more marked inferiority in speed. The British had also a comfortable superiority in cruisers and destroyers — eight armored and twenty-six light cruisers, against eleven of the last; eighty destroyers against sixty-three.

Another advantage gained since the outbreak of war was in the sphere of knowledge. For the British had not only gained from occasional contacts a clearer idea of the capacity of the enemy's weapons, but had discovered his signal-code. In August 1914, the German light cruiser *Magdeburg* had been sunk in the Baltic, and clasped in the arms of a drowned under-officer the Russians had found the cipher and signal books of the German navy, as well as their squared maps of the North Sea. These were sent to London, and thereafter, by intercepting the enemy's enciphered wireless messages, the British Intelligence was able to obtain advance information of many of the enemy's movements. Although suspicion led the enemy to make variations in their codes and maps, their efforts to seal up the leakage of information were offset by the development of directional wireless as a means of locating ships. And this was the source of the one naval battle of the war — Jutland.

In January 1916, a new commander was appointed to the

German High Seas Fleet. This was Admiral Scheer, the nominee of Admiral von Tirpitz, and an advocate of a more aggressive war policy. The pressure of the British blockade and the relaxation of the German submarine blockade — under pressure from President Wilson — combined to provide an urge to action. And a rumored division of the British fleet, to protect the coast from raids, came as an encouragement to action. In mid-May Scheer crystallized his plan. A cruiser raid on Sunderland was intended to draw out part of the British fleet to counter it, and lying in wait for this detachment would be the German submarines with the High Seas Fleet behind, ready to pounce. The submarines were duly dispatched, but bad weather prevented reconnaissance by the German airships. Without this safeguard Scheer would not move, and thus the submarines exhausted their sea-going endurance. On May 30, Scheer decided to abandon his plan, and the use of his submarines, for an alternative. This was to send the Scouting Force, of battle and light cruisers, under Admiral Hipper, to demonstrate off the Norwegian coast, while he followed, out of sight. He calculated that the danger to the British cruiser patrol and shipping might draw part of the British fleet to the spot and give him a chance to destroy it. Hipper steamed north early in the morning of the thirty-first, with Scheer fifty miles astern.

Already, the previous evening, the impending departure of the Germans, although not their purpose, was known to the British Admiralty, and the Grand Fleet was ordered to sea. Jellicoe, with the main section of the fleet, sailed eastward by 10.30 P.M. for a rendezvous some fifty miles off the Norwegian coast, being joined on the way by Jerram's squadron from Invergordon. Beatty with the battle-cruisers, reënforced by four of the latest *Queen Elizabeth* type battleships, sailed simultaneously from Rosyth (near Edinburgh) with orders from Jellicoe to reach by 2 P.M. on the thirty-first a spot sixty-nine miles south-southeast of the main rendezvous. From this, if no enemy had yet been sighted, Jellicoe would sweep southwards towards Heligoland Bight, while Beatty was ordered to close to within sight of him.

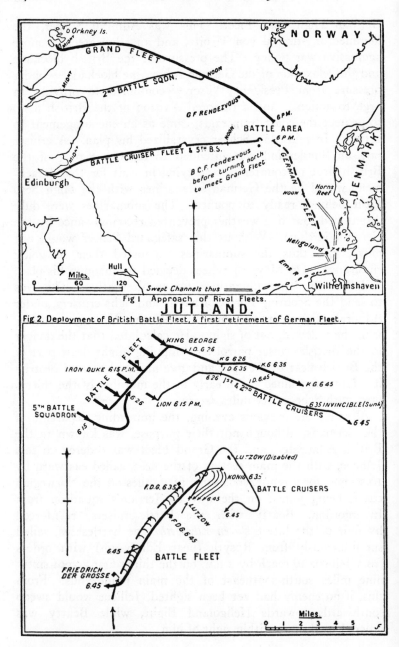

Fig 1 Approach of Rival Fleets.

JUTLAND.

Fig 2. Deployment of British Battle Fleet, & first retirement of German Fleet.

Beatty reached his own rendezvous at the assigned hour and was just turning north towards Jellicoe when the *Galatea*, one of his screen of light cruisers, sighted a stray merchant steamer and, instead of turning with the rest, continued east-southeast to examine her. This was the first of many jests of fate. For simultaneously a German light cruiser, screening Hipper's western flank, also sighted the steamer and decided to investigate. Within a few moments the two unsuspecting rivals had sighted each other — and warned their respective superiors. Thereby the strange steamer not only brought on the Battle of Jutland, but probably cost the British a decisive victory. For if this chance meeting had not occurred, the two forces might not have met until they were further north — when the Germans would have been further from shelter and nearer the jaws of Jellicoe.

Minutes were now to be momentous. Controversy as to their use has been acrid, but much of the criticism on both sides seems pedantic — more apt for the proverbial armchairs, although here occupied by professional sailors, than for the vague conditions in the North Sea on the afternoon of May 31, 1916.

At 2.20 P.M. the *Galatea* signaled, "Enemy in sight. Two cruisers, probably hostile, bearing southeast, course unknown." The sound of guns from the distant *Galatea* had just been heard when, at 2.32 P.M., Beatty turned again southeastwards to cut off the retreat of the enemy cruisers. Unfortunately his signal to turn, made by flags, was not read, owing to smoke and want of wind, by Evan-Thomas's squadron of battleships which had been following five miles astern. In consequence Evan-Thomas did not turn until 2.40 P.M., and thereby found himself ten miles behind Beatty's battle-cruisers.

It has been argued that the signal should have been made, more simply and effectively, by searchlight flashes — an argument that seems irrefutable. It has been argued that Evan-Thomas should have turned on his own initiative, as he must have seen Beatty turning — an argument which seems highly disputable in view of his general orders and his ignorance of Beatty's tactical intentions. On the other side, it has been contended, first, that Beatty himself should have acted earlier; second, that he should also have given Evan-Thomas the chance to close up to him — either by continuing on his northward course while Evan-Thomas was turning, or, still better, by swinging towards him before turning. But th's ideal perhaps unduly discounts the conditions — physical and psychological. Both Jellicoe and Beatty had been steaming leisurely, with hope of an encounter waning as the hours passed, and all the more because the Admiralty had signaled that, by directional wireless, the enemy fleet had been located still at its anchorage. Yet another unlucky mishap.

If fair account be taken of the hazy situation, Beatty would seem to have taken his decision with all reasonable promptness. As for the decision itself, he had every reason, from past experience, to fear that the German cruisers would give him the slip, and little reason to suspect that they masked a greater force. At the most he might meet the German battle-cruisers, and they were only five in all, while he had six. If his temperament was impetuous rather than calculating, both past experience and the general strategic situation would here seem to justify his action in forfeiting extra strength to gain extra minutes.

Finding that the enemy cruisers were apparently following the *Galatea* northwestwards, Beatty himself gradually changed his course until he was steaming northeast. Thereby he and Hipper were converging towards each other, and about 3.30 P.M. they came in sight of each other. Hipper promptly turned to fall back towards his own battle fleet and Beatty duly turned on a parallel course. At 3.45 P.M. both sides opened fire at a range of about nine miles. Owing to bad light the British miscalculated the range, and so not only lost the advantage that their guns outranged the Germans, but made poor shooting. In contrast, the British were silhouetted against the western sky. Just after 4 P.M. catastrophe burst upon the British. A shell from the *Lutzow*, Hipper's flagship, plunged into the midship turret of the *Lion*, Beatty's flagship. With both legs shattered, Major Harvey of the marines managed, before he died, to call down the voice tube the order to flood the magazines — and thereby saved the ship from being blown up. But the *Indefatigable*, hit by a salvo of three shells from the *Von der Tann*, dropped out of the line and, hit again, turned over and sank with a thousand men. Fortunately, at this critical moment Evan-Thomas, by cutting the corners, had come within range, and his accurate fire disturbed the accuracy of the Germans' — although the poor quality of the British shells, which burst without penetrating their armor, saved the Germans from vital injury. And at 4.26 P.M. they scored afresh, when the battle-cruiser *Queen Mary*, hit by a salvo, blew up and sank with her crew of twelve hundred — her grave and their grave marked by a gigantic pall of smoke eight hundred feet high. Thus Beatty was reduced from six ships to four, against five. About this time also, the *Princess Royal* vanished momentarily in an ominous cloud of smoke and spray, and a signalman on the *Lion* laconically reported, "*Princess Royal* blown up, sir." Whereupon Beatty as curtly said to his flag captain, "Chatfield, there seems to be something wrong with our damned ships to-day. Turn two points to port" — nearer the enemy.

It was a tribute to his cool nerve, although the crisis had really passed with the entry of Evan-Thomas into the fight. That entry marred the trap which Scheer was planning for Beatty. For, instead of steering to catch Beatty between the two jaws formed by Hipper and his own main fleet, Scheer was forced to steam direct to Hipper's aid.

At 4.33 P.M. Goodenough's light cruiser squadron, two miles ahead of the *Lion*, sighted battleships to the southeast, and signaled the news to Beatty. Goodenough boldly held to his course until he could definitely identify the High Seas Fleet, and then sent a wireless message direct to Jellicoe — who had already quickened his pace towards Beatty.

Beatty also held his course until he had sighted Scheer's battleships, and then, at 4.40 P.M., turned about to run north towards Jellicoe. The turn was well timed to let Beatty's force, now the bait, be seen by Scheer without letting it come within range of Scheer's guns. But the signal to turn, again made by flags, was again missed by Evan-Thomas, who held to his southward course until he had passed Beatty running north. Thereby he came under fire from Scheer's leading battleships, and became both the bait to Scheer and the shield to Beatty during the run north.

Danger during Beatty's turn, which was made in succession round a fixed point, was partly averted by the disconcerting and gallant attacks of the British destroyers. Two had been crippled and, drifting helplessly between the oncoming lines of battleships, with glorious impudence fired their last torpedoes before they were riven by shells. German destroyers chivalrously stopped to pick up the survivors.

Meantime the two great fleets were rushing towards each other, Scheer in ignorance, Jellicoe in knowledge of his enemy's approach — but not of his exact course. But upon such detailed knowledge Jellicoe's own dispositions must depend. Unfortunately the haze over the North Sea was mental as well as physical. Beatty, leading the run north, had lost touch with Scheer's fleet and even with Hipper's, which was steaming roughly parallel to him in the mist. And, although Evan-Thomas was still in touch with Scheer, he sent no reports. The only messages Jellicoe received came at the very start of the retirement, four from Goodenough and one from Beatty, whose wireless had been shot away — so that he had to transmit the message through a third ship. But the importance of this lack of information of the enemy can be, and has been, exaggerated. For the German fleet did not vary its course and the real trouble came from British errors in reckoning their own position — on the part of both Jellicoe's and Beatty's flagships. The result was that when the two came in sight of each other the *Lion* was found to be some seven miles further west than Jellicoe had anticipated. And, as a corollary, the enemy also were sighted on the starboard bow — *i.e.*, on Jellicoe's right front instead of straight ahead. More frequent reports of the position of Beatty's fleet might have provided, through averaging, a more accurate reckoning.

Jellicoe was advancing south in a compact mass of six parallel columns, like a six-pronged comb, four miles wide from flank to flank. This is not a fighting formation, for only a minimum of the total guns would be able to fire, forward, if an enemy was met. To deliver the maximum fire the ships must bring their broadsides to bear, and must form into line of battle. If the enemy were found directly ahead, each column had only to wheel to the right or left for the whole fleet to be in line, firing their broadsides at the enemy. The Grand Fleet only required four minutes to make this deployment, but it required that the enemy should be in exactly the right position. An alternative method, if the enemy lay to a flank, was for one of the columns — normally a wing column — to steam on while the remainder wheeled to follow in its wake. In this case the fleet would still be able to form a single chain within four minutes, but would take much longer to straighten their line.

Let us now see what actually happened. Jellicoe had dispatched the 3rd Battle-Cruiser Squadron (Hood) to support Beatty, but owing to the error in reckoning already mentioned it moved too far eastward. Thereby it became unintentionally the upper jaw of a trap into which the unconscious Hipper was putting his head. Hipper meantime was still running parallel to, but out of sight of, Beatty. At 5.40 P.M. Hipper suddenly sighted Beatty afresh — to the westward — and, coming under fire, swerved more to the eastward. Then he heard Hood's guns opening fire on his light cruisers. Alarmed, he turned away to the southeast at 6.34 P.M., only to see his light cruisers attacked by four of Hood's destroyers, which he imagined to be the forerunners of Jellicoe's main fleet. So he swerved again, to the southwest.

Meantime, Jellicoe and Beatty had not sighted each other until just before 6 P.M., although their advanced cruisers had made visual contact at 5.30 P.M., when about five miles apart. At 6.01 P.M., Jellicoe flashed the question, "Where is the enemy's battle fleet?" No answer came. Beatty was busily intent on his own "disappearing" opponent, Hipper — following him on a long outer curve which, incidentally, was carrying Beatty across Jellicoe's front. At 6.10 P.M. Jellicoe repeated his question, and four minutes later Beatty, almost simultaneously with Evan-Thomas, reported the enemy's bearing. The two reports enabled Jellicoe to judge Scheer's rough position, although not the course he was steering — which, actually, was northwestward in Hipper's wake.

Within a minute of Beatty's report Jellicoe had made his decision and given the order to deploy — on his left wing. Two minutes later his right wing opened fire, as it was wheeling to the left. It has been argued that he should have deployed earlier; but this would have meant acting on uncertain information, and the risk of putting himself in an unfavorable position. It has been argued that he should have deployed on his right; but this would have meant the risk that the enemy crossed the head of his line before he could cross theirs, and the certainty that until the line was straightened out — twenty-two minutes later — only a part, if a growing part, of his fleet could fire. It has been argued, by Churchill, that he might have deployed on one of the centre divisions and thereby have saved seven minutes, besides gaining the advantage of deploying within closer, yet not too close, reach to the oncoming foe. This, however, was a manœuvre rather more complex and less practised, and would at least have meant that the fire of the left fork of the tail was temporarily masked.

Jellicoe's actual deployment ensured that he would have time to cross the head of the enemy's line — the historic and deadly manœuvre of "crossing the T" — and also that none of his battleships would have their fire masked by others while the chain was straightening. Nor does there seem much actual substance in the criticism that a chance was lost by deploying further away from the enemy. Rather was it gained. For Scheer had no intention of fighting the Grand Fleet unless at an advantage.

Thus, in fact, he no sooner saw that Jellicoe's line — obscured for a time by the smoke of the cruiser action in the intervening space — was likely to "cross the T" than he made, at 6.30 P.M., an instant turn about. This was a deft emergency manœuvre whereby each ship turned about simultaneously; it enabled the whole line to slip out of range in the minimum time. His precipitancy was due to the fact that he mistook Hood's battle-cruisers for Jellicoe's leading battleships, and so thought the British manœuvre was further advanced than it was in reality. His mistake was to his opponent's disadvantage. For Jellicoe had actually signaled at 6.29 P.M. for his line to turn south-southeast by subdivisions, in order to get closer to the enemy, but had canceled the order on finding that his tail had not yet straightened out. Nor had it done so when Scheer made his "somersault" turn, under cover of a torpedo attack and a smoke screen. This hid Scheer's retirement for the few minutes before he was swallowed up in the mist. Although several of his leading battleships had suffered heavy hits, the only complete loss had been one of Hipper's light cruisers, the *Wiesbaden*. And, before disappearing, Hipper had destroyed another British battle-cruiser, the *Invincible*, and one armored cruiser, and had left a second sinking.

But the potentially vital fact in Scheer's retirement was that he had turned westward — away from his own harbors. If he had sighted the British battle fleet on his flank, as would have happened if Jellicoe had deployed in any other way, the natural course for Scheer would have been, not to turn about, but to turn right — and so retire towards his own harbors. Thus the best justification for Jellicoe's choice is that it gave him the opportunity to cut off Scheer's path of retreat. It also placed Scheer against the western sky.

This opportunity Jellicoe promptly exploited. To give direct chase to Scheer, when his own line was already six miles astern of Scheer, and only two hours' daylight remained, was a move that promised little. It would also have exposed the battle fleet to the very risk of running into mines dropped and torpedoes fired by the enemy, which Jellicoe was intent to avoid.

Instead, at 6.44 P.M. he ordered each division to turn southeast — so that they were once more in six columns echeloned back like a staircase from left to right. In the next quarter of an hour he made two more partial turns. The effect was to bring him round in a gradual curve between the unseen Germans and their line of retreat, while edging closer to them. Only the coming darkness and the increasing mist threatened the advantage gained by his skillful manœuvre. One criticism,

however, appears reasonable — that, either on Beatty's initiative or Jellicoe's orders, the battle-cruiser fleet, whose essential rôle was that of "feelers" for the battle fleet, might have
swung round more sharply and sought to keep touch with
the enemy. Actually, the battle-cruisers were further away
than the battle fleet from the enemy.

The enemy, however, was about to make touch himself —
to his own danger. Having slipped out of one trap, he almost
slipped into another, created mainly by his own miscalculation.
For, after steaming west for about twenty minutes, Scheer
suddenly reversed his direction and steamed east again — to
appear out of the mist at about the same point as before. He
claimed in his subsequent dispatch that his idea was to strike
a second blow so as to keep the initiative, and maintain German prestige. The claim is at his own expense, for no good
tactician would steam into the middle of the superior British
fleet for such a purpose. The logical hypothesis is that he
expected to cross the tail of the British fleet, thereby gaining
the chance to punish part of it and regaining his path home.
For, as already mentioned, he had mistaken Hood's squadron
for the van of the battle fleet and so he overestimated the distance that the battle fleet had moved. Hence, when Scheer
appeared out of the mist at 7.10 P.M. he was opposite the centre
of the "stepped" British line.

Its rear squadron, being nearest, opened fire first — at a
range of only about five miles. Within the next few minutes
the greater part of the British fleet joined in. But, with a perhaps excessive fear of partial exposure, Jellicoe ordered his
rear squadrons to form astern of him — in non-technical language, to wheel eastward and follow in his wake. Thereby
he drew them further away from the enemy. And at this
moment Scheer had also decided to go away. Indeed, he was
in such a hurry to get out of Jellicoe's jaws that he not only
performed a fresh "somersault" manœuvre, less neat than
before, under cover of smoke screens and destroyer attacks,
but also launched his battle-cruisers in a "death ride."

The destroyers proved the most effective of these agents of
his salvation, for, seeing their torpedoes loosed, at long range,

Jellicoe swung his ships away by two quick turns of two points each (22.5 degrees in all). This turn away was a long-practised method which the majority opinion in the navy approved as the best expedient, and only a minority opposed on the score that the torpedo danger was overrated, and that its adoption tended to abnegate the offensive value of the battleship. A decision between these opinions is difficult. One can only draw the logical conclusion that, if the precaution was essential, it was confession of the weakness of the battleship, and of the ease with which its offensive movements could be paralyzed by an infinitely less expensive instrument of war. At Jutland the justification for the precaution is that only one British battleship was hit by a torpedo, and the justification for the minority opinion is that this battleship was so little affected that it kept its place in the line.

As a means of freeing the German fleet the destroyer attack was not only the most effective but the cheapest, for only one destroyer was sunk — by a counter-stroke of the British light cruisers — while the German battle-cruisers suffered heavily. The *Lutzow* was disabled before the "death ride" began, and the other four were hit repeatedly in the few minutes before a signal of recall from Scheer reprieved them.

The tactical effect of the destroyer attack was that while the German fleet was going west the British fleet was going the opposite way. A quarter of an hour later, satisfied that the torpedo attack had spent itself, Jellicoe corrected his turn away, but continued on a course almost due south. Not until 8 P.M. did he turn west. In this delay there seems to be ground for criticism. For to maintain his tactical advantage of being across the enemy's line of retreat, it was desirable both to shepherd him away from his own coast and to keep touch with him so that he had less chance of slipping past the British mobile barrier in the dark.

By one school of criticism much emphasis has been given to the fact that after sighting the enemy again at 7.40 Beatty sent a further wireless signal to Jellicoe ten minutes later: "Submit van of battleships follow battle-cruisers. We can then cut off whole of enemy's battle fleet." But excellent as this

sounds, and was its meaning, its historical value is rather
diminished by the fact that, before it was decoded and handed
to him, Jellicoe had already turned the battle fleet west, while
Beatty was merely going southwest, according to his last
message. Moreover, the German fleet was already cut off
from its base. Perhaps Beatty meant "head off" — his own
next order to his light cruisers, to locate the head of the enemy's
line, which was now steaming south, suggests this explanation.
Moreover, he succeeded in heading off the enemy on his own,
for when they came under his fire, about 8.23 P.M., they
promptly sheered off to the westward again. And by checking
their course south this encounter helped them in slipping past
the British tail later.

The best, indeed the only, chance of closing with the Germans had passed in the half hour following their 7.20 P.M. turn
away. The great question that remained was whether Jellicoe
could continue to bar their way during the night so that he
could reëngage at dawn with a whole day's light before him,
and thereby profit from his strategic advantage — now added
to superior strength.

When the blanket of darkness spread across the sea about
9 P.M., it not merely accelerated the haziness of the day, but
changed it to blindness. The battleships lost their advantage
of range, the torpedo-craft gained the advantage of coming to
close range with minimum risk. And all ships would have
difficulty in distinguishing friend from foe.

Jellicoe wisely rejected the hazard of a night battle, for it
would have meant staking his double advantage on a pure
gamble. Thus his problem was to prevent the enemy from
finding an open way home during the five and a half hours
before daylight. There were three likely routes, each leading
to a swept channel through the mine-fields which covered the
approaches to the Heligoland Bight and the German harbors.
One, on the east, was past Horn Reefs and down the Frisian
coast; a second, more central, eventually led past Heligoland;
the third, in the extreme southwest, was entered near the
German coast and led eastward past the mouth of the Ems.
The distance to this was one hundred and eighty miles, and,

being the furthest, it was the least obvious choice. Hence Jellicoe might justly fear that an astute enemy might take it — but for one factor. This was the inferior speed of the German fleet compared with his own. If the Germans had enjoyed equal or greater speed, the Ems route would have offered them more chance and scope for evading an uncertain guard during the hours of darkness. Lacking it, they were wise to take the greater immediate risk of the shorter route.

Jellicoe, however, was unwilling to uncover one completely in order to cover the others more closely. And he chose a "beat" which certainly reconciled as far as was possible the difficulties of covering all. Indeed, it left the Germans only one good chance — that of slipping behind Jellicoe and taking the Horn Reefs passage. Hence, one would anticipate that Jellicoe would be especially sensitive to any signs of an attempt to pass astern of him.

At 9.17 P.M. Jellicoe ordered the fleet to take up night cruising stations — the battleships being closed up in three parallel columns. The course of the fleet was to be due south, and the speed seventeen knots. The destroyers were massed five miles astern, a disposition which prolonged the moving barrier, protected the rear of the battle fleet against torpedo attacks, and, above all, prevented the risks of mistaken identity in the darkness. If the battleships sighted destroyers, or the destroyers battleships, each would know that the dim shapes were those of an enemy. Beatty had already taken station with the battle-cruisers ahead of and on the western, or enemy, flank of the battle fleet. The historical significance of his night position is that it made impossible any attempt of the Germans to outstrip or pass south of the British, and so might have provided a further cause for sensitive suspicion of an attempt to pass astern. The formation of the Grand Fleet might be likened metaphorically and symbolically to that of the traditional British lion, Beatty's battle-cruisers and light cruisers being the nose and ears, and the destroyers the lion's tail. The nose was to smell nothing, the ears to hear something, the tail to be twisted, but the lion as an entity to remain as majestically unmoved as those surrounding Nelson's column.

One preliminary remains to be mentioned — Scheer's intention. It was simple, not subtle, and to that extent simplified the problem of parrying it. Desperation, at the morning's dire prospect, seems to have inspired it. For he took the shortest route home — by Horn Reefs — prepared to lose heavily but determined to break through. Unlike Jellicoe, he could at least feel that the luck lurking in a night encounter was more likely to be a friend than otherwise to his bold course. To enhance his prospects and safety he posted his lame battle-cruisers and old battleships in rear and covered his van with destroyer and light-cruiser tentacles.

The scene was set. Would the monarchs of the seas, taking the call, clash in blind battle? Thus the anticipation. But only the tinkle of the jester's bell was heard from the darkened stage. And when light came, the stage was empty.

The first tinkle came at 9.32 P.M. when the *Lion*, Beatty's flagship, inquired by flashing-lamp of the *Princess Royal*, "Please give me challenge and reply now in force, as they have been lost." The reply seems to have been seen, in part, by an enemy ship. For, about half an hour later, several cruisers were sighted by the *Castor*, which was leading one of the British destroyer flotillas. They took the initiative and challenged her by making part of the British secret challenge for the day. As, however, they next switched on their searchlights and opened fire, the *Castor* replied in a similar unfriendly fashion, but several of her attendant destroyers withheld their torpedoes from a natural doubt as to the true identity of the cruisers. But the effect of this mischance, and missed chance, can be exaggerated. For, from 10.20 P.M. to 11.30 P.M., the British tail was repeatedly in action with the enemy, who were trying to elbow their way through. At 10.20 P.M. they "elbowed" Goodenough's light cruisers, but sheered off after the light cruiser *Frauenlob* had been sunk by a torpedo from the badly battered *Southampton*. In the next hour the British destroyers suffered the contusion and caused confusion. The light cruiser *Elbing* was rammed by the battleship *Posen* and left sinking, while the British destroyer *Spitfire* acted up to her name by ramming the battleship *Nassau*. She not only "got

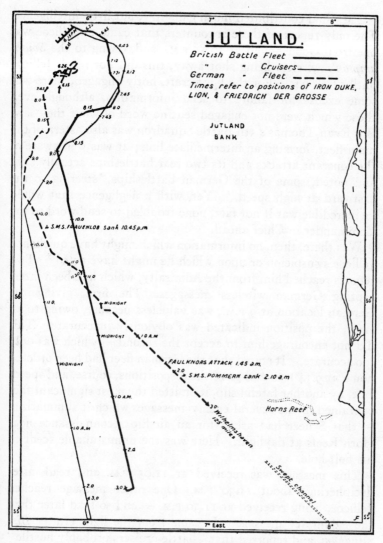

away with" this act of impertinence, but with a long strip of
Nassau's plating as proof of her prowess. Once more the
German fleet sheered off, but veered in afresh about 11.30 P.M.
and this time broke through, although harassed by the British
hornets for over an hour at the cost of four of their number.

They had contributed much gallantry, but little intelligence. The only report of these encounters that came to Jellicoe was one from Goodenough at 10.15 P.M., and, owing to the *Southampton's* wireless being shot away, this did not reach Jellicoe until 11.38 P.M. For the light craft, hotly engaged, there was some excuse for failure to send information, although even those which were not engaged sent no word of what they saw. But Evan-Thomas's 5th Battle Squadron was also astern of the main fleet, forming an intermediate link; it was well aware of the constant attacks and its two rear battleships actually saw, and noted, some of the German battleships "steering to the eastward at high speed." Yet, with a negligence that would be incredible was it not fact, none troubled to send word to the Commander-in-Chief ahead.

Was there, then, no information which might have quickened Jellicoe's suspicion or upon which he might have acted? Two reports reached him from the Admiralty, which had been intercepting German wireless messages. The first, giving the German location at 9 P.M., was valueless because, owing to an error, the position indicated was obviously inaccurate. This did not encourage him to accept the second — which was only too accurate. It stated that the German fleet had been ordered home at 9.14 P.M. and gave the dispositions, course, and speed. But, by another fateful slip, it omitted the most significant fact contained in the several enemy messages which it summarized — that Scheer had asked for an airship reconnaissance near Horn Reefs at daylight. Here was the unmistakable scent to his bolt-hole.

This message was received at 11.05 P.M. and read, after deciphering, about 11.30 P.M. One other message reached Jellicoe, being received at 11.30 P.M. — and so read later than the Admiralty message. It came from the light cruiser *Birmingham*, and reported that "battle-cruisers probably hostile" were in sight, steering south and well to the westward. Unfortunately, the *Birmingham* had sighted them at a moment when they had sheered away from the British torpedo attacks. If Jellicoe already distrusted the Admiralty message, upon which he took no action, it was natural that he should regard the two later reports from the *Southampton* and *Birmingham* as support to his doubts.

Yet, it is curious, and not easy to explain, that he should have been so insensitive to the definite indication of fighting astern. For, apart from these two reports, the recurrent firing was heard and the flashes seen both by his flagship and the other battleships. That this fire was obviously from light guns did not, it is true, reveal the presence of enemy battleships, but it was no proof that they were not there, for at night battleships would naturally be using their secondary armament if engaged with British light craft. More curious still is the fact that Jellicoe made only one attempt, at 10.46 P.M., to inquire the source of the firing, and the wording of his signal suggests a preconceived idea that it was merely an enemy destroyer attack. Thus, in sum, the conclusion is that while Jellicoe's lack of certain knowledge was due to the neglect of his subordinates, his lack of suspicion is the measure of his own responsibility — and the salvation of Scheer.

One more serious contact occurred before the German fleet was at last safely free. In the dim light before dawn it was sighted by Captain Stirling's 12th Destroyer Flotilla. The exception, when he should have been the rule, Stirling sent a wireless report to Jellicoe at 1.52 A.M., before he engaged the enemy, and another during the action. His attack torpedoed and sank the German battleship *Pommern*, and thereby achieved more than the whole Grand Fleet had done. But his reports did not reach Jellicoe, presumably owing to a wireless failure. Thus the British battle fleet continued serenely on its course southward, and the German on its course homeward.

When daylight came Jellicoe turned about, at 2.39 A.M., and steamed northward, expecting to see the German fleet and seeing only an empty sea. Then came another Admiralty message to say that the German fleet was close to Horn Reefs, and this time its evidence was accepted. After searching for enemy stragglers, and finding none, the Grand Fleet in turn steamed homeward. Its total loss had been three battle-cruisers, three armored cruisers, and eight destroyers to the German one battleship, one battle-cruiser, four light cruisers, and five destroyers. In officers and men, the British had lost 6097 killed to the German 2545, and 177 prisoners to none.

Thus the one naval "battle" of the World War was but a casual item in the long butcher's bill. Its value as a battle was in every sense negligible. To trace to it the ultimate and bloodless surrender of the German fleet two and a half years later is absurd, confounding mere sequence with causation. If Jutland did little to encourage the Germans to provoke a decisive clash at sea, it did little to discourage them. They had won the first game, against the battle-cruisers, and superior gunnery had yielded them honors "above the line"; they had been outmanœuvred in the second game, with honors easy, and had scored several tricks in the third before the game had been broken off. As they could not hope to gain the rubber because of their opponent's stronger hand, the interruption left them at least a flattering sense of their own skill. As a new and untried creation the German navy inevitably suffered an inferiority complex in face of a navy which enjoyed a matchless roll of victories and the "Nelson tradition." Jutland had dissipated this fear of the untried in face of the known unknown.

Within twelve weeks the German fleet was to make a bolder bid to take the British at a disadvantage. Covered by airship patrols, it advanced close to the English coast on August 19 with the idea of bombarding Sunderland as a bait to draw the Grand Fleet south on to a waiting ambush of submarines. Battle was again baulked by caution and an accident. One of Beatty's advanced cruisers was torpedoed, and Jellicoe, suspecting instead a new-laid mine-field, turned back and steamed north for two hours. When he again came south the German fleet had gone. For Scheer had received a report of a strong British force — actually the light force from Harwich — coming up from the south, and hastily assumed that this was the Grand Fleet. If so, it had not only evaded his trap, but, turning the tables, threatened to cut him off. Hence he turned for home.

For the British navy, Jutland would better not have been fought at all. However unpalatable the admission, it undoubtedly depreciated British naval prestige in the eyes of Allies and the home public more than the inspiring feats of individual gallantry and the fact of Britain's continued supremacy at sea could redeem. That supremacy was to ensure the ultimate downfall of German power to continue the war. But no victorious battle helped, as such a battle might, to shorten the gloomy and costly process of exhaustive slaughter on land. Jutland merely ensured what was already ensured without a battle, so long as the British navy maintained its passive superiority of strength.

Here was the general aspect. On the technical side, Jutland was more significant, if not more productive of enthusiasm. It showed that the German standard of gunnery was far higher than complacent or patronizing opinion in England had recognized, and it tended, less fairly, to reflect unfavorably on British gunnery, owing to the lapse of some, and the lack of opportunity of other, elements of the fleet. In material, Jutland showed also that the Admiralty and its technical advisers had failed to foresee or profit by experience as well as the Germans. Against the inferior armor-piercing qualities of the British shells must be set — but not offset — the fact of insufficient protection of the British ships against plunging fire, and especially against the flash from an explosion in a gun-turret passing down into the magazine. This was the probable cause of the mysteriously sudden end of the *Queen Mary* and *Indefatigable*. More debatable, perhaps, were the results of the policy of building huge battle-cruisers in which a large degree of protection was sacrificed for a small increase in speed. Speed in itself confers indirectly a high degree of protection, but essentially through diminishing the target, in the sense of making it more difficult for the enemy to hit. For effective protection in this way a diminution of size is required, not merely a diminution of armor for the sake of a few extra knots.

The tactical side of Jutland has aroused still more criticism and controversy than the technical side. Criticism of its foundation is less easy to counter than criticism of the actual direction. The naval neglect of tactical study, the absence of tactical textbooks, and the secrecy which by custom had enshrouded the meagre instructions, have ever been a source of wonder to soldiers, who know from history and experience that good and flexible tactics in an army are essentially the product of ceaseless reflection and discussion by many minds. "La critique est la vie de la science." Students of military history know that the attempt to keep tactics secret defeats its own end — and its own employer. There was no mystery in the tactics by which Alexander's Macedonians, the Romans, the Mongols, Gustavus's Swedes, Frederick's Prussians, Wellington's Peninsular infantry, won their repeated triumphs. Only a matchless harmony of execution, through practice and understanding, which gave them the advantage no rival and imitator could overtake. Secrecy leads to rigidity of tactics; open discussion and criticism to flexibility and the well-attuned initiative of subordinates when confronted with the unexpected. The basic criticism of naval tactics during the World War period is that they undermined the basis of tactics — elasticity. Moreover, the fleet fought at Jutland as a single body, as did armies in the days before Napoleon developed the system of independent divisions. Tactically, the fleet was an armless body. Thus, however skillfully Jellicoe manœuvred his fleet, he could not justly hope to paralyze his opponent's freedom of movement. And to pin an opponent is the vital prelude to a decisive manœuvre; this dual act gives a double meaning to the old maxim, "Divide to conquer." The British fleet was all too truly "one and indivisible."

Subject to this dominant proviso, Jellicoe's handling of the fleet during the day of May 31 may fairly be adjudged a very able if cautious performance when we take full account of the obscure conditions. In 1916 this obscurity had reached an extreme, for aircraft reconnaissance had not yet been adequately developed as a corrective to the long ranges developed by progress in guns. As for Jellicoe's oft-criticized deployment on the left wing, it was probably the best in the circumstances, although praise of it is apt to overlook the fact that it was not free from trouble. For it meant that Beatty's battle-cruisers took longer to get clear of the front of the battle fleet and so masked its fire and caused checks — the very objection which has been brought against Churchill's suggested alternative of deploying from the centre.

The lessons of the night have already been summed up, and the only further question is whether Jellicoe might not have seized the opportunity to forestall the enemy's attempt to break through by using his torpedo craft offensively instead of defensively as his pendent tail. But if, discounting all criticisms, we admit that Jellicoe's handling of the battle fleet was the flawless masterpiece that numerous naval admirers argue, the admission only strengthens the belief that the worst fault of the Jutland battle was that it was ever fought.

VI

1917 — THE STRAIN

DESPITE incessant provocation for two years, since the *Lusitania* incident, President Wilson held to his neutral policy, and if his excess of patience angered many of his own people, it was at least the means of consolidating American opinion and reconciling it as a whole to intervention in the war. Meantime he strove by speech and by the agency of Colonel House — his unofficial ambassador — to find a basis of peace on which the belligerents could agree. This effort was doomed to failure by his misunderstanding of the psychology of the warring peoples and of people at war. He was still thinking in terms of traditional warfare, between governmental policies, while the conflict had long since passed into the wider sphere of the struggle of peoples dominated by primitive instincts and chained by their own catch-phrases to the chariot wheels of Mars-mechanized.

The declaration of the unlimited submarine campaign brought convincing proof of the futility of these peace hopes and of the reality of the German intentions, and, when followed by the deliberate sinking of American ships and an attempt to instigate Mexico to action against the United States, President Wilson hesitated no longer, and on April 6, 1917, America entered the war against Germany.

Her potential force in man-power and material was illimitable. But, even more unready than Britain in 1914, it must be long in exerting more than a moral influence, and Germany confidently anticipated that the submarine campaign would take decisive effect within a few months. How near her calculation came to fulfillment the record of 1917 and 1918 bears witness.

The year 1916 had closed in gloom for the Entente. The

simultaneous offensive on all fronts, planned a year before, had misfired, the French army was at a low ebb, the Russian still lower, the Somme had failed to produce visible results in any way proportionate to its cost, and another fresh Ally had been overrun. At sea the negativeness of Jutland was a disappointment, and, although Germany's first submarine campaign had been abandoned, a stronger one was threatened. To offset these debits, the Entente could only show the capture of distant Baghdad and the limited Italian success at Gorizia in August, whose value, however, was mainly that of a moral fillip to Italy herself.

Among the Allied peoples and their political representatives there was a growing sense of depression. On the one hand it took the form of dissatisfaction with the conduct of the war, and, on the other, of discouragement over the prospects of a victorious conclusion to the war, and a tendency to discuss the possibilities of a peace by negotiation. The first-named tendency was the earlier to come to a head and was signalized in London, the political mainspring of the Allies, by the replacement of Asquith's Government on December 11 by one with Lloyd George as its chief. The order of precedence in events had a significant effect. For Lloyd George had come into power as the spokesman of a widespread demand for a more vigorous as well as more efficient prosecution of the war.

The second tendency received an impulse from the German peace move of December 12, after the fall of Bucharest, which proposed an opening of peace discussions. This suggestion was rejected as insincere by the Allied Governments, but it afforded the opportunity for President Wilson, on whose behalf Colonel House had long been sounding the belligerent Governments as to the prospects of mediation, to invite these to define their war aims as a preliminary to practical negotiation. The German reply was evasive, the Allied replies were considered by their opponents unacceptable as a basis of discussion, and the tentative peace moves subsided. But while this wave of depression was surging on the "home-front," the Allied Commanders continued optimistic. In November Joffre assembled, at Chantilly, a further conference of the Commanders at which it was agreed that the Germans were in great difficulties on the western front, and that the situation of the Allies was more favorable than it had ever been.

The fighting strength of the British army in France had grown to be about 1,200,000 men, and was still growing. The fighting strength of the French army had been increased by the incorporation of native troops to some 2,600,000, so that, including the Belgians, it was estimated that the Allies disposed of about 3,900,000 men against about 2,500,000 Germans.

Joffre, however, declared that the French army could maintain its strength for one more great battle, and that thereafter it must progressively decline, as France had no longer a sufficient number of men of military age to replace losses. He therefore warned Haig that during the coming year the burden must fall more and more upon the British army. It was also agreed that in view of these factors the relative superiority of the Allies on the western front would be greater in the spring of 1917 than at any time which could be foreseen with certainty. In consequence it was decided to take the earliest opportunity of pressing the advantage gained on the Somme, and to continue the process of exhausting the enemy's reserves as preparation for an effort which should be decisive. An alternative proposal was made by General Cadorna that the French and British should coöperate in a combined thrust from the Italian front against Austria with the object of knocking this weaker partner out of the war. But it was rejected by the French and British Commanders, despite Lloyd George's espousal of it at the Allied conference held in Rome in January. Their objection was that it involved a fresh diversion of strength away from the main front, where alone, they held, success could have decisive results.

The Entente plan for 1917 was soon to be complicated by changes in the command. French opinion had tired of the meagre results of Joffre's attrition strategy, and the method of the limited objective had fallen into disfavor because of the unlimited losses on the wrong side, which accompanied it without apparent gain. They contrasted the dull course of Joffre's strategy with the brilliant results gained by Mangin at Verdun, in the autumn, under Nivelle's direction, and as a result Joffre gave place to Nivelle, who promised a real breakthrough. His confidence so inspired Lloyd George, the new British Prime Minister, that Haig was subordinated to him for the forthcoming operations — an arrangement which violated the axiom that a general cannot direct one force while exercising executive command of another. For carrying out a plan essentially audacious, Nivelle had two further handicaps: he failed to convert several of his subordinates to the idea, and he was given less rein by the Government than his predecessor. Again, while Joffre had intimated that the British must take the chief part, Nivelle changed this policy, and, in his desire to conserve the glory for France, overlooked how severely the French fighting power had been strained. Joffre's plan had been for a convergent attack on the great German salient Lens-Noyon-Reims, first against its west flank and then against its south flank — the British to attack north of the Somme, including but extending beyond the old battle ground, and the French south of it to the Oise. The attacks were to begin early in February and to be followed by the main French attack in Champagne. Nivelle's change was to ask the British to take over more of the front — south of the Somme — in order to release French troops for the Champagne blow, and as a result the start was postponed a month.

Before the plan could be put in operation, the Germans had dislocated it. Ludendorff's first step had been to set on foot a complete programme for the reorganization of German manpower, munitions, and supplies. While this was developing, he intended to stand on the defensive, hoping that the new submarine campaign would either decide the issue or pave the way for a decisive blow on land when his reserves of men and material were ready. As a "coefficient of safety" in face of the Somme offensive, he had previously ordered a new line of defense, of great artificial strength, to be built across the chord of the arc Lens-Noyon-Reims. Early in the new year, anticipating the renewal of the Entente advance on the Somme, Ludendorff hurried on the completion of this rear line and arranged for the utter devastation of the whole area inside the arc. There was a satirical, or satyrical, aptness in the code-word for this programme of destruction — "Alberich," the name of the malicious dwarf in the Nibelung Saga. The Crown Prince Rupprecht thought of resigning rather than carry out these extreme measures, but satisfied his conscience by refusing to sign the order for them. Houses were demolished, trees cut down, and even wells contaminated, while the wreckage was littered with a multitude of explosive booby-traps. And on the night of March 12 the German forces began a methodical retirement, by stages, to the new line called by them the "Siegfried" and by the Allies the "Hindenburg" line. A consummate manœuvre, if unnecessarily brutal in application, it showed that Ludendorff had the moral courage to give up territory if circumstances advised it. The British, confronted with a desert, were inevitably slow in pursuit, and their preparations for an attack on this front were thrown out of gear, limiting them to the sector around Arras, where the front was unchanged.

On April 9 Allenby's Third Army opened the spring offensive at this point, taking the long-sought Vimy ridge, but failed to develop its initial success, and continued the attack too long after the resistance had hardened. This costly action was ostensibly prolonged in order to take the pressure off the French. For the French thrust between the Somme and the Oise had also been stultified by the German retirement, and the main attack on April 16 east and west of Reims was a worse fiasco with a dangerous sequel. With a prolonged bombardment giving away any chance of surprise and without first drawing away the German reserves, the idea of a rapid break-through was doomed to fail. The high hopes that had been raised caused the greater reaction, and the troops were weary of being thrown against barbed wire and machine-guns to no apparent effect.

Accentuated by service grievances, mutinies occurred in the French armies, and no less than sixteen corps were affected. The flame of revolt broke out in a regiment of the 2nd Colonial Division on May 3, and, although momentarily extinguished, soon spread, to the tune of such cries as "We will defend the trenches, but we won't attack!" "We are not so stupid as to march against undamaged machine-guns!" The fact that the mutinies always occurred when the troops were ordered into the line is clear proof that disgust with their leadership rather than seditious propaganda was the real cause of revolt. A significant sidelight is that cases of desertion in the French army rose from 509 in 1914 to 21,174 in 1917. So general was the rot that, according to the Minister of War, only two divisions in the Champagne sector could be relied on fully, and in places the trenches were scarcely even guarded.

The savior of the situation was General Pétain, and his instrument a change of policy based on psychology. On April 28 the Government had made him Chief of the General Staff as a brake on Nivelle's reckless offensive, and on May 15 they took the wiser and more honest step of appointing him to replace Nivelle. For a month he traveled along the front by car, visiting nearly every division, summoning both officers and men to voice their complaints. Essentially patriarchal and not familiar, he inspired confidence both in his firmness and in his promises. Tours of duty in the trenches were equalized, regularity of leave ensured, rest camps improved. Within a month calm was restored — at the price of only twenty-three executions, although more than a hundred of the ringleaders were deported to the colonies.

But if the French army was convalescent, Pétain had still to revive its fighting confidence and power. To this end he first reorganized its training and tactics on the basis that firepower should economize man-power, and then aimed to test his newly sharpened blade in easy tests that should not risk blunting it again. Thus, for the rest of the year the British bore the brunt of the campaign. Their strength in France was now at its highest — sixty-four divisions, supplied with an abundance of artillery and ammunition. The strain on them, however, was increased by the failure of Russia to make any effective contribution to the pressure on Germany, owing to the revolution which broke out in March. Haig decided to keep the Germans occupied by carrying out the original plan for an offensive in Belgium, but if the principle was right, the method and choice of site were opposed to all the experience of history.

The initial move was an attack on the Messines ridge in order to strengthen out the Ypres salient and attract the enemy's reserves. Carried out on June 7 by the Second Army under Plumer (with Harington as Chief of Staff), it proved a model example of the "limited" attack, in which the surprise-effect of nineteen huge mines, simultaneously exploded, and supplemented by an overwhelming artillery concentration, was exploited just as far as, and no further than, the point where the German "numbness" began to wear off.

This coup was tardily followed on July 31 by the main attack at Ypres, which, hampered in execution by the heavy rain, was foredoomed by its own destruction of the intricate drainage system of the area. The British Command had persevered for two and a half years with the method of a prolonged preparatory bombardment, believing that quantity of shells was the key to success, and that, unlike all the great captains of history, they could forego the aid of surprise. The offensive at Ypres, which was finally submerged in the swamps of Passchendaele in early November, threw into stronger relief than ever before the fact that such a bombardment blocked the advance for which it was intended to pave the way — because it made the ground impassable. The discomfiture was increased by the new German defensive method of thinning the front defenses and using the men so saved for prompt local counter-attacks. The defense was built up of a framework of machine-guns distributed in concrete "pill-boxes" and disposed in great depth. On the British side the profitless toll of this struggle in the mud was to some extent mitigated by better staff work when the direction of the attack was progressively handed over to Plumer's Second Army.

Three months of dreadful struggle came to an end with the British no appreciably nearer their immediate object of driving the Germans from their submarine bases in the Belgian ports, and if they had worn down the German strength, they had worn down their own still more.

The 1917 campaign in the west closed, however, on a note

brighter in promise if not in accomplishment. Appreciating from the first days the futility of using tanks in these Flanders swamps, the Tank Corps headquarters looked around for an area where they could try out a new and different method. They drew up a project for a large-scale raid to scour a canal-enclosed "pocket" near Cambrai, where the rolling downland lent itself to tank movement. The basic idea was the release of a swarm of tanks without any preparatory bombardment to give warning of the attack. When their hopes at Ypres waned, the British Command adopted the scheme, but transformed it into a definite offensive with far-reaching aims, for which they had not the resources because of the drain of Ypres. It was to be carried out by Byng's Third Army with six divisions, and the date was fixed for November 20. Led by nearly four hundred tanks, the attack came as a complete surprise, and despite minor checks achieved a penetration far deeper and at less cost than any past British offensive. But all the available troops and tanks were thrown in to the first blow, and no reserves were at hand to exploit the success. The cavalry, as always on the western front, proved unable to carry out this rôle.

Thus the advance died away, and on November 30 the Germans launched a counter-stroke against the flanks of the salient created by the British advance. In the north it was parried but in the south broke through, and a disaster was narrowly averted. But if Cambrai closed in disappointment, it revealed that surprise and the tank were the combination by which the trench-barrier could be unlocked. Meanwhile Pétain, after overhauling his instrument, the French army, sought to test its readiness for 1918. In August a stroke by Guillaumat's army at Verdun recovered all the remainder of the ground lost in 1916, and in October Maistre's army flattened the southwest corner of the German front, seizing the Chemin des Dames ridge.

The Collapse of Russia. The temporary breakdown of the French fighting power was not the worst of the troubles which together crippled the Entente offensive in 1917. The collapse, first partial and then complete, of Russia was a loss which even the entry of America into the war could not possibly compensate for many months, and before the balance was restored the Western Allies were to be perilously near the brink of defeat. Russia's enormous losses, due to her defective machine, but incurred in sacrifice for her Allies, had undermined the moral even more than the material endurance of her forces. Revolution broke out in March, superficially against the corrupt *entourage* of the Tsar, but with more deep-seated moral causes beneath. The Tsar was forced to abdicate and a moderate Provisional Government climbed into the saddle, but without reins. This was only a makeshift, and in May another succeeded it, more Socialist in tendency and outwardly led by Kerensky. While clamoring for a general peace and undermining discipline by a system of committee control suitable to a trade-union but not to the field of battle, Kerensky imagined he could send troops against the enemy by platform appeals. Brusilov succeeded Alexiev in the Supreme Command, and on July 1 the army gained some initial success against the Austrians, especially in the region of Stanislau, only to stop as soon as real resistance was met, and to crumble directly the Germans counter-attacked. By early August the Russians had been driven out of Galicia and the Bukovina, and only policy halted the Austro-German forces on the frontiers of Russia itself. Since the departure of Hindenburg and Ludendorff in 1916, Hoffmann had been in real control of the eastern front; his clever combination of strategy and policy did much to complete the paralysis of Russia, and thus release German troops for use in the west. In September the Germans took the opportunity to practise their new artillery methods, for future use in France; their surprise attack, under Hutier's command, achieved the capture of Riga with scarcely a show of opposition. Next month the Bolsheviks under Lenin overthrew the wordy Kerensky, imposed their self-constituted rule on the Russian people, and sought an armistice with Germany, which was concluded in December.

The Break-Through in Italy. The defection of Russia did not end the Entente tale of woe. Each autumn, with demoralizing regularity, Germany had seized an opportunity to eat up one of the weaker Allies. In 1915 it had been Serbia's fate, in 1916 Rumania's, and now it was to be Italy's turn, or so the Germans intended. Ludendorff's decision, taken in September, was determined by the appeals of the Austrian authorities, who felt that their troops could not endure the strain of another defensive battle on the Italian frontier. In May, Cadorna had attacked once more on the Isonzo front, but an Austrian counter-attack in the Carso sector had retaken part of the small gains. Losses, however, were more nearly balanced than formerly. The question of Allied coöperation on the Italian front was raised afresh without result, but Cadorna, nevertheless, initiated in August an "eleventh battle of the Isonzo." Capello's Second Army captured a large part of the Bainsizza plateau, north of Gorizia, but a long-sustained effort brought no further success and Cadorna was forced to break off the offensive after four weeks' struggle. But it had so strained the resistance of the debilitated Austrians that, in Ludendorff's words, "it became necessary to decide for the attack on Italy in order to prevent the collapse of Austria-Hungary."

Ludendorff had a difficult problem to solve, Russia had not yet capitulated, the front there was already weakly held for its extent, and the British offensive in Flanders made impossible a large withdrawal of troops from France. As he could only scrape together six German divisions, and the Austrians' quality was lower than ever, he came to the conclusion that the only chance of decisive results was to pick out a particularly weak sector which coincidently offered scope for a strategic exploitation of the break-through. This was found in the Tolmino-Caporetto sector. On October 24, after a short bombardment, the blow was launched and pushed deep down the western slopes of the mountains, imperiling the Italian forces to both south and north. On October 28 the advance reached Udine, the former Italian general headquarters, and on October 31 the Tagliamento.

Not the least significant feature of this offensive was the way it was prepared, by a moral bombardment. Propaganda had been exploited for months as a means of sapping the Italian discipline and will to resist. But its effect can be exaggerated; the most formidable propaganda, as with the French in April, was that supplied by the attrition strategy of the Italian Command, which had sickened the troops by its limited results at unlimited cost.

But the result also surprised Ludendorff, who with his slender forces had not calculated on such distant objectives as were now possible of attainment. As the direct pursuit was slowing down, he belatedly tried to switch troops from the left wing to Conrad's army which flanked the north of the Venetian salient, but was foiled by the inadequacy of the railways. Even so, Cadorna, with his centre broken through, only saved his wings by a precipitate retreat to the line of the Piave, covering Venice, leaving 250,000 prisoners in the enemy's hands. The same day Cadorna was superseded in supreme command by Diaz. Italy's Allies had begun to rush reënforcements, two army corps, one British and one French, to her aid, and on November 5 their political and military chiefs arrived at Rapallo for a conference, out of which sprang the Allied Council at Versailles, and ultimately a unified command.

The invaders had outrun their transport, and the resistance of the Italians, morally braced by the emergency, succeeded in holding the Piave in face of direct assaults and strenuous efforts by Conrad to turn their left flank from the Trentino. At the beginning of December, the British and French, who had been waiting in reserve in case of a fresh break-through, moved forward to take over vulnerable sectors, but the attack was only renewed in the north, and on December 19 it came to an end with the coming of the snows. If Caporetto seriously damaged Italy, it also purged her, and after an interval of recuperation she was to vindicate herself at Vittorio Veneto.

The Capture of Jerusalem. Once more a distant theatre of war provided the sole triumph of the Entente cause during the year — this time in Palestine. The second reverse at Gaza, in April 1917, had led to a change of command, Murray being succeeded by Allenby, who was strong enough and fortunate enough to obtain the adequate force for which Murray had asked in vain. The British Government was anxious for a spectacular success to offset the moral depression of the Nivelle failure and the decline of Russia, and the British General Staff desired to dislocate the Turks' attempt to recapture Baghdad by drawing away their reserves.

Allenby took over in July and devoted the first three months to intensive preparations for an autumn offensive, when the season would be suitable. The command was reorganized, the communications developed, and his own headquarters moved forward from Cairo to the front. By complete secrecy and ruses he deceived the Turks as to the point of attack. The defenses of Gaza were bombarded from October 20 onwards, and an attack followed on November 1 to pin the enemy and draw in his reserves. Meanwhile, as a necessary preliminary to the real blow, the inland bastion of Beersheba was seized by a convergent manœuvre on October 31, a prelude to the decisive attack on November 6, which broke through the enemy's weakened centre and into the plain of Philistia. Falkenhayn, now in command at Aleppo, had also been planning an offensive, but the better communications of the British decided the race, and although Falkenhayn tried to stem the tide by a counter-stroke against Beersheba, the breaking of his centre compelled a general retreat. The pursuit was hampered, owing to lack of water, but even so, by November 14, the Turkish forces were driven apart in two divergent groups, the port of Jaffa was taken, and Allenby wheeled his main force to the right for an advance inland on Jerusalem. He gained the narrow hill passes before the Turks could block them, and, after a necessary pause to improve his communications, brought up reserves for a fresh advance, which secured Jerusalem on December 9. By the time the winter rains set in the British had expanded and consolidated their hold on the region. As a moral success the feat was valuable, yet, viewed strategically, it seemed a long way round to the goal. If Turkey be pictured as a bent old man, the British, after missing their blow at his head, — Constantinople, — and omitting to strike at his heart, — Alexandretta, — had now resigned themselves to swallowing him from the feet upwards, like a python dragging its endless length across the desert.

The Clearing of East Africa. The year 1917 witnessed another overseas success, the clearing of German East Africa, although not the close of the campaign. More than a year elapsed after the rebuff at Tanga before a serious attempt was made to subdue the last German stronghold on the African continent. To spare troops from the main theatres was difficult, and the solution was only made possible by the loyal co-operation of the South African Government. In February 1916, General Smuts was appointed to command the expedition and formed the plan of a drive from north to south through the difficult interior, in order to avoid the fever-rampant plain on the coast. In conjunction with this central wedge, a Belgian force under Tombeur was to advance eastwards from Lake Tanganyika, and a small British force under Northey was to strike in from Nyasaland in the southwest. The Germans under Lettow-Vorbeck were weak in numbers but handled with masterly skill, and with all the advantages of an equatorial climate, a vast and trackless region, — mountainous in parts and covered with dense bush and forest, — to assist them in impeding the invader. From Dar-es-Salaam on the coast to Ujiji on Lake Tanganyika ran the one real line of rail communication, across the centre of the colony. After driving the Germans back across the frontier and seizing the Kilimanjaro gap, Smuts moved direct on this railway at Morogoro, over 300 miles distant, while he dispatched a force under Van Deventer in a wide sweep to the west to cut the railway further inland, and then converge on Morogoro. Lettow-Vorbeck delayed this manœuvre by a concentration against Van Deventer, but Smuts's direct advance compelled him to hurry his force back, and thus enabled Van Deventer to get astride the railway.

However, Lettow-Vorbeck evaded the attempt to cut him off and fell back in September on the Uluguru Mountains to the south. The Belgians and Northey had cleared the west and the net had been drawn steadily closer, confining Lettow-Vorbeck to the southeast quarter of the colony. Early in 1917 Smuts returned to England, and Van Deventer conducted the final operations which ended with Lettow-Vorbeck avoiding envelopment to the end, slipping across the frontier into Portuguese Africa. Here he maintained a guerilla campaign throughout 1918 until the general Armistice. With an original force of only 5000, 5 per cent being Europeans, he had caused the employment of 130,000 enemy troops and the expenditure of £72,000,000.

The Mastering of the Submarine. The military side of 1917 is thrown into shadow by the naval, or more strictly the economic, side. The vital issue turned on the balance between Germany's submarine pressure and Britain's resistance. April was the worst month. One ship out of every four which left the British Isles never came home. The Allies lost nearly a million tons of shipping, 60 per cent of it British, and although the German navy's promise of victory by the end of the month was proved a miscalculation, it was clear that, ultimately, the continuance of such a ratio of loss must starve the civilian population and prevent the maintenance of the armies. Britain, indeed, had only food enough for another six weeks.

The Government sought to counter the menace by the indirect means of rationing, increasing home production, and the expansion of shipbuilding; by the direct means of the system of convoys with naval escorts, and a counter-offensive against the submarine, aided by new devices to detect the presence of submarines and the use of thousands of patrol craft. The most effective counter-measure, that of penning the Germans in their bases by close-in mine-fields, was hindered by the British failure to obtain a real command of the North Sea, through a decisive victory. The British Destroyer Flotillas daringly laid thousands of mines in the channels left by the Germans through the Heligoland Bight, but their ceaseless efforts were largely foiled by the German mine-sweepers, which were able to work freely under the protection of the German fleet. Nevertheless these mines hindered and delayed the passage of the U-boats and increased that demoralizing nerve-strain on the U-boat crews which was, above all, the cause of the decline of the submarine campaign. Too few submarines and trained crews in proportion to the task, and too great a strain upon them, spelled ultimate collapse.

But the British crisis of the spring of 1917 was averted less by an offensive than by a defensive method. For the convoy system was the main agent of salvation. The method of patrolled areas had been continued, despite its proven futility of 1916, during the early months of 1917. As Churchill says, "In April the great approach route to the southwest of Ireland was becoming a veritable cemetery of British shipping." And other cemeteries were only small by comparison. Besides 516,000 tons of British shipping, 336,000 tons of Allied and neutral were buried beneath the waves during April, and the direct loss of food and raw materials to the island kingdom was augmented by the growing unwillingness of neutral shipping to take the risk of supplying such a customer. Only the "guts" of her merchant-seamen in going to sea after being several times torpedoed lay between Britain's stomach and starvation. And the blindest blunder of the British Admiralty was in opposing the introduction of the convoy system in face of the futility of their other methods to avert the close-looming disaster. At last the advocacy of younger officers was decisively reënforced by Mr. Lloyd George's intervention, and in April voyages under convoy were sanctioned as an experiment on the Gibraltar and North Sea routes. The first left Gibraltar homeward-bound on May 10. Crowned by unmistakable success, the convoys were extended to the transatlantic routes when the arrival of American flotillas under Admiral Sims increased the number of destroyers available for escorts. The loss of shipping in such convoys was reduced to a bare one per cent, and when, in August, the convoys were extended to outward-bound shipping, the British loss fell next month below the 200,000 ton level. Meantime the offensive campaign — now reënforced by special submarine chasers, aircraft, and the new horned mines — exacted an ever-rising toll of submarines, and by the end of 1917 the menace, if not broken, was at least subdued. If the British people had to tighten their belts, and their food rationing, they were now secure against starvation.

During the early months of 1918 the number of German submarines declined as steadily as their losses rose, until in

May fourteen were lost out of one hundred and twenty-five on service, while the effect of those that were operating declined disproportionately to their number. In all, the German war loss totaled one hundred and ninety-nine submarines, of which one hundred and seventy-five fell victims to the British navy. And of the various weapons the mine claimed forty-two and the depth charge thirty-one submarines. Hunted from the narrow seas, the U-boats were even shut out from the ocean during the last phase by a vast mine-barrage, laid mainly by the American navy, across the 180-mile-wide passage between Norway and the Orkney Islands. It consisted of no less than 70,000 mines, of which the British laid 13,000. This was a direct counter to the main submarine operations against the ocean-brought supplies of Great Britain.

The shorter-range operations of the small submarines from the Belgian coast were crippled by the perfected barrage across the Straits of Dover, by the daring attack of Admiral Keyes's force on the night of April 22, 1918, — which for a time blocked up the exit from Zeebrugge, — and by the progressive demoralization of the U-boat crews. Yet the removal of the menace should not lead to an underestimate of its powers for the future. The 1917 campaign was launched with only one hundred and forty-eight submarines and from the most unfavorable strategic position. Great Britain lay like a huge breakwater across the sea approaches to northern Europe, and the submarines had to get outside through narrow and closely watched outlets before they could operate against the arteries of supply. And, despite these handicaps, they almost stopped the beat of England's heart.

The Economic Reënforcement. In restoring circulation, America's first aid became a potent factor long before her military assistance. It embraced her provision of light craft to reënforce the British anti-submarine fleet, her rapidly developed construction of new mercantile ships, and still more her financial aid. By July 1917, Britain had spent over £5,000,000,000, her daily expenditure had risen to £7,000,000, and the burden of financing her Allies as well as her own efforts was straining even her resources, when America's aid came to ease the pressure. In the first months after her entry into the war, the appeals for loans came as a shock to Congress. Unable from remoteness and inexperience to realize the inevitable costs of the war, a large section of the American public felt that its new associates were trying to dip their hands too freely into the capacious pockets of Uncle Sam. Thus Mr. McAdoo, the Secretary of the Treasury, could satisfy neither the Allies nor the American public, the former feeling that he was stinting them and the latter crying that he was spending the nation's money like a drunken sailor. Hence further loans were vigorously opposed in Congress. Northcliffe graphically, if perhaps hyperbolically, summed up the situation when he cabled, "If loan stops, war stops."

Actually, up to mid-July the United States had advanced £229,000,000 to the several Allies, with the restriction that this was to pay for supplies bought in the United States, while Britain in the same period had added £193,000,000 to the £900,000,000 already lent to her Allies — without such restriction. On the top of this fresh strain came the fear of having to sell securities in order to liquidate the earlier "Morgan loan" — with consequent damage to British credit. Mr. Balfour, then Secretary for Foreign Affairs, was so alarmed that he cabled to Colonel House, "We seem on the verge of a financial disaster which would be worse than defeat in the field. If we cannot keep up exchange neither we nor our Allies can pay our dollar debts. We should be driven off the gold basis, and purchases from the U.S.A. would immediately cease and the Allies' credit would be shattered." The danger was met by the action of the United States Treasury in continuing monthly advances, despite opposition, until a coördinated Interallied finance council could be created; by the formation of an official purchasing commission to take over the unofficial functions formerly fulfilled by J. P. Morgan and Company on behalf of the British Government; and by sending Lord Reading to Washington as a combined political and financial representative to oil, by frankness and sympathy, the creaking machinery of demand and supply. The overwhelming success of the Liberty Loan campaign was at least an equal asset. Advances to the Allies were authorized at a maximum average monthly rate of $500,000,000. By the end of the year the problem itself was shifting its basis. For, owing to the vast needs and purchases of the American Government for its own forces, the supply of credit to the Allies began to exceed that of the supply of goods. The difficulty of the Allies was now that of obtaining the material they needed for munitions rather than of obtaining the money to pay for it.

While America's entry into the war thus secured the position of the Allies, it also conferred one great offensive benefit even before America's armies threw their weight into the scale. No longer was the grip of the naval blockade hampered by neutral quibbles, but instead America's coöperation converted it into a strangle-hold under which the enemy must soon grow limp, since military power is based on economic endurance. As a party to the war, the United States, indeed, wielded the economic weapon with a determination, regardless of the remaining neutrals, far exceeding Britain's boldest claims in the past years of controversy over neutral rights. Thus the surface blockade of Germany began to tighten coincidently with the flagging of the submarine blockade of Britain.

The Air. Another new form of action reached its crest at the same time as the submarine campaign. As the submarine was primarily an economic weapon, so was the aeroplane primarily a psychological weapon. The explosive bullet had virtually ended the Zeppelin raids in 1916, but from early in 1917 aeroplane raids on London grew in intensity until by May 1918 the air defenses were so thoroughly organized that the raiders thereafter abandoned London, as a target, for Paris. If the stoicism of the civil population took much of the sting from a weapon then in its infancy, the indirect effect was serious, interrupting business and checking output in industrial centres, as well as drawing off, for defense, many aircraft from the front. In reply the British formed an Independent Air Force, under Trenchard, which carried out extensive raids into Germany during the closing months of the war, with marked effect on the declining *morale* of the "home front."

To relate the action of aircraft in the military sphere is not possible, for it formed a thread running through and vitally influencing the whole course of operations, rather than a separate strategic feature. But a brief outline of the evolution of aircraft action in the field may help to complete the strategic picture. Military appreciation of air values was a slow growth, and the advocates of aircraft had an uphill struggle for recognition. Until the Italians used aircraft extensively against the Turks in Tripoli, 1911–1912, general military opinion was aptly represented by General Foch's comment when watching the *Circuit de l'Est:* "That is good sport, but for the army the aeroplane is worthless." Even in 1914 the proportion of military aircraft was puny, and their application more limited than with the Italians two years earlier.

In the first month of the war visual reconnaissance was the only rôle allotted and no provision was made for air combat or bombing. For the inadequacy of its air service and defective information the German army paid a heavy price during the invasion of France. But the Royal Flying Corps, although bringing only forty-four machines across the Channel, twice rendered invaluable service. One reconnaissance unmasked the initial attempt to outflank the British army at Mons, and another discovered Kluck's historic swerve towards the Marne.

In September the sphere of air coöperation was enlarged to embrace observation of targets for the artillery, communication being at first by colored lights and eventually by wireless telegraphy. In September also, photography from the air was tried, but its potential value was not recognized by General Headquarters until 1915. By March a special aeroplane camera was supplied, and air photography henceforth developed continuously, although long handicapped by dependence on captured German lenses for the large scale cameras. A fresh form of coöperation was tried in 1915, although not fully applied until 1916. This was the contact patrol, whereby commanders were informed of the situation of their own infantry during battle, and of threatened counter-attacks by the enemy.

The pursuit of this air coöperation by both sides simultaneously, as well as the desire to baffle the enemy's observation, had naturally led to air fighting, and this, in turn, to a struggle for supremacy in the air. Rifles and pistols were the only weapons available at the outset, so that air combat bore the appearance of an exhilarating and uncertain new form of game-shooting. Soon, however, light machine-guns were fitted, although the fighting rôle was mainly restricted to "pusher" type aeroplanes, as, on a tractor type, the propeller hindered fire in a forward direction. In May 1915, the Germans produced a new and fast Fokker fighting machine equipped with an interruptor gear which enabled the gun to fire through the orbit of the revolving propeller without risk of hitting the blades. The Fokkers inflicted heavy losses among the British machines, and, for a time, gained air superiority for the Germans.

The Allies replied to this menace not only by new machines but by new methods. The "fighters" were concentrated in special squadrons, instead of being distributed among all, and these squadrons were to seek out their opponents behind the opposing front, thus enabling their own reconnaissance and artillery machines to work undisturbed. This method of offensive patrols was successfully tried by the French at Verdun in February 1916, and developed by the British on the Somme, where for some weeks the Germans were almost driven out of the air. The offensive was also extended to the enemy's aerodromes — an extension which recalled the historic naval maxim that the enemy's coasts were the frontiers of Britain. Already, in October 1914, British naval aircraft operating on the Belgian coast had raided the Zeppelin sheds at Düsseldorf and Cologne, destroying one airship; another was destroyed next month in a raid from Belfort on Friedrichshafen.

Although the raids on aerodromes from 1916 onwards did not often succeed in inflicting serious material damage, they had a marked moral effect, for once pilots were safely back in their own aerodrome they were apt to feel that their share of risk was complete. An unforeseen addition was all the worse to bear when the nerve-tension had been relaxed, and when they were taken at a disadvantage on the ground.

The Allied air supremacy of 1916 was not long maintained.

The Germans challenged it with improved types of single-seater fighting machines and with the so-called "circus" system whereby special fighting squadrons were formed — under a picked leader who picked his own pilots — and were successively switched to any part of the front where the higher command desired air superiority to be gained. The most famous of these "circuses" were those of Boelcke and Baron von Richthofen.

By these means the Germans regained the upper hand early in 1917. But the Allies soon retorted with fresh machines and gradually won back a superiority in the air which was never lost again — although never so marked as in the summer of 1916. Because of the three-dimensional conditions of air warfare, a command of the air could never be attained in the sense that a command of the sea was possible, and the object became a superiority which should ensure a local and temporary command of the air when needed.

The year 1917 was marked also by an increasing development of the method of fighting and flying in formation, which tended to replace the Homeric combats of individual champions — whose mounting score of victims had been followed with the excitement that formerly awaited the victims of a Red Indian scalping expedition or the news of a test-match. Henceforth, knight-errantry yielded to tactics and air-fighting gradually assumed the more developed forms of warfare, although carried out on a different plane. By the end of the war an attack was often delivered by formations of fifty or sixty machines which manœuvred — the actual squadrons compact — with the aim of breaking up the enemy's formation.

Thus they became cavalry of the air, and the resemblance was heightened by another new form of air action, used with great effect in the later stages of the war. This was the attack on ground troops. So long as the rival armies were firmly embedded in trenches, air attack had small scope, although occasionally it came to the relief of hard-pressed packets of infantry. But when the British front broke, in March 1918, all the available fighter squadrons, French as well as British, were concentrated to strike at the advancing enemy. Their overhead counter-attacks during this crisis were an important factor in stemming the German onrush, and one that has been inadequately recognized by military historians. Still greater opportunities came when the enemy tide ebbed in the autumn. After the breaking of the Bulgarian, Turkish, and Austrian fronts alike, air attacks on the retreating columns both hastened and completed the break-up of the enemy armies.

Air attack on the communications, supply depots, ammunition dumps, and billets of the armies had been developed much earlier. The battle of Neuve-Chapelle, in March 1915, marked the first organized attempt to prevent the arrival of enemy reënforcements, and at Loos, in September, a more extended bombing plan was applied against the German railways. Results were small, however, owing to lack of experience, deficiency of equipment, and the want of machines to maintain the intensive bombardment essential for causing an effective stoppage. If a railway was damaged before the battle, it could be repaired in time for the passage of reënforcements; and, unless repairs were hindered by continuous bombing, supplies and ammunition would reach the enemy troops before they began to run short. The first lesson was learned and applied in the later battles of the war, when the bombing of communications played a regular part, but the second lesson was never fully applied, owing to lack of bombing aircraft. The very eagerness with which the armies had eventually embraced aircraft as immediate auxiliaries — for reconnaissance, artillery observation, and the protection of these duties — limited the supply of aircraft for rôles of indirect coöperation, and curtailed their exploitation of the bombing weapon.

Perhaps, also, their concentration on these auxiliaries blinded the armies to the greater possibilities of crippling their opponents by hunger. The Germans, especially, neglected opportunities of inflicting decisive injury — as a senior staff officer of the British Second Army revealed a few years ago. This army received the bulk of its supplies from Calais and Boulogne, and in front of these bases were held only three days' reserves of food and ammunition, apart from three days' supplies with the fighting troops. To serve the front

there were two double lines and one single; to meet the normal needs of the troops seventy-one trains a day were needed
— three-quarters of the total capacity of the three lines.   With
this narrow margin of safety, the blocking of one line would
have sufficed to dislocate the whole system, while the blocking
of more than one line would have brought a catastrophe.   To
cause such a block would have been the easier because outside
Calais there was a junction of two of the lines, and near St.
Omer two converged.   Moreover, a block at Arques, near St.
Omer, would even have cut off the troops from the three days'
reserves, which lay in depots farther back along the two lines
which converged at this point.   It is not difficult to picture
the situation which would have arisen if an effective and sustained bombing attack had been launched in April 1918, to
coincide with the German army's attack, when this area was
congested with British and French troops who were trying to
dam the breach in the front.

The Allied Commanders, also, on the western front, were
unwilling to spare sufficient aircraft for a real test of the effect
of bombing communications.   Yet, there was a significant
hint of its potency when on July 16, 1918, the bombing of
an ammunition train at Thionville station stopped all traffic
along this important section of the German communications
for forty-eight hours — the forty-eight hours before the Allied
counter-stroke on the Marne which turned the tide of the war.

At sea, the Germans, relying on their submarines, fortunately failed to explore the possibilities of air attacks on merchant shipping, or on the ports where that shipping had to
unload its freight.   And the Allies could not, as their enemy
had no shipping in use.   There was one fleeting glimpse of
such action; as early as August 12, 1915, a British seaplane,
launched from a seaplane carrier near the Dardanelles, gained
the distinction of being the first to torpedo a ship.   The most
valuable service rendered by naval aircraft during the war
was in anti-submarine patrolling and escorting convoys — a
purely protective rôle.

Not until late in the war was there any attempt on the Allied
side to attack the enemy's "home" front save for spasmodic

raids by a handful of British naval aircraft, as well as by the French. Nor, in the light of human nature, was independent air action likely to be developed so long as this new weapon was handled by and divided between the land and sea forces. The essential fusion between the two parts was delayed until April 1918, when the Royal Air Force was created. As a sequel, the Independent Air Force was formed in June, under Trenchard, who had been the dynamic leader of the British military air arm in France. In the few months that remained, the repeated and expanding raids of Trenchard's force accelerated the moral disintegration of Germany, and, by their moral effect at least, hampered the production of munitions in the Rhineland. Even so, the significance of this force was more in promise than fulfillment, for it was barely a quarter of its intended strength when the Armistice came. Similarly, the effect of the German air raids on England should be assessed in the light of the fact that the largest raid was carried out by less than forty bombers.

Propaganda. The beginning of 1918 witnessed the development and thorough organization of another psychological weapon, when Lord Northcliffe, who had been the head of the British War Mission in the United States, was appointed " Director of Propaganda in Enemy Countries," and for the first time the full scope of such a weapon was understood and exploited. Northcliffe found his best blade in President Wilson's speeches, which with idealism, if not with entire realism, unvaryingly distinguished between Germany's policy and the German people, and emphasized that the Allied policy was to liberate all people, including the Germans, from militarism. This blade, sharpened by the armorer, Colonel House, was trenchantly wielded by Northcliffe with the aim of severing the common ties which held together the enemy nations and their rulers. But these ties were stout enough to turn any blade until they had been frayed by military pressure. In July 1917 the effect of President Wilson's speeches, acting upon war-weariness and anti-militarism in Germany, produced a parliamentary revolt, and under Erzberger's management the Reichstag passed a peace resolution, which foreswore terri-

torial annexations. But the only effect was to break Bethmann-Hollweg, the unhappy rope in the tug-of-war between
the military and the political parties. The parliamentary
representatives of the German people were as helpless to withstand the iron will of the General Staff as was Imperial Austria,
now utterly sick of, and only anxious to abandon, the war
which she had provoked. These peace movements received
small practical response from the enemy democracies. For
President Wilson, as their spokesman, reiterated the declaration that they would negotiate no peace with military autocracy. His encouragement to the enemy peoples to throw off
this control was excellent in precept but vain in fact when
addressed to those who were so firmly manacled. They were
not Houdinis.

In January 1918 there was, indeed, a significant attempt at
popular revolt, when over a million German workers joined
in a general strike, but this was soon quenched and even forgotten in the fresh exhilaration of the great offensive. Only
when the military machine itself began to crumble could the
slaves of the machines free themselves from the grip, or propaganda help them in loosening it. Perhaps only then did an
active will to peace reënforce their mere passive weariness of
war. The inner strength of militant patriotism lies in the fact
that it is not merely a gag but a drug.

1917 — THE STRAIN

Scene I

THE HALT AND LAME OFFENSIVE — ARRAS, APRIL 1917

On April 9, 1917, the British armies in France entered upon what they had hoped was to be the final and decisive campaign of the World War. To the ordinary observer the day was a brilliant contrast to all previous offensives, but it proved yet another mirage in the military desert. This was perhaps inevitable before zero hour.

The Arras offensive had its roots deeply embedded in the Battles of the Somme, 1916. Its strategic conception sprang from the Somme, for, in conjunction with the other attacks — stillborn or prematurely deceased — planned for the spring of 1917, it was an effort to complete the overthrow of German power and man-power which it was believed that only the onset of winter had prevented on the Somme. Its strategic failure was the outcome partly of the situation produced by the Somme and partly of the inability of the Higher Command to forget the barren methods employed on the Somme. And the germ of the Arras plan dated from the time of the Somme.

For as early as June 1916 a plan known as the Blaireville project had been drawn up for a blow near Arras to take place as a supplement to the Somme offensive. Postponed because of the immense casualties on the Somme, which drew off all available forces to that human sump-pit, it was revived and extended in October as part of the spring plan. The gradual British advance eastwards on the Somme had left a German-held bulge between it and Arras — a bulge of which Gommecourt formed the westernmost point. This bulge seemed to offer the opportunity for a right- and left-hand blow on the respective sides, converging towards Cambrai. If successful this might not only cut off the German forces holding

the bulge, but create a gap too wide for the German reserves
to block, and so pave the way for an advance towards Valenciennes and against the enemy's line of communications and
retreat through the Belgian "trough."

On November 18, 1916, the Allied Commanders-in-Chief
met at Chantilly to discuss their plans for 1917, and the outcome was that early in February the British Fourth and
Fifth Armies should resume their Somme offensive on the
southern side of the Gommecourt bulge, while the Third Army
(Allenby) struck on the northern side from Arras. After
gaining Monchy-le-Preux, Allenby was to push southeast to
close the German lines of retreat along the Cojeul Valley, and,
if possible, the Sensée Valley also. In conjunction, the First
Army (Horne) was to attack mmediately north of the Third
and form a defensive flank, and the French to attack south
of the Somme. Three weeks later the main French blow was
to be launched in Champagne — an undue delay if the two
main blows were to react on each other.

But the whole scheme was dissolved by a combination of
French and German action. The French action took the form
of dismissing their Commander-in-Chief, Joffre, whose bubble
reputation had been pricked by the unconcealable evidence
of ill-preparedness at Verdun and, less justly, by the lack of
success on the Somme. He was replaced by Nivelle, the popular hero of the Verdun *ripostes*, whose appointment caused
a change in the plan for 1917 — in the sense of giving the French
a more spectacular rôle. In consequence the British had to
take over more of the front, while friction was created by the
dictatorial attitude of Nivelle towards his *vis-à-vis* and by the
intrigues of his staff to procure Haig's removal. But the worst
effect of the change was that it caused a delay in the Allied
offensive. And before it could begin the Germans had dis-
rupted its foundation — by a strategic withdrawal not merely
from the Gommecourt bulge, but from the whole of their old
and indented front between Arras and Soissons. An absurd
attempt was made to picture this as a British triumph and the
fruit, even if a little late in garnering, of the Somme offensive.
It was the fruit, but not in the sense which the British Com-

ARRAS, April, 1917.

Scale of Miles.

LENS

VIMY RIDGE

Thelus

Drocourt

Gavrelle

R. SCARPE

Fampoux

ARRAS

Railway Triangle   Feuchy

St Sauveur
Ronville

TELEGRAPH
HILL

Monchy
le Preux.

Cojeul R.

Wancourt   Guemappss

Heninel

Sensee R.

CAMBRAI
10 m.

Croisilles   Bullecourt

Queant

Original Front Line.
Hindenburg Line.
Drocourt-Quéant Switch.
Line on 24th April.

F.

mand suggested — for the method of petty limited attacks pursued throughout the autumn had given the Germans ample opportunity to dig, literally and metaphorically, a pit for their assailants. Straightening their front by retiring to the newly built Hindenburg Line, they left the British to follow laboriously through the intervening desert which, with immense thoroughness of destruction, they had created. By nullifying the Allies' preparations for attack, this withdrawal restricted them to the sectors on the two flanks of the evacuated area.

The main rôle in the British attack thus fell to the Third Army under Allenby. If he could break through the old defenses just to the north of where the Hindenburg Line ended, he would automatically take this line in flank and rear. But in anticipation of such a move the Germans had dug a switch line from Quéant, near the northern end of the Hindenburg Line, through Drocourt — covering the rear of the old defenses north of Arras. Thus Allenby's whole chance of strategic success depended on whether he could reach and break through this partially completed switch-line — some five miles behind the front system — before the German reserves could arrive in strength. Surprise was the only key which could open this gate. Because of this the real drama of the Arras offensive lies in the preliminary discussions and preparations even more than in the battle itself.

Surprise had been discarded in the Somme offensive, except on July 14 — indeed, this master-key of all the great captains of history had been rusting since the spring of 1915. The two means by which surprise could be obtained, and the Drocourt–Quéant switch reached in time, were by launching a mass of tanks or by a hurricane bombardment, brief but intense. The first means became impossible owing to the slowness in delivering new tanks after the discouraging reports made upon them in 1916, so that sixty old machines were all that could be scraped together. Allenby and his artillery adviser, Holland, were anxious to have the shortest possible bombardment, and originally proposed that it should last only forty-eight hours. If this, according to later standards, was more than forty hours too long, it was a tentative step in the direction of surprise. But the Higher Command was faithful to the theory of prolonged bombardment, and had a deep-rooted distrust of such an innovation. Nevertheless Allenby stood firm until General Headquarters hit upon the deft device of promoting his artillery adviser to another sphere and replacing him by one who shared their view. Then the plan of a five days' bombardment, preceded by three weeks of "wire-cutting," was adopted — to the doom of surprise and the abnegation of a break-through.

In smaller points Allenby still sought for surprise, notably in linking up the underground sewers and quarries of Arras, St. Sauveur, and Ronville, in order to shelter two divisions which were to pass underground and leapfrog through the leading divisions. Another feature of the plan was that, after the three assaulting corps of the Third Army had broken the enemy's first system of defense, the Cavalry Corps (Kavanagh) and XVIII Corps (Maxse) were to pass through in the centre between the human buttresses, and drive forward towards the switch line. Partly for concealment, the daring risk was taken of moving this pursuit force through the city of Arras, whose houses extended almost up to the front line. This plan, refreshingly ingenious, was vitiated, however, not only by the absence of initial surprise, but by the comparatively narrow front of the opening attack — about twelve miles. Thus the central bottle-neck was, in turn, so narrow that its end could be easily stopped. Ludendorff, in his Vilna offensive in the autumn of 1915, had revealed a better method — a dual penetration by two horns goring their way into the enemy's front, while through the wide gap between the horns the pursuit force unexpectedly issued.

A fundamental defect of the Arras plan, moreover, was the width of its base compared with its fighting front — the routes of supply and reënforcement all converging on Arras, with the result that the narrow mouth of this bottle-neck became utterly congested. When the initial attack failed to make the progress anticipated, this congestion was increased by the arrival of the cavalry in the forward area — although the experience of 1915 and 1916 had shown that such advance was futile unless and until a wide path had been swept clear of the enemy.

Yet, if the strategic object was practically forfeited before zero hour on April 9, the tactical success was at first a vivid and enheartening contrast to all previous British offensives. The new British gas-shell was most effective in paralyzing the defending artillery, for it not only compelled the gun crews to keep on their gas-masks for hours at a time, but, by killing off the horses like flies, prevented ammunition from being brought up. The attack was delivered by the VII, VI, and XVII Corps of the Third Army and the Canadian Corps of the First Army. On the extreme right, or south, lay Snow's VII Corps, with the 21st Division near Croisilles forming a pivot on which the rest of the Corps — the 14th, 30th, and 56th (1st London) Divisions — advanced. To their left lay Haldane's VI Corps, with the 3rd, 12th, and 15th Divisions attacking and the 37th Division waiting to leapfrog through and seize the key position of Monchy-le-Preux. The marshy valley of the Scarpe, the boundary between the VI Corps and its neighbors, separated the British right and left wings. North of the Scarpe the attack was entrusted to Fergusson's XVII Corps, composed of the 9th, 34th, and 51st Divisions, with the 4th to leapfrog through the 9th on the Corps' right. Furthest north of all, Byng's Canadian Corps was to assault the ill-omened Vimy Ridge, which had so long proved an impregnable barrier to the Allied forces. The capture of a large part of the ridge on April 9 gained all the greater *éclat* from the fame — or, to the Allies, ill-fame — which this ridge had acquired. The Canadians' feat was as finely prepared as it was executed. Yet it is but just to recognize that in one important condition the task was easier than further south, for the very fact of attacking uphill gave the attackers here better artillery observation and drier ground than those who had to traverse the sodden or marshy area near the Scarpe.

At 5.30 A.M. the assaulting infantry moved forward on the whole front, covered by a superbly timed creeping barrage, and in less than an hour almost the whole German first-line system was captured. North of the Scarpe the success continued, and after the leading divisions had gained their three successive objectives, the 4th Division passed through on the

Corps' right, and by seizing Fampoux breached the last German line in front of the Drocourt–Quéant switch. But south of the Scarpe the German resistance, first at the Railway Triangle and Telegraph Hill, then on the Wancourt–Feuchy line, — helped by machine-guns from Monchy-le-Preux Hill, — was so strong that it badly delayed, although it could not stop, the advance of the 12th and 15th Divisions. Thus the reserve 37th Division could not pass through that day, and behind them the cavalry had moved up, not only in vain, but to add to the congestion.

The results of the opening day had been greater and quicker, in both prisoners and progress, than in any previous offensive — yet they had extinguished the dim hope of a strategic break-through. A contributory factor was the misuse of the tanks. With only sixty machines available, it would have been wiser to concentrate them in aid of the vital effort to gain Monchy-le-Preux instead of spreading them over the front. The error was repeated in the next phase, whereas, if all available tanks had been concentrated on the south side of the salient formed by the first day's attack, they could have taken the German resistance in enfilade, and might have rolled it up.

So on April 10 the Third Army butted direct at a stiffening resistance, with its guns too far back to support the infantry. Not until the morning of April 11 did the arrival of four tanks help a battalion of the 37th Division to seize Monchy-le-Preux — driving in a wedge which was, however, too narrow and too late.

That same morning part of Gough's Fifth Army launched a converging assault from the south against the Hindenburg Line, in an attempt to relieve the pressure of German opposition to the Third Army. It was a desperate remedy for a despairing situation. For this army, after painfully toiling over the evacuated area, had been able neither to make the preparations nor to bring up the artillery necessary for a normal trench attack, far less an assault on the massive defenses of the Hindenburg Line. The difficulty led to a novel expedient, which contained the germ of the method which was

triumphantly successful later at Cambrai.   But instead of 381
tanks, as at Cambrai, only eleven could be gathered.   As
artillery support was deficient, this handful of tanks acted as
a mobile barrage and wire destroyer, leading the 4th Australian Division and 62nd Division against the Hindenburg
Line near Bullecourt.   And not only was this line stormed,
south of Bullecourt, but two tanks penetrated nearly a mile
beyond into Riencourt, clearing this village for the Australians
who pressed on their heels.   This astonishing little effort, however, was marred by the failure of the troops who had been
detailed to protect the right flank of the advance, and a counter-
attack from this direction captured the tanks and many
Australians, forcing the infantry back to their starting line.
With better security the gain might have been held, but the
British could hardly have done more, as the obstinate German
resistance at Heninel and Wancourt, to the right of the Third
Army, prevented any chance of the two armies joining hands.
Next morning a gallant assault by the 21st and 56th (1st
London) Divisions conquered these two bastions, but the
increasing intensity of German counter-attacks brought the
first and main phase of the offensive to a close on April 14.
If strategic success had been missed, 13,000 prisoners and 200
guns had been taken.

The next phase had little result to put in relief against the
depressing total of British casualties.   The French offensive
of April 16 on the Aisne, to which Arras had been the prelude, proved a worse downfall, shattering Nivelle's extravagant hopes and predictions, and burying his career in its ruins.
The British were not ready to resume their offensive until a
week later, and although Haig decided to continue "the full
pressure of the British offensive . . . in order to assist our
Allies," there was by then no French advance to assist.   On
April 23 and 24 Allenby pushed forward his line, at heavy
cost and against heavy pressure, to include Guemappe and
Gavrelle.   At a conference of the army commanders on April
30, Haig showed that he placed little faith in the possibility of
a further French offensive, but decided to continue his own attacks, "to move steadily forward up to a good defensive line."

Despite fruitless assaults and sacrifices on May 3 and 5, "bald-headed" assaults which showed more obstinacy than imagination or care, this line was not reached, and the offensive which had been prolonged to so bitter a conclusion was at last broken off. The British offensive centre of gravity was then transferred to the north — to open as brilliantly at Messines on June 7, and to fade out still more miserably in the swamps of Passchendaele in October.

1917 — THE STRAIN

Scene II

THE SIEGE-WAR MASTERPIECE — MESSINES

On June 7, 1917, took place a battle which on the morrow was hailed as a brilliant military achievement, and which to-day, unlike so many historically tarnished "masterpieces" of 1914–1918, stands out in even higher relief. For we appreciate now that the capture of the Messines Ridge by General Plumer's Second Army was almost the only true siege-warfare attack made throughout a siege-war. It was also one of the few attacks until late in 1918 in which the methods employed by the command completely fitted the facts of the situation.

But if to-day its abiding historic interest lies in its perfect suitability of method, at the time this was overshadowed, and rightly, by its value as a moral tonic. Perhaps this was almost too strong a stimulant to those not in direct charge of the operation, leading them to place too high hopes in the subsequent operations at Ypres, where the conditions were different and the methods also. But such a reflection does not dim the value of Messines, which came as a tonic badly needed after the depressing end of the spring offensive at Arras and on the Aisne.

While Pétain was striving to rally and rejuvenate the French army, Haig decided to transfer the weight of his attack to Flanders, and, as a preliminary step to his main action at Ypres, to fulfill his long-formed plan of securing the high ground about Messines and Wytschaete as a flank bastion to the Ypres advance. For, while in German possession, it gave the enemy complete observation of the British trenches and forward battery positions, enabled them to command the communications up to the Ypres salient, and to take in enfilade, or even reverse, the trench positions therein.

Preparations had been begun nearly a year before, although their real development dated from the winter. Thus, when Haig asked Plumer, on May 7, when he would be ready to deliver the Messines attack, Plumer was able to say, "A month from to-day" — and keep his promise exactly. The calm confidence of this businesslike statement betrays no sign of the anxiety suffered, nor does it do justice to the will-power demanded of Plumer in carrying through his purpose.

The key factor in the success was the simultaneous explosion of nineteen great mines, containing 600 tons of explosives and involving the tunneling of 8000 yards of gallery since January, in the face of active counter-mining by the enemy. A couple of months before the attack it was reported to Plumer that the Germans were within eighteen inches of the mine at Hill 60, and that the only thing to do was to blow it. Plumer was firm in his refusal, and equally staunch under the wearing strain of ominous rumors and reports throughout the following weeks. His justification came at 3.10 A.M. on June 7, when this mine went up along with eighteen others — only one out of twenty had been blown up by the Germans.

Another example of his will-power was in withstanding strong and insidious pressure from General Headquarters to change his artillery adviser. Before the Arras offensive the same thing had happened with the Third Army, and Allenby's artillery plan had been radically modified — to the loss of all hope of surprise — by the removal of his artillery adviser to another sphere and his replacement by one who gave a different opinion. But, before Messines, Plumer resisted all attempts at a change, and finally quelled them by saying flatly that as long as he was responsible he intended to have his own men. If Plumer could be strong in resisting expert advice at need, no commander was more keen to secure it from all sources, and none weighed it more carefully — as a foundation for his own decision. In Harington he had a Chief of his General Staff who blended intellect with sympathy, and their happy combination was a symbol of the coöperation which was diffused throughout the Second Army staff, and through them to the fighting troops.

Trust and receptiveness to ideas and criticisms were the keynotes of the Second Army. They were instanced in the schools and courses behind the front, where free questioning and criticism were encouraged, while an answer and a reason to any point raised were always forthcoming. They were also marked in the preparation of an attack. Where other high commanders were apt to lay down a series of objectives which their troops must gain, Plumer's method was to suggest certain provisional lines, and then to discuss them, and each fraction of them, with the corps and divisional commanders concerned, adjusting the several objectives to the local conditions and opinions until a final series was pieced together like a mosaic, on which all were agreed.

Further, the impartial common sense of his judgment was shown by the fact that, although he could oppose technical advice from General Headquarters when it conflicted with reality, he welcomed it when it coincided. The western front in 1914–1918 was preëminently an engineers' war, yet historians will be perplexed at the small part played by engineers in its direction, and the overweening influence of cavalry and infantry doctrine in the attempt to solve its problems. Messines, however, was in sharp contrast, for here the methods and the training were largely based on a manual, S. S. 155, compiled by the engineers from their special knowledge and experience of siege warfare.

For Messines was to be a strict siege operation, the capture of a fortified salient at the minimum cost of lives by the maximum substitution of mind (in preparation) and material (in execution) for human bodies. Mines, artillery, tanks, and gas all played their part. But a contrary wind curtailed most of the scheme of gas projection, and the effect of the mines and artillery was so overwhelming that the tanks were hardly needed. On the centre corps front alone, of about three miles, a total of 718 guns and howitzers, 192 trench mortars, and 198 machine-guns was concentrated. Thus the artillery strength here was approximately one gun to every seven yards of front, or 240 to the mile.

The fact that the attack would converge against a salient

increased its chances, but it complicated the staff, troop, and artillery organization of the attack. For the sectors of each attacking corps were of varying depths, and contracted more and more in width up to the final objective which was the chord of the arc forming the salient. As, however, it was a siege operation, without any attempt at exploitation or a break-through, it was easier to avoid the congestion which had occurred at Arras. And the problem was further simplified by the plan of so allotting sectors that five of the divisions had sectors of equal breadth from front to rear, while the four which filled the interstices had smaller tasks. Further, when the main ridge was captured, fresh troops were to leapfrog through to gain the final Oosttaverne line across the base of the salient.

Meticulous organization and forethought marked every stage of the preparation, and this was based on personal touch, — staff officers continually visiting the units and trenches, — not on paper reports and instructions. Another feature was the special intelligence scheme, whereby the information obtained from prisoners, ground and air observation and reconnaissance, photography, wireless interception, and sound ranging, was swiftly conveyed to an army centre, established for a fortnight at Locre Château, and then sifted and disseminated by summaries and maps.

The bombardment and wire-cutting began on May 21, were developed on May 28, and culminated in a seven days' intense bombardment, mingled with practice barrages to test the arrangements. The consequent forfeiture of surprise did not matter in the Messines stroke, a purely limited attack, in contrast to that at Arras, where it had been fatal to the hope of a break-through. For, although there was no surprise, there was surprise-effect, produced by the mines and the overwhelming fire, and this lasted long enough to gain the short-distanced objectives that had been set. The point, and the distinction between actual surprise and surprise-effect, are of significance to the theory of warfare.

Behind the barrage nine infantry divisions, with three more close up in reserve, were to advance to the assault. On the right (or south flank) was the II Anzac Corps (Godley) composed of the 3rd Australian, New Zealand, and 25th Divisions, with the 4th Australian Division behind. In the centre came the IX Corps (Hamilton-Gordon), the attack here being led by the 36th, 16th, and 19th Divisions, with the 11th in reserve. On the left was the X Corps (Morland), composed of the 41st, 47th, and 23rd Divisions, backed up by the 24th.

At 3.10 A.M. on June 7 the nineteen mines were blown, wrecking large portions of the Germans' front trenches. Simultaneously the barrage fell. When the débris and shock of the mines subsided, the infantry advanced, and within a few minutes the whole of the enemy's front line system was overrun, almost without opposition. Resistance stiffened as the penetration was deepened, but the training of the infantry and the efficiency of the barrage, based on the finest shades of calculation, enabled continuous progress to be made, and within three hours the whole crest of the ridge was secured.

The New Zealand Division had cleared the intricate fortifications of Messines itself — here the pace of the barrage was regulated to 100 yards in fifteen minutes instead of the general pace of 100 yards in three minutes. The garrisons of Wytschaete and the White Château held out for some time, but the first village was captured after a fierce struggle by troops of the 36th (Ulster) and 16th (Irish) Divisions in a combined effort — a feat of symbolical significance. Perhaps the most difficult sector was that of the 47th (2nd London) Division, which had not only to overcome the highly fortified position of the White Château, but had the Ypres-Comines canal as an oblique interruption across its line of advance. The Londoners, however, overcame both, and by 10 A.M. the objective of the first phase was reached along the whole attacking line. While it was being consolidated, over forty batteries were moved forward to support the next pounce.

At 3.10 P.M. the reserve divisions and tanks leapfrogged through, and within an hour almost the whole of the final objective was captured. Some 7000 prisoners had been taken, apart from dead and wounded, at a cost to the attacker of only 16,000 casualties. The success had been so complete

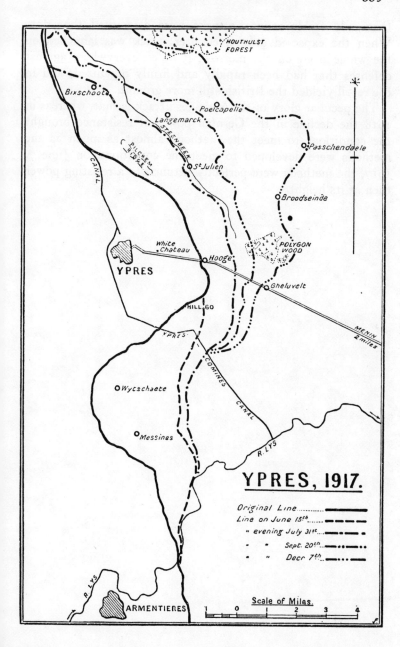

HOUTHULST FOREST

Bixschoote

Poelcapelle

Langemarck

STEENBEEK

CANAL

PILCKEM RIDGE

St Julien

Passchendaele

Broodseinde

White Chateau

Hooge

POLYGON WOOD

YPRES

HILL 60

Gheluvelt

YPRES

MENIN 2 miles

COMINES CANAL

Wytschaete

R. LYS

Messines

YPRES, 1917.

Original Line ....
Line on June 15th ....
"   evening July 31st ....
-   "   Sept. 20th ....
-   "   Dec. 7th ....

R. LYS

ARMENTIERES

Scale of Miles.

1   0   1   2   3   4

that only feeble counter-attacks were attempted that day. When the expected general counter-attack was launched on the whole front on the morrow, it failed everywhere against defenses that had been rapidly and firmly organized, and in the recoil yielded the British still more ground.

The peculiar glory of the Messines attack is that, whereas in 1918 the decline in the German power of resistance brought the conditions to meet the methods almost as much as the methods were developed to meet the conditions, on June 7, 1917, the methods were perfectly attuned to a resisting power then at its height.

1917 — THE STRAIN

SCENE III

THE "ROAD" TO PASSCHENDAELE

ON July 31, 1917, began what is termed the Third Battle of Ypres. And it is symbolical of its course and its issue that it is commonly spoken of by the title of "Passchendaele," which in reality was merely the last scene of the gloomiest drama in British military history. Although called the Third Battle, it was not a battle, but rather a campaign, with the fighting more defined than the purpose — of the nature so familiar in the military annals of Flanders, and the Low Countries generally. And, like its German forerunners of 1914 and 1915, it achieved little except loss — in which, again, it repeated the earlier history of this theatre of war. So fruitless in its results, so depressing in its direction, was this 1917 offensive, that "Passchendaele" has come to be, like "Walcheren" a century before, a synonym for military failure — a name black-bordered in the records of the British army. Even the inexhaustible powers of endurance and sacrifice shown by the combatants, or the improved executive leadership which did much in the later stages to minimize their sufferings, tend to be not merely overshadowed, but eclipsed in memory by the futility of the purpose and result.

What was the origin and what the object of "Third Ypres"? An offensive in this sector had formed part of Haig's original contribution to the Allied plan for 1917. Its actual inauguration had been postponed by the unfortunate turn of events elsewhere. When the ill-success of the opening offensive in the spring at Arras and in Champagne was followed by the threatened collapse of the French army as a fighting force, Haig's "first-aid" treatment was to allow the British offensive at Arras, by the Third Army, to continue for some weeks longer, with the general object of keeping the Germans occupied, and with the local object of reaching a good defensive line. When successive thrusts, against an enemy now fully warned and strengthened, failed to reach this line, Haig decided to transfer the main weight of this effort northward to Flanders, as he had originally intended. His loyalty to his Allies, and his acute sense of the common interest, inspired him to press on with an offensive policy, even though French coöperation was lacking. His remarks at the conference of the army commanders on April 30 show that in his own mind he had practically written off the French share as a bad debt on the balance-sheet of 1917.

It is right to emphasize that, in May, Haig's opinion of the policy to pursue was reënforced by the Prime Minister, who, having committed himself to the Nivelle gamble for victory, was equally ardent to continue the offensive. It is just, however, to recognize that on cooler reflection he subsequently tried in vain to check the policy which he had countenanced. For if the ominous condition of the French army, the crisis at sea caused by the submarine campaign, and the need to second the still possible Russian offensive combined to justify Haig's decision in May, the situation had radically changed before the main offensive was actually launched on July 31. In war all turns on the time factor. By July the French army, under Pétain's treatment, was recuperating, if still convalescent, the height of the submarine crisis was past, and the revolutionary paralysis of the Russian army was clear. Nevertheless, the plans of the British High Command were unchanged. The historian may consider that insufficient attention was given to the lessons of history, of recent experience, and of material facts in deciding both upon the principle of a major offensive and upon its site. The axis of the attack diverged from, instead of converging on, the German main communications, so that an advance could not vitally endanger the security of the enemy's position in France. Haig, curiously, was to adopt here the same *eccentric* direction of advance which a year later his advice prevented Foch and Pershing from taking on the other flank of the western front. Thus an advance on

the Belgian coast offered no wide strategic results, and for the
same reason it was hardly the best direction even as a means
of pinning and wearing down the enemy's strength on a profitable basis.   Moreover, the idea that Britain's salvation from
starvation depended on the capture of the submarine bases on
this coast has long since been exploded, for the main submarine
campaign was conducted from German ports.   In fairness,
however, one should add that this mistaken belief was impressed on Haig by the Admiralty.

Worse still, the Ypres offensive was doomed before it began
— by its own destruction of the intricate drainage system in
this part of Flanders.   The legend has been fostered that these
ill-famed "swamps of Passchendaele" were a piece of ill-luck
due to the heavy rain, a natural and therefore unavoidable hindrance that could not be foreseen.   In reality, before the
battle began, a memorandum was sent by Tank Corps Headquarters to General Headquarters pointing out that, if the
Ypres area and its drainage were destroyed by bombardment,
the battlefield would become a swamp.   This memorandum
was the result of information from the Belgian "Ponts et
Chaussées" and local investigation — although it would seem
that such vital facts might have been known and appreciated
long before.   The area had been reclaimed from marshland
by centuries of labor, and in consequence the farmers of the
district were under penalty to keep their dikes clear.   Land
used for pasture was such because it was subject to flooding
and too wet for cultivation.   In the disregard of this warning
is epitomized the main and inevitable cause of the barren
results of the "Passchendaele offensive."

Perhaps the very brilliance of the preliminary stroke at
Messines on June 7 had helped to raise unfounded expectations over what was in conception and purpose a totally
different operation.   Nearly two months passed before the
preparations for the main advance were completed, and during that interval the Germans had ample warning to prepare
counter-measures.   These comprised a new method of defense,
as suited to the waterlogged ground as the British offensive
methods were unsuited.   Instead of the old linear systems of

trenches they developed a system of disconnected strong points and concrete pill-boxes, distributed in great depth, whereby the ground was held as much as possible by machine-guns and as little as possible by men. While the forward positions were lightly occupied, the reserves thus saved were concentrated in rear for prompt counter-attack, to eject the British troops from the positions they had arduously gained. And the further the British advanced the more highly developed, naturally, did they find the system. Moreover, by the introduction of mustard gas the Germans scored a further trick, interfering seriously with the British artillery and con-centration areas.

Thus, when the fully expected blow fell, the Crown Prince Rupprecht was so far freed from his usual pessimism as to record in his diary, "My mind is quite at rest about the attack, as we have never disposed of such strong reserves, so well trained for their part, as on the front attacked." This actual front was held by the troops of the German Fourth Army (Sixt von Arnim).

The main rôle in the British attack was given to Gough's Fifth Army, with one corps of the Second Army playing a subsidiary part on the extreme right. On July 22 the bom-bardment opened, by 2300 guns, to continue for ten days, until at 3.50 A.M. on July 31 the infantry advanced on a fifteen-mile front to the accompaniment of torrential rain. On the left substantial progress was made, Bixschoote, St. Julien, and the Pilckem ridge being gained, and the line of the Steenbeek reached. But in the more vital sector round the Menin road the attack was repulsed. And the rain con-tinued day after day, postponing the next major attempt, and hastening the conversion of the undrainable ground into a swamp, in which first the tanks and ere long even the infantry were bogged.

The second blow, on August 16, was a diminished replica of the first in its results. The left wing was again advanced across the shallow depression formed by the little valley of the Steenbeek and past the ruins of what had been Langemarck. But on the right, where alone an advance might have a strategic effect, a heavy price was paid for nought, and even the tally of prisoners shrank to a mere two thousand. Nor did men feel that the enemy's skillful resistance and the mud were the sole explanation of their fruitless sacrifice. Complaints against the direction and staff work in Gough's army were general and bitter, and their justness seemed to receive recognition when Haig extended the Second Army's front northward to include the Menin road sector, and thereby entrusted to Plumer the direction of the main advance towards the ridge east of Ypres. It was a thankless task at the best, for the experience of war attested the futility of pressing on in places where failure had already become established, and it seemed heavy odds that the laurels earned by Messines must become submerged in the swamps beyond Ypres.

Yet, in the outcome, the reputation of Plumer and the Second Army Staff, headed by Harington, was enhanced — less because of what was achieved in scale than because so much more was achieved than could reasonably have been expected in so hopeless a venture. The definition of genius as "an infinite capacity for taking pains" had both an example and a confirmation in the Plumer-Harington combination. Applying, as at Messines, siege-warfare methods to a task that was more a siege than a battle, their plan was that of a series of shallow advances, not pressed beyond the point where the artillery support was outrun, and leaving both the infantry fresh enough and the artillery close enough to deal with the inevitable counter-attacks.

Bad weather and the need for preparation delayed the resumption of the offensive until September 20, but that morning the Second Army attack, on a four-mile front, achieved success in the area of previous failure — on either side of the Menin road. Fractions of six divisions, the 19th, 39th, 41st, 23rd, 1st and 2nd Australian (infantry were kept down to the minimum with artillery at the maximum), advanced at 5.40 A.M. By 6.15 A.M. the first objective was gained almost unopposed, and, with the exception of one or two strong points, the third and last objective was gained soon after midday, and the counter-attacks were repulsed by fire. A fresh spring on

September 26 and another on October 4 — the last a larger one on a six-mile front, by troops of the 37th, 5th, 21st, and 7th Divisions, the 1st, 2nd, and 3rd Australian Divisions, and the New Zealand Division — gave the British possession of the main ridge east of Ypres, with Gheluvelt, Polygon Wood, and Broodseinde, despite torrents of rain, which made the battle-field a worse morass than ever. And on each occasion the majority of the counter-attacks had broken down under fire, a result which owed much to the good observation work of the Royal Flying Corps and the quick response of the artillery. Some 10,000 prisoners were swallowed in the three bites, and this widening maw frightened the enemy into modifying his elastic tactics and strengthening his forward troops — to their increased loss under the British artillery fire.

These attacks had at least done something to restore prestige, if they could have little strategic effect on a campaign which was foredoomed, and in which both the time and the scope for extensive penetration had long since vanished. Unhappily, the Higher Command decided to continue the pointless offensive during the few remaining weeks before the winter, and thereby used up reserves which might have saved the belated experiment of Cambrai from bankruptcy. For, having wasted the summer and his strength in the mud, where tanks foundered and infantry floundered, Haig turned in November to dry ground — where a decisive success went begging for lack of reserves.

At Ypres, minor attacks on October 9 and 12 advanced the line a trifle, and then, after an interval, a combined attack by the Fifth Army and the French was tried, with small result, on October 22. On October 26, the Second Army, in torrents of rain as usual, made a fresh effort, which was less successful than before, owing to the exhaustion caused by pushing forward over a morass and to the fact that the mud not only got into and jammed rifles and machine-guns but nullified the effect of the shell-bursts. The attackers' troubles were augmented by the enemy's increasing use of mustard gas, and by his renewed adoption of his tactics of holding the bulk of his troops well back for a counter-attack. Thus when, on November 4, a sudden advance by the 1st Division and 2nd Canadian Division gained the empty satisfaction of occupying the site of Passchendaele village, the official curtain was at last rung down on the pitiful tragedy of "Third Ypres." It was the long overdue close of a campaign which had brought the British armies to the verge of exhaustion, one in which had been enacted the most dolorous scenes in British military history, and for which the only justification evoked the reply that, in order to absorb the enemy's attention and forces, Haig chose the spot most difficult for himself and least vital to his enemy. Intending to absorb the enemy's reserves, his own were absorbed.

Perhaps the most damning comment on the plan which plunged the British army in this bath of mud and blood is contained in an incidental revelation of the remorse of one who was largely responsible for it. This highly placed officer from General Headquarters was on his first visit to the battle front — at the end of the four months' battle. Growing increasingly uneasy as the car approached the swamp-like edges of the battle area, he eventually burst into tears, crying, "Good God, did we really send men to fight in that?" To which his companion replied that the ground was far worse ahead. If the exclamation was a credit to his heart it revealed on what a foundation of delusion and inexcusable ignorance his indomitable "offensiveness" had been based.

The only relief to this sombre review is that a bare fortnight later was enacted, on a different stage, and with a technique suggested in early August, a "curtain-raiser" which was to be developed into the glorious drama of autumn 1918.

1917 — THE STRAIN

SCENE IV

THE TANK SURPRISE AT CAMBRAI

ON November 19, 1917, the German troops in front of Cambrai were contemplating with undisturbed minds the apparent normality and comparative tranquillity of the British lines opposite them; contrasting their own security in the massively fortified and comfortable trenches of the Hindenburg Line with the unsavory lot of their comrades struggling in the shell-churned mud-holes of the Ypres salient; indulging in self-congratulation not only on the impregnability of their famous line, but on the pertinacity of the unteachable English who had so engulfed themselves at Ypres that there could surely be no danger of any other assault elsewhere before winter came.

On November 20, 381 tanks, followed by a relatively small proportion of infantry, rolled forward in the half-light upon the astonished Germans without even the courtesy of a preliminary bombardment to announce their coming. Always good hosts, the Germans might well feel aggrieved at the omission of a warning which had customarily given them four or five days' notice to prepare a suitable reception.

On November 21 the bells of London rang out in joyous acclaim of a triumphant success that seemed a foretaste of victory, perhaps at no distant date. And Ludendorff, back at the German Supreme Command, was hurriedly preparing emergency instructions for a general retreat. Both the bells and Ludendorff were premature — although prophetic — by some nine months.

For on November 30 came a German retort so full of menace that the public thereafter showed a strong distaste for premature celebrations. Applause changed to reproaches; the cause of the disasters was the subject of inquiry; and in public opinion the name of Cambrai came to be associated more with the ultimate reverse than with the initial success. Actually, however, the fuller knowledge now available suggests that the black date in the national calendar should be the twentieth, and not the thirtieth, of November. Yet gloomy as is this page of World War history, it forms one of the most striking examples of the proverb that "every cloud has a silver lining." If November 20, 1917, is in itself a tragedy of errors, its eventual effect on the fortunes of the Allies was beneficent — pointing and paving the way to the victorious method of 1918, and, to take a still longer view, it is seen to be one of the landmarks in the history of warfare, the dawn of a new epoch. Thus we may say that the joy-bells, if immediately wrong, were ultimately right.

These eleven days form perhaps the most dramatic of all episodes in the World War. Yet, sensational as was their course in its abrupt change of fortune, the real story of Cambrai lies beneath the surface. First is the question of its origins, of paramount importance because it ushered in a new cycle of warfare. Its initial source is to be found nearly two years, and its immediate source nearly four months, earlier.

The guiding idea of those who sponsored the tank in infancy had been to release it unexpectedly in a large concentration, and this idea had, as we have seen, not only been formulated but worked out in detail as early as February 1916 — seven months before a driblet of tanks were launched on the Somme under conditions which violated all the essentials therein laid down. Fortunately, in 1917, the headquarters of the Tank Corps in France, although unlike General Headquarters they had not seen this memorandum, had come by experience to similar ideas. Further, the eternal yet too often underrated principle of surprise was deeply rooted in their minds, and thus when insight apprised them in the very first days of Third Ypres — the Passchendaele offensive — that the "mudlark" was futile, an alternative project was quick to blossom.

The chief General Staff Officer, Colonel Fuller, on August 3, 1917, drew up a plan for a great tank raid in a more suitable sector. In the preface to it this significant example of prevision may be read: "From a tank point of view the Third Battle of Ypres may be considered dead.   To go on using tanks in the present conditions will not only lead to good machines and better personnel being thrown away, but also to a loss of *morale* in the infantry and tank crews, through constant failure. From an infantry point of view, the Third Battle of Ypres may be considered comatose.   It can only be continued at colossal loss and little gain."

Then came the alternative proposal: "In order to restore British prestige and strike a theatrical blow against Germany before the winter, it is suggested that preparations be at once set on foot to take St. Quentin."   It was further pointed out that the operation was strategically a sound one as a preparatory step to an advance towards Le Cateau, and then Valenciennes, the following year.   Discussion of this project brought out the objection that it required a combined British and French operation, which might lack the simplicity and smooth working essential for the novel method to succeed. Therefore, on August 4, a second project was framed, for a tank raid south of Cambrai.   The word "raid" should be stressed, for, as originally conceived, the object was "to destroy the enemy's personnel and guns, to demoralize and disorganize him, and not to capture ground."   As the preliminary notes stated: "The duration of the raid must be short — eight to twelve hours — so that little or no concentration of the enemy may be effected for counter-attack." Had this been followed there would have been no need to lament the thirtieth of November.   "The whole operation may be summed up as 'advance, hit, retire.'   Big raids of this description will not only reduce the enemy's fighting power, but will reduce his initiative with reference to any big battle which at the time may be in progress."   For this raid a force of three tank brigades of two battalions each, and "one, or better, two, divisions of infantry or cavalry," with extra artillery, was suggested, operating on an 8000-yard front. The object, as proposed, was "to raid the reëntrant formed by the L'Escaut–St. Quentin Canal between Ribecourt-Crevecœur-Banteux."   The raiding force was to be divided into three groups, the main one to scour the country in this canal-enclosed pocket, while smaller groups formed offensive flanks on each side to protect the main operation. "The essence of the entire operation is surprise and rapidity of movement. Three hours after zero the retirement might well begin, the tanks and aeroplanes operating as a rearguard to the dismounted cavalry retiring with their prisoners."

The proposed sector lay in the area of the Third Army, under General Sir Julian Byng, and on August 5 the detailed project was taken informally to him by one of the Tank Corps brigadiers. Byng was receptive to the idea, although inclined to expand it from a raid into a break-through attack to gain Cambrai. Next day he went to General Headquarters, saw Haig, and suggested a surprise attack with tanks at Cambrai in September. The Commander-in-Chief was favorable, but his Chief of Staff, General Kiggell offered strong objections on the ground that the army could not win a decisive battle in two places at once, and should rather concentrate every possible man in the Ypres sector — which, incidentally, he never visited until the campaign was over. Thus the enlarged idea helped to postpone the raid, as the refusal to recognize reality at Ypres postponed the attack at Cambrai until too late for decisive results to be possible.

The historian, while respecting Kiggell's emphasis on the principle of concentration, may doubt whether Ypres was a suitable site for the fulfillment of this principle, and may also hold that distraction of the enemy's force has ever been an essential complement to concentration — of one's own effort.

Kiggell's objections sufficed to dissuade Haig, who still valued the tank as only "a minor factor.' Thus the Cambrai project was postponed indefinitely, while the High Command persevered with their hopeless efforts in the Passchendaele swamps. But neither Byng nor the Tank Corps were willing to let the idea drop, and certain opinions at General Headquarters were in accord, so that, as the Ypres offensive became a more palpable failure, a readier ear was lent to an alternative which promised to redeem British prestige. Finally, in mid-October, the Cambrai plan was sanctioned, and fixed for

November 20. But now the situation had changed for the worse, for, if the plan were crowned with success, that success must be barren for want of reserves to reap the harvest. The reapers were engulfed at Passchendaele.

It is just to recognize that if General Headquarters had missed the opportunity, General Headquarters had now perhaps a surer appreciation than the Third Army Command of the limitations imposed by their lack of means. Kiggell urged that Bourlon Hill merely should be the first objective, followed by a lateral exploitation northward, and Haig put a time-limit on the operation. But the Third Army orders were more ambitious in scope and objectives, despite the fact that all their available infantry divisions and tanks were being thrown into the initial break-through effort.

Byng's plan was (1) to break the German defensive system, the famous Hindenburg Line, in the neck between the Canal de L'Escaut and the Canal du Nord; (2) to seize Cambrai, Bourlon Wood, and the passage over the River Sensée; (3) to cut off the Germans in the area south of the Sensée and west of the Canal du Nord; and (4) to exploit the success towards Valenciennes. The force allotted for this ambitious plan comprised the III (Pulteney) and IV (Woollcombe) Corps, each of three infantry divisions, the Cavalry Corps (Kavanagh) of two divisions, a total of 381 fighting tanks, and roughly 1000 guns. Thus of the original project only the fundamental idea, the tank method, and the locality remained. Otherwise there were marked alterations, and in these lay the germ of disaster. The raid had been transformed into a large-scale offensive, with far-reaching aims. Instead of securing a "pocket" and withdrawing, an organized advance was to be made up a narrow "lane," bounded by two canals. A protection to a raid, these became a danger to such an attack, circumscribing the action of the tanks and preventing the formation of tank offensive flanks. Otherwise the ground was good, mostly rolling downland, excellent for tank movement; it was marked by two features, the Flesquières-Havrincourt ridge and Bourlon Hill.

The fundamental weakness of the general plan, however,

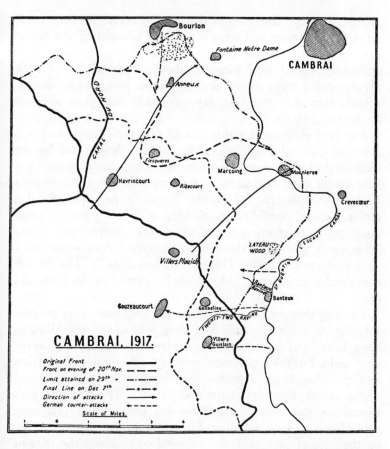

CAMBRAI, 1917.

Original Front
Front on evening of 20ᵗʰ Nov. — — —
Limit attained on 29ᵗʰ " —·—·—·
Final Line on Dec 7ᵗʰ —+—+—
Direction of attacks →
German counter-attacks ←—————

Scale of Miles.

was not topographical, but the complete lack of reserves, unless the two cavalry divisions can be considered such — and the futility of so regarding them was amply shown in their fresh inability, in face of modern weapons, to influence the action. The six divisions employed in the initial attack were all that the Third Army Commander had at his disposal — for a plan that visualized a penetration beyond Cambrai to Valenciennes! It is extremely difficult to understand what was in mind as to the future, for without reserves complete success could only mean the creation of an excessively deep and narrow salient, requiring scores of divisions to hold it. It is true that the Guards and one or two other divisions could be made available, and were ultimately brought to the scene, but they were too far away for prompt intervention. The situation, indeed, had some reminder of Loos. The French also moved a corps to the Senlis-Péronne area just before the attack, but after the first day were told that they were no longer required!

The best comment on this lack of reserves is contained in a story of General Franchet d'Esperey, which one has on the authority of the officer to whom the words were spoken. A long motor ride, in search of information, brought him to a British headquarters at Albert. Entering, he interrogated a senior General Staff Officer, flinging at him a string of crisp questions as to the progress of the attack, its frontage, depth. Then came the final, the vital question: "And where were your reserves?" "Mon Général, we had none." The French commander exclaimed, "Mon Dieu!" turned on his heel, and fled.

Turning now to the tank plan, the problems were to gain surprise, to cross the wide and deep obstacle of the Hindenburg Line, and to ensure coöperation between the infantry and tanks for their common security. Careful organization and the absence of a preliminary bombardment contributed to the accomplishment of the first object. The difficulty presented by the Hindenburg Line was overcome by devising super-fascines, huge bundles of brushwood, which were carried on the nose of each tank and released on reaching the edge of the Hindenburg trenches; the tanks, working in sections of three, had thus the power to cross three successive obstacles. Thirdly, a strictly drill attack was worked out and practised by which in each section an advanced-guard tank moved about 100 yards ahead of the two main-body tanks, keeping down the enemy's fire and protecting the main body as they led the infantry forward. The infantry, moving in flexible file formations, followed immediately behind the main-body tanks. While the tanks cleared a way for them through the deep belts of enemy wire and subdued the hostile machine-gun fire, the infantry acted as "moppers-up" to the tanks and were also ready to protect them from the enemy's guns at close quarters. The one fault of the tank plan was that, against expert advice, the tanks attacked on the whole frontage instead of against selected tactical points, with the result that no tank reserves was kept for use in the later stages.

The preparations for the battle were made with great skill and secrecy, while, to mislead the enemy as to the scale and frontage of the attack, gas and smoke attacks, dummy attacks with dummy tanks, raids and feints, were carried out on a wide front both north and south of the real sector of attack.

Nevertheless, one man nearly undid the secrecy of a multitude. A prisoner from an Irish regiment gave information of the coming attack, and of the concentration of tanks, but fortunately he was not believed and the German Army Commander, General von der Marwitz, reported on the eighteenth that there was no likelihood of an attack. But on the nineteenth a British telephone message, "Tuesday Flanders," was overheard near Bullecourt, and, as it sounded like a combined date and code-word, quickened German suspicions. That night the troops were ordered to be especially alert, and Marwitz hastily utilized a division, just detraining from Russia, to strengthen his defenses. But if the Germans now anticipated an attack, they also expected the usual preliminary bombardment — and its absence assured the British attack the essential surprise-effect. That effect was accentuated by an early morning mist, as in almost all the successful thrusts of the war.

At 6.20 A.M. on November 20 the tanks and infantry moved forward to the attack on roughly a six-mile front, and gained a demoralizing initial success at all points save in the left centre in front of Flesquières. The main cause of this one serious check was that the commander of the 51st Division, Harper, preferred a method of his own instead of conforming to the formations devised by the Tank Corps, and adopted in all the other divisions. His advance tanks were called "rovers," and went much further ahead, and the infantry formations were not as well fitted for close coöperation with tanks as those laid down. The separation seems to have been inspired by his expressed feeling that the whole Cambrai plan was "a fantastic and most unmilitary scheme" — when on the staff of General Headquarters he had resisted the development of machine-guns, and now was equally skeptical of tanks. The result was that the infantry were too far behind the tanks, lost the gaps in the wire, and were stopped by machine-gun fire. An officer who examined the battlefield afterwards could only find three small heaps of machine-gun cartridge cases, from which it would appear that a handful of machine-guns held up a whole division — a fact which sheds a striking light on the future of infantry action in open country. The loss of touch between the infantry and tanks lay also at the root of the losses which befell the tanks when they came over the ridge and under the close fire of several German batteries, for infantry accompanying them could have picked off the gunners. Here occurred the famous incident of the solitary German artillery officer who was reputed to have "knocked-out" sixteen tanks single-handed. It must go into the catalogue of historic legends, for only five derelict tanks were to be seen at this point after the attack had moved on, and an intelligence officer who examined the ground found marks which showed clearly that three batteries had been in position there to engage the tanks. It is possible that all save one gun, and one gunner, had been silenced, as was claimed, but impressions in the heat of battle are sometimes misleading. The feat has, however, an ironical significance in the fact that it was blazoned to the world by the British General Headquarters. The incentive of a mention in dispatches was not accorded to enemy feats performed at the expense of the infantry or cavalry.

The effect of this battlefield incident has also been magnified. On the right the 12th, 20th, and 6th Divisions secured their objectives rapidly, though the 12th had severe fighting at Lateau Wood. The 20th Division passed through and captured Masnières and Marcoing, securing the passage of the canal at both and even the bridge intact at the latter. On the left of the 51st the 62nd Division made a brilliant advance, advancing by nightfall as far as Anneux, over two miles in the rear of Flesquières. The Flesquières resistance was thus only an islet, cut off and overlapped by the waves which swept round its flanks and on to Marcoing, Anneux, and even to the edge of Bourlon Wood. A penetration of five miles had been made — the equivalent of months of heavy fighting and heavier losses on the Somme and at the Third Battle of Ypres. Decisive success was within the grasp of the British forces, the enemy's three main lines of defense had been overrun, only a half-finished line and the open country lay beyond. But the original divisions and the tank crews were exhausted, and apart from one squadron of the Canadian Fort Garry Horse the two cavalry divisions could contribute nothing toward fulfilling their rôle of exploitation.

On November 21 local reserves made some further progress. Flesquières was evacuated by its surviving defenders in the early hours, and after dawn the 51st and 62nd Divisions pressed rapidly on, clearing the German salient formed by this resistance on the first day and carrying the tide of the British advance as far as Fontaine-Notre Dame, one and a half miles beyond the high-water mark of November 20. But on the right little ground was gained — a fresh German division had arrived just in time to occupy the rear line of defense early on the twentieth.

Haig's time-limit of forty-eight hours had expired, but owing to the menace of the uncaptured Bourlon Hill to the new British position, as well as the hope of an enemy withdrawal and the desire to relieve the enemy pressure on Italy, he decided to continue the offensive and, somewhat belatedly, placed a few fresh divisions at the disposal of the Third Army. But the Tank Corps, the essential cause of the early success that had apparently surprised the British as much as the German Command, was tired out, men and machines — all had been staked on the first throw.

The fresh attacks met with more failure than success against an enemy now braced to meet the danger. On November 22 the Germans recaptured Fontaine-Notre Dame; on the twenty-third, the 40th Division with tanks captured the whole of Bourlon Wood, but the attempts on Bourlon village and Fontaine-Notre Dame failed. Bitter and fluctuating fighting

followed; both villages were won, and lost again. And meanwhile the Germans, with prompt initiative and consummate
skill, were preparing a deadly counter-blast. Unfortunately
there seems to have been a disposition in the superior command,
with certain exceptions, to discredit the numerous warning
signs of the gathering storm, and even to find amusement in
the anxiety displayed by those whose clearer vision was soon
to be attested. This attitude was apparently due to over-
confidence — partly induced by the easy success of November
20, and partly due to a belief that the Passchendaele offensive
had absorbed all the enemy's reserves. The effect of Passchendaele, indeed, was always overrated.

In contrast, General Snow, commanding the VII Corps on
the southern flank of the wedge driven into the German front,
had forecast both the place and the date of the counter-stroke
nearly a week before. His subordinate commanders, particularly in the 55th Division (Jeudwine), which adjoined the
III Corps, had reported a host of corroborative evidence —
that the enemy artillery were registering on spots never bombarded before, that German aircraft were flying over the lines
in large numbers, and that the British reconnaissance machines
were "shelled off" certain areas where the enemy could concentrate under cover. Late on November 29 the 55th Division
was so convinced of the imminent menace that Jeudwine asked
that the neighboring III Corps might put down a counter-
preparation with "heavies" on the Banteux Ravine just before
daylight next morning, but his request was not met.

And next morning the Germans repaid the tank surprise by
one which was similar in principle if different in method.
Unheralded by any long artillery preparation, a short, hurricane bombardment with gas and smoke shell paved the way
for the infiltrating advance of the German infantry — the
prototype of the German offensive method of spring, 1918, as
the British attack had been the prototype of the Allied offensive method of summer and autumn, 1918. Emerging from
the sheltered assembly position of Banteux and Twenty-Two
Ravines at the very moment when the unfulfilled counter-
preparation would have opened, the German stream trickled

through the weak points in the British line; then, expanding into a broad torrent which submerged the villages of Gonnelieu and Villers Guislain, swept over gun positions and headquarters, and surged forward to Gouzeaucourt. The menace of disaster was immeasurable, but, fortunately, the complementary attacks on the north of the salient, round Bourlon Wood, were brought to a standstill, and the emergency declined with the recapture of Gouzeaucourt by the superb counter-attack of the Guards' Division and a later effort of the 2nd Tank Brigade. For a time, indeed, there was a chance to "redouble" and score heavily off the Germans, disordered by this success and hampered by their narrow penetration. But rejecting Snow's plea for a flank riposte by the cavalry, the Army Commander directed his cavalry head-on against the Germans, and they were soon held up. Thus the invaders were able to consolidate their hold and even to resume their erosion of the British position. During the next few days continued German progress, especially towards Villers Plouich, and British lack of reserves rendered the British position in the Masnières-Bourlon salient so precarious that the greater part of the original gains had to be evacuated. A sombre sunset after a brilliant sunrise.

One shadow which still lingers is that undeservedly thrown on the regimental officers and men by superior officers anxious to exculpate themselves. The official court of inquiry pinned the blame on the troops, ascribing the surprise to their negligence and also asserting, contrary to facts, that they had failed to send up S.O.S. flares. Even Byng declared, "I attribute the reason for the local success on the part of the enemy to one cause and one alone — namely, lack of training on the part of junior officers and N.C.O.'s and men." Haig, however, who had been kept in the dark as to the warnings, was an exception to the "general" rule. In sending his report home, he generously assumed the whole responsibility — although he also sent home several of the subordinate commanders.

It is thus due for history to record, from the records, that many of the junior leaders were acutely alive to the danger and gave vain warnings to their superiors. And as for their resistance, it was more than anyone had a right to expect of troops who had been kept in action continuously since their attack on November 20. For military history, indeed, the lesson of Cambrai is that the welcome renaissance of the essential principle of surprise was offset by a fundamental breach of the principle of economy of force — both in adjusting the end to the means and in appreciating the capacity and limits of human endurance.

1917 — THE STRAIN

Scene V

"CAPORETTO"

In the chill and sodden gloom of an autumn morning amid the mist-wreathed peaks of the Julian Alps came a rumbling. Before its echoes finally subsided, the Allied cause had been shaken to its foundations. The first rumors of disaster, which were far from exaggerating the reality, came like a thunderclap to the Allied peoples, if not to all their leaders, for 1917 hitherto had seen the Allies on the offensive in all theatres.

The year had begun with the expectation of a sure progress towards victory, of a vast combined offensive culminating in the overthrow of the Central Powers, and if the mirage of early victory had been slowly fading before the evidence of stubborn resistance and heavy losses, the public were still unprepared for a definite change of rôle from attack to defense. More especially was this unexpected in Italy, for while there was obvious ground for qualms over Russia, the Italians had been attacking during August and September, and the cables had given the impression that the tide of battle was flowing strongly in their favor. And for once, in a war when the output of fiction was greater than that of fact, these reports were correct.

If the gain in ground was small, the moral and material effect on the already war-rotted Austrians was large, and, as Ludendorff records, "the responsible military and political authorities of the dual monarchy were convinced that they would not be able to stand a continuation of the battle and a twelfth attack on the Isonzo." Thus "in the middle of September it became necessary to decide for the attack on Italy in order to prevent the collapse of Austria-Hungary." So urgent was the need that Ludendorff was forced to abandon his preparations for the offensive in Moldavia, which he had intended as the *coup de grâce* to Russia's crumbling resistance. Even so, where could he raise sufficient troops for converting the Austrian defensive into an effective offensive ? The British pressure at Passchendaele and the mere length of his immense fronts in France and Russia absorbed his resources until he could force peace on Russia. All he could spare was his slender general reserve of six divisions, which had already been his instrument in countering the Kerenski offensive — Russia's final flicker — and in the coup which captured Riga. His adviser in the strategic design of operations, Major Wetzell, was, however, of the opinion that the application of even this small force at a "soft" spot, such as the sector between Flitsch and Canale, would suffice to lame if not to break the Italian menace.

The result proved him right — the trouble was that it unduly exceeded the most sanguine expectations. And it was due to the fact that it was expanded to a more ambitious plan — without increase of means — than was originally intended in the "germ" scheme, which Waldstätten, of the Austrian General Staff, had brought to the German Command on August 29. This original scheme was for a break-through at Tolmino, followed merely by rolling up the Isonzo front. Caporetto and Cambrai were to have a curious kinship.

Ludendorff sent General Krafft von Delmensingen on a special mission to reconnoitre the ground and report on the scheme. Krafft had led the Alpine Corps in the Rumanian campaign, and was thus an expert in mountain warfare. He found that the Austrians had managed to retain a small bridgehead on the west bank of the Isonzo at Tolmino, and this afforded a jumping-off point for the projected attack. Guns were got up mostly by hand and at night; the infantry came up by seven night marches, taking no vehicles, but carrying their ammunition, equipment, and supplies on the men or on pack animals. Thus the twelve assault divisions and 300 batteries concentrated undiscovered by the Italians, owing partly to able precautions, partly to the country, and partly to the inadequate air reconnaissances of the enemy.

What of the Italians? The Commander-in-Chief, Cadorna, was undoubtedly a man of more than ordinary ability, but, like certain other famous commanders, his intellectual power was offset by his lack of touch with and understanding of the fighting troops. With such men, also, their mental remoteness is often accentuated by the natural isolation in which those in high military position are placed. Considering the comparatively slender weight of the attack, he had enough men and guns to withstand it successfully, but his distribution of them was unsuited to the conditions of the various sectors. Troops already too highly tried were kept too long in the positions of greatest strain. Thus, the combination of faulty distribution with the enemy's unerring eye for the vulnerable spot produced, with other factors, an Austro-German success out of all proportion to the means.

Capello, commanding the Second Army, dissatisfied with the defensive suitability of the positions on which the Italian offensive had stopped, had wished to forestall the attack by a flank thrust northwards from the Bainsizza Plateau, but was overruled by Cadorna, who was not only conscious of his shortage of reserves but had belatedly come to doubt the value of offensive methods. In this he was at least wiser than his subordinate, who, alike in offensive spirit, in his manner as a commander, and as the victim of the Germans' new offensive method, was the Gough of the Italian army. Cadorna had full warning of the enemy's intention from his intelligence and from deserters, — Czech and Transylvanian officers, — but he did not feel sufficiently sure of the real direction of the enemy's attack to justify him in committing his reserves beforehand.

Yet it is at least curious that, as information specifically pointed to the Caporetto sector, on its fifteen-mile frontage there were only posted two battalions to the mile compared with eight to the mile further south. The very fact that this had long been a quiet sector, where both sides sent troops to rest, might have aroused the suspicions of the Italian command. But Capello actually refused the appeal of his left wing here for reënforcements. Perhaps he was the less patient towards arguments because he should have been a patient in hospital. Instead, with misguided pertinacity he stayed in bed at his headquarters, and only yielded the reins of command the day after his front collapsed.

The Italian frontier province of Venezia formed a tongue pointing towards Austria. It was flanked on the south by the Adriatic and on the east and north by the Julian and Carnic Alps — beyond which lay the Austrian Trentino. The six German divisions, with nine Austrian, formed the attacking Fourteenth German Army, under General Otto von Below, with whom was Krafft as Chief of Staff and guiding brain. These troops were to climb the mountain barrier at the tip of the tongue, while two Austrian armies, under Boroevic, were to advance along the stretch of lower ground near the Adriatic shore.

The difficulties of organizing and deploying an attack in the mountains were ably overcome, and, after four hours' gas shell and one hour general bombardment, the attackers moved forward in the drizzle of snow and rain, and in many places rapidly overcame the resistance of infantry, who, owing partly to the breakdown of telephone communication, were but fitfully supported by their own artillery. But the misty conditions were the greater factor in the success, as they were the next March in France; they provided the element of surprise which proved the only and indispensable key to open a way through the enemy's front. Although the right and left wings of the attacking army were delayed by sturdy resistance in the rear positions, the centre group (four divisions) under Stein penetrated completely at Caporetto, and through this breach reserves were pouring by evening. The effect was to make the whole defensive position untenable and to ease the task of the attacking right wing (three and a half Austrian divisions) under Krauss, which now pushed forward almost unchecked down the Val d'Uccea, the shortest line to turn the river barrier of the Tagliamento. This enveloping advance nullified Cadorna's efforts to dam the breach, efforts which also broke down owing to the difficulty of pushing reserves up the narrow mountain roads already congested by troops which had no stomach left for fighting. This convinced Cadorna of the necessity of ordering a general retreat to the Tagliamento, as Capello had earlier urged, and it was successfully achieved after two critical days — October 30 and 31.

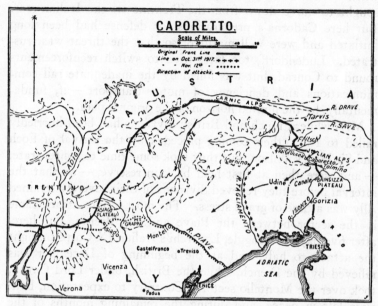

Fortunately the pursuing enemy had suffered from hitches in movements and supply, as well as an increasing friction between the German and Austrian commanders. Their attempt to achieve a surprise capture of the crossings was foiled, and although in a deliberate attack one of Krauss's Austrian divisions got across at Cornino on November 2, Cadorna had had breathing space to make preparations for a further retreat to the Piave. Although large bodies of troops were cut off by the enemy's pincer-like advance, the main armies succeeded in reaching the Piave by November 10, thus reforging their line. Yet its links were very thin. Nearly 600,000 men had been lost, and the Second Army, which had suffered the direct blow, was practically out of action as a force. At this juncture Cadorna gave place to Diaz, whose supreme value was that he understood the mind of the soldiers, and knew how to reinvigorate their morale, playing, in fact, the same rôle as Pétain in France earlier that year.

Three days later a fresh menace developed, on November 12, when Conrad's troops (Austrian Tenth and Eleventh Armies) sought to move down from the Trentino on the Italian rear. But here Cadorna's preparations for defense had been long initiated and were well matured, so that the threat was frustrated. Ludendorff, too late, tried to switch reënforcements round to Conrad, but was foiled by the inadequate rail communications and deficiency of motor transport — if, fundamentally, by the limited horizon of the original plan.

Meanwhile, French and British divisions had been hurriedly railed to Italy, their coming preceded by the arrival of Foch and Sir Henry Wilson, but they took some time to concentrate, — and were then at first held back in reserve, — so that the interval before they relieved divisions of their severely strained Ally was a time of grave stress. The most serious attack came in the sector between the Piave and the Brenta, but here, after five days of struggle, Laderchi's Italian IX Corps brought the attack to halt, and at the beginning of December was relieved by the French, while the British, under Lord Cavan, took over the Montello sector. Contrary to expectation, both were left in peace, and during the remaining months of the campaign the enemy's attack was confined to renewed efforts by Conrad and Krauss further to the northwest, in the Asiago and Grappa sectors. If these imposed a fresh tax on the weary Italians, it was psychologically worth while, for this successful and stalwart resistance by its vindication of their fighting power laid the moral foundations for the Italian *revanche* of 1918.

Reviewing the drama of Caporetto in the clearer light of history, there is reason to think that excessive emphasis was placed on the effect of enemy and seditious propaganda, and that the major reason for the crumbling resistance early was the same as in France that spring — that the troops were morally tired, and that the result of being hurled endlessly against machine-gun defenses had worn down their fighting spirit. The presence of imminent disaster to their country set a new light upon the position, and gave a sacrificial impulse to a duty which, on the Piave line, fighting "with their backs to the wall," they honorably and gallantly fulfilled.

Strategically, however, the most critical stage was past with the passing of Tagliamento, for henceforth what Clausewitz called the "friction of war" so upset the attackers' communications that their power and speed fell off badly. Some of the causes have been mentioned. But one, which was to operate again next spring in France, deserves emphasis. The well-filled supply depots of the Italian army were too great a temptation to the undernourished enemy, the desire to eat quenched the desire to pursue, and sudden congestion of the stomach accelerated the congestion of the advance. It is significant that even a German divisional commander, General Lecquis, could exult more at the capture of two or three chickens apiece by his men than of many prisoners, and regarded the possession of a few pigs "as the height of human felicity."

VII

1918 — THE BREAK

THE middle years of the World War had been, in a military sense, a tussle between a lean Hercules and a bulky Cerberus. The Germanic Alliance was weaker in numbers but directed by a single head, the Entente stronger in numbers but with too many heads. Owing to their own excessive losses, diffusion of effort, and the collapse of Russia, the Entente at the end of 1917 were faced with the grim fact that the numerical balance had been reversed, and months must elapse before the prospective stream of America's new divisions should tilt the scales once more in their favor. The emergency paved the way for the creation of a unified command, but it still needed disaster to bring it into being.

At the conference at Rapallo n November, the formation of a Supreme War Council was decided upon, to be composed of the principal Ministers of the Allies, with military representatives, and to sit permanently at Versailles. If the fundamental defect was that it mere y substituted a formal for an informal committee, a further flaw was that the military representatives had no executive status. In the economic sphere, where deliberation rather than instant action was necessary, it led to a real improvement in the combination of shipping, food, and munition resources. Militarily, it was futile, for it set up a dual advisership — the Versailles representatives on the one hand and the chiefs of the national General Staffs on the other. Yet it is fair to add that this "dead end" was due to a British obstruction.

Both the Americans and the French desired to give this committee executive power and an executive head, and Pétain logically supported the proposal, which came from Colonel House and General Bliss. But the fundamental offset to its wisdom was that it eliminated the essential control of strategy by the statesman, while the suggested composition of the council repeated the error of the Nivelle era. For it was to consist of the national Commanders-in-Chief and Chiefs of Staff, and thus whichever member was chosen as president would have his freedom of judgment and execution hampered by his responsibility to and for his own national army. Moreover, in fulfillment, the proposal would mean that the council would have a French chief — as the French realized when they supported and the British when they opposed the proposal. In rejecting it Lloyd George was guided not only by a wise objection to a purely military council, but by his feeling that British opinion was not ripe for it, and that Haig's resistance to another Nivelle solution would be supported by the public at home. Moreover, the suggested inclusion of the Chiefs of Staff introduced a personal complication, for the last thing that Lloyd George desired was to strengthen the influence of Sir William Robertson upon the conduct of the war. Rather was he hoping to sidetrack Robertson, whom he held responsible for the futile and costly strategy of 1917, in favor of Sir Henry Wilson, his nominee for the Versailles committee. And while he sought to make Versailles independent of the narrow purview of the British General Staff, Clemenceau was equally intent to make it merely a microphone for the French General Staff, to amplify its "voice."

In default of agreement the military representatives — now Generals Weygand, Wilson, Bliss, and Cadorna — were merely technical advisers. But as the menace of the German attack grew closer and with it the need for common action, this advisory body was converted into a military executive committee to handle an Interallied general reserve, a fresh compromise which set up a dual control — the Commanders-in-Chief and the Versailles committee.

If concentration of control was lacking, so also was concentration of force. Since early in November the stream of German troop-trains from east to west had been steadily swelling. When the 1917 campaign opened, there had been a proportion of nearly three Allies to two Germans — actually in March one hundred and seventy-eight British, French, and Belgian divisions against one hundred and twenty-nine German divisions. Now the Germans had a slight advantage, with the likelihood of augmenting it. But the Allied statesmen, recalling how often their own offensive had failed with equal or greater superiority of force, were slow to appreciate the gravity of the menace or to respond to the sudden fall in the temperature of military opinion. Nor could they agree to draw reënforcements from the other fronts.

The Italians strove against any withdrawal of the Allied contingents from their front, and the French opposed any reduction of the Salonika force. Lloyd George went further and urged an offensive in Palestine, a scheme which was sanctioned on the understanding that no reënforcements should be sent there from France, but which also meant that none would come from there to France. Robertson, the Chief of the Imperial General Staff, disagreed both with this Palestine plan and with the creation of the Versailles executive committee, and resigned, being succeeded by Sir Henry Wilson. The position was still further weakened by the insistence of Clemenceau, the new French Premier, that the British should extend their front south to the Oise — a further fourteen miles. This meant that Gough's Fifth Army was dangerously stretched out and took over ill-prepared defenses on the very sector that Ludendorff was about to strike. Meantime, the German strength had increased to one hundred and seventy-seven divisions by the end of January, with thirty more to come. The Allied strength, owing to the dispatch of divisions to Italy and the breaking up of others because of the French shortage of drafts, had fallen to the equivalent of one hundred and seventy-three — counting as double the four and a half large-size American divisions which had arrived. For the French and British had been constrained to follow the Germans in reducing their divisions from twelve to nine battalions each.

The prolonged waste of soldiers' lives in the swamps beyond Ypres had led Lloyd George and his Cabinet to withhold reënforcements for fear of encouraging fresh squandering. This undoubtedly weakened Haig's initial power of resistance to the German onslaught, yet it is just to point out that it was weakened more — in quality as well as quantity — by the 400,000 British casualties suffered in the offensive of the latter part of 1917. Moreover, we should not forget that the Government had the heavy responsibility of being the trustee for the lives of the nation. The real ground of criticism is that it was not strong enough to make a change in, or place a check upon, a command which it did not trust, while supplying the reënforcements necessary for defense. And for this lack of moral strength the public must share the blame, for they had already shown themselves too easily swayed by clamor against political interference with the generals, and too prone to believe that the politician is invariably wrong on such occasions. The civilian public, indeed, is apt to trust soldiers too little in peace, and sometimes too much in war.

These political handicaps, and the accompanying tendency of politicians to work deviously towards what they dare not demand openly, were also seen in the project for a unified command. The Prime Minister, indeed, had gone so far in December as to disclaim faith in his own long-sought cure. Instead he sought a palliative in an Interallied executive committee, under Foch's chairmanship, which should control a common general reserve of thirty divisions. This scheme was decisively annulled by Haig, who, when called on by Foch for his contribution of seven divisions, replied that he could spare none. He preferred to make an arrangement with Pétain for mutual support.

When the test came, a week later, this broke down, and Haig then took a foremost part in hastening and facilitating the appointment of a generalissimo, which he had formerly opposed. For the actual breakdown the blame has been commonly thrown upon the French, and there is no question that Haig understood from Pétain on March 24 that if the Germans continued their rapid progress the French reserves would have to be used to cover Paris. But in fairness it is essential to add that, whereas the original compact had only pledged the aid of some six French divisions, Pétain actually sent nine by March 24, and twenty-one (including four of cavalry) by

March 26. If these reënforcements were perhaps slower coming into action than in dispatch, it does not affect the fact that the original pledge was amply exceeded. Thus the fundamental fault would seem to lie in trusting to an arrangement for such slender support by either Ally.

The German Plan. On the German side the submarine panacea for victory had been replaced by a military panacea, and hopes were perhaps exaggerated by the unexpected collapse of Russia. But although Ludendorff promised victory in the field, he did not disguise the fact that a western offensive would be a far harder task than the conquests in the east. He realized also that it would be a race between the effect of Germany's blow and the arrival of American reënforcements, although he hoped to win the race. To secure the rear of his offensive, a definite peace was wrung from the Bolshevik Government of Russia by a military demonstration, and also forced on Rumania. And to secure, if possible, the economic base of his offensive, the Ukraine was occupied for its wheat supplies, with little resistance except from Czechoslovak troops who had formerly been taken prisoners from the Austrian army.

Ludendorff's next problem was to decide his first point of attack. The sector between Arras and St. Quentin was chosen, on the western face of the great salient formed by the German front in France. The choice was governed by tactical reasons, — this sector was the enemy's weakest point and the ground offered fewer difficulties than elsewhere, — although Ludendorff had in mind the possibility of separating the Allied armies and driving the British back against the Channel coast, where they would be too closely penned in to evade his blows. From the experience of the vain Allied attacks Ludendorff had drawn the deduction that "tactics had to be considered before purely strategical objects which it is futile to pursue unless tactical success is possible." Hence he formulated a strategical plan based on the new, or resurrected, principle of taking the tactical line of least resistance. Presumably he hoped by firm control to guide these tactical movements to a strategic destination. If so, he failed.

Where did the fault lie? The general view at the end of the

war was that the tactical bias had led Ludendorff to change direction and dissipate his strength. That if the Franco-British Command had previously erred by aiming at the strategically correct target without enough attention to the tactical diffi-culties the German Command had followed it with an equal if opposite error by concentrating on tactical success at the expense of the strategical goal. But a closer examination of the German documents since available, and of Ludendorff's own orders and instructions, throws a different light on the question. It would seem, indeed, that the real fault was that Ludendorff failed to carry out in practice the new principle he had adopted in theory; that he either did not grasp, or shrank from, the full implication of this new theory of strategy. For in fact he dissipated too large a part of his reserves in try-ing to redeem tactical failures and hesitated too long over the decision to exploit his tactical successes. Ludendorff's strategy in the east had been so masterly and so farsighted that his indecision and short-sight in the west are difficult to explain. Perhaps he himself was feeling the strain of directing so many vast operations; perhaps it was that he missed the strategical insight and balanced view of Hoffmann, who, after being at his side throughout the 1914–1916 campaigns, had stayed in the east when Ludendorff went to the Supreme Command. The modern vice of seniority prevented Germany from making the fullest use of the man who perhaps approached nearer to military genius than any other general of the war.

In any case the campaign leaves the impression that Luden-dorff had neither his former clearness as to the goal nor the same grip on the changing situations. But in the organization of the attacks his powers were at their highest level. Surprise was to be the key which should open a gate in the long-locked front. The most thorough arrangements were made for concealing and for exploiting the attacks, and the surprise effect of the short but intense bombardment was increased by lavish use of gas and smoke shell. Further, while Ludendorff had settled to strike first on the Somme sector, to which blow the code-name "Michael" was given, he also began prepara-tions for successive attacks at other points, which, besides being in readiness for the future, helped to mystify the enemy. Two were on the British front and one on the French — "St. George I" against the Lys sector, "St. George II" against the Ypres sector, and "Blücher" in Champagne.

The "Michael" attack was to be made by the German Seventeenth, Second, and Eighteenth Armies (sixty-three divisions in all) on the forty-three mile front Arras-St. Quentin-La Fère, but its main force was intended to be exerted north of the Somme, and, after breaking through, the Seventeenth and Second Armies were to wheel northwest and press the British army against the coast, while the river and the Eighteenth Army guarded their flank.

The assault was launched on March 21, and the surprise was greatly helped by an early morning mist. But while the thrust broke through completely south of the Somme, where the defense — but also the attacking force — was thinnest, it was held up near Arras, a check which reacted on all the attack north of the river. Ludendorff, violating his new principle, spent the following days in trying to revive his attack against the strong, and strongly held, bastion of Arras, maintaining this direction as his principal line of effort. Meantime he kept a tight rein on the Eighteenth Army, which was advancing in the south without serious check from its opponents. As late as March 26 he issued orders which restrained it from crossing the Avre and tied it to the pace of its neighbor, the Second, which in turn was held back by the very limited success of the Seventeenth Army near Arras. Thus we see that in reality Ludendorff was bent on breaking the British army by breaking down its strongest sector of resistance in a direct assault. And because of this obsession he failed, until too late, to throw the weight of his reserves along the line of least resistance south of the Somme. The intended wheel to the northwest might have come to pass if it had been made after passing the flank, and thus been directed against the rear of the Arras bastion. On March 26 the attack north of the Somme (by the left wing of the Seventeenth Army and the right of the Second Army) was visibly weakening as the price of its hard-earned gains. South of the Somme the left of the Second Army reached, and was now to be embarrassed by, the desert of the old Somme battlefields — a brake on progress and supply. The Eighteenth Army alone was advancing with unslackened impetus.

This situation led Ludendorff to adopt a new plan, but without relinquishing his old. He ordered for March 28 a fresh and direct attack on the high ground near Arras — by the right of the Seventeenth Army, and to be followed by a Sixth Army attack just to the north between Vimy and La Bassée. But the promising situation south of the Somme led him to indicate Amiens as an additional main objective. Even so, he restrained the Eighteenth Army from pushing on to turn the flank of the Amiens defenses without further orders! On March 28 the fresh Arras attack was launched, unshielded by mist or surprise, and failed completely in face of the well-prepared resistance of Byng's Third Army. Only then did Ludendorff abandon his original idea and direct his main effort, and some of his remaining reserves, towards Amiens. But meantime he ordered the Eighteenth Army to mark time for two days. When the attack was renewed it made little progress in face of a resistance that had been afforded time to harden, and Ludendorff, rather than be drawn into an attrition struggle, suspended the attempt to reach Amiens.

He, however, had missed vital arteries and decisive results by the narrowest of margins. By March 27 the advance had penetrated nearly forty miles and reached Montdidier, cutting one railway to Paris; by March 30 the German flood was almost lapping the out-works of Amiens. Eighty thousand prisoners and 975 guns had been taken. Once the crust was broken, the very elaboration of the methods of communication built up during three years of static warfare caused the greater flux behind the front. The extent of the retreat was primarily the measure of the loss of control by the British commanders.

Disaster had driven the Allies to an overdue step, and on Haig's appeal and Lord Milner's intervention Foch had been appointed on March 26 to "coördinate" the operations of the Allied armies. If he had fallen into disfavor owing to the heavy cost of his attacks in Artois during 1915 and the barren fruit of the Somme in 1916, his will-power and energy earned and created confidence. On April 14 he was definitely made Commander-in-Chief of the Allied armies. But before this a fresh German menace had developed — though not intended as such.

With a large part of his reserves holding the vast bulge south of the Somme, Ludendorff turned, if without much confidence and merely as a diversion, to release, on April 9, his "St. George I" attack. Its astonishing early success against a weakened front led him to convert it bit by bit into a major effort. The British were desperately close to the sea, but their resistance stopped the German tide, after a ten-mile invasion, just short of the important railway junction of Hazebrouck, and an attempt to widen the front towards Ypres was nullified by Haig's swinging his line back just before and by the gradual arrival of French reënforcements. Haig complained strongly that Foch was too slow in sending French reserves northward, but the event justified Foch's reluctance to commit himself thither and his seeming excess of optimism in declaring that the danger was passed. Ludendorff had doled out reserves sparingly, usually too late and too few for real success; so apprehensive that his new bulge would become another sack that, after the capture of Kemmel Hill, when opportunity opened its arms, he stopped the exploitation for fear of a counter-stroke.

Thus Ludendorff had fallen short of strategic results; on the other hand he could claim huge tactical successes — the British casualties were over 300,000. The British army had been badly mauled; and although fresh drafts to the number of 140,000 were hurried out from England and divisions brought back from Italy, Salonika, and Palestine, months must elapse before it could recover its offensive power. Ten British divisions had to be broken up temporarily, while the German strength had now mounted to two hundred and eight, of which eighty were still in reserve. A restoration of the balance, however, was now in sight. A dozen American divisions had arrived in France and, responding to the call, great efforts were being made to swell the stream. At the crisis in March, Pershing, the American Commander-in-Chief, even relaxed his inflexible opposition to partial or premature use of the American troops so far as to declare that they were at Foch's disposal for use wherever required. It was an inspiring gesture — although in practice he continued to keep a tight hold on his troops and, with rare exceptions, only allowed them to take over parts of the front as complete divisions.

For Germany the sands were running out. Realizing this, Ludendorff launched his "Blücher" attack between Soissons and Reims, on May 27. Falling by surprise with fifteen divisions against seven, it swept over the Aisne and reached the Marne on May 30, where its impetus died away. This time the German superiority of force had not been so pronounced as before nor aided by nature's atmospheric cloak. It would seem that the extent of the opening success was due in part to the strategic surprise — the greater unexpectedness of the time and place of the blow — and in part to the folly of the local army command in insisting on the long-exploded and obsolete method of massing the defenders in the forward positions — there to be compressed cannon-fodder for the Germans' massed artillery.

But once again Ludendorff had obtained a measure of success for which he was neither prepared nor desirous. The surpriser was himself surprised. The attack had been conceived merely as a diversion, to attract the Allied reserves thither preparatory to a final and decisive blow at the British front in Flanders. But its opening success attracted thither too large, yet not large enough, a proportion of the German reserves. Blocked frontally by the river, an attempt was made to push west, but it failed in face of Allied resistance — notable for the appearance of American divisions at Château-Thierry, where they gallantly counter-attacked.

Ludendorff had now created two huge bulges, and another smaller one, in the Allied front. His next attempt was to pinch out the Compiègne "tongue" which lay between the Amiens and Marne bulges. But this time there was no surprise, and the blow on the west side of the "tongue," June 9, was too late to coincide with the pressure on the east. A month's pause followed.

Ludendorff, though anxious to strike his long-cherished decisive blow against the British in Belgium, considered that their reserves here were still too strong, and so again decided to choose the line of least tactical resistance, hoping that a heavy blow in the south would draw off the British reserves. He had failed to pinch out the Compiègne "tongue" on the west of his Marne salient; he was now about to attempt the same method on the east, by attacking on either side of Reims. But he needed an interval for rest and preparation, and the delay was fatal, giving the British and French time to recuperate, and the Americans to gather strength. The British divisions previously broken up had now been reconstituted, and as a result of an urgent appeal made to President Wilson in the crisis of March, and the provision of extra shipping, American troops had been arriving at the rate of 300,000 a month since the end of April. By mid-July seven American divisions were ready to help in resisting the next, and final, German stroke. Five more were being acclimatized to front-line conditions away on the Alsace-Lorraine sector, and five with the British, while another four were assembled in the American training area.

The tactical success of his own blows had been Ludendorff's undoing. Yielding too late to their influence, he had then pressed each too far and too long, so using up his own reserves and causing an undue interval between each blow. He had driven in three great wedges, but none had penetrated far enough to sever a vital artery, and this strategic failure left the Germans with an indented front which invited flanking counter-strokes.

The Turning of the Tide. On July 15 Ludendorff launched his new attack, but its coming was no secret. East of Reims it was foiled by an elastic defense, and west of Reims the German penetration across the Marne merely enmeshed them more deeply to their downfall — for on July 18 Foch launched a long-prepared stroke against the other flank of the Marne salient. Here Pétain, who directed the operation, turned the key which Ludendorff lacked, using masses of light tanks to lead a surprise attack on the Cambrai method. The Germans managed to hold the gates of the salient open long enough to draw back their forces into safety and straighten their line. But their reserves were depleted, Ludendorff was forced to postpone, if not yet to abandon, the offensive in Flanders, and the initiative definitely and finally passed to the Allies.

Foch's first concern was to keep it, by giving the enemy no rest while his own reserves were accumulating. To this end he arranged with Haig, Pétain, and Pershing for a series of local offensives, aimed to free the lateral railway communications and to improve the position of the front ready for further operations. To Haig he proposed an attack in the Lys sector, but Haig suggested instead the Somme area as more suitable. Rawlinson, commanding the British Fourth Army in front of Amiens, had already submitted to Haig a plan for a large surprise attack there, and Foch agreed to this in place of his own proposal. He also placed under Haig the French First Army (Debeney) to extend the attack to the south. Rawlinson's army was doubled, and by skillful precautions the enemy were kept in the dark until, on August 8, the attack was delivered — with four hundred and fifty-six tanks. The blow had the maximum shock of surprise, and south of the Somme the troops of the Australian and Canadian Corps rapidly overran and overwhelmed the German forward divisions. By August 12, when the advance came to a halt through reaching the tangled wilderness of the old 1916 battlefields, if also through lack of reserves, the Fourth Army had taken 21,000 prisoners at a cost of only 20,000 casualties. Great, if not fully exploited, as a material, it was far greater as a moral success.

Ludendorff has said: "August 8 was the black day of the German army in the history of the war. . . . It put the decline of our fighting power beyond all doubt. . . . The war must be ended." He informed the Emperor and the political chiefs that peace negotiations ought to be opened before the situation became worse, as it must. The conclusions reached at a Crown Council held at Spa were that "we can no longer

hope to break the war-will of our enemies by military operations," and "the object of our strategy must be to paralyze the
enemy's war-will gradually by a strategic defensive." In other
words, the German Command had abandoned hope of victory
or even holding their gains, and hoped only to avoid surrender
— an insecure moral foundation.

On August 10 Foch issued a fresh *directive* for the preparation
of an "advance" by the British Third Army "in the general
direction of Bapaume and Péronne." Meantime he wished
Haig to continue the Fourth Army's frontal pressure, but Haig
demurred to it as a vain waste of life and gained his point.
Economy of force was henceforth to be added to the advantages
of the new strategy now evolved. Thus the momentum of the
Fourth Army had hardly waned before the Third Army moved.
From then on Foch beat a tattoo on the German front, a series
of rapid blows at different points, each broken off as soon as its
initial impetus waned, each so aimed as to pave the way for the
next, and all close enough in time and space to react on each
other. Thus Ludendorff's power of switching reserves to
threatened spots was restricted, as his balance of reserves was
drained.

On August 10 the French Third Army had struck to the
south; then on August 17 the French Tenth Army still further
south; next on August 21 the British Third Army, followed
by the British First Army on August 26. Ludendorff's order
to the troops holding the Lys salient to retire was hastened in
execution by the attacks of the re-formed British Fifth Army,
and by the first week in September the Germans were back
on their original starting line — the strong defenses of the
Hindenburg Line. And on September 12 Pershing completed
the series of preliminary operations by erasing the St. Mihiel
salient — the first feat of the Americans as an independent
army. Pershing had originally intended to make this a step-
ping-stone to an advance towards the Briey coal-fields and the
eastern end of the Germans' main lateral railway near Metz,
but the project was abandoned for reasons that will be referred
to later. Thus no exploitation of the success was attempted.

The clear evidence of the Germans' decline and Haig's

assurance that he would break the Hindenburg Line where
the German reserves were thickest persuaded Foch to seek
victory that autumn instead of postponing the attempt until
1919. All the Allied armies in the west were to combine in a
simultaneous offensive.

The Collapse of Bulgaria. But before it could develop, an
event occurred in the Balkans which, in the words of Ludendorff, "sealed the fate of the Quadruple Alliance." He had
still hoped to hold fast in his strong lines in the west, falling
back gradually to fresh lines if necessary, and with his strategic
flanks in Macedonia and Italy covered, while the German
Government was negotiating for a favorable peace. At the
same time there was alarm as to the moral effect of the western-
front defeats on the German people, their will-power already
undermined by shortage of food, and perhaps also by propaganda.

But on September 15 the Allied armies in Salonika attacked
the Bulgarian front, which crumbled in a few days. Guillaumat, who had succeeded Sarrail in December 1917, had prepared the plan for an offensive, and when recalled to France
in the crisis of July as Governor of Paris he won over the Allied
Governments to consent to the attempt. His successor in
Salonika, Franchet d'Esperey, concentrated a Franco-Serb
striking force, under Michich, on the Sokol-Dobropolye sector,
west of the Vardar, where the Bulgarians trusted to the strength
of the mountain ridges and were weak in numbers. On September 15 Michich attacked, and while the British attack at
Doiran pinned a large part of the Bulgarian reserves, he broke
right through towards Uskub. With their army split into
two parts, the Bulgarians, already tired of the war, sought an
armistice, which was signed on September 29. Franchet
d'Esperey's achievement not only severed the first root of
the Central Alliance, but opened the way to an advance on
Austria's rear.

The First Peace Note. The capitulation of Bulgaria convinced Ludendorff that it was necessary to take a decisive
step towards securing peace. While he was scraping together
a paltry half-dozen divisions to form a new front in Serbia and

arranging a meeting with the political chiefs, Foch's grand assaults fell on the western defenses, September 26–28, and the line threatened to crack.

The German Supreme Command lost its nerve — only for a matter of days, but that was sufficient, and recovery too late. On the afternoon of September 29, Ludendorff was studying the problem in his room at the Hotel Britannique at Spa — an ominously named choice of headquarters! Examination only seemed to make it more insoluble, and in a rising outburst of fear and passion he bemoaned his troubles — especially his lack of tanks — and berated all those whom he considered as having thwarted his efforts — the jealous staffs, the defeatist Reichstag, the too humanitarian Kaiser, and the submarine-obsessed navy. Gradually he worked himself into a frenzy, until suddenly, with foam on his lips, he fell to the floor in a fit. And that evening it was a physically as well as mentally shaken man who took the precipitate decision to appeal for an armistice, saying that the collapse of the Bulgarian front had upset all his dispositions — "troops destined for the western front had to be dispatched there." This had "fundamentally changed the situation in view of the attacks then being launched on the western front," for though these "had so far been beaten off, their continuance must be reckoned with."

This remark refers to Foch's general offensive. The American attack in the Meuse-Argonne had begun on September 26, but had come practically to a standstill by the twenty-eighth. A Franco-Belgo-British attack had opened in Flanders on the twenty-eighth, but if unpleasant did not look really menacing. On the morning of the twenty-ninth, however, Haig's main blow was falling on the Hindenburg Line, and the early news was disquieting.

In this emergency, Prince Max was called to be Chancellor to negotiate a peace move, with his international reputation for moderation and honor as its covering pledge. To bargain effectively and without confession of defeat he needed, and asked, a breathing space "of ten, eight, even four days, before I have to appeal to the enemy." But Hindenburg merely reiterated that "the gravity of the military situation admits of no delay," and insisted that "a peace offer to our enemies be issued at once," while Ludendorff plaintively chanted the refrain, "I want to save my army."

Hence, on October 3, the appeal for an immediate armistice went out to President Wilson. It was an open confession of defeat to the world, and even before this — on October 1 — the Supreme Command had undermined their own home front by communicating the same impression to a meeting of the leaders of all political parties. Men who had so long been kept in the dark were blinded by the sudden light. All the forces of discord and pacifism received an immense impulse.

While the German Government was debating the conditions for an armistice and questioning Ludendorff as to the situation of the army for further resistance if the terms were unacceptable, Foch continued his military pressure.

The Breach of the Hindenburg Line. The plan of the general offensive embraced a series of convergent and practically simultaneous attacks: —

1 and 2. By the Americans between the Meuse and the Argonne Forest, and by the French west of the Argonne, both in the direction of Mézières — beginning on September 26.

3. By the British on the St. Quentin-Cambrai front in the general direction of Maubeuge — beginning on September 27.

4. By the Belgian and Allied forces in the direction of Ghent — beginning on September 28.

The general aspect was that of a pincer-like pressure against the vast salient jutting south between Ypres and Verdun. The attack towards Mézières would shepherd that part of the German armies towards the rather difficult country of the Ardennes and away from their natural line of retreat through Lorraine; it was also dangerously close to the hinge of the Antwerp-Meuse line which the Germans were preparing in rear. The attack towards Maubeuge would threaten the other main line of communication and retreat through the Liége gap, but it had further to go. In these attacks, the Americans had the hardest natural obstacle; the British had to face the strongest defenses and the heaviest weight of enemy troops.

Pershing's attack opened well, adding surprise to its superi-

ority in numbers, — approximately eight to one, — but soon
lost impetus owing to the difficulties of supply and exploitation
in such country. When it was eventually suspended on
October 14, after bitter fighting and severe losses, the American
army was still far distant from the vital railway. A new force,
it was suffering the growing pains which the British had passed
through in 1915–1916. Pershing's difficulties were enhanced
by the fact that he had waived his own proposal for an exploitation of the St. Mihiel success towards Metz in view of Haig's
objection to a move which, however promising in its ultimate
aim, would diverge from the general direction of the other
Allied attacks. Foch's original plan for the general offensive
had accordingly been readjusted, and in consequence Pershing
had not only a more difficult sector, but a bare week in which
to prepare his blow. The shortness of time led him to use
untried divisions instead of switching the more experienced
divisions used at St. Mihiel. But in the outcome Haig's insistence was proved unnecessary, for the British attack broke
through the Hindenburg Line before the Meuse-Argonne
attack had drawn away any German division from his front.

Haig, by pushing forward his left wing first, facilitated the
attack of his right on the strongest section of the Hindenburg
Line, the Canal du Nord, and by October 5 the British were
through the German defense system, with open country beyond.
But on this front the attackers had actually fewer divisions
than the defenders,[1] their tanks were used up, and they could
not press forward fast enough to endanger the German retreat.

Within a few days the Supreme Command became more
cheerful, even optimistic, when it saw that breaking into the
Hindenburg Line had not been followed by an actual break-
through of the fighting front. More encouragement came from

[1] On September 25, the eve of Foch's general offensive, there were fifty-seven German divisions facing forty British and two American divisions along the Hindenburg
Line between, roughly, St. Quentin and Lens. In the Meuse-Argonne sector twenty
enemy divisions opposed thirty-one French and thirteen large-strength American
divisions — a total equivalent of at least sixty normal-size Allied divisions. The German divisions had shrunk to an abnormally small size, but this fact does not affect the
historical comparison of odds met by the right and left pincers respectively of the Allied
offensive.

reports of a slackening in the force of the Allies' attacks, particularly in the exploitation of opportunities. Ludendorff still wanted an armistice, but only to give his troops a rest as a prelude to further resistance and to ensure a secure withdrawal to a shortened defensive line on the frontier. By October 17 he even felt he could do it without a rest. It was less that the situation had changed than that his impression of it had been revised. It had never been quite so bad as he had pictured it on September 29. But his first impression, and depression, had now spread throughout the political circles and public of Germany, as the ripples spread when a pebble has been dropped in a pool.

The combined pressure of the Allied armies, and their steady advance, were loosening the will-power of the German Government and people. The conviction of ultimate defeat, slower to appeal to them than to the army chiefs, was the more forcible when it was realized. And the indirect moral effect of military and economic pressure was accentuated by the direct effect of peace propaganda, skillfully directed and intensively waged by Northcliffe. The "home front" began to crumble later, but it crumbled quicker than the battle front.

The Collapse of Turkey. The offensive planned for the spring in Palestine had been interrupted by the crisis in France and the consequent withdrawal of most of Allenby's British troops. The depletion was made up by reënforcements from India and Mesopotamia, and by September Allenby was again ready to take the offensive. He secretly concentrated, on the Mediterranean flank, the mass of his infantry, and behind them the cavalry. Meantime Lawrence and his Arabs, appearing out of the desert like unseen mosquitoes, menaced the enemy's communications and distracted their attention. At dawn on September 19 the western mass attacked, rolling the Turks back northeast towards the hilly interior — like a door on its hinges. Through the open doorway the cavalry passed, riding straight up the coastal corridor for thirty miles, before swinging east to bestride the Turkish rear. The only remaining way of retreat was eastwards across the Jordan, and this was closed with shattering effect by the British air-bombers. Completely trapped, the main Turkish armies were rounded up, while Allenby's cavalry exploited the victory of Megiddo by a swift and sustained pursuit which gained first Damascus and finally Aleppo. Defenseless and threatened with a direct advance of Milne from Macedonia on Constantinople, Turkey capitulated on October 30.

The Collapse of Austria. The last Austrian attempt at an offensive on the Italian front, in conjunction with the German assaults in France, had been repulsed on the Piave in June. Diaz waited until conditions were ripe for an offensive in return, until Austria's internal decay had spread and she was without hope from Germany. On October 24 Cavan's army moved to seize the crossings of the Piave, and on October 27 the main attack opened, driving towards Vittorio Veneto to divide the Austrians in the Adriatic plain from those in the mountains. By October 30 the Austrian army was split in two, the retreat became a rout, and the same day Austria asked for an armistice, which was signed on November 4.

The Curtain Falls on the Western Front. Already, on October 23, President Wilson had replied to the German requests by a note which virtually required an unconditional surrender. Ludendorff wished to carry on the struggle in hopes that a successful defense of the German frontier might damp the determination of the Allies. But the situation had passed beyond his control, the nation's will-power was broken, and his advice was in discredit. On October 26 he was forced to resign.

Then, for thirty-six hours, the Chancellor lay in coma from an overdose of sleeping draught after influenza. When he returned to his office on the evening of November 3, not only Turkey, but Austria, had capitulated. If the situation on the western front was felt to be rather easier, Austrian territory and railways were now available as a base of operations against Germany. Several weeks before, General von Gallwitz had told the German Chancellor that such a contingency, then unrealized, would be "decisive." Next day revolution broke out in Germany, and swept rapidly over the country. And in these last days of tremendous and diverse psychological strain the "reddening" glare behind was accentuated by a looming cloud on the Lorraine front — where the renewed American pressure, since November 1, was on a point more sensitive than other parts, a point where "they must not be allowed to advance if the Antwerp-Meuse line was to be held any longer." If this continued, the Rhine and not the frontier would have to be the next line of resistance.

But hourly the revolution was spreading, fanned, as peace negotiations were delayed, by the Kaiser's reluctance to abdicate. Compromise with the revolutionaries was the only chance, and on November 9 Prince Max handed over to the socialist Ebert. Germany had become a republic in outward response to President Wilson's demand and in inward response to the uprising of the German people against the leaders who had led them into disaster. The German fleet had already mutinied when their commanders sought to send them out on a forlorn hope against the British. And on November 6 the German delegates had left Berlin to treat for an armistice.

In the days previous to their arrival the Allies had been anxiously debating the terms, but here the voice of Foch was clear and decisive, for President Wilson suggested that the terms should be left to the decision of the military chiefs. Haig, supported by Milner, urged moderation : "Germany is not broken in the military sense. During the last weeks her armies have withdrawn fighting very bravely and in excellent order. Therefore . . . it is necessary to grant Germany conditions which she can accept . . . the evacuation of all invaded territories and of Alsace-Lorraine is sufficient to seal the victory." The British also feared the danger of guerilla warfare and considered that the German army should be kept undemobilized as a safeguard against the spread of Bolshevism.

Foch agreed that "the German army could undoubtedly take up a new position, and that we could not prevent it." But he disagreed with Haig's conditions and insisted not only that the Germans must hand over a third of their artillery and half their machine-guns, but that the Allies must occupy the Rhineland, with bridgeheads on the east bank of the Rhine. Only by holding the Rhine would the Allies have a guarantee that Germany could not subsequently break off the peace negotiations, whereas Haig's proposals would facilitate the German withdrawal to and consolidation of a new position of resistance. Foch also intimated privately to Clemenceau that the occupation would "serve as a pledge for security as well as for reparations."

Pershing went even further than Foch and protested against granting any armistice. Foch, however, answered such objections logically : "War is only a means to results. If the Germans now sign an armistice under our conditions those results are in our possession. This being achieved, no man has the right to cause another drop of blood to be shed." The real results he sought by his terms went, however, beyond the armistice. Once the German army was out of the way France might then be able to frame the peace on her terms and not on those of President Wilson. Thus the ironical result of the President's action in allowing the soldiers to settle the armistice conditions was that he nullified the peace conditions set out in his Fourteen Points — and gave the Germans a just complaint, if not a realistic objection, that they had been entrapped to their doom by his promises.

The next point of difference was whether reparations should be mentioned in the armistice. The British objected, but the French insisted. Clemenceau cleverly and disarmingly argued, "I wish only to make mention of the principle," and advocated the vague but comprehensive formula, "reparations for damages," while the French Finance Minister strengthened its potential effect by inserting the innocent-looking reservation that "any future claims or demands on the part of the Allies remain unaffected." With greater innocence Colonel House swallowed this clause, and through his support it was added to the terms.

The next question was that of the naval terms, and here the national positions were reversed. Foch, having made his own terms so severe, was anxious to lighten the naval terms and to demand merely the surrender of submarines. He asked somewhat scoffingly : "As for the German surface fleet, what do you fear from it ? During the whole war only a few of its units have ventured from its ports. The surrender of these units will be merely a manifestation, which will please the public but nothing more." But Sir Eric Geddes, the First Lord of the Admiralty, reminded Foch that it was the British fleet which "held in check" the German fleet, and pointed out that if the latter was left intact the war-strain on the former would continue until peace was settled. Lloyd George suggested that as an effective but less humiliating compromise the naval terms should demand the internment and not the surrender of the German surface ships. This solution was agreed upon, although the Admiralty only gave way under protest, and the final demand, apart from the surrender of one hundred and fifty submarines, was for the internment "in neutral ports, or, failing them, Allied ports" of ten battleships and six battle-cruisers, besides light craft. Owing to the difficulty of finding an adequate neutral port, their ultimate destination became the British base of Scapa Flow. One important effect of this prolonged discussion was that the terms to Germany were not settled until Austria had capitulated — an effect which, as Lloyd George shrewdly foresaw, enabled the Allies to "put stiffer terms to Germany" with less chance of refusal.

The Germans' acceptance of these severe terms was hastened less by the existing situation on the western front than by the collapse of the "home front," coupled with exposure to a new thrust in the rear through Austria. The Allied advance in the west was still continuing, in some parts seeming to gather pace in the last days, but the main German forces had escaped from the perilous salient, and their complete destruction of roads and railways made it impossible for supplies to keep pace with the advancing troops. A pause must come while these communications were being repaired, and thus the Germans would have breathing space to rally their resistance. The advance reached the line Pont à Mousson-Sedan-Mézières-Mons-Ghent by November 11, — the line of the opening battles in 1914, — but strategically it had come to a standstill.

It is true that, to meet this situation, Foch had concentrated a large Franco-American force to strike below Metz directly east into Lorraine. As the general Allied advance had almost absorbed the enemy's reserves, this stroke, if driven in deeply and rapidly, promised the chance of turning the whole of this new line of defense along the Meuse to Antwerp and might even upset his orderly retreat to the Rhine. But it is unlikely that this Lorraine thrust, prepared for November 14, would have solved the hitherto insoluble problem of maintaining the initial momentum of advance after an initial break-through. Foch did not think so. For when asked how long it would take to drive the Germans back across the Rhine if they refused the armistice terms, he replied, "Maybe three, maybe four or five months. Who knows?" And his post-war comment on this Lorraine offensive was: "Its importance has always been exaggerated. It is regarded as the irresistible blow that was to fell and administer the knock-out to the Boche. That's nonsense. The Lorraine offensive was *not* in itself any more important than the attack then being prepared in Belgium, on the Lys."

More truly significant was the decision on November 4, after Austria's surrender, to prepare a concentric advance on Munich by three Allied armies, which would be assembled on the Austro-German frontier within five weeks. In addition Trenchard's Independent Air Force was about to bomb Berlin on a scale hitherto unattempted in air warfare. And the number of American troops in Europe had now risen to 2,085,-000, and the number of divisions to forty-two, of which thirty-two were ready for battle. The internal situation and the obvious external developments which could be calculated were the factors which produced Germany's decision to capitulate — not any single and hypothetical blow on the strongest part of her front. With revolution at home, the gathering menace on their southern frontier, and the continued strain on their western, the German delegates had no option but to accept the drastic terms of the armistice, which was signed in Foch's railway-carriage in the Forest of Compiègne at 5 A.M. on November 11. And at eleven o'clock that morning the World War came to an end.

1918 — THE BREAK

SCENE I

THE FIRST BREAK-THROUGH

At 4.30 a.m. on March 21, 1918, the sudden crash of some four thousand German guns heralded the breaking of a storm which, in grandeur of scale, of awe, and of destruction, surpassed any other in the World War. By nightfall a German flood had inundated forty miles of the British front; a week later it had reached a depth of nearly forty miles, and was almost lapping the outskirts of Amiens; and in the ensuing weeks the Allied cause itself was almost submerged.

These weeks rank with those of the Marne in 1914 as the two gravest military crises of the World War. In them Germany came desperately near to regaining that lost chance, and best chance, of victory, which she had forfeited in early September, 1914. And to the people of Britain at least the risk seemed even worse, because more fully realized and because their stake was greater.

No episode of the war is so studded with question marks as that on which the curtain rose, March 21, 1918. Why, when the Allies had been attacking with superior force for two years, were they suddenly fighting "with their backs to the wall"? Why, after the public had been assured that Interallied coöperation was assured and a generalissimo unnecessary, was one urgently demanded and appointed? Why, when the Allies had made so little visible impression on the German front in two years of constant offensive, were the Germans able to tear a huge hole in the Allied front within a few days? Why, as this breach so far exceeded in size the dream-aims of its Allied forerunners, did it fail to obtain any decisive results? In seeking the answers to these several "whys" lies the main interest of March 21 for history.

The primary cause of the sudden British change from the offensive to the defensive lay in the fact that the German fighting strength on the western front was increased by 30 per cent between November 1917 and March 21, 1918, while the British strength fell by 25 per cent, compared with the previous summer. The bulk of these fresh German troops were transferred from the Russian front, where Ludendorff, as a preliminary to his great bid for victory in the west, had wrung a definite peace from the Bolshevik Government, and also from Rumania. But if these facts explain the change, the causes of its abruptness and extent lie beneath the surface. Chief among them was that the British Command had dissipated its credit, both in balance of man-power and with the Government. This doubly unfortunate result was due to the strategy which can be summarized adequately in a single word, manifold in its ill-omened significance — "Passchendaele."

Conscious of his responsibility to the nation, and personally distrustful of Haig's judgment, Mr. Lloyd George placed a firm check on the flow of reënforcements to France lest they should be poured down another offensive drain-pipe. Friction between the two was almost inevitable, because of their extreme contrast of temperament and training. The one a volatile Welshman; the other a stubborn and taciturn Scot. The one with a magnetic power of drawing even the unwilling to him; the other with an impregnable capacity for holding even the most willing at a distance. The one infinitely adaptable; the other inflexibly consistent, and persistent. In the one, speech and thought so closely coincided that they became fused, while with the other the opening of the mouth automatically cut out the action of the brain. Anecdotes of Haig's inarticulateness, to the point of unintelligibility, are many. One of the best is of the occasion when, presenting the prizes to an Aldershot cross-country team, all that he could get out was: "I congratulate you on your running. You have run well. I hope you will run as well in the presence of the enemy."

Again, Lloyd George was as receptive to ideas as he was critical of the pretensions of hierarchical wisdom, and he constantly sought to gather a variety and diversity of opinions as

a broad basis for judgment. Haig, as his own admiring biographer, General Charteris, confesses, "had not a critical
mind," and neither knowledge of, nor interest in, affairs outside his own military work. And he took over the command
"genuinely convinced that the position to which he had now
been called was one which he, and he alone in the British army,
could fill." When to his rigidly disciplined outlook was added
this feeling of divine right, it raised an almost impassable
barrier of character between him and the Prime Minister.
Neither made much effort to surmount it, and growing distrust on both sides — a distrust of Haig's military and Lloyd
George's personal methods — steadily heightened it.

Throughout the months following Passchendaele and preceding the German offensive, Lloyd George was assiduously
seeking an opportunity to take the power out of Haig's hand,
as he feared to remove him from his place. His solution was
the Supreme War Council in control of a general Interallied
reserve. But the scheme was thwarted by Haig's action. For,
having no belief in the method of battle control by committee,
he shattered it by his refusal to contribute his small quota of
seven divisions. Whatever the just strength of his objection
to the method on principle, his action is not easy either to understand or to justify. For, convinced as he was that the German
attack was coming on his front, and conscious of his shortage
of reserves, it seems curious that he should not risk a contribution of seven divisions in order to draw from a pool of thirty.
He chose, instead, to rely on an arrangement with Pétain for
mutual support, whereby in case of need he might be reënforced by six to eight French divisions. This was far less than
Haig could hope for from the general reserve, if formed. Moreover, Haig's distrust of French fulfillment of such promises
had for years been so marked, his tongue so caustic about
them, that it is astonishing that he should have pinned his
faith to a small and purely French promise when he could
have had a much larger promise from a board on which there
was a British representative.

This excessive trust on the part of the British Command,
like the Government's withholding of reënforcements, may

well have been due to an apparently well-grounded belief in the power of their defense to stop a German attack. Why should the Germans succeed where the British had so often failed? The only close approach to a break-through by the British had been at Cambrai, with the tanks — and Haig knew that it was almost impossible for the Germans to have built tanks in quantity.

But in his defensive calculations, as in his offensive actions throughout the past two years, he seems to have underrated the infinite value of surprise, which for three thousand years of recorded warfare has proved the master-key to victory. The real significance of the Cambrai attack on November 20 previous had been that it had revived the use of such a key, forging it from an amalgam of armor and the caterpillar track. Unhappily, the effect of this tank key was largely lost because when inserted in the lock Haig had not the power to turn it fully, through exhausting his strength in the Passchendaele mud.

In the counter-attack of November 30 the Germans had used a key similar in principle if different in design — a short sharp bombardment with gas and smoke shell, followed up by an inrush of infantry, specially trained in the new infiltration tactics. It would seem that by the following March the British had not sufficiently taken this lesson to heart. For, though the Fifth Army's subsequent excuses of weak numbers and a long line were just, Gough had expressed confidence beforehand in his power to resist the onslaught.

But when Gough's original front was forced, an inadequate preparation and coördination of the measures to block the enemy's path further back were revealed. He had failed to arrange for the blowing up of certain causeways and General Headquarters had not given him a definite order. Worse still was the confusion caused by the fact that in the case of the more important railway bridges this duty was entrusted to the railway authorities instead of the local commanders, and in this way the vital railway bridge at Péronne was allowed to fall undestroyed into German hands.

If this was good luck for the Germans, their thorough and

skillful preparations for the initial assault had earned them success — although here again fortune favored them.

For the effect of the gas-gained surprise was immensely increased by Nature, which in the early hours of March 21 provided a thick mist that cloaked the infiltrating assailants as much as it masked the defending machine-guns. Without this aid it is questionable how far the German tactical surprise would have succeeded, and in this lay the essential inferiority of the German means of surprise, compared with that at Cambrai and later, on August 8, 1918, which was achieved by armored machines.

These not only formed the main material from which the key was manufactured, but provided the power to press it home and turn it. In contrast, Ludendorff had to depend on unarmored infantry to exploit the opening created by the brief but intense bombardment with gas-shell. For he had failed to grasp the significance of the tank and neglected to develop it in time; only in August 1918, when it was used to strike him a mortal blow, did he put it in the "urgent" class of war material.

But the German plan was distinguished by a research for tactical surprise more thorough and far-reaching than in any of the earlier operations of the war. The Germans significantly record that "Haig's dispatches dealing with the attacks of 1917 were found most valuable, because they showed how not to do it." To Ludendorff's credit he realized that the obvious is an obstacle that superior weight cannot compensate, and, once created, can rarely overcome. And he sought to effect and develop surprise by a compound of many deceptive elements. It is to his credit also that, unlike Falkenhayn, who merely wanted officer clerks, he surrounded himself with able assistants. Captain Geyer compiled the new training handbooks, while Colonel Bruchmüller had emerged from retirement to become the famous artillery "battle-piece" producer. With a prophetic play upon his name he was known as "Durchbruchmüller" — Break-through Müller. Under his superintendence the masses of artillery were brought up close to the front line in concealment, and opened fire without previous "registration" through the method he had introduced. The infantry were trained in new infiltrating tactics, of which the guiding idea was that the leading troops should probe and penetrate the weak points of the defense, while the reserves were directed to back up success, not to redeem failure. Special reconnaissance parties were assigned simply for the task of sending back early news of progress. The ordinary lines of attacking infantry were preceded by a dispersed chain of "storm" groups, with automatic rifles, machine-guns, and light mortars. These groups were to push straight through wherever they could find an opening and leave the defenders' "strong points" to be dealt with by the succeeding lines. The fastest, not the slowest, must set the pace, and no effort was made to keep a uniform alignment. Further, "the inclination of leaders to assemble their troops and get them in hand after a certain objective has been reached must be suppressed." "If the troops know the instructions of the commanders they can go on of themselves." The assaulting divisions were brought up overnight, those of the second line to a position only about a mile behind the first, and the third only ten miles back. All reserves started moving forward at zero, so as to be at hand when wanted. And when a second-line division was so used it came under the control, not of a higher commander sitting in rear, but of the first-line division commander, who had his finger on the pulse of the battle.

On November 11 at Mons — prophetic date and place — the German "leaders" had met in conclave to decide on the date and place of the forthcoming offensive. Naturally, according to German custom, the issue was thrashed out, not between the nominal commanders, but between their chiefs of staff — Ludendorff, Kuhl (Crown Prince Rupprecht's), Schulenberg (German Crown Prince's), together with Ludendorff's own strategical adviser, Major Wetzell. Kuhl and Schulenberg each wanted the attack to be made on the front of their own army groups — Kuhl indicating Flanders and Schulenberg the Verdun sector. Wetzell was inclined to support Schulenberg, arguing that an attack on the flanks of Verdun, a salient, would forestall any future Franco-American offensive at that delicate point, and, after defeating the French, the whole German strength could be turned against the British. Ludendorff, however, rejected this scheme on the score that the ground was unfavorable, that a break-through at Verdun would lead nowhere decisive, and that the French army had recuperated too well after nearly a year's undisturbed convalescence. He laid down as a first principle that "the British must be defeated," and thought that the drain of Passchendaele would make them an easy prey. But he disagreed with Kuhl's proposal to strike, between Ypres and Lens, towards Hazebrouck, as it would meet the main mass of the British, and this low ground would be long in drying. He favored instead an attack around St. Quentin, although Wetzell contended that it would be slowed down in crossing the old devastated area on the Somme, and was within easy reach of French reënforcements. A final decision was put off, and Rupprecht noted in his diary, "Ludendorff underestimates the toughness of the British."

In December, Wetzell tried to reconcile, and sagely combine, the two projects, by dividing the offensive into two acts — first, a wide-front attack on both sides of St. Quentin, and, second, a fortnight later, a break-through in Flanders towards Hazebrouck. The first act was only to be carried far enough to draw the British reserves southward. Wetzell summed up: —

We shall not, in my opinion, succeed in obtaining our object by *one* great attack at *one* place, however carefully it is prepared . . . we can only shatter their front by a clever combination of successive, definitely related, mutually reacting attacks on different parts of the front, finally in the direction of Hazebrouck.

It was to be left to Foch to adopt his method without acknowledgment. For, after further conferences, Ludendorff decided on January 27 in favor of the St. Quentin attack (known by the code-name "Michael") and against the Hazebrouck attack "St. George," which was only kept in mind and not in immediate readiness.

A further complication arose. The front from the Belgian coast to St. Quentin was under Rupprecht, and for political as well as personal reasons it was considered necessary to give the German Crown Prince a chance of redeeming his discredit at Verdun in 1916 — which was really Falkenhayn's. Hence he was given a share in the offensive by employing the Eighteenth Army (Hutier), which belonged to his army group, on the southern flank of the main offensive. It is a moot question whether he could not have helped better, if less gloriously, by using it for a diversion at Verdun, in order to draw the French reserves away from, instead of towards, the intended breach in the British front.

In a broad sense, Ludendorff's chosen sector, which extended from Arras to La Fère, fulfilled his new principle of taking the line of least resistance, for it was the weakest in defenses, defenders, and reserves. Moreover, it was close to the joint between the French and British armies, and so lent itself to a separation. But although it was true, as a generalization, that this sector was comparatively weak, the classification was loose and inaccurate. The northerly third of it was strong and strongly held, by Byng's Third Army, with fourteen divisions (four in reserve), while the bulk of the British reserves were on this flank, which also could and did receive support more quickly from the other British armies which lay to the north. The remaining two-thirds of the sector upon which the German blow fell was held by Gough's Fifth Army. The central part facing Marwitz's army was held by seven divisions (two in reserve). The southern part facing Hutier's army was also held by seven divisions (one in reserve).

But Ludendorff gave Below's army near Arras nineteen divisions for the initial attack, by its left wing only, on a nine and a half mile frontage. South of it came Marwitz's army. As the British salient towards Cambrai was not to be attacked directly, but pinched out, this four-mile stretch was adequately occupied by two German divisions, and Marwitz had eighteen divisions for his nine and a half mile attack frontage. On the extreme south, either side of St. Quentin, came Hutier's army. Ludendorff gave it only twenty-four divisions to attack on a twenty-mile frontage. Hence we see that it had only half the proportionate strength of the other armies. Despite his principle, he was distributing his strength according to the enemy's

strength and not concentrating against the weakest resistance. The direction given in his orders emphasized this still more. The main effort was to be exerted north of the Somme, for, after breaking through, Below and Marwitz were to wheel northwest, rolling up the British front, while the river and Hutier formed a screen to cover their flank. Hutier's army was merely an offensive flank guard. This plan was to be radically changed in execution, and to have the appearance of following the line of least resistance, because Ludendorff gained rapid success where he desired it little and failed to gain success where he wanted it most.

What of the British meantime? As the result of a war game played at Versailles, Sir Henry Wilson had forecasted that the enemy attack would come on the Cambrai-Lens sector, but that the Germans would wait to deliver it until about July 1, when their training and accumulation of forces would be complete. Wilson was somewhat outside the mark in place and still more out in time. Haig's intelligence was more accurate, although it did not foresee the full southward extension of the attack. As the time drew near signs multiplied sufficiently to enable Haig to calculate the date. On March 18 German prisoners captured near St. Quentin gave the date as the twenty-first, and on the evening of the twentieth Maxse's XVIII Corps was able through raiding to establish the certainty of the morrow's attack.

Thus it is true to say that no strategic surprise was obtained. Nor was it even obtainable under the conditions of 1918 in France. But with the opposing armies spread out in contact along the far-flung line of entrenchments, a quick breakthrough followed by a rapid exploitation along the line of least resistance might promise such a decisive upset as normally is only attainable by choosing the line of least expectation. The hurricane bombardment opened at 4.30 A.M. on the twenty-first, concentrating for two hours on the British artillery and then, reënforced by mortars, turning on the trenches. Almost all telephone cables were severed and wireless sets destroyed, while the fog made visual signaling impossible. Thus the troops were made dumb and the commander blind. At 9.40 A.M., or in some parts earlier, the German infantry advanced under cover of a creeping barrage, supplemented by low-flying aircraft.

The British outpost zone was overrun almost everywhere by midday, but this was inevitable and had been foreseen. But the northern attack met such stubborn resistance against the right of Byng's army that it had not seriously penetrated the main battle zone even by the night of the twenty-second, and, despite putting in successive reënforcements, the capture of Vaulx-Vraucourt was then the high-water mark of its progress. On most parts of Gough's army front the battle-zone resistance was just as firm, but the flood found a way through on the twenty-first near La Fère, on the extreme right, at Essigny, and at Ronssoy. The resistance of the 21st Division at Epéhy for a time checked this last breach from spreading northward, but it began to crumble so deeply that the neighboring sectors were affected. Southward, again, near St. Quentin, the line sagged still more deeply, and on the night of the twenty-second Gough was driven to order a general retirement to the line of the Somme. He was hurried into this precipitate decision by a mistaken report that the enemy was already across the Crozat Canal at Jussy and so behind his right flank. Early next morning the Péronne bridgehead was abandoned. Several of Gough's subordinate commanders were even more vague or misled as to the situation, control lapsed, and gaps occurred. The worst was at the joint between Byng's and Gough's armies, and this the Germans speedily accentuated. And a new danger arose further south at the joint between the British and French.

But Ludendorff, continuing to ignore his new principle, was only intent to nourish the attack near Arras, where progress was disappointing. Meantime Hutier, once across the Crozat Canal, was pressing swiftly forward, almost without check save from his own limited rôle. On the twenty-third Ludendorff again emphasizes in his orders that Below's is the principal effort, reënforces it by three divisions, and indicates that the Sixth and Fourth Armies, still more to the north, will chime in to help it. Two days later, when the check to Below has become still clearer, Ludendorff arranges that Below's hitherto passive right wing shall strike direct at Arras on the twenty-eighth, in order to overcome this strong place which is hampering and enfilading Below's attacking left wing. And on the twenty-ninth the Sixth Army, reënforced by six or seven divisions, is to extend the attack northwards between Arras and Lens — with Boulogne as its goal! Meanwhile Hutier is actually told not to pass the line Noyon-Roye for the time being.

On the twenty-sixth Ludendorff begins to doubt Below's chances and to turn his eyes south. But, instead of throwing his weight thither, he merely makes it a second principal effort. And, even so, it is to be towards Amiens by Marwitz's army, while Hutier is told not to cross the Avre without fresh orders. This means that the army which has all the difficult ground of the old 1916 Somme battlefields to cross is pushed on, while the army that has a smoother path is held back. The apparent explanation, and the extraordinary flux of Ludendorff's thought, are revealed in a later sentence of the order which shows that he is contemplating a vast fan-like movement in which three armies are to wheel south towards Paris while Below and his neighbors wheel north to crush the British against the sea-coast. The grandiose conception was far beyond Ludendorff's resources in reserves. It would seem that for the moment he was intoxicated with success, and, like Moltke in August 1914, was counting his chickens before they were hatched. Another parallel with 1914 was that the army commanders' reports of progress outstripped their actual stages of advance. Even they, however, were less futuristic than the Kaiser, who, according to Rupprecht, "announced a complete victory" on March 21.

On the twenty-seventh Hutier reached Montdidier, a penetration of nearly forty miles, but next day Ludendorff had a cold douche of reality when Below's Arras attack with nine divisions collapsed under a storm of fire from the expectant defense. No mist came to the aid of the attackers.

Ludendorff then put a belated stop to Below's vain efforts and countermanded the Sixth Army's attack intended for the morrow. Amiens was made the main objective, and Marwitz was given all the reserves at hand — nine divisions. But Hutier had to pause for two days until four fresh divisions reached him. By this time the surge toward Amiens was almost stagnant, its impetus having slackened far less because of the resistance than because of the exhaustion of the troops and the difficulties of supply. Roads were blocked, transports scuppered, and reserves harassed by the British air attacks, which here played a vital part. When the attack was renewed on March 30 it had little force and made little progress in face of a resistance that had been afforded time to harden, helped by the cement of French reserves which were now being poured into the sagging wall. That day was the first on which their artillery, arriving later than the infantry, had come into action in force. Even so, there was a moment of crisis when the

Germans captured the Moreuil Wood ridge, which was not only at the joint between the French and British but commanded the crossings of the Avre and Luce where they joined. And these covered the main Amiens-Paris railway. But the menace was warded off by a swift counter-stroke of the Canadian Cavalry Brigade, made on the initiative of and led by General Seely, ex-War Minister turned Murat The ridge was regained, and, although lost again next day by other troops, the coup seems to have extinguished the now flickering flame of German energy. Nearly a week passed before, on April 4, a further German effort was made by fifteen divisions, of which only four were fresh. Meeting a reënforced defense, this had still less success.

Seeing that his new effort was too late, Ludendorff then suspended the attack towards Amiens. At no time had he thrown his weight along the line of fracture between the British and French armies. Yet on March 24 Pétain had intimated to Haig that if the German progress continued along this line he would have to draw back the French reserves southwestwards to cover Paris. How little more German pressure would have been needed to turn the crack into a yawning chasm! The knowledge is one more testimony to the historical truth that a joint is the most sensitive and profitable point of attack.

The supreme features of this great offensive are, first, the immensity of its outward results compared with those of any previous offensive in the west; second, its ineffectiveness to attain decisive results. For the first it would be both unjust and untrue to blame the British troops. They achieved miracles of heroic endurance, and the prolonged resistance in most of the battle zone is the proof. The real cause of the subsequently rapid flow-back lay in the frequent breakdown of control and communication. During three years of trench warfare an elaborate and complex system, largely dependent on the telephone, had been built up, and when the static suddenly became fluid the British paid the inevitable penalty of violating that fundamental axiom of war — elasticity.

On the German side, Arras was the actual rock on which

their plan broke. It is probable that military conservatism cost them dear. For Bruchmüller has revealed that while Hutier's army carried out his surprise-bombardment designs, Below's in the north clung to their old-fashioned methods, refusing to dispense with preliminary ranging. Once again, and near the Somme again, Below's conventional military mind had proved the best asset to the British army.

But a more fundamental cause of the German failure was Ludendorff's own limitations. He had sufficient receptiveness to see a new truth, but not sufficient elasticity or conviction to carry it out fully in practice. The principle of following the line of least resistance was too novel for one who from his youth had been saturated in the Clausewitzian doctrine of striking at the enemy's main force. "The British must be defeated" was his catchword, his vision was bloodshot, and he could not realize that in strategy the longest way round is often the shortest way there — that a direct approach to the object exhausts the attacker and hardens the resistance by compression, whereas an indirect approach loosens the defender's hold by upsetting his balance.

In the actual execution of the offensive by the German troops there is another cause of failure that has been commonly overlooked and yet is of great significance. It is the physical effect on ill-nourished troops of breaking into an area full of well-filled supply depots, and the psychological effect of discovering that the enemy is so much better fed and equipped than themselves — that they have been nourished only with lies about the result of the U-boat campaign and the enemy's economic condition. This dual effect is to be traced in many sources of evidence. One of the most illuminating and trustworthy is the war-diary of the German poet and novelist, Rudolf Binding.

On March 27 he records : —

Now we are already in the English back-areas . . . a land flowing with milk and honey. Marvellous people these, who will only equip themselves with the very best that the earth produces. Our men are hardly to be distinguished from English soldiers. Everyone wears at least a leather jerkin, a waterproof . . . English boots or some other beautiful thing.

The horses are feeding on masses of oats and gorgeous foodcake . . . and there is no doubt the army is looting with some zest.

On the next day follows a highly significant entry : —

To-day the advance of our infantry suddenly stopped near Albert. Nobody could understand why. Our armies had reported no enemy between Albert and Amiens. . . . Our way seemed entirely clear. I jumped into a car with orders to find out what was causing the stoppage in front. Our division was right in front of the advance and could not possibly be tired out. It was quite fresh. . . .

As soon as I got near the town I began to see curious sights. Strange figures, which looked very little like soldiers, and certainly showed no sign of advancing, were making their way back out of the town. There were men driving cows . . . others who carried a hen under one arm and a box of note-paper under the other. Men carrying a bottle of wine under their arm and another one open in their hand. . . . Men staggering. Men who could hardly walk. When I got into the town the streets were running with wine. . . .

I drove back to Divisional Headquarters with a fearful impression of the situation. The advance was held up, and there was no means of setting it going again for hours.

It proved hopeless, and the officers were powerless, to collect the troops that day, while the sequel he records was that "the troops which moved out of Albert next day cheered with wine and in victorious spirits were mown down straight away on the railway embankment by a few English machine-guns."

But the intoxication due to loot was even greater and more general than that due to wine, and the fundamental cause of both was "the general sense of years of privation." A staff officer even stops a car, when on an urgent mission, to pick up an English waterproof from the ditch. And in this intoxication the Germans not only lose their chance of reaching Amiens, but ruin sources of supply invaluable to the maintenance of their own advance — wrecking waterworks for the sake of the brass taps. The cause of this senseless craving is revealed in their impression that "the English made everything either out of rubber or brass, because these were the two materials which we had not seen for the longest time." "The madness, stupidity, and indiscipline of the German troops is shown in other things as well. Any useless toy or trifle they seize and load into their packs, anything useful which they cannot carry away they destroy."

Once this plunder was exhausted the reaction was all the greater and the contrast of their own paucity with the enemy's plenty the more depressing. As hopes of military success fade and with them the hope of again nourishing their stomachs, and souls, on the enemy's supplies, a moral rot sets in rapidly.

Anyone with personal experience of war knows how the thought of food and of civilized comfort fills the soldier's horizon. How far was the German army's sudden moral decline from July onward, when the last attack proved abortive, due not only to increasing hunger but to the eye-opening conviction of the enemy's greater material power of endurance?

Propaganda and censorship could hide the difference so long as the front was an inviolable wall of partition. But when the Germans broke through the British lines and into the back-areas the truth was revealed to the German troops. Is the historical verdict, penetrating beneath the surface of military statistics and acreage to the psychological foundation, then to be that the British disaster of March 1918 was a stroke of fortune for those who suffered it? If so, it seems a pity that the solution was not tried earlier. Instead of conducting unwilling "frocks" round the front, the British Command might have arranged visits for Germans to its back-areas — that "land flowing with milk and honey." Or at least it might have designedly released a proportion of its prisoners after they had been suitably entertained! Such a strategy would certainly have supplied the imagination which many found so lacking in the military leadership.

1918 — THE BREAK

Scene II

THE BREAK-THROUGH IN FLANDERS

On April 9, 1918, the first anniversary of the abortive British attempt to break through the deadlocked trench front in Artois, the Germans made a more successful attempt — in the reverse direction. This was the second move in Ludendorff's gigantic offensive campaign which had begun on March 21. Springing from around Neuve-Chapelle, where, three years before, the first British attempt to break the deadlock had penetrated half a mile deep in all, a narrow German jet of attack swept away the opposing Portuguese and before noon on the ninth had penetrated to a depth of over three miles. To the north, but happily not to the south, the flanks of the breach crumbled, and, with fresh jets playing upon the British front, more sectors gave way.

By the next day twenty-four miles of frontage had been engulfed, and on the twelfth, Sir Douglas Haig issued his historic order of the day: "There is no other course open to us but to fight it out. Every position must be held to the last man. . . . With our backs to the wall and believing in the justice of our cause, each one of us must fight on to the end." To the British public, and even perhaps to the British forces, this message came like a thunderclap, awakening them to the graveness of the danger and seeming almost to convey a warning that hope had gone and only honor remained — to go down fighting with their faces to the foe.

Yet at that moment, and still more during the following days, it is probable that the least sanguine and most depressed man was not in the British ranks, but behind the advancing enemy — Ludendorff himself. On March 21 and the next days Ludendorff had seen his carefully contrived strategical plan — for his great bid for victory — going astray. The rapidity with which progress was made where he did not want it, and its slowness where he did want it, had driven him unwillingly to press on towards Amiens across the desert of the old Somme battlefields, instead of wheeling northwards from the Somme. With the repulse of his delayed assault on the Arras bastion on March 28, he had been forced to relinquish definitely his plan of rolling up the flank of the British armies and penning them back against the coast, isolated from their Allies.

But his thrust towards Amiens failed, however narrowly, to reach its destination — through its belatedness and difficulties of supply. In desperation, rather than in reflection, Ludendorff clutched at Wetzell's rejected scheme, and decided to launch the "St. George" attack against the Ypres-Lens sector. But he had pressed "Michael" too long and too far. Not only was he short of reserves, but he had to accumulate fresh supplies and ammunition, and switch his heavy artillery northwards. Conferences on April 1 and 2 showed that the offensive could not be ready until the ninth. And, instead of thirty-five additional divisions, only eleven could be sent in time. With a sense of ironic humor, the attack was rechristened "Georgette." Ludendorff was in luck at the start, but it was an elusive and delusive form of luck. The luck was that his opening blow fell on the front of the 2nd Portuguese Division, which was just about to be relieved by two British divisions, and had in the meanwhile been stretched to hold the whole corps sector.

The less agreeable aspect — for Ludendorff — of this piece of luck was somewhat unkindly epitomized in the comment that the Portuguese ruined Ludendorff and saved their Allies by running away. For, although the extension and development of this attack were "according to plan," Ludendorff never seems to have been whole-hearted in pursuing it. From the point of view of his strategy, and its interests, he either pressed the attack too hard or did not press enough.

The clearest evidence of this irresolution — and depression — is to be found in the captured archives of the Fourth German Army, which attacked in this sector. And their evidence is a better guide than any carefully prepared post-war apologia. They have the further advantage that they fell into enemy hands before any judicious adulterations could be made in the interests of high commanders' reputations. These German records show the General Staff Officers, Lossberg for the Fourth Army, Kuhl for the Army Group, and Ludendorff at the Supreme Command, settling all affairs without even the pretense of consulting their respective superiors, Sixt von Arnim, Rupprecht, and Hindenburg. They also show Ludendorff doling out divisions with a parsimonious hand, usually too late and inadequate in number for real success; so apprehensive that his new bulge would become another sack that at the moment of supreme opportunity he stops the German advance for fear of a counter-attack.

But all this was hidden from the British commanders and men. They only knew the enemy's blows, not his doubts and disquietude. And if he felt himself in a sack, they felt themselves in a mincing machine — with an unpleasant likelihood of their minced remains being ejected into the sea. That is the sort of wall that an army does not relish having at its back. Whereas on the Somme there had at least been ample room to withdraw, in the north the British troops, bases, and communications were all crowded into and passed through a narrow "throat" of land sensitive to the least pressure and all too easy to strangle. Apart from the coast railway, the only lateral line of communication ran through St. Pol-Lillers-Hazebrouck, barely fifteen miles behind the front trenches. Thus it was that a ten-mile German penetration, reached on April 12, and, happily, never deepened appreciably, was as menacing, if not more so, than forty miles had been on the Somme.

The strain was all the more severe because it fell on troops already strained. Besides the Portuguese, only one — the 55th — of the six divisions between the La Bassée and the Ypres-Comines Canal was not already battle-worn, having come to this front on relief from the battle in the south. Strained, they were also stretched. The drain on Haig's re-

serves and the greater importance of the vital bastion of high
ground, Arras-Givenchy, had caused a distribution of strength
by which this handful of divisions had to hold a front of twenty-
four miles.   Worst of all, the greatest stretching of all fell on
those who could least bear it.   The Portuguese corps had been
holding a six-mile front, on both sides of Neuve-Chapelle.
It had been in the line for a long time, and increasing cases of
insubordination had been a warning of declining morale.   The
remedy applied was an inverted example of military judgment.
General Horne, the First Army Commander, reshuffling his
dispositions, withdrew the 1st Portuguese Division, all but one
brigade, from the line on April 5.   The 2nd also was to be
relieved by British divisions on the night of April 9, but meanwhile it was given the whole corps sector to hold.   We might
aptly coin the phrase "First Army aid" as a satirical definition
for misguided first aid.   Horne's solution is the more curious
in that he had been warned by his "Q" staff that the convergence of German railways made the Lys sector the most
probable point of attack; indeed, the only point where an
attack could be mounted.   They had, further, sought permission to prepare special supply dumps fifteen miles in rear
to meet the danger of a break-through here, but had been
rebuffed.   Happily, they began preparations — without his
knowledge.   And the existence of these dumps helped to ease
the emergency that followed.

For at 4.05 A.M. on the ninth an intense bombardment was
opened on the eleven-mile front between the La Bassée Canal
and Armentières; the flanks of this sector were deluged with
mustard gas — an indication that they were to be paralyzed
but not immediately attacked.   At 7.30 A.M., after a slackening in the bombardment, small groups of German infantry
began to move forward, and at 9 A.M., after the bombardment
had swelled again for an hour, the assault was launched by a
mass of nine divisions of the German Sixth Army — against
three.   Once more, as on March 21, nature afforded it a cloak
in the form of a thick mist.   At the southern extremity the
55th (a Lancashire Territorial division) held on to Givenchy
firmly, opposing so unshakable a resistance as not only to

break the attack, but to dissuade the German Command from subsequent attempts to extend it southwards.

But in the centre the Germans swiftly overran the Portuguese positions.   It is a reasonable criticism that there was an

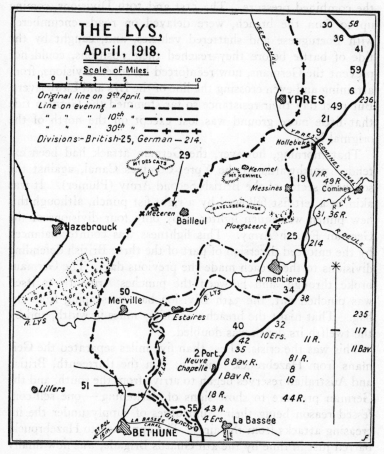

THE LYS,
April, 1918.

Scale of Miles.

Original line on 9th April.
Line on evening "   10th "
"   "   "   30th "
Divisions:- British-25, German — 214.

error of judgment in leaving this division even for a few days with a front more than double that of the 55th on its flank. The sturdy resistance of King Edward's Horse and the 11th Cyclist Battalion checked the German onrush, and helped, with that of the reserve brigade of the 55th Division, to prevent the Germans from crumbling away the southern flank.   This resistance, indeed, tended to shepherd the German advance into the northwesterly direction, which it took more and more.

But on the northern flank of the break-through the 40th Division, its own flank laid bare, was partly overwhelmed by the combined pressure. The 51st and 50th Divisions, coming up to dam the breach, were delayed on roads encumbered with Portuguese and shattered vehicles, and, caught by the tide of battle before they reached their positions, could not prevent the Germans, now reënforced by seven divisions, from attaining and even crossing the line of the Lys and Lawe rivers. But next day their resistance so far stemmed the German tide that little more ground was lost except on the north of the original bulge.

That morning, however, the German attack had been extended northwards to the Ypres-Comines Canal, against the southern sector of the British Second Army (Plumer). It was akin to a left-fist followed by a right-fist punch, although this new punch was much lighter — by only four divisions of the German Fourth Army. This lightness was counter-balanced by the enforced diversion of part of the three British defending divisions to the breach made the previous day. The Germans broke through, and between the punches Armentières itself was pinched out, the 34th Division barely escaping from the bag. That night the breach was thirty miles in width, and by the twelfth its depth was doubled.

This was the crisis. Less than five miles separated the Germans from Hazebrouck junction. On the thirteenth, British and Australian reserves began to arrive from the south, and the German pressure to show signs of slackening — one self-confessed reason being their "difficulties of supply under the increasing attacks from the air." The approach to Hazebrouck, barred just in time by the 4th Guards Brigade, was now finally bolted by the 1st Australian Division, and the remaining German pressure was exerted almost entirely on the northern half of the breach.

Plumer now took over charge of all except the southern fringe of the battle area, and to shorten his line, as well as to forestall a fresh extension of the German attack, he began an unhurried withdrawal from the Ypres salient to a line just in front of the immortal town. This was a wise and clear-sighted move, even though it abandoned the few square miles of mud which had been purchased at so terrible a price the previous autumn.

Although the enemy gained Bailleul and the Ravelsberg Ridge on the fifteenth, he was then stopped at Meteren and in front of Kemmel Hill, and by the eighteenth the storm subsided. Meantime storms of another type had been raging behind the front. Foch's appointment as Generalissimo did not seem to Haig to have brought him the prompt support he had expected. Ever since the tenth, and, indeed, before, he had been pressing Foch for French aid and active share in the battle. On the fourteenth an acrimonious conference took place at Abbeville, and next day Haig made the stricture "that the arrangements made by the Generalissimo were insufficient to meet the military situation."

Foch, on the other hand, was, perhaps to the point of hazard, intent on husbanding his reserves for an offensive. In his opinion, on April 14, "la bataille du nord est finie" — where to many observers it looked rather as if the British army was "finie." As usual he illustrated his opinion by a parable — of the rings made by dropping a stone into water, the successive rings growing less marked until the water became still. To hard-pressed Allies these parables were apt to be irritating. But his prediction proved right, even though, as at Ypres in 1914 and 1915, the British troops suffered a terrible strain in proving him right.

Contrary to what has been alleged, five French divisions arrived behind the British front as early as the fourteenth. But their intended counter-attacks, as at Ypres in 1915, did not at first materialize. Let it be said, however, in justice and as a matter of tactical interest, that British counter-attacks throughout this battle achieved consistently little gain, at heavy loss. On the eighteenth a French division took over Kemmel Hill, and next day the remainder entered the line. On the twenty-fifth the Germans resumed their offensive, but only on a limited front. The famous Kemmel Hill was captured from the French, and the British to the north were also forced back. For a few hours a last opportunity was vouch-safed to the Germans, but through Ludendorff's intervention they refrained from exploiting it. After a final, costly, and more abortive assault on the twenty-ninth, the German offensive was abandoned.

As General Edmonds, the official historian, has penetratingly remarked, "it is easy to see why Ludendorff collapsed after the eighth of August, 1918 — on the twenty-ninth of April he was already well on the way to despair."

1918 — THE BREAK

Scene III

THE BREAK-THROUGH TO THE MARNE

Four battle-worn British divisions were "resting" in a quiet sector north of the Aisne, between Reims and Soissons, far detached from the rest of the army. They had been sent to the French front, after strenuous exertions in the battles of the Lys, in return for French reënforcements which had gone north to aid the British in the later stages of that "backs to the wall" struggle. On the tranquil Aisne they could recuperate while still serving a useful purpose as guardians of the trench-line.

It was too quiet to be true. But the uneasiness of the local British commanders — shared by certain of their French neighbors — was lightly discounted by their French superiors. On May 25 they received from French headquarters the message that "in our opinion there are no indications that the enemy has made preparations which would enable him to attack to-morrow." Next morning the French captured two prisoners who told of the impending attack, but the Higher Command had no plan to meet it, and, even so, did not warn the troops until late in the day. Too late!

For at 1 A.M. on May 27, 1918, a terrific storm of fire burst on the Franco-British front between Reims and north of Soissons, along the famous Chemins-des-Dames; at 4.30 A.M. an overwhelming torrent of Germans swept over the front trenches; by midday it was pouring over the many unblown bridges of the Aisne, and by May 30 it had reached the Marne — site and symbol of the great ebb of 1914. After nearly four years a menace deemed forever past had returned to a point that endowed it with demoralizing symbolism.

Happily, it proved to be "thus far and no farther." Like the two great preceding offensives of March 21 and April 9, that of May 27 achieved astonishing captures of ground and prisoners, but it brought the Germans little nearer to their strategical object. And, even more than its predecessors, its very success paved the way for their downfall. To the reasons for this we shall come. But why, a month after the last onslaught, in the north, had come to an end; why, when there had been this long interval for preparation and for examination of the situation by a now unified command, should a surprise greater than any before have been possible? This is perhaps the most interesting historical question of the battle.

It has long been known, of course, that the French Higher Command, the one directly concerned with the safety of the Aisne sector, did not believe in the likelihood of an attack. Nor did the British Higher Command, which, however, was concerned with the front in the north, and expected a further onslaught there. If not justified by the event, the British had some cause for expecting it, as German disclosures have since attested.

But the Intelligence Service of another of the Allies, better placed to take a wide survey, did give the warning — only to be disregarded until too late. On May 13, a fortnight after the fighting in Flanders had died away, the British Intelligence came to the conclusion that "an attack on a broad front between Arras and Albert is intended." Next day this was discussed at a conference of the Intelligence section of the American Expeditionary Force, and the head of the Battle-Order section, Major S. T. Hubbard, gave a contrary opinion, holding that the next attack would be against the Chemin-des-Dames sector, between May 25 and 30. Among the reasons given were that, as surprise was the keynote of the German method, this sector was one of the few where it was now possible; that it was all the more likely to be chosen because regarded by the Allies as secure and as a resting ground for tired divisions; that its feasible frontage corresponded well with the limited German resources available at the moment, and that this hypothesis was confirmed by the ascertained location of the German troops, particularly of certain picked divisions.

The warning in detail was conveyed to the French General Headquarters, but fell on deaf ears. Why should credence be given to an opinion coming from such an amateur army, not yet tested in battle, over the verdict of war-tried and highly developed Intelligence services? The warning was reiterated, however, and Colonel de Cointet, Chief of the French Intelligence, was won over to its acceptance. But now, as at Verdun two years before, the Operations branch opposed until too late the view of its own Intelligence. This time, however, it was less blameworthy, for it was tugged the other way by the comforting assurances of General Duchêne, Commander of the Sixth French Army, in charge of the Chemin-des-Dames sector.

This general, indeed, bears a still heavier responsibility, for he insisted on the adoption of the long-exploded and wasteful system of massing the infantry of the defense in the forward positions. Besides giving the enemy guns a crowded and helpless target, this method ensured that, once the German guns had made a bloated meal of this luckless cannon-fodder, the German infantry would find practically no local reserves to oppose their progress through the rear zones. In similar manner all the headquarters, communication centres, ammunition depots, and railheads were pushed close up, ready to be dislocated promptly by the enemy bombardment.

Pétain's instructions for a deep and elastic system of defense had evidently made no impression on General Duchêne, so that it was still less a matter for wonder that the protests of junior British commanders met with a rebuff — and the conclusive "J'ai dit." It was unfortunate also, if perhaps less avoidable, that when the four British divisions forming the IX Corps (Hamilton Gordon) arrived from the north at the end of April, their depleted ranks filled up with raw drafts from home, they were hurried straight into the line, as the best place to complete their training.

The central backbone of the Aisne defenses was formed by the historic Chemin-des-Dames ridge north of the river. The eastern half of this "hog's back" was to be held by the British, with the 50th Division (H. C. Jackson) on the left, next the

8th Division (Heneker), and beyond the end of the ridge, in the low ground from Berry-au-Bac along the Aisne and Marne canal, the 21st Division (D. G. M. Campbell), joining up with the French troops covering Reims. The infantry of the 25th Division (Bainbridge) was in reserve.

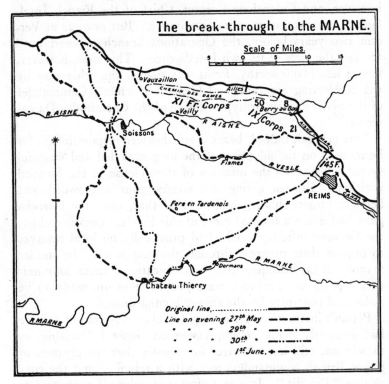

The break-through to the MARNE.

Scale of Miles.

Original line. ————
Line on evening 27th May ———
   "   "   29th " ———·———
   "   "   30th " ——··——
   "   "   1st June. +—+—+

Altogether the French Sixth Army front was held by four French and three British divisions, with three and one respectively in reserve. Against these tired or raw troops, in the main attack from Berry-au-Bac westwards, fifteen German divisions, all but one brought up fresh, were to fall upon five, with two more for the subsidiary attack between Berry-au-Bac and Reims, while seven German divisions lay close up in support.
Even so, the German superiority was not so pronounced as

in the March and April offensives, whereas both the rapidity and the extent of their progress were greater. Yet this time the tactical surprise of the assault was unaided by the heavy ground mists which had previously helped so much by wrapping the Germans' initial advance in a cloak of invisibility. And they had a series of extraordinarily difficult obstacles to cross. The conclusion is, therefore, that the advantage was due in part to the strategic surprise — the greater unexpectedness of the time and place — and in part to the folly of exposing the defenders so completely to the demoralizing and paralyzing effect of the German bombardment — by 3719 guns on a front of under forty miles. This last, indeed, was a form of surprise, for the object of all surprise is the dislocation of the enemy's morale and mind, and the effect is the same whether the enemy be caught napping by deception or allows himself to be trapped with his eyes open. Further, the Germans' success on May 27, 1918, deserves study and comparison with their other offensives, whose success was almost in mathematical ratio to their degree of surprise. This final year, indeed, read in the light of previous years, affords fresh proof that surprise — or, more scientifically, the dislocation of the enemy's mental balance — is essential to true success in every operation of war. A lesson oft-repeated, oft-ignored. At the bar of history any commander who risks the lives of his men without seeking this preliminary guarantee is condemned. And peoples who count their dead to-day may well feel that the trial, and the sentence, if the verdict be "guilty," should not wait so long.

Let us pass to the events of May 27. For three and a half hours the unfortunate troops had to endure a bombardment unparalleled, according to the verdict of the more experienced sufferers, in its intensity. And the ordeal of those hours of helpless endurance, amid the ever-swelling litter of shattered dead and untended wounded, was made more trying by the troops having to crouch, semi-suffocated in gas-masks. Then the grey waves advanced — a relief, if only of action, at last. Three-quarters of an hour later they had reached the crest of the ridge in the centre, near Ailles. This uncovered the flank of the left British division, the 50th, forcing its survivors to fall back down the other slope. Next to it the 8th Division was being forced to give way, although two of its brigades held stubbornly for a time on the north bank of the Aisne.

Here the 2nd Devons earned imperishable glory and a citation in the French Orders of the Day — by sacrificing themselves almost to a man in a stand which gained breathing space for fresh resistance to take form in rear. On the British right, the attack on the 21st Division developed later; this division was awkwardly placed with the swampy Aisne and Marne canal running through the centre of its battle zone, but most of it was successfully extricated and withdrawn west of the canal. By midday the situation was that the Germans had reached and crossed at most points the Aisne from Berry-au-Bac to Vailly — helped by the fact that General Duchêne had been belated in giving the order to blow up the bridges. Hitherto the German progress had been evenly distributed, but in the afternoon a heavy sagging occurred in the centre, at the junction of the French and British wings, and the Germans pushed through as far as Fismes on the Vesle. This was natural, both because it is an habitual tendency, and because the heaviest weight — more than four to one — of the assault had fallen on the two French divisions in the centre and the left of the 50th Division adjoining them.

This sagging, together with the renewed German pressure, compelled a drawing back of the flanks. On the east, or British, flank this operation was distinguished by a remarkable manœuvre of the 21st Division, which wheeled back during the night through hilly wooded country, while pivoting on and keeping touch with the Algerian division, which formed the right of the army.

After a pause in the morning of May 28, the Germans forced the passage of the Vesle, and on the twenty-ninth they made a vast bound, reaching Fère-en-Tardenois in the centre and capturing Soissons on the west, both important nodal points, which yielded them quantities of material. The German troops had even outstripped in their swift onrush the objectives assigned to them, and had done this despite the counter-attacks which Pétain was now shrewdly directing against their sensitive right flank. On the thirtieth the German flood swept on to the Marne, but it was now flowing in a narrowing central channel, for this day little ground was yielded by the Allied right flank, where the four British divisions — the 8th and 50th now merely remnants — had been reënforced by the 19th (Jeffreys), as well as by French divisions. Next day what remained of the original four was relieved by the French, who now took over command from the IX Corps, although fractions of them still remained in the fighting line for another three weeks as part of the 19th Division.

But from May 31 onwards the Germans, checked on the side of Reims and in front by the Marne, turned their efforts to a westward expansion of the great bulge — down the corridor between the Ourcq and the Marne towards Paris. Hitherto the French reserves had been thrown into the battle as they arrived, in an attempt to stem the flood, which usually resulted in their being caught up and carried back by it. On June 1, however, Pétain issued orders for the further reserves coming up to form, instead, a ring in rear, digging themselves in and thus having ready before the German flood reached them a vast semicircular dam which would stop and confine its now slackening flow. When it beat against this in the first days of June its momentum was too diminished to make much impression, whereas the appearance and fierce counter-attack of the 2nd American Division at the vital joint of Château-Thierry was not only a material cement, but an inestimable moral tonic to their weary Allies.

In those few days of "flooding," the Germans had taken some 65,000 prisoners, but whereas this human loss was soon to be more than made up by American reënforcements, strategically the Germans' success had merely placed them in a huge sack which was to prove their undoing less than two months later. As in each of the two previous offensives, the tactical success of the Germans on May 27 proved a strategical reverse, because the extent to which they surprised their enemy surprised, and so upset the balance of, their own command.

For, as the disclosures of General von Kuhl have revealed,

the offensive of May 27 was intended merely as a diversion, to attract the Allied reserves thither preparatory to a final and decisive blow at the British front covering Hazebrouck. But its astonishing opening success tempted the German Command to carry it too far and too long, the attraction of success attracting thither their own reserves as well as the enemy's. Nevertheless, we may justly speculate as to what might have resulted if the attack had begun on April 17, as ordered, instead of being delayed until May 27, before the preparations were complete. The Germans would have worn out fewer of their reserves in ineffectual prolongations of the Somme and Lys offensives, while the Allies would have still been waiting for the stiffening, moral and physical, of America's man-power. Time and surprise are the two supreme factors in war. The Germans lost the first and forfeited the second by allowing their own surprise to surprise themselves.

1918 — THE BREAK

Scene IV

THE SECOND BATTLE OF THE MARNE, JULY 1918

How apt, if how strange, the historical coincidence by which, as the Marne had been the first high-water mark and witnessed the first ebb of the tide of invasion in 1914, so four years later it was destined to be the final high-water mark from which the decisive ebb began. For on July 15, 1918, the shell-churned wastes around Reims were the scene of the last German offensive on the western front. The tide of German success was definitely stemmed, and three days later the ebb began under pressure of the great Allied counterstroke.

But although the first day marked the last German bid for victory, the actual attack was by no means the Germans' supreme effort, nor had it the decisive aims popularly ascribed to it at the time. For Ludendorff still adhered to his guiding idea that the British, severely shaken in the great battles of March and April, should be the target for his decisive blow and that their front in Flanders should be the stage on which he would produce this final drama of victory.

Thus, as has already been told, the spectacular May 27 attack when the Germans, pouring over the Chemin-des-Dames, across the Aisne and to the Marne, seemed to menace Paris itself, was conceived merely as a diversion to draw the Allied reserves away from Flanders. And its rapid success, surprising Ludendorff as much as his attack surprised Foch, dug a pitfall for the Germans by luring their own reserves thither to exploit and retain this apparent windfall.

So also with the June 9 attack, less bountiful in its fruits, that had been launched near Compiègne to break down the buttress of Allied territory that lay between the huge salients created by the German "pushes" of March and May. When, instead, this German attack was broken off by Ludendorff, with little gained, but his own reserves still further drained, he considered "the enemy in Flanders still so strong that the German army could not attack there yet." So he planned a further diversion — to be made by forty-seven divisions attacking on either side of Reims. The principal blow was to be delivered by the First (Mudra) and Third (Einem) Armies, driving towards Châlons, while the Seventh Army (Boehn) sought to cross the Marne near Dormans and to converge with the main advance in the direction of Epernay.

But the sands of time were slipping out for the Germans, and American reënforcements, like the sands of the shore in potential number, were slipping into the Allied line of battle, there to become a cement for this grievously strained rampart. Appreciating this, Ludendorff intended his Flanders attack, once more towards the nodal point of Hazebrouck, to follow on the twentieth, only five days after the Reims diversion. On July 16 actually, as soon as the Reims attack was under way, artillery and aircraft were sent off by train to the Flanders front, and Ludendorff himself moved to Tournai to supervise the staging and production of his decisive drama.

But the curtain was never to rise upon it. The Reims diversion had not even the brilliant opening success of its predecessors, and on July 18 the Allied counter-stroke so jeopardized the Germans' situation that Ludendorff felt compelled to postpone, if not yet to abandon, the fulfillment of his dream. The reason why the German offensive "fell flat" on July 15 was that east of Reims it was played to an empty "first night" house. One of the great stories of the war which everybody knows is that of the "elastic defense," in face of which the German onslaught lost its momentum before it reached the real position of the French resistance. Statesmen and generals have vied with each other in acclaiming the brilliance of "Gouraud's manœuvre." Alas! the story must be consigned to its place with many others in the museum of war legends.

The manœuvre was entirely due to Pétain, that cool, un-

emotional company director of modern war and shrewd economist of human lives who, called to be Commander-in-Chief
after the Nivelle fiasco of 1917, had systematically worked
to rebuild the French army and to restore the stability of its
man-power and morale that had been so undermined by the
extravagant offensive policy of Joffre and Nivelle from 1914
to 1917.

Not content merely to reorganize, Pétain had set himself
to ensure against a recurrence of the trouble by tactics that
should be both an economy of force and an economy of the
nervous force of the combatant. To this end, one method was
an elastic defense in depth, allowing the initial shock and impetus of the enemy's attack to be absorbed by a thinly held
forward position, and then awaiting him on a strong position
in rear, when the enemy's troops would be beyond the range
of the bulk of their supporting artillery.

This method Pétain had sought to apply against the German attack of June 9, but, although partially successful, its
full effect was lost through the reluctance of the local commanders, still clinging to their old offensive dogmas, to reconcile themselves to a voluntary yielding up of a few square
miles of worthless ground. And before July 15, when the
coming German attack was definitely expected, a week's argument was required before Pétain could persuade the lion-
hearted Gouraud, who commanded the French Fourth Army
east of Reims, to adopt this elastic manœuvre.

But even when we have ascribed it to the right source, the
accumulation of historical error is not fully corrected. For the
method was not the revolutionary innovation that it has been
termed. The Germans, in fact, had used it on September
25, 1915 — nearly three years before — to discomfit the great
French autumn offensive in Champagne. And the underlying idea can be traced back another two thousand years —
to Cannæ, where Hannibal applied it against the Romans in
a distinctly more subtle and decisive way.

But it sufficed, even in the mild way of 1918, to thwart the
German attack east of Reims, where its effort was immeasur-
ably strengthened by the German failure to achieve a surprise

such as had marked their earlier offensives of 1918. Even the exact hour was discovered by an evening raid on July 14, and thus before the German infantry advanced from their trenches they had been trapped and riven by the French artillery counter-preparation. They withered away before the machine-guns of the French outpost line, and the shrunken remnants that passed beyond failed to make even a crack in the main position.

But the dramatic nature of this repulse east of Reims has obscured the fact that it was not the whole battle. West of Reims the front had only been stabilized for a month since the last German thrust, and the newly improvised position was a handicap to the execution of the elastic method by commanders who were slow to grasp it. Thus here the German attack deepened the corner of the great bulge made in May, and not only pushed across the Marne, but behind Reims, so that it threatened to undercut this pivot of the Allied resistance. If the threat had an important influence on the French plan for the counter-stroke, its physical progress was stopped on July 16. The German attack had degenerated into local actions, disconnected and therefore useless, while the French artillery and aircraft, by bombarding the Marne crossings, made it difficult for the Germans to obtain supplies. Next day a queer hush of expectation spread over the far-flung battlefield. The stage was set for the great "revanche."

In an event so significant for the history of the world, the main historical interest is to determine its causes. The chief among them is to be found, not by any analysis of military art, but by a process far more true to the character of the World War — that of drawing up a balance-sheet of the previous six months' transactions. When Ludendorff opened his campaign he had a credit balance of 207 divisions, 82 in reserve. Now he had only 66 "fit" divisions in reserve, most of them really so "watered down" that they could hardly be counted as sound assets.

If these operations had made serious inroads into the Franco-British balance of man-power, the Allies had at least averted liquidation, and now, in July, ample and increasing

American drafts were being paid into their account. Like a promissory note, this American aid was of incalculable value in restoring their credit — their morale and confidence — even before it made good their material losses. Pétain, the military economist, had appreciated this primary factor long before, when he had said, "If we can hold on until the end of June our situation will be excellent. In July we can resume the offensive; after that victory will be ours."

If this simple calculation of time and numbers has the effect of attenuating the popular image of an inspired "Foch counter-stroke" wresting victory from the jaws of defeat, it is regrettable, but it is reality. Unfortunately, even what remains suffers in examination, and in the outcome a further reduction. War is a masculine activity, and so it is perhaps natural that the feminine maxim, "Il faut souffrir pour être belle," should be inverted. For in military history it is both easy and pleasant for all concerned to make an image of beauty, whereas it is not only hard for the seeker to reach the truth, but the subject usually suffers in consequence.

The riddle of July 18, 1918, might aptly be put in terms of the old conundrum: "When is a counter-stroke not a counter-stroke?" Foch's mystical faith in the almighty power of the offensive "will to conquer" had long since been shown at the Marne in 1914 — where day after day he had ordered attacks, apparently oblivious of the reality that his exhausted troops could do and did nothing more than cling precariously to their ground.

Then at Ypres, the same year, he had spurred on Sir John French to order ambitious attacks, while actually the British troops were barely resisting superior numbers. On these occasions the result justified the spirit, if not the letter, of his instructions. But when the German gas attack made a hole in the Allied line at Ypres, in April 1915, Foch's refrain of "Attaquez," and his unredeemed promises of a French attack, caused Sir John French to waver almost nightly from the resolve to withdraw and straighten out the line, as Smith-Dorrien, to his cost, urged from the outset. Thus, when this common-sense course was ultimately followed, the British had merely lost not only Smith-Dorrien's services but many lives to no purpose.

When Foch was rehabilitated in 1917 this "offensive" instinct still dominated him, and when the crisis of March 1918 called him to the Supreme Command he had hardly set about his unenviable task of restoring the battered front of the Allies before he was dreaming of fresh offensives. Even before the new collapse of the Aisne front in May he had issued a "directive" to Haig and Pétain for attacks to free the lateral railway near Amiens and Hazebrouck.

If this project showed his practical belief in his theory of freedom of action, it is also evidence that he had no idea of luring the Germans into vast salients which he could cut off in flank — which was the conception subsequently extolled by popular propagandists. Similarly, the truth of the great counter-stroke of July 18 is that it was not conceived, by Foch at least, as a counter-stroke at all. But the refrain "Attaquez" was chanted so continually that sooner or later it was bound to coincide with a "psychological moment" — as on July 18.

In the meantime Ludendorff's keenness in pursuing a similar policy, and the wariness of Pétain and Haig, helped to prevent the Allied forces from becoming seriously involved in a premature offensive before the balance of numbers changed. In contrast, it was the oft-derided economist, Pétain, the "cautious," who had conceived the plan of the defensive-offensive battle as it was actually waged — first a parry to the enemy's thrust and then a riposte when he was off his balance. On June 4 he had asked Foch to assemble two groups of reserves at Beauvais and Epernay respectively with a view to a counter-stroke against the flank of any fresh German advance. The first group, under Mangin, had been used to break the German attack of June 9, and was then switched a little further east to a position on the west flank of the German salient between Soissons and Reims which bulged towards the Marne.

Foch, however, planned to use it for the strictly offensive purpose of a push against the rail centre of Soissons. While this was being prepared, the Intelligence Service made it clear that the Germans were about to launch a fresh attack near Reims. Foch thereupon determined to anticipate it, not retort to it, by launching his offensive on July 12. Pétain, however, had the contrary idea of first stopping and then smiting the enemy when the latter had entangled himself. And, perchance curiously, the French troops were not ready on July 12, so that the battle was fought rather according to Pétain's than to Foch's conception. But not altogether. For Pétain's plan had comprised three phases: first, to hold up the German attack; second, to launch counter-strokes against the flanks of the fresh pockets it was likely to make on either side of Reims; third, and only third, when the German reserves had been fully drawn towards those pockets, to unleash Mangin's army in a big counter-offensive eastward along the baseline of the main bulge — the enemy's rear — and so close the neck of the vast sack in which the German forces south of the Aisne would be enclosed.

Events and Foch combined to modify this conception. As already narrated, the German attack west of Reims had made an unpleasantly deep pocket, penetrating well over the Marne and threatening to take in rear the natural buttress formed by the Montagne de Reims. To avert the danger, Pétain was driven to use most of the reserves he had intended for the second phase of the counter-stroke. And to replace them he decided to draw from Mangin's army, and to postpone the latter's counter-offensive — already ordered by Foch for July 18.

When Foch — full of eagerness and with his spirit still more fortified, if that was possible, by Haig's promise to send British reserves — heard of Pétain's action, he promptly countermanded it. Hence on July 18 the French left wing [1] was launched to its counter-offensive while the defensive battle was still in progress in the centre and on the right wing. This

[1] The spearhead of this consisted of Mangin's Tenth Army, which had ten divisions in the first line (including the American 1st and 2nd Divisions), six divisions and Robillot's Cavalry Corps in the second line, and the British 15th and 34th Divisions in reserve. Mangin struck at 4.35 A.M., using his massed tanks on the Cambrai method without any artillery preparation. The left of Degoutte's Sixth Army, on Mangin's inner flank, chimed in one and a half hours later, after a preliminary bombardment. Degoutte's subsidiary rôle was marked by the fact that he had only seven divisions (among them the American 4th and 26th) in the first line and one in the second; he was later reënforced by the American 42nd, 32nd, and 28th Divisions, which bore the main burden in the final stage of the advance to the Vesle.

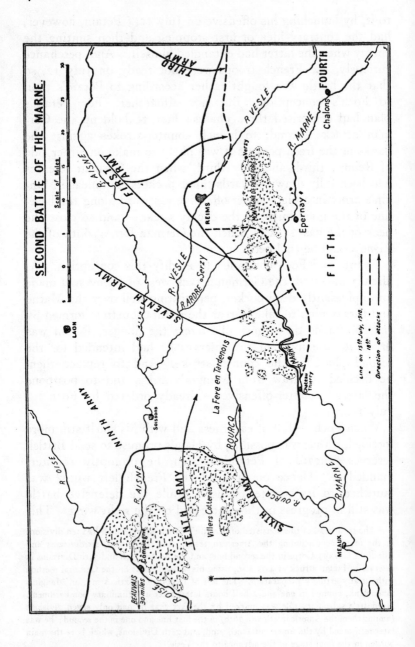

SECOND BATTLE OF THE MARNE.

Scale of Miles

Line on 15th July, 1918.
" " 18th "
Direction of attacks

meant that the second phase of Pétain's plan had to be dropped out, and, instead of the right wing attracting the Germans' reserves in order to enable the left wing to fall on their naked back, the left wing's offensive eased the pressure on the right wing.

To compensate as far as possible the initial passivity of the right wing,[1] the British reserves (51st and 62nd Divisions) which were sent thither were used to relieve the defending troops "on the move," passing direct to an attack. In the centre,[2] American reserves were similarly used, and thus a general pressure began along the whole face of the great salient.

But this convergent pressure did not begin until July 20, and by that time the opening surprise — due to the sudden release of a mass of tanks without any preliminary bombardment — of the left wing's attack was over and its impetus slackening. Thus the Germans, fighting hard for breathing space, gained the time they required to draw the bulk of their forces out of the sack, even though they left 30,000 prisoners and much material behind. And, once they were safely back on a straight and much shortened line along the Vesle, Ludendorff felt able, on August 2, to order preparations for fresh attacks in Flanders and east of Montdidier.

Six days later his offensive dreams were finally dissipated; but it is historically important to realize that it was not the second Battle of the Marne, "Foch's great counter-stroke," which dissipated them. This July 18 counter-stroke, conceived as such by Pétain and amended by Foch, was by no means decisive in its results. It may be that Foch's impetuosity robbed him of such results; that Pétain's oft-criticized caution would have been more fruitful and collected a larger "bag."

Nevertheless, if the battle had no clearly decisive material or even moral effect on the Germans, the first taste of victory after such deep and bitter draughts of defeat was an incalculable moral stimulant to the Allies, and perchance its depressing effect on the German morale was more insidiously damaging

---

[1] Berthelot's Fifth Army, comprising nine divisions.

[2] De Mitry's Ninth Army, comprising six divisions (including the 3rd American) with the 28th American and a French one in reserve.

428 THE REAL WAR — 1918

than was at first visible. So that Foch, who was ever concerned only with moral factors, which cannot be mathematically calculated, may well have been content. He had gained the initiative, and he kept it. That was enough; results mattered little. For his strategy was simple, not the complex masterpiece of art which legend has ascribed to him. It was best expressed in his own vivid illustration: "War is like this. Here is an inclined plane. An attack is like the ball rolling down it. It goes on gaining momentum and getting faster and faster on condition that you do not stop it. If you check it artificially you lose your momentum and have to begin all over again."

1918 — THE BREAK

SCENE V

THE "BLACK DAY" OF THE GERMAN ARMY — AUGUST 8

AUGUST 8, 1918, is a date which grows ever larger on the horizon of the historian. So far as any one event of the campaign in the west can be regarded as decisive, it is the great surprise east of Amiens that occurred on this day. And that decisiveness is above all a proof that the moral element dominates warfare.

For although August 8 was "a famous victory," the most brilliant ever gained by British arms in the World War, and, better still, the most economical, neither its tactical nor its visible strategic results were sufficient to explain its moral effect. Its 16,000 prisoners on the first day, and 21,000 all told, were a handsome prize compared with that of any previous British offensive, but a trifle in proportion to the vast forces then deployed on the western front, and in relation to such triumphs of the past as Worcester, Blenheim, Rossbach, Austerlitz, and Sedan. Its initial penetration of six to eight miles, and ultimate twelve miles, was, again, excellent by 1915–1917 standards, but in March the Germans had penetrated thirty-eight miles in the reverse direction without achieving any decisive result. Studied on the map, the advance of August 8–21 merely flattened out the nose and indented one cheek of the shallow German salient Arras-Montdidier-Noyon. It was far from reaching any vital link of the enemy's communications, or even cutting off the troops in that salient.

Yet it unhinged the mind and morale of the German Supreme Command. It led the Kaiser to say: "I see that we must strike a balance. We are at the end of our resources. The war must be ended." It made Ludendorff take a similarly despondent view — "The war would have to be ended."

In comparing the impression made upon him by the dramatic counter-stroke of July 18 on the Marne and that of August 8, there is a remarkable contrast. And in this contrast lies the answer as to which was the more decisive of the two. For after July 18 he had by no means lost hope. He seems to have treated this reverse as hardly more than an unfortunate incident, and as late as August 2 was ordering preparations for four fresh attacks, including his cherished Flanders blow, if on a reduced scale in comparison with his original intention.

But after August 8 these dreams vanish. There is an abandonment of any idea of returning to the offensive and, more significant still, no adoption of an alternative strategy. Mere passive resistance to the enemy's kicks cannot be called a strategical plan. Only when it was too late did he formulate the design of a purposeful evacuation of France as a preliminary to a fresh campaign beyond the frontier. By then, however, the moral collapse of the German Command had spread to the German people.

After the war Ludendorff delivered his considered opinion that "August 8 was the black day of the German army in the history of the war." The adjective "black" is peculiarly apt, for when faintness follows a sudden shock the blackening of the vista is the symptom which precedes the loss of consciousness and the consequent paralysis of the faculties. Thus, the primary interest in the story of August 8 is to trace how this shock came about. On July 12, Foch, irrepressibly eager to begin his cherished but oft-postponed idea of returning to the offensive, made this proposal to Haig : —

The first offensive to be launched on the British front should be one starting from the front Festubert-Rebecq, with a view to freeing the Bruay mines and forbidding the communication centre of Estaires. . . .

Five days later Haig replied that he saw "no advantage in an advance over the flat and marshy region between Rebecq and Festubert," and made the suggestion, instead : —

The operation, in my opinion, which is of the highest importance and which I proposed to you, as before, should be executed as soon as possible, is to push forward the Allied front to the east and southeast of Amiens so as to free that town and the railway. The best way to carry out this object is to make a combined Franco-British operation, the French attacking south of Moreuil and the British north of the Luce.

To realize this project I am preparing plans secretly for an offensive north of the Luce, direction east. . . . In liaison with this project the French forces should, in my opinion, carry out an operation between Moreuil and Montdidier. . . .

This letter, from the archives, sheds light on several momentous points of post-war controversy. First, as to the origin of the offensive, it shows not only that it was purely of British conception, but also that it was a "limited" conception — a narrow-fronted "shove" to secure for Amiens and the railway a rather wider margin of safety. The question is often mooted whether the idea sprang from the Commander-in-Chief, Haig, or from the Fourth Army Commander, Rawlinson. Here the words "as before" suggest that Haig had priority, for it was the brilliant little surprise operation at Hamel on July 4 and its revelation of the decline of German morale which inspired Rawlinson with the idea of a wider offensive.

However, there is little in the question of priority, for the defensive advantage of freeing Amiens was obvious. Indeed, the fact that Rawlinson's inspiration should not have come until after Hamel suggests his deeper appreciation of the moral element. The exploitation of an enemy's moral disintegration is fundamentally an offensive purpose.

Second, as to the plan of the offensive, the letter seems to contradict the claim, made in *Sir Douglas Haig's Command* and elsewhere, that the British were forced by Foch, against their will, to let the French share in the operation — thereby increasing what Clausewitz termed the inevitable "friction" of war. Rawlinson certainly, and rightly, argued against it as inimical to the surprise he sought.

But the letter shows that it was Haig's proposal. It is true that he proposed leaving a gap of a few miles between the French and British attacks. But both were purely frontal and strategically shoulder to shoulder. A richer offensive prospect was perhaps offered by a convergent attack on the two flanks of the salient, north of Albert and well south of Montdidier, respectively. But, for the former, a trench-filled belt of the old Somme battlefields was a difficulty, and subsequent events do not support the view that another army would have brought off such a surprise as the Fourth did south of the Somme.

The enlargement of the original project was due to Foch, who, on August 5, directed that if the initial attack was successful, it was to be continued by pushing southeast towards Ham. If the attacks against the southern flank of the salient which Humbert's and Mangin's armies began on August 10 and 17 respectively could have coincided with that of the British, greater material profits might have been yielded. As it was, the close coöperation of Debeney's army immediately adjoining the British did little to compensate its inevitable hindrance to the plan of surprise. For, lacking tanks, it could not dispense with a preliminary bombardment, and this could not begin, without forfeiting the general surprise, until the British advance started.

Greater material profits, however, could hardly have increased the moral effect of August 8 on the German Command. And this effect came from the shock of perhaps the most complete surprise of the war. How it was achieved is an object-lesson for future soldiers, for, like all the masterpieces of moral dislocation in military history, it was a subtle compound of many deceptive factors. Too often surprise is treated as an incidental, to be gained by a simple choice of date or place.

Its foundation was the sudden loosing of a swarm of tanks — 456 in all — in place of any preliminary artillery bombardment. This method, inaugurated at Cambrai the previous November, had been repeated by the French on July 18. Before Amiens it was enhanced by manifold devices. Secrecy was sought by holding the preliminary conferences always at different places, by concealing reconnaissances, and by informing the executants at the latest moment compatible with readiness — divisional commanders did not know that an attack was intended until July 31, and the fighting troops not until thirty-six hours before the start. Even the War Cabinet in London was kept in the dark, and in that august

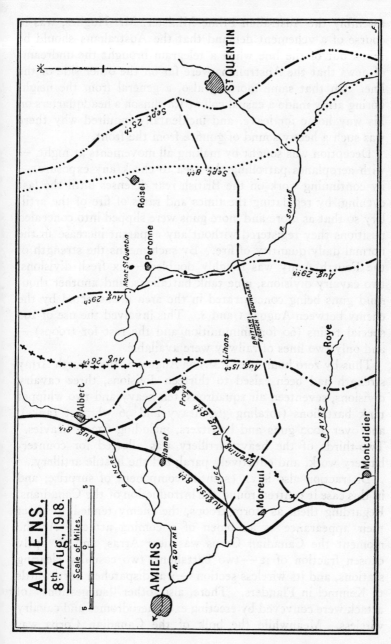

AMIENS,
8th Aug., 1918.

Scale of Miles

5   0   5

St Quentin

Roisel

Peronne

Mont St Quentin

Roye

Albert

Proyart

Hamel

Montdidier

Moreuil

Amiens

Sept. 25th

Sept. 8th

Aug. 29th

Aug. 29th

Aug. 26th

Aug. 15th

Aug. 8th

Aug. 8th

Evening Aug. 8th

BRITISH FRENCH BOUNDARY

R. SOMME

R. SOMME

R. ANCRE

R. LUCE

R. AVRE

R. RAYRE

assembly the Australian Prime Minister, Mr. Hughes, was in course of a vehement demand that the Australians should be taken out of the line when a telegram brought the undreamt of news that the Australians were far on the other side of the line. On that same morning also, a general from the neighboring army made a casual call at Rawlinson's headquarters on his way home for leave, and incidentally inquired why there was such a heavy sound of gunfire from the front.

Deception was sought by making all movements at night, — with aeroplanes patrolling the area to check any exposure, — by continuing work on the British rear defenses until the last evening, by regulating the times and rates of fire of the artillery so that as more and more guns were slipped into concealed positions they registered without any apparent increase in the normal daily quantity of fire. By such means the strength of the Fourth Army was roughly doubled — six fresh divisions, two cavalry divisions, nine tank battalions, and another thousand guns being concentrated in the area unsuspected by the enemy between August 1 and 8. This involved the use of 290 special trains (60 for ammunition and the rest for troops) — and only two lines of railway were available.

Thus by zero hour (4.20 A.M.) on August 8, the Fourth Army strength had been raised to thirteen divisions, three cavalry divisions, seventeen air squadrons, ten heavy and two whippet tank battalions (totaling 360 heavy and 96 whippet tanks), and over 2000 guns and howitzers, including 672 "heavies." Two-thirds of the heavy artillery was allotted for counter-battery work, and effectively paralyzed the hostile artillery.

Distraction also is an essential component of surprise, and in this case it centred round the introduction of the Canadians. Regarding them as storm troops, the enemy tended to greet their appearance as an omen of a coming attack. At the moment the Canadian Corps was near Arras, and an aptly chosen fraction of it — two battalions, two casualty clearing stations, and its wireless section — was dispatched northwards to Kemmel in Flanders. There, also, other "suggestions" of attack were conveyed by erecting extra aerodromes and cavalry wireless. Meanwhile the bulk of the Canadian Corps was filtered down to the Somme, where various ingenious rumors were circulated among the British troops to account for its appearance.

The Fourth Army dispositions were that the main punch was to be delivered south of the Somme, by the Canadian Corps (Currie) on the right and the Australian Corps (Monash) on the left, next the river, whilst the III Corps (R. H. K. Butler) advanced north of the river to safeguard the flank of the main punch. But the Canadians did not move into the front line until a few hours before the assault, and meantime the Australians extended their front as far south as the Amiens-Roye road, relieving the French, and thereby lulling the Germans into a false sense of security. For what enemy would expect attack from a force which was spreading itself out defensively?

The whole front of attack was about fourteen miles long, and on the German side was held by six skeleton divisions (averaging barely 3000 effectives apiece) of General von der Marwitz's Second Army. Their weakness of numbers was accentuated by weakness of defenses, and in their rough forward line there were none of the usual deep dugouts to safeguard morale until the hour of trial.

Five days before the attack an enemy raid captured an Australian post, and three days later a local attack fractured the III Corps front and took two hundred prisoners. But such information as the enemy gained only deluded him further.

Thus when, an hour before sunrise on August 8, the British tanks swept forward, with the barrage and infantry advance simultaneous, the blow had the maximum shock of surprise. Shrouded by a thick ground mist, it fell on an enemy who had done nothing to strengthen his position by entrenchments, and the Canadians and Australians — matchless attacking troops — surged irresistibly over the enemy's forward divisions. Only north of the Somme, where tanks were few, was there a partial check. To accelerate the momentum all reserves were set in motion at zero hour — copying the Germans' example of March 21. Soon, too, armored cars were racing down the roads, to spread confusion behind the German front, even shooting up an army-corps staff at breakfast in Proyart.

The day's final objective (six to eight miles distant) was gained over most of the front except the extreme right and left. But the next day saw slight progress and rather spasmodic pressure, and thereafter the attack flickered out as rapidly as it had blazed up. Why this strange contrast? Why was not so complete a break-through completed by a dramatic finale? Partly, it would seem, because the advance had now reached the edge of the old Somme battlefields of 1916, a tangled waste of rusty wire and derelict trenches which was a brake on movement, reënforcement, and supply. It is well to remember that the problem of maintaining continuity of advance was never solved in the World War. Again, the original front of attack had not been wide, and it is significant that almost all successful advances in the World War seem to have been governed by a law of ratio, the depth of the penetration being roughly half of the frontage of attack.

Another reason was, as at Cambrai, the lack of reserves. The introduction of the local reserves of the Fourth Army was well timed, but when its thirteen divisions had been engaged, all that were available were three divisions assembled by Haig in the area. Moreover, the Germans, in contrast, succeeded in reënforcing their original six divisions with eighteen reserve divisions by August 11 — ten more than had been estimated.

A fourth cause of the stoppage was inherent in the form of the attack. For, being strictly frontal, the more it pushed back the enemy the more it consolidated their resistance. This is always the defect of a frontal attack unless an organized force can be rushed through and placed on the enemy's rear. The cavalry as usual were allotted the rôle of exploitation. This time they rendered serviceable help in gaining and holding certain localities until the infantry came up, but such help was but a slender thing compared with the true rôle of cavalry in past history. Greater results might have been attained if the ninety-six whippet tanks, instead of being tied to the cavalry, had been used independently to pass through the gap and make a concentrated thrust southeastwards against the rear of the German army facing the French — as was suggested by the Tank Corps.

But from the broad strategic viewpoint there was, or was evolved, this time a method behind the lack of reserves. On August 10 Haig had visited this front and studied the situation at close quarters. In consequence, when Foch urged a continuance of the Fourth Army's frontal pressure, Haig demurred to it as a vain waste of life. In a letter of August 14 he told Foch that he had stopped the further attack prepared for next day, and that he was preparing an attack by the Third Army north of Albert.

Foch objected to the delay involved by this alternative step, but at a conference at Sarcus next day Haig stubbornly held to and gained his point. As a result the Third Army struck on August 21, the First Army further north on the twenty-eighth, while the Fourth Army seized the opportunity of this distraction of the enemy to resume their advance, the Australians gaining Mont St. Quentin and Péronne on the thirty-first, and thereby turning the barrier of the upper Somme. These operations marked the new strategy of successive attacks at different but closely related points, each attack broken off and succeeded by a fresh as soon as its initial impetus was spent.

It would be unjust, as many British writers have done, to claim that Haig initiated this strategy. For it is to be clearly traced in the successive attacks already begun by the French to the south — Debeney's left wing on the eighth, his right on the ninth, Humbert's army on the tenth, and Mangin's on the twenty-first. But Haig appears to have appreciated first its potentialities for economy of force. While Foch was filled with the idea of maintaining the pressure, Haig was seized with the idea of pressure at the most economical expenditure of life. The Fourth Army's bag of 21,000 prisoners from August 8–12 had cost only 20,000 casualties.

To the success of this strategy the surprise of August 8 and its effect on the German Command had contributed greatly. Their instinctive response to the shock was to hurry to the spot all possible reënforcements, and thereby they drained their reserve funds to bankruptcy point. The reserves of the army group of Prince Rupprecht, which held the front from the sea to the Somme district, fell from thirty-six to nine by August 16. Rupprecht's own resolution had done much to bring the British advance to a halt by preventing the local army commanders from carrying out their first panic decision to fall back behind the upper Somme. But this very resolution, perhaps, cost the Germans more in the end.

Thus, in sum, the decisiveness of August 8 came from the dislocation of thought or will, or both, throughout the whole hierarchy of the German Command. The history of 1914–1918 repeated the experience of all history that, except against an exhausted or already demoralized foe, decisive success in war is only possible through surprise. And that surprise must be a compound of many subtle ingredients.

1918 — THE BREAK

SCENE VI

MEGIDDO — THE ANNIHILATION OF THE TURKISH ARMIES

ON September 19, 1918, began an operation which was both one of the most quickly decisive campaigns and the most completely decisive battles in all history. Within a few days the Turkish armies in Palestine had practically ceased to exist. Whether it should be regarded primarily as a campaign or as a battle completed by a pursuit is a moot question. For it opened with the forces in contact and hence would seem to fall into the category of a battle, but it was achieved mainly by strategic means, with fighting playing a minor part. This fact has tended to its disparagement in the sight of those who are obsessed with the Clausewitzian dogma that blood is the price of victory — and hold, as a corollary, that no victory is worthy of recognition which is not sanctified by a lavish oblation of blood. But Cæsar's triumph at Ilerda, Scipio's near Utica, Cromwell's at Preston, and Moltke's, though opportunist rather than sought for, at Sedan, each had the same "pale pink" complexion. In each, strategy was so effective that fighting was but incidental. Yet no one can deny that decisiveness both as victories and on the course of history. A more serious "depreciation" of this final campaign-battle in Palestine lies in the fact that Allenby had a superiority of over two to one in numbers, and more in terms of weapon-values.[1] In addition the morale of the Turks had so declined that it is often argued that Allenby had merely to stretch out his hand for the Turkish army, like an overripe plum, to fall into it. There is force in these contentions. But

[1] Allenby's fighting strength was 12,000 sabres, 57,000 rifles, and 540 guns. He estimated the Turkish strength at 2000 sabres, 32,000 rifles, and 402 guns. This figure is about double Liman von Sanders's estimate, which, however, seems to be a vague calculation rather than a statistical computation.

most of the "crowning mercies" of modern history, from Worcester to Sedan, have seen almost as great a disparity of strength and morale between victors and vanquished. And in 1918 Allenby had to outwit such able commanders as Liman von Sanders and Mustapha Kemal, not such men as those who thrust their heads into the sack at Sedan.

When full deduction is made for the advantageous conditions of September 1918, the conclusion remains that the triumph immortalized by the already immortal name of Megiddo is one of history's masterpieces by reason of the breadth of vision and treatment. If the subject was not a difficult one, the picture is almost unique as a perfect conception perfectly executed.

The question is often asked as to whose was the conception. Was it that of the titular commander? Or did it spring from some gifted subordinate? When the victories of Hindenburg on the Russian front are discussed, even the man in the street speaks of Ludendorff's strategy — and the student of war goes still deeper, or lower, and muses on the unassessable influence of Hoffmann's military genius. But with Megiddo it is possible to dispel doubt, through the unanimous evidence of those most intimately concerned. The broad conception sprang entire from Allenby's mind, whatever the credit due to his assistants for working out its executive details. "Grew," indeed, would be a better word than "sprang," for the original conception was of more modest dimensions — to break through the Turkish front near the coast and, wheeling inwards, turn the flank of their forces in the Judæan Hills. But, returning one day from a ride during which he had been studying the problem, Allenby suddenly unfolded the plan as it was executed, in all its almost breath-taking scope. It abundantly fulfilled Napoleon's maxim that "the whole secret of the art of war lies in making oneself master of the communications." If Allenby had a superiority of strength he was going to use it to make himself master not of one, but of every one, of the Turkish communications. And the success of his attempt to do so owed much to the complementary fact that he had taken thorough measures to be master of his own communications.

The three so-called Turkish "armies," each hardly more than the strength of a division, drew nourishment through a single stem — the Hejaz railway running south from Damascus. At Deraa a branch ran out westwards; crossing the Jordan at Jisr el Mejamie, just north of Beisan, it forked at El Afule in the Plain of Esdraelon, one line going to the sea at Haifa and the other turning south again through the hills of Samaria to Messudieh Junction. This line fed the Seventh (Mustapha Kemal) and Eighth (Jevad) Turkish armies which held the front between the River Jordan and the Mediterranean Sea. The Fourth Army (Jemal) east of the Jordan was fed by the main Hejaz railway.

Now, to cut an army's lines of communication is to dislocate its physical organization. To close its lines of retreat is to dislocate its morale. And to destroy its lines of "intercommunication" — by which orders and reports pass — is to dislocate it mentally, by breaking the essential connection between the brain and the body of any army. Allenby planned to achieve not a single but the triple dislocation, and the third element was not the least important to the success of his plan.

The convergence of both roads and railways made Deraa, El Afule, and, to a less extent, Beisan the vital points in the Turks' rear. To get a grip on El Afule and Beisan would sever the communications of the Seventh and Eighth Armies and also close their lines of retreat, except for the extremely difficult outlet to the desolate region across the Jordan eastwards. To get a grip on Deraa would sever the communications of all three armies and the best line of retreat of the Fourth. But it was considerably further from the British front.

El Afule and Beisan, however, lay within a sixty-mile radius, and hence were within the range of a strategic cavalry "bound," provided that these vital points could be reached without interruption or delay. The problem was, first, to find a line of approach unobstructed by nature, and, second, to ensure that the enemy could not block it by force. How was it solved? The flat coastal Plain of Sharon afforded a corridor to the Plain of Esdraelon and Vale of Jezreel, in which El Afule and Beisan respectively lay. This corridor was interrupted by

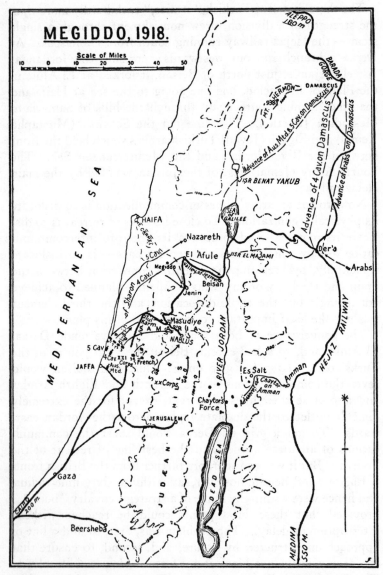

MEGIDDO, 1918.

Scale of Miles

10   0   10   20   30   40   50

MEDITERRANEAN SEA

ALEPPO 180 m.

BARADA GORGE

MT HERMON 9383

DAMASCUS

Advance of Aus.Mtd.& Cav.on Damascus

JISR BENAT YAKUB

SEA of GALILEE

Advance of 4 Cav.on Damascus

Advance of Arabs on Damascus

HAIFA

of CARMEL

5 Cav.

Nazareth

El 'Afule

JISR EL MAJAMI

Megiddo

Valley of Jezreel

Beisan

Der'a

Arabs

of Sharon 4 Cav.

Jenin

Masudiye

Tul Karm

S A M

NABLUS

RIVER JORDAN

Es Salt

Chaytor on Amman

Amman

HEJAZ RAILWAY

5 Cav XXI

Cav.XXI Corps

JAFFA

Aus. Mtd.

French

xx Corps

Advance of Chaytor on Amman

JERUSALEM

Chaytor's Force

JUDEAN

DEAD SEA

Gaza

CAIRO 200 m.

Beersheba

MEDINA 550 M.

---

only a single door, so far back that it was not guarded by the Turks, formed by the narrow mountain belt which separates the coastal Plain of Sharon from the inland Plain of Esdraelon.

But the entrance to the corridor was firmly bolted and barred by the trenches of the Turkish front. Allenby planned to use his infantry to force this locked gate and swing it back, as on a hinge, northeastwards, so leaving a clear path for his cavalry. But, having passed through the front gate, they would still have to get through the back door. This the Turks could easily close if they had time and warning. Speed on the part of the cavalry was essential. But not sufficient. The attention and reserves of the Turks must be distracted. Even so, there was still a risk. War experience had shown how easily cavalry could be stopped, and a handful of men and machine-guns would suffice to block the two passes through the intermediate mountain belt. To avert this risk the Turkish Command must be made deaf and dumb as well as blind. In this complete paralysis of the Turkish Higher Command lie the main significance and the historical value of the victory of Megiddo.

Let us watch how it was achieved. For it Allenby had two comparatively novel tools — aircraft and Arabs. Feisal's Arabs, under the guiding brain of Colonel Lawrence, had long been harassing, immobilizing, and demoralizing the Turks along the main Hejaz railway. Now they were to contribute more directly to the final stroke by the British forces. On September 16 and 17, emerging like phantoms from the desert, they blew up the railway north, south, and west of Deraa. This had the physical effect of shutting off the flow of Turkish supplies temporarily — and "temporarily" was all that mattered here. It had the mental effect of persuading the Turkish Command to send part of its scanty reserves towards Deraa.

The Air Force contribution was in two parts. First, by a sustained campaign it drove the enemy's machines out of the air. This campaign was carried so far that ultimately the fighters "sat" above the Turkish aerodrome at Jenin to prevent their machines even taking off. Thus it closed the enemy's air eye during the period of preparation. Secondly, when the moment came for the execution of Allenby's plan, the Air Force made the enemy's command deaf and dumb by decisively bombing their main telegraph and telephone exchange at El Afule — a stroke in which Ross-Smith, who later made history by his flight to Australia, helped England to make history. In addition, the enemy's two army headquarters at Nablus and Tul Keram were bombed, and at the second, the more vital, the wires were so effectively destroyed that it was cut off throughout the day both from Nazareth and from its divisions in the coastal sector. Another and earlier form of air activity was, if less military, perhaps of even wider strategic effect. This was the dropping not of bombs but of an equal weight of illustrated pamphlets showing the physical comforts which the Turkish soldier enjoyed as a prisoner of war. Its appeal to half-starved and ragged men was none the less for being imponderable.

But if the air and the Arabs were perhaps the two most vital factors in "unhinging" the enemy preparatory to the actual push, the plan had also the wide and purposeful variety of ruses which marks the masterpieces of military history. By these Allenby sought to divert the enemy's attention away from the coast to the Jordan flank. In this aim he was helped by the very failure of two attempted advances east of the Jordan, towards Amman and Es Salt, during the spring. Then, throughout the summer, he kept a cavalry force, periodically relieved, in the stifling heat of the Jordan Valley, to hold the enemy's attention. When the cavalry were ultimately moved surreptitiously across to the other flank, their camps were not only left standing, but new ones added, while 15,000 dummy horses of canvas filled the vacated horse lines. Mule-drawn sleighs created dust-clouds; battalions marched by day toward the valley — and returned by night in lorries to repeat this march of a stage army; a hotel was taken over in Jerusalem and elaborately prepared for the mythical reception of General Headquarters; new bridging and wireless activity fostered the illusion; Lawrence sent agents to bargain for vast quantities of forage in the Amman district.

And all the time more and more troops were filtering down by night marches to the other flank near the sea, there to be concealed in orange groves or in camps already standing. By these means Allenby increased his two-to-one superiority, on the front as a whole, to a five-to-one superiority on the vital sector — unsuspected by the enemy. For some time Liman von Sanders had certainly anticipated a big attack, and, indeed, had thought of frustrating it by a voluntary retirement to a rear line near the Sea of Galilee. "I gave up the idea, because we would have had to relinquish the Hejaz railway . . . and because we no longer could have stopped the progress of the Arab insurrection in rear of our army. On account of the limited marching capacity of the Turkish soldiers and of the very low mobility of all draft animals, I considered that the holding of our positions to the last gave us more favorable prospects than a long retirement with Turkish troops of impaired morale."

Although he feared an attack near the coast, he feared still more the effect of one east of the Jordan, and even at the last hour the warning of the first given by an Indian deserter on September 17 was offset by the more positive news of the Arab attacks on the vital railway at Deraa. Deceived by his own preconceived idea, Liman von Sanders was, indeed, too ready to believe that this deserter was a tool of the British Intelligence, and his story a blind to cover Allenby's real purpose. Further, Liman von Sanders rejected the plea of Refet Bey, commanding the coastal sector, who wished to withdraw his troops a mile so that the British bombardment might waste itself on empty trenches. Forbidding Refet to withdraw an inch, he ensured that he should go back a hundred miles, to Tyre, leaving his army behind — dead or prisoners.

On the night of September 18 began what was both the last move of the "distracting" preparation and the first move of the real action. The 53rd Division, which formed Allenby's extreme right, made a spring forward in the hills on the edge of the Jordan Valley. Thereby they would be a step on their way towards closing the only way of retreat — across the Jordan eastwards — left open to the Turks when the main move had fulfilled its encircling purpose.

Far away to the west by the sea all was quiet. But at 4.30 A.M. 385 guns opened fire on the selected frontage. For a quarter of an hour only, they maintained an intense bombardment, and then the infantry advanced, under cover of a rapid lifting barrage. They swept, almost unchecked, over the stupefied defenders and broke through the two trench

systems, shallow and slightly wired — by western-front standards. Then they wheeled inland, like a huge door swinging
on its hinges. Of this door, a French contingent and the 54th
Division formed the hinged end; then, with a five-mile
interval, the 3rd Indian, 75th, and 7th Indian Divisions formed
the middle panel; and the 60th Division, by the sea, the outside panel. The latter reached Tul Keram by nightfall. But
what survived of the Turkish Eighth Army had long before been
pouring back through the defile to Messudieh in a confused
crowd of troops and transport. And upon this hapless mob
the British aircraft had swept down with bombs and bullets.

Meantime, through the opened door had ridden the three
cavalry divisions of the Desert Mounted Corps (Chauvel).
By evening they had reached the Carmel Range, the "intermediate door," sending detachments with their armored cars
to secure the two passes. By morning they were across. One
brigade descended on Nazareth where the enemy's General
Headquarters lay, ignorant of the events of the past twenty-
four hours because cut off from all communication with its
fighting body. Liman von Sanders, however, escaped through
a failure to block the northern exit of the town, and after a
vigorous street-fight the cavalry were forced to retire.

The real strategic key, however, was now not at Nazareth
but at El Afule and Beisan. These were reached at 8 A.M. and
4.30 P.M. respectively — to Beisan the 4th Cavalry Division had
covered seventy miles in thirty-four hours. Passing through
the Carmel Range in its wake, the Australian Mounted Division turned south to Jenin to place a closer barrier across the
Turks' line of retreat. The enemy's only remaining bolt-hole
was east over the Jordan — which flows swiftly, with few fords,
through a deep and winding trough, 1300 feet below sea level
at the Dead Sea end. He might have reached this but for the
Air Force, as the infantry advance was making slow progress
through the hills in face of the stubborn Turkish rearguards.
Early in the morning of September 21, the British aircraft
spotted a large column — practically all that survived of the
two Turkish armies — winding down the steep gorge from
Nablus to the Jordan. Four hours' continuous bombing and

machine-gunning reduced this procession to stagnation, an inanimate chaos of guns and transport. Those who survived were merely scattered fugitives. From this moment may be timed the extinction of the Seventh and Eighth Turkish Armies. What followed was but a rounding up of "cattle" by the cavalry.

Only the Fourth Army, east of the Jordan, remained. This, delaying too long, did not begin to retire until September 22. A broken railway and the Arabs lay across its line of retreat to Damascus. And four days later the 4th Cavalry Division moved east from Beisan to intercept it, while the other two converged directly on Damascus, its goal. Escape was impossible, but its fate was different from that of the other armies, a rapid attrition under constant pin-pricks rather than a neat dispatch. In this pursuit the Desert Mounted Corps co-operated with, and, for the first time, met, their real desert Allies, hitherto an invisible and intangible factor. Their presence, and identity, was disclosed when a messenger reported, "There's an Arab on the top of the hill over there in a Rolls-Royce; talks English perfectly and in the hell of a rage!" For no pursuit could be fast enough to satisfy Lawrence's ardent spirit as he urged his Arabs on toward the city of desire. To a British cavalry officer with an apt gift of phrase their march looked "like some strange Oriental version of an old-time Epsom road on Derby Day," but they outpaced the 4th Cavalry Division.

The fragments of the Turkish Fourth Army were finally headed off and captured near Damascus, which was occupied on October 1. On the previous day the garrison had been intercepted by the Australian Mounted Division as it was trying to escape through the Barada Gorge (the Biblical "Abana"). Sweeping the head of the fugitive stream with machine-guns from the overhanging cliffs, the Australian Light Horse rolled it back to Damascus, there to swell the "bag" of prisoners to 20,000.

The next move was a fitting conclusion to this chapter of history. The 5th Cavalry Division was dispatched to advance on Aleppo, two hundred miles distant, in conjunction with an Arab force. Its armored cars led the way and dispersed such slight opposition as was met, reaching the outskirts of Aleppo on October 23. Two days later the leading cavalry brigade came up. A combined attack was arranged for next morning, but during the night the Arabs slipped into and captured the town on their own. The British force, too weak to press the retreat of the garrison, was awaiting reënforcements from Damascus when the capitulation of Turkey on October 31 wrote "finis" to the campaign. During a brief span of thirty-eight days the British had advanced three hundred and fifty miles and captured 75,000 prisoners — at a cost of less than 5000 casualties.

In a war singularly barren of surprise and mobility, those keynotes of the art of war, their value had been signally vindicated at the last, and in one theatre at least. Surprise and mobility had virtually won the victory without a battle. And it is worth noting that the Turks were still capable of holding up the infantry attack until the "strategic barrage" across their rear became known and produced its inevitable, and invariable, moral effect.

Because a preliminary condition of trench-warfare existed the infantry and heavy artillery were necessary to break the lock. But once the normal conditions of warfare were thus restored, the victory was achieved by the mobile elements — cavalry, aircraft, armored cars, and Arabs — which formed but a fraction of Allenby's total force. And it was achieved, not by physical force, but by the demoralizing application of mobility. A new light on Napoleon's dictum that the moral is to the physical as three to one.

SCENE VII

THE BATTLE OF A DREAM — ST. MIHIEL

FOR four years a wedge sixteen miles deep lay embedded in the flank of the main French armies. It was the most marked, and most "ugly," feature of the whole irregular front between the Swiss border and the Belgian coast. Along this long irregular line of trenches salients were numerous, and of all sizes, but none was so acute as that which came down from the heights of the Woevre to the Meuse at St. Mihiel — and even protruded beyond the river. All that time it galled France bodily and mentally, for although it was not in itself a convenient springboard for a fresh German offensive it might easily become a menace if a new wedge were driven in on the other side of Verdun; worse still, it crippled the prospects of any French offensive into Lorraine. For such an offensive, whether launched from the Verdun or from the Nancy sector, would not only suffer the menace of St. Mihiel in its rear but would be difficult to nourish — because the St. Mihiel salient interrupted the railways from Paris to Nancy and from Verdun to Nancy. This handicap was all too clearly manifest in 1916, when the army defending Verdun fought half-choked and always in danger of being suddenly strangled.

For two more trying years the defenders of Verdun had to bear the semi-suffocation of their windpipe. And then, at the end of the first hour of September 12, 1918, three thousand guns pealed a message of deliverance. Four hours later, deafened yet exhilarated by the thunder of their guns, the infantry of the First American Army advanced from their own trenches across the pulverized earth that had held the enemy trenches. Twenty-four hours later the two sharp points of the American forceps, cutting into each side, met midway, and the ugly fang was removed.

America's First Army had fought its first battle and won its first victory, as an army.   The achievement was not merely a good augury but a vindication — especially of Pershing. And it was an invaluable tonic both to the army which fought and to the nation behind it, while a proportionate disillusionment to the Germans, who had questioned, even more strongly than her Allies, America's power to produce an effective army.

Apparently, the extraction of the St. Mihiel fang was also one of the most perfectly complete pieces of strategic dentistry in the war.   Actually, the operation was less satisfactory, and roots were left to cause trouble later.   In part, the incompleteness was due to the faulty action of the forceps; in part to the dentist; but still more to the long-concealed fact that the dentist's arm was jogged.   Yet there is still a question — whether the operation could have been more effective even if the dentist had not suffered interference.

To answer it, we must examine the cause and course of the operation.   It was the fulfillment of a dream and a scheme which almost coincided with the entry of the United States into the war.   Indeed, Pershing and his Staff had come to Europe in June 1917 with their eyes fixed on St. Mihiel and their minds on Metz, behind it.   The British, they knew, were committed to operations in Flanders and northern France, an area which, despite its drawbacks — mud especially — was nearest to their home base and gave them the shortest lines of communication with the Channel ports.   The offensive operations of the French had all been carried out in the sector north of Paris and it was natural that they should concentrate to cover their capital.

The choice of the easterly sector facing and flanking Metz was the natural one for the Americans, because it clashed least with their Allies' lines of supply and was easiest of access from their own base ports in the Bay of Biscay.   Moreover, this sector was obviously the Germans' most sensitive point, because a thrust there needed to penetrate only a short distance before it would imperil the stability of the whole German position in France — which formed a vast salient jutting southwards between Verdun and Ypres.   For to sever the eastern end of the great lateral railway Metz-Maubeuge would at least restrict the free movement of reserves and supplies, and, more significant still, would "turn" the flank of all the successive lines to which the German armies could withdraw short of their own frontier. Further, such a thrust promised the vital economic result of releasing the Briey iron region and threatening the Saar basin — upon which the Germans largely depended for their munitions. To pinch off the St. Mihiel salient was not only a necessary preliminary to a secure offensive, but was a local operation well suited to the first test of a new force.

But the American Expeditionary Force was more intent to conserve its strength until maturity than had been the British. A year passed before it was ready, and before that the Germans had intervened elsewhere to compel a further postponement. Not until August 1918, when the German tide had begun to ebb, was Pershing able to collect his scattered divisions — which had just helped in stemming it — and to form them into the first all-American army. And even so it had to depend on the French for most of its artillery and on the French and British for part of its aircraft.

On July 24 the commanders of the Allied armies met at Bombon to discuss their future action. The outcome was very modest. Foch did not choose to look far ahead and merely called for a series of local attacks to free his lateral railways. The first was delivered on August 8 in front of Amiens, and its dramatic evidence of the moral rot that had set in among the German troops changed the whole picture. On August 11 the newly formed staff of the First American Army moved to the St. Mihiel area, and there developed their plan to a far more ambitious one than had been suggested at Bombon — from that of freeing the French lateral railways to that of threatening the German. Not merely to pinch off the salient but to break through its baseline, where ran the "Michel" Line as an inner barrier against any sudden rupture of the front. The plan framed by General Hugh Drum, the Chief of Staff, visualized the use of fifteen American divisions — each more than twice the strength of a French or British division — and four French divisions. Pershing approved the plan on August 15 and Foch two days later. Indeed, Foch added to it not only six more French divisions, but an extension of the frontage and the direction "to strike the heaviest blow possible and secure the maximum results."

But on August 30 Foch came to the American Headquarters at Ligny-en-Barrois with a radically different plan. The change was due to Haig's intervention. August 8 and its sequel had given him a clear perception of the German decline and, disregarding the cautious counsels of his government, he was now willing to test his judgment and risk his reputation by assaulting the ill-famed Hindenburg Line — the strongest defenses on the whole German front. But he was anxious to reduce the risk of failure and increase the profit of success; he therefore urged Foch to change the main American attack from a divergent to a convergent direction. It would thus, he calculated, have a quicker and stronger reaction upon the German armies facing him, and by loosening their grip would ease his task — as he would similarly ease that of the Americans.

Foch lent his ear the more readily to Haig's argument because his own horizon had enlarged. He now felt that the war might be finished in 1918, instead of 1919. And his enthusiastic assurance led him to transform his new method of alternating attacks at different points into a simultaneous general offensive — "Tout le monde à la bataille." By it he seems to have hoped not merely to stretch and crack the German resistance, but even to cut off and surround the German armies between his converging pincers — British on one side and American on the other. Pétain, when consulted, was quite agreeable to the change of plan, which promised to draw the German reserves to either flank and leave the French a clearer path in the centre.

Thus when Foch came to Ligny-en-Barrois he proposed that the St. Mihiel plan should be modified to a mere excision of the salient. This operation was to be a preliminary, and safeguard, to the rear of the American main attack — now to be launched northwest towards Mézières instead of northeast towards Metz. Foch further proposed that while Pershing's army operated on the easier ground west of the Argonne, a Franco-American army under a French commander should attack the more difficult sector between the Argonne Forest and the Meuse. He also proposed to send General Degoutte to hold Pershing's hand and guide his tactical decisions.

The change of plan came as a shock to Pershing, and the other proposals as an affront. The interview was lively and the atmosphere grew heated. Foch hinted that he would appeal to President Wilson — and the threat had as little effect on Pershing as when previously used. Foch implied that Pershing was trying to shirk his share of the battle, and Pershing retorted that he was fully ready to fight "as an American army." Foch ironically suggested that even for St. Mihiel Pershing could not raise an all-American army, but had to depend on his Allies for guns, tanks, and aircraft. Pershing retaliated with the reminder that by Allied request the Americans had shipped only infantry and machine-guns during the spring crisis.

Foch wisely dropped the argument and left Pershing to "chew the cud." Next day Pershing, after reflection, wrote to Foch. He recognized the potential value of the convergent attack, but dwelt upon the difficulties of American participation. "Since our arrival in France our plans . . . have been based on the organization of the American army on the front St. Mihiel-Belfort. All our depots, hospitals, training areas, and other installations are located with reference to this front and a change of plans cannot be easily made." Then he dealt with Foch's second proposal, contending that "it is far more appropriate at the present moment for the Allies temporarily to furnish the American army with the services and auxiliaries it needs than for the Allies to expect further delay in the formation of the American army."

Pershing did not attempt to hide his dislike of limiting the St. Mihiel attack, and suggested that instead of switching at once to the Meuse-Argonne he should exploit the St. Mihiel attack to the full and later, if necessary, mount a fresh attack

"either in the region of Belfort or Lunéville."   Not yet vouch-
safed an intuition of victory that autumn, he suggested that
these attacks would fit in with the ultimate American aim of
taking charge "during January and February" of " the sector
from St. Mihiel to Switzerland."   "However," he said, "it is
your province to decide as to the strategy of operations, and I
abide by your decision."

On one question he was unshakable.   "I can no longer agree
to any plan which involves the dispersion of our units."
"Briefly, our officers and soldiers alike are, after one experience, no longer willing to be incorporated in other armies.
. . . The danger of destroying by such dispersion the fine
morale of the American soldier is too great."   "If you decide
to utilize the American forces in attacking in the direction of
Mézières I accept that decision, even though it complicates
my supply system and the care of my sick and wounded, but
I do insist that this American Army be employed as a whole."

The result of this letter was a conference between Foch,
Pétain, and Pershing on September 2, whereat Pershing gave
up his own plan for a share in Foch's, and Foch conceded Pershing's claim to American unity.   The concession was wrung
from him by his own realization that without the Americans
his right pincer would have a weak and worn point.   And, as
Pershing preferred to attack east of the Argonne, where supply
would be easier, although the ground was more difficult, he
obtained his preference.

The one outstanding question was that of St. Mihiel.   Foch
wanted the general offensive to open by September 20 at the
latest, and suggested that the St. Mihiel attack should be abandoned.   Pershing and his staff decided that they must first
cut off the St. Mihiel wedge to safeguard the rear of their
Meuse-Argonne attack.   Again, their claim was conceded.
But it meant that they could not switch divisions from one
battle to the other in time, and that a number of raw divisions
had to be used for the Meuse-Argonne attack.   In addition,
the St. Mihiel attack was two days, and the Meuse-Argonne
six days, behind time-table.

Each attack interfered with the other.   And the conse-

quences were compound not simple. The first effect was
upon the American dispositions. Instead of fifteen double-
sized American divisions, which were available, only seven
were used in the attack. Although this was a more than

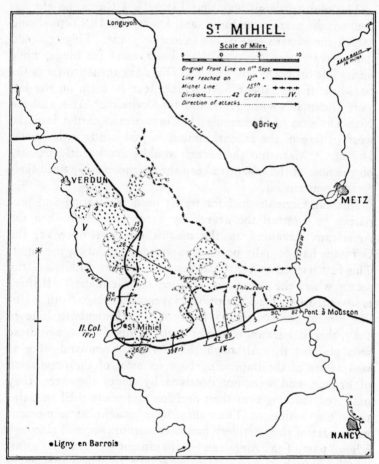

ST. MIHIEL.

Scale of Miles.

Original Front Line on 11ᵗʰ Sept. ——
Line reached on 12ᵗʰ . ▬▬▬
Michel Line 15ᵗʰ . ＋＋＋＋
Divisions .... 42 Corps .... IV.
Direction of attacks ....

ample provision for the task, ensuring a numerical superiority
of about eight to one over the Germans, the actual distribution was curious. For while six divisions (including two of
Regulars) formed the right pincer, only one National Guard
division formed the left. What had happened was that in-

stead of reshuffling the entire dispositions the left pincer had been severely fined down, and the objectives rigorously limited. Foch, indeed, suggested that the left wing attack should be abandoned.

The plan in detail was that Liggett's I Corps, on the extreme right nearest the hinge, and Dickman's IV Corps should attack the eastern face of the salient at 5 A.M. Liggett would demonstrate with the 82nd Division against the hinge, while on its left his 90th, 5th, and 2nd Divisions thrust towards the base-line of the salient. Attacking next to them on the left were Dickman's 89th, 42nd, and 1st Divisions. At 8 A.M. the 26th Division of Cameron's IV Corps would thrust into the western face of the salient, aiming to join hands with the 1st Division. Meantime the French would exert a gentle pressure on the nose of the salient to keep the defenders busy until their retreat was cut off.

But the Germans had for weeks been meditating and preparing to forestall the attack by a retreat. And when the Americans advanced to the assault on September 12, the Germans had actually begun this withdrawal during the night. This fact has led to a satirical description of St. Mihiel as "the sector where the Americans relieved the Germans." If there is some truth in the description, it is not the whole truth. Unlike the bigger strategic retreat to the Hindenburg Line in 1917, this withdrawal worked out to the disadvantage of those who planned it. Although the German Command were as well aware of the impending blow as most of the population of France, and were not deceived by feints elsewhere, they hesitated too long over their decision and made their preparations too leisurely. Thus they were caught at a moment when part of their artillery had been withdrawn, and although a large part of the American bombardment — from 2971 guns, mostly French — was wasted on empty trenches, the longer range fire trapped some of the retiring Germans on the roads. Moreover, the comparative shortness of the bombardment, due largely to Liggett's insistence on the need for surprise, prevented the Germans gaining a comfortable start in their withdrawal. And the swift onrush of the American 2nd and

42nd Divisions, especially, upset their methodical arrangements.

But Pershing's plan was also too inelastic. Before midday Liggett's divisions had reached their final objectives and, soon after, their second day's objectives on the high ground north of Thiaucourt! The rapidity of their advance was accelerated by Liggett's instructions that units should press on as long as possible, without checking to keep alignment with their neighbors. Dazed and unsupported by their own artillery, the Germans made practically no resistance. But Pershing felt himself tied by Foch's instructions and refused Liggett's plea for a further bound — which might have ruptured the Michel Line. Dickman's and Cameron's converging corps reached their day's objectives with almost equal ease. But there, tied too closely to Pershing's apron strings, they came to a halt and awaited further orders.

Too late, Pershing tried to exploit his opportunity. If the German roads out of the salient were jammed, so also were his own roads into it. His orders for Dickman and Cameron to resume their advance did not reach the troops until after dark. And thus all but some four thousand of the forty or fifty thousand Germans in the bag slipped out before the neck was drawn tight by the junction of the two American corps at Vigneulles next morning. Nevertheless, Liggett had taken over 5000 prisoners, and the other two corps, together with the French, had taken as many in their original advance. The total came to 15,000, and, more remarkable, 443 guns, for a cost of less than 8000 casualties. If the result did not entirely satisfy the Americans, they could console themselves with the thought that this first attempt was no different from the past offensives of their Allies in failing to reap the harvest of an initial success.

During the thirteenth and fourteenth, Dickman and Cameron wheeled up, with the French 2nd Colonial Corps between, into alignment with Liggett facing the Michel Line. Then and there the battle was broken off. The only serious fighting had been borne by Liggett's corps, which had met with counter-attacks owing to the menacing direction of its advance — the enemy was willing to evacuate the salient, but had no intention of allowing his base-line to be crossed.

What might have happened if Pershing had not been prevented from trying his original plan? There is no doubt that the Germans were immensely relieved that Pershing did not follow up his success, or that in their view a further advance in this direction would have been a greater menace than the Mézières direction of the Argonne offensive. Pershing's own view was emphatic: "Without doubt, an immediate continuation of the advance would have carried us well beyond the Hindenburg Line [the Michel Line was an extension of the main Hindenburg Line] and possibly into Metz." Dickman was still more pungent: "The failure to push north from St. Mihiel with our overwhelming superiority in numbers will always be regarded by me as a strategical blunder for which Marshal Foch and his staff are responsible. It is a glaring example of the fallacy of the policy of limited objectives. . . ."

On the other hand, Liggett, who proved himself perhaps the soundest reasoner and strongest realist in the American army, has declared: "The possibility of taking Metz and the rest of it, had the battle been fought on the original plan, existed, in my opinion, only on the supposition that our army was a well-oiled, fully coördinated machine, which it was not as yet." He has also pointed out that although the attack between the Meuse and Argonne came as a greater surprise to the Germans, they were able to throw in reserves so rapidly as to block the original breach by the third day. And even if the Michel Line had been broken, an advance from St. Mihiel would then have met a fresh obstacle, especially on its right, in the defenses of Metz. Significant also is the matured verdict of General von Gallwitz, the opposing German Army Group Commander: "An overrunning of the Michel position I consider out of the question. In order to capture this position a further . . . operation on a very large scale would have been required." It is well to remember that for decisive results Pershing would at least have had to reach the Longuyon-Thionville stretch of the lateral railway, a further twenty miles beyond the Michel Line, and to have gone far enough beyond it to interrupt the line running back from Longuyon through Luxembourg. It would have demanded a penetration deeper and quicker than any yet achieved by the Allies on the western front. With an untried army this was surely a remote hope.

Yet there is one factor of which criticism has taken no account; a factor which endowed Pershing's original plan with a peculiar advantage. Almost every attempted break-through in the war had been based on the idea of a single penetration. Among the few exceptions had been the simultaneous Artois and Champagne attacks on September 25, 1915. But although in form a dual penetration, the effect was that of two single ones, for they were too far apart to cause any prompt sagging and collapse of the sector between. The convergent Argonne and Cambrai thrusts of Foch's new plan had also the same appearance of duality, but an even wider interval between them.

Now duality is the very essence of war, although curiously overlooked. Everyone recognizes the advantage which even a light-weight boxer has in using two fists against a one-armed opponent. So in war the power to use two fists is an inestimable asset. To feint with one fist and strike with the other yields an advantage, but a still greater advantage lies in being able to interchange them — to convert the feint into the real blow if the opponent uncovers himself. Nor should duality be limited to the force. Duality of objective, of which Sherman was the supreme exponent, enables the attacker to get his opponent on the horns of a dilemma, and, by mystifying him, to obtain the chance of surprising him, so that if the opponent concentrates in defense of one objective the attacker can seize the other. Only by this elasticity of aim can we truly attune ourselves to the uncertainty of war.

Returning from the general to the particular, we can recognize that the St. Mihiel salient offered the chance of attempting the yet untried method of dual penetration under almost ideal conditions. If two powerful attacks had broken through the flanks of the salient, — and better still, beyond them to right and left, — the defenders in the centre would have dissolved into chaos and been securely "caged." Through this collapsed centre a fresh force might then have driven, with a clear path between the two protecting wings. What we know of the incompleteness of the base-line defenses and the time taken before they were completely garrisoned suggests that, on September 12 and 13 at least, they could have been ruptured on a wide front. On a smaller scale, the actual attack fulfilled this process as far as it went, but the wings were then held back and there was no fresh force to pass through the centre.

But it is still a question how far the Americans could have advanced beyond the breach. And here the main factor would not have been defenses or defenders, but supplies. The road blocks and transport difficulties actually experienced in the limited advance do not encourage an optimistic answer. It is more likely that the eventual result would have justified Liggett's opinion and Napoleon's axiom: "With a new army it is possible to carry a formidable position, but not to carry out a plan or design." And the last weeks of the war were to show that even experienced armies could not solve the problem of maintaining supplies during a sustained advance, even though almost unopposed. For bulk cancels experience.

1918 — THE BREAK

Scene VIII

THE BATTLE OF A NIGHTMARE — THE MEUSE-ARGONNE

ALTHOUGH a far greater battle in scale, the Meuse-Argonne is less significant, except to the combatants, than St. Mihiel. Strategically and historically, it may even be viewed as an appendix to the unfinished and partly unwritten story of St. Mihiel.

In the first place, the ultimate aim was more idealistic than realistic. It was based on the idea that the Ardennes formed an impenetrable back wall to the great German salient in France, and that if the Allies could reach and close the exits east and west they would cut off the German armies in the salient. But the impassability of the Ardennes has been much exaggerated, especially in Haig's reports. Actually, the Ardennes were traversed by numerous roads and several railways, so that though the severance of the routes east and west might complicate the German withdrawal, this would be imperiled only if the objective were attained very rapidly. As always in war, everything turned on the time factor.

To reach the lateral railway from the Meuse-Argonne sector, the Americans would have to advance thirty miles. And, to be effective, they would have to advance more rapidly than from the St. Mihiel sector, because their thrust would be aimed close to the main German armies instead of, like the projected St. Mihiel thrust, close to the German frontier. The attempt, and hope, were fundamentally unreal. To cross these thirty miles of difficult country, they would first have to break through the German front, and then, some eight miles behind it, would meet the untouched defenses of the Kriemhilde section of the Hindenburg Line. Pershing might have confidence in the capacity of his untried army, but his faith, like that of the French in 1914 and 1915, was to founder on the rock

of machine-guns. Pétain, if he underestimated the effect of
other factors, was closer to reality when he predicted that the
Americans might cover a third of the distance before the winter.
That, roughly, was as far as their original attack reached, and
there they stuck, until other factors, unforeseen by Pétain,
intervened to relieve them.

In the second place, the Meuse-Argonne attack did not
fulfill its immediate aim — the Haig-inspired aim for which
Pershing had sacrificed his own plan. For the left wing attack
broke through the Cambrai-St. Quentin section of the Hindenburg Line, the strongest artificially, before the Meuse-Argonne
attack had drawn off any German divisions from the British
front. Thus the result justified Haig's confidence, but not
his precaution, proving that his troops could break through
without indirect help to ease their path. The strength of
the defenses was nullified by the weakening morale of the
defenders.

The irony of the result was increased by the fact that while
fifty-seven German divisions faced the left wing attack by
forty British and two American divisions, only twenty German divisions were present to oppose the right wing attack by
thirteen American and thirty-one French divisions — the
equivalent of at least sixty ordinary strength divisions. The
difference of result may be explained, in part, by the differing
degree of experience, and in part by the difference of conditions. The left wing attack opened with the British close on
the edge of the Hindenburg Line, while on the right wing the
Americans had to conquer a deep series of defenses before they
could assault their section of the Hindenburg Line. And
before they reached it their attack had lost its momentum.

Thereafter, although stubborn American assaults at heavy
cost caused the Germans to draw off, on balance, a further
sixteen divisions from the French front, the strategic effect
was small. For with shrewd strategic sense the French in the
centre appreciated that decisive results depended on the rapid
penetration and closing of the pincers, and so did not unduly
hasten the retreat of the Germans facing them. In their
skillful advance they usually kept a step in rear of their Allies

on either flank, moving forward by successive bounds when the enemy had been shouldered back. For the first two years they had borne the main burden of the fighting. If their commanders had been slow to learn how to economize life, they, and still more their men, had learnt it now. Perhaps a shade too well. But it is not for those who were fresh in the evening of the war to complain of excess of caution in those who had suffered the full heat of the day, since dawn.

On the other hand, criticism of the disappointingly early check of the Meuse-Argonne attack has been too apt to over-look the handicap of excessive freshness. The trouble was not merely that the troops were fresh — perhaps it was mostly that the arrangements were fresh. The Americans had scarcely a week of real preparation — an astonishing contrast with the months which preceded the French and British offensives of 1915, 1916, and even 1917. Even though the German fighting power and morale were now in decline, such haste would have put an almost superhuman strain on any troops. Yet it was demanded of new troops with a new organization. Popular opinion might complain of the frequency with which the ma-chine jammed; the miracle is that it did not collapse and, instead, was rapidly repaired to move forward anew.

It is equally creditable to the Higher Command that the opening attack achieved so high a degree of surprise. This preparatory success owed much to the ingenuity of the Intel-ligence section in creating the most artistic mirage of an offen-sive further east, near the Vosges.

Thus when the real offensive was launched, the twenty-mile front of attack was held by only five German divisions, all emaciated, and all but one composed of low-grade troops. Against them were thrown nine American divisions, with three more in close reserve — a superiority in fighting strength of about eight to one. There were three more divisions in army reserve. But, owing to the difficulty of withdrawing and switching troops from St. Mihiel, only one regular division could be used at the outset, and only three had previous battle experience.

The attack was preceded by a three hours' intense bombardment from 2700 guns and accompanied by 189 small tanks. It is significant to note that the proportion of tanks was much larger than in the Allied offensives of July 15 and August 8. It is also noteworthy, in view of Pershing's pre-St. Mihiel hint to Foch, that all the artillery was French-made, and half of it manned by the French, as also were forty-seven of the tanks.

Pershing's plan was far-reaching. It certainly cannot be criticized as circumscribed or short-sighted, for the attacking troops were expected to reach and break through the Kriemhilde line on the first day, an advance of over eight miles, and were to exploit the success during the night, so that the second morning would find them in open country, and almost half-way to Sedan and the lateral railway. Unfortunately, Pershing's orders were by no means clearly worded.

Foch, in a personal note, had intimated that the American army must not let itself be tied by the pace of its neighbor, Gouraud's French Fourth Army, and added, "There is no question of fixing . . . fronts not to be passed without a new order, such a restrictive indication tending to prevent exploitation of opportunities. . . ."

Unfortunately, Pershing's orders to his corps had this very tendency, however far-reaching his aim. Bullard's III Corps on the right and Liggett's I Corps on the left were to drive in wedges on either flank of the commanding height of Montfaucon, thus helping Cameron's V Corps in the centre, which was to sweep over Montfaucon and on to the Kriemhilde line "without waiting for advance of the III and I Corps." This provision was wise, but less happily their advance was to be "based upon the V Corps." Here lay the germ of paralysis.

For when the assault was launched, at 5.30 A.M. on September 26, the V Corps, which had its flanks protected, made far less progress than its neighbors — although its left division, the 91st, was a happy exception. On the right of the V Corps, the 4th (Regular) Division of Bullard's Corps penetrated deeply past the flank of Montfaucon, while the 80th and 33rd near the Meuse made good progress. On the left wing of the army, which had the most difficult task and ground,

Liggett's orders paved the way for a good start. Thus the 35th Division neatly circumvented the formidable obstacle of Vauquois by an encircling advance, and then, with the 28th Division on their left, drove a wedge nearly four miles deep up the Aire Valley just east of the Argonne Forest. Through the forest itself moved the 77th Division, which had the difficult task of linking up with the French on the west side.

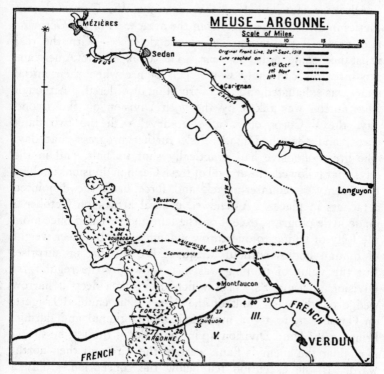

Then, however, Pershing's orders for a halt on reaching the corps' objective were construed as putting a brake on the advance, and it was difficult to get up momentum again after the six hours' delay. A method that was sound in siege warfare was, as Liggett's insight told him, a mistake when faced with a weak and temporarily demoralized enemy. The Americans had, as yet, neither the training nor organization for methodical siege warfare, and the best chance of decisive suc-

cess lay in swamping the defense by a human torrent in the
first flush of surprise before the enemy could bring up reënforcements. With the brake put on prematurely, the advance
thereafter slowed down and became spasmodic along the whole
front. Guns could not get forward to support the infantry,
control lapsed, and supplies frequently failed, through inexperience accentuating the natural difficulties of the ground.

All these factors helped the success of the Germans' own
tactics in drawing the sting from the attack. For the Germans
had repeated the method of elastic defense — with the real
resistance some miles in rear. The unexpectant Americans
ran into this cunningly woven belt of fire when their initial
spurt was exhausted and their formation disordered. Although
Montfaucon was taken by the 79th Division on the second
day, the V Corps only came up level with the two flank
corps, and they had made little further progress that day.
The great offensive had practically shot its bolt, and in the
days that followed, the arrival of fresh German divisions enabled
the enemy to counter-attack and force back the disjointed
attackers in places. A renewed general attack on October 4
made little progress, except on the left, and revealed once more
the folly of trying to overthrow machine-guns by sheer weight
of human bodies without adequate fire support or surprise.
But the value of training was also shown by the regular 1st
Division in Liggett's Corps which drove in a deep if narrow
wedge on the east bank of the Aire. This enabled Liggett,
on October 7, to try a manœuvre both original and daring;
bringing the 82nd Division up in the wake of the 1st, he swung
it against the enemy's flank west of the Aire and then northward. If the execution fell below the conception — only a
tithe of the division came into action — so that the chance of
cutting off the enemy troops in the Argonne was lost, the threat
at least persuaded the enemy to retire from the forest while
there was time, and by October 10 the American line had
passed and was clear of this hampering obstacle.

Meantime, the all too obvious failure to fulfill the original
plan had provoked widespread reactions behind the front.
Clemenceau visited Foch and bitterly remarked, "Those

Americans will lose us our chance of a big victory before winter. They are all tangled up with themselves. You have tried to make Pershing see. Now let's put it up to President Wilson." The complaint was rather unfair, in view of the fact that the advance of Gouraud's army was well behind that of the American, if by design. But Foch was more generous, or more fully aware of the firmness of Pershing's position, and replied, "The Americans have got to learn sometime. They are learning now, rapidly." Pétain, indeed, had made the strategically sound suggestion of giving charge of the Argonne Forest sector to a separate army, half French and half American, under General Hirschauer, but Pershing saw in it only a fresh political manœuvre, and had rejected it firmly.

Pershing, however, overhauled his own army — and its commanders. The inactive forces east of the Meuse were formed into the Second American Army, to be commanded by Bullard, while Liggett was given charge of the First and of the Meuse-Argonne attack. Pershing himself retained the superior direction of both, and left Hugh Drum to continue as Chief of Staff to Liggett. Dickman succeeded Liggett in the I Corps, and Hines succeeded Bullard, while Cameron was replaced by Summerall. Other commanders of all grades fell beneath Pershing's sickle almost as fast as their men beneath the scythe of the German machine-guns.

But for a time these changes made little impression on the Germans. The next general attack on October 14 achieved little at large cost — both of men's lives and generals' reputations — and with its failure even the Higher Command realized that the offensive had reached stalemate. An attempt to press on, with exhausted troops and disordered communications, could exercise no pressure adequate to be any appreciably greater relief to the other Allied armies. Moreover, the British left wing of the Allied offensive, in which the 27th and 30th American Divisions shared, had already broken through the last defenses of the Hindenburg Line and by October 5 had emerged into open country, with only natural obstacles, mileage, and a devastated area to hinder its advance.

Liggett, who now took charge, was wise to realize that in

the circumstances it was far better to rest and reorganize his forces for a sure bound as soon as possible than to sacrifice lives in attempting the impossible. While utilizing the breathing space not only to replenish his ranks and supplies but to improve his communications and overhaul his organization, he carried out local operations to obtain a good jumping off line for the fresh bound. Further, he recast not only the tactics but the plan. Pershing had proposed that the American left should strike first, followed in turn by the remaining corps to the right. This meant battering first at the naturally strong and heavily wooded Bois de Bourgogne area due north of the Argonne, where also the enemy were in strongest force. Liggett preferred to drive a broad wedge in the centre and so outflank the Bois de Bourgogne, threatening its encirclement in conjunction with the advance of the French Fourth Army to the west.

It was well conceived; for when Liggett unleashed his forces on November 1, this area was the only one which showed resisting power, and by next day the enemy rearguards there had disappeared and were falling back as fast as on the rest of the American front. If the Germans were offering little resistance, the very rapidity of the pursuit — outstripping the French on the flank — imposed almost as great a strain; and it was a tribute to the overhaul that the First Army machine functioned much more smoothly than in the earlier phase. And this despite the execution of a most difficult manœuvre by which the whole army wheeled progressively to the right during the course of the pursuit, ready for an attack northeastwards — against the strong position between the Meuse and Chiers rivers to which the enemy had retired. This wheel was a preliminary to an advance towards Metz, but the Armistice now rang down the curtain.

Strategically, this move was more important (because the Germans here were more sensitive) than the now incidental arrival of the left wing on the Carignan-Sedan section of the lateral railway. This railway had been brought under artillery fire as early as November 3, and had been reached by the infantry four days later, but the Germans had already slipped out of the bag. Indeed, the advance to this point, although an exhilarating finish, was chiefly significant in showing the "liberties" that could be and were taken at the finish. With a somewhat brusque disregard of French feelings, Pershing issued a message that he wished the American army to have "the honor of entering Sedan" — although it was now in the French sector of advance. Pershing added the encouragement or incitement: "Boundaries will not be considered as binding." The message was passed to the corps without being shown to Liggett, and as a result the 42nd Division on the left of the army raced for Sedan. But the vague wording produced a still more unmilitary, indeed, a burlesque, result. For the 1st Division — Pershing's favorite — from the centre corps had also started to race thither by night, crossing the divisions of the I Corps and throwing them into confusion as it impetuously swept through them. It capped the farce by taking prisoner the commander of the 42nd Division. Liggett, however, intervened with prompt action and vigorous language — to restrain both divisions and allow the French the courtesy of entering Sedan, thus to wipe out the bitter memory of 1870.

The historian who scans the whole horizon of the war must recognize that this last offensive, beginning on November 1, had only a supplementary influence, for Ludendorff had fallen from power — his plea for a renewed stand on the German frontier rejected — and the enemy were already suing for peace before Liggett struck. Nevertheless it was well that the Armistice had tarried long enough to allow the offensive of November 1 to take place. For it provided a counterpoise to the bitter memories of the first phase — more truly, the first battle — of the Meuse-Argonne, and a proof that when purged and refined by experience the American army could produce leadership and staff work worthy of the gallant sacrifice of the fighting troops — the American nation in arms.

EPILOGUE

EVERY anniversary of the Armistice kindles emotions and memories such as no other day in the year has at present the power to do. For those who shared in the experiences of those four and a quarter years of struggle the commemoration does not stale with repetition. But the mood in which it is commemorated has undergone subtle changes. On the original Armistice itself the dominant note was a sigh of relief, of infinite volume, most restrained among those who had the most direct cause for relief, most exuberant, perhaps, among those who least appreciated the relief.

The earlier anniversaries were dominated by two opposite emotions. On the one hand grief — a keener sense, now that the storm had passed, of the vacant places in our midst. On the other hand, triumph — flamboyant only in rare cases, but nevertheless a heightened sense of victory, that the enemy had been laid low. That mood again has been modified.

Armistice Day has become more a commemoration than a celebration. The passage of time has refined and blended the earlier emotions, so that, without losing sense of the personal loss and of quiet thankfulness that as a nation we proved our continued power to meet a crisis graver than any in past annals, we are to-day conscious, above all, of the general effects on the world and on civilization. In this mood of reflection we are more ready to recognize both the achievements and the point of view of our late enemies, and perhaps all the more because we realize that both the causes and the course of war are determined by the folly and the frailty rather than by the deliberate evil of human nature.

The war has become history, and can be viewed in the perspective of history. For good it has deepened our sense of fellowship and community of interest, whether inside the nation or between nations. But, for good or bad, it has shattered our faith in idols, our hero-worshiping belief that great men are different clay from common men. Leaders are still necessary, perhaps more necessary, but our awakened realization of their common humanity is a safeguard against either expecting from them, or trusting in them, too much. It has been for the benefit both of history and of future generations that the past decade has seen such a flood of evidence and revelations, of documents and memoirs. That most of the actors are still alive provides an invaluable check in sifting the evidence, while the historians themselves have been so immersed in the atmosphere of war that they have a certain immunity from the abstract theorizing which an historian in his cloistered study fifty years later so easily contracts. We know nearly all that is to be known. The one drawback is that the flood has been so huge that only the student has been able to cope with its investigation.

What caused that astonishingly sudden collapse and surrender of Germany which, as by a miracle, so it seemed, lifted the nightmare load of war from Europe? To arrive at a satisfactory answer it is not sufficient to analyze the hectic weeks of negotiation and military success which preceded November 11. Even in the military sphere we need to go back to August 8 — the day which filled the German Command with the conviction of defeat — and to July 18, which witnessed the visible turning of the tide. And if we go back thence we must go back further, to March 21; for the decline of Germany's military power is not explicable without reference to the consummation of that military effort, and consumption of her military resources, in the great series of offensives which opened in the spring of 1918.

We ought, however, to go back further still. Indeed, if the historian of the future has to select one day as decisive for the outcome of the World War he will probably choose August 2, 1914 — before the war, for England, had yet begun — when Mr. Winston Churchill, at 1.25 A.M., sent the order to mobilize the British navy. That navy was to win no Trafalgar, but it was to do more than any other factor towards winning the war for the Allies. For the navy was the instrument of the blockade, and as the fog of war disperses in the clearer light of these post-war years that blockade is seen to assume larger and larger proportions, to be more and more clearly the decisive agency in the struggle. Like those "jackets" which used to be applied in American gaols to refractory prisoners, as it was progressively tightened so did it first cramp the prisoner's movements and then stifle his breathing, while the tighter it became and the longer it continued, the less became the prisoner's power of resistance and the more demoralizing the sense of constriction.

Helplessness induces hopelessness, and history attests that loss of hope and not loss of lives is what decides the issue of war. No historian would underrate the direct effect of the semi-starvation of the German people in causing the final collapse of the "home-front." But leaving aside the question of how far the revolution caused the military defeat, instead of *vice versa*, the intangible all-pervading factor of the blockade intrudes into every consideration of the military situation.

This, during the last year of the war, is studded with "ifs." If Germany, instead of throwing all her military resources into a series of tremendous offensives in 1918, had stayed on the defensive in the west, while consolidating her gains in the east, could she have averted defeat? Militarily, there seems little doubt that she could. In the light of the experience of 1915, when the Allies had 145 divisions in the west to Germany's 100, and when the German trench systems were a frail and shallow bulwark compared with those of 1918, it is difficult to see that the Allies could have breached it, even if they had waited until the inflowing tide of American man-power had restored to them the relative numerical superiority that they had enjoyed in 1915.

And if so, in face of the accumulating cost of vain assaults, would they not eventually have inclined towards a compromise peace? A peace, peradventure, which, in return for the relinquishment of Belgium and Northern France, might have conceded to Germany part or the whole of her gains in the east. Yet, as we ask the question, and militarily find an optimistic answer difficult, the factor of the command of the sea comes to mind. For it was the strangle-hold of the British navy which, in default of a serious peace move, constrained Germany to carry out that *felo de se* offensive of 1918. She was dogged by the spectre of slow enfeeblement ending in eventual collapse.

Perhaps if she had adopted such a war policy of defense in the west, offense in the east, after the Marne in 1914, or even, after 1915, continued the policy which she had that year temporarily adopted, the prospect might have been brighter and the story different. For on the one hand, she could have consummated unquestionably the dream of "Mittel-Europa," and on the other, the blockade was still a loose grip, and could hardly have been drawn effectively tight so long as the United States remained outside the conflict. But in 1918 the best chance had passed.

Another big "if," often mooted, is the question whether, even in the autumn of 1918, Germany could have avoided capitulation. Would the fighting front have collapsed if the war had gone on after November 11? Was capitulation inevitable, or could the German armies have made good their retreat and stood firm on their own frontiers? German opinion largely says "yes" to the latter question, and blames the surrender on the "home front." Many open-minded and diligent students of the war among the Allies are inclined to agree that it was possible from a military point of view. But again the naval aspect intervenes. Even if the German armies, and the German people, roused to a supreme effort in visible defense of their own soil, had managed to hold the Allies at bay, the end could only have been postponed. The most that history is likely to concede is that they might have held on long enough, tightening their belts, for the Allies, already weary, to sicken of the effort, and thus concede more favorable terms than those of Versailles.

Having disposed of the "ifs," having emphasized the fundamental cause of the Armistice, — Britain's sea-power, her historic weapon, the deadliest weapon which any nation has wielded throughout history, — let us turn to examine the immediate causes of the Armistice. How did victory come?

Here military action bulks large. Other factors contributed, apart from the naval. If we do not accept entirely, we should not discount unduly, the unwilling tribute paid by the Germans to the effectiveness of Allied, and especially of British, propaganda. In the later stages of the war it was skillfully directed and intensively developed.

If now, when passions are stilled, the memory of some of the "facts" that were exploited is disturbing to our sense of fair play and lies uneasily on the stomach, we realize equally that such forms of propaganda neither stimulated our own people nor discouraged the enemy. It was the kernel of essential truth upon the bigger issues which was digested by the German people and, by leading them to question both the honesty of their leadership and the hope of success, weakened the will to continued sacrifice.

Nevertheless, though we should recognize the value of the more discriminating propaganda, its effect was rather in supplementing and completing the military successes than in paving the way for them, as German spokesmen have often contended. There is significant evidence on this point to be found in the memoirs of Prince Max of Baden, a man whose high-minded patriotism and sincerity command the respect of both friend and foe, and whose book is perhaps the most valuable of all war memoirs yet published. Unintentionally and unconsciously, he shows in casual passages, easily missed, that when German arms were temporarily in the ascendant, moderation was forgotten in exultation, even among the more sober.

In March 1918, he quotes even a pacifist as exuberantly crying, "Never worry ! . . . What an experience ! . . . World dominion." And another representative of moderate opinion "let the cat out of the bag" in saying meditatively, "It would seem that we need n't say no to Briey and Longwy" — revealing that intoxication of spirit which, more fundamentally than any ill intention, was responsible for Germany's war guilt.

In face of such widespread intoxication, propaganda could only be secondary to military action. Thus we are left with the sure conclusion that the success of the Allied armies was chief among the immediate causes of Germany's capitulation on November 11.

That conclusion does not necessarily, or even naturally, imply that at the moment of the Armistice the German armies were on the brink of collapse. Nor that the Armistice was a mistaken concession — as some among the Allies, usually those whose fighting was done with their tongue, were so loud in proclaiming at the time.

Rather does the record of the last "hundred days," when thoroughly sifted, confirm the immemorial lesson of history — that the true aim in war is the mind of the enemy command and government, not the bodies of their troops; that the balance between victory and defeat turns on mental impressions and only indirectly on physical blows. That in war, as Napoleon said and Foch endorsed, "it is the man, not men, who counts."

The reiteration of this great truth is to be found in the war's last phase. Great as were the stimulus and visible success of the tide-turning battle on the Marne in July, Ludendorff was still planning and preparing fresh offensives thereafter. If he was chagrined, he does not appear to have been so disillusioned as he was after his own outwardly successful attack on the Lys in April.

But the Fourth Army surprise attack before Amiens on August 8 was a dislocating moral blow. Prince Max put August 8 in its true light psychologically, when he defined it as "the turning point." Even so, to develop the conviction of failure into the conviction of hopelessness required to compel surrender, something more was needed. It came not from the western front, but from a despised "side-show," — Salonika, — long condemned by Allied military opinion and scornfully ridiculed by the Germans as their "largest internment camp." With Bulgaria's collapse, the back gate to Austria, as well as to Turkey, and through Austria to Germany, stood ajar.

The immediate issue of the war was decided on September 29 — decided in the mind of the German Command. Ludendorff and his associates had then "cracked," and the sound went echoing backwards until it had resounded throughout the whole of Germany. Nothing could catch it or stop it. The Command might recover its nerve, the actual military position might improve, but the moral impression, as ever in war, was decisive.

Yet, let us once again emphasize that the fundamental causes of the decision are more various than the acts which immediately produced it.

The truth is that no one cause was, or could be, decisive. The western front, the Balkan front, the tank, the blockade, and propaganda have all been claimed as the cause of victory. All claims are justified; none is wholly right, although the blockade ranks first and began first. In this warfare between nations, victory is a cumulative effect, to which all weapons — military, economic, and psychological — contribute. Victory comes, and can only come, through the utilization and combination of all the resources existing in a modern nation, and the dividend of success depends on the way in which these manifold activities are coördinated.

It is even more futile to ask which country won the war. France did not win the war, but unless she had held the fort while the forces of Britain were preparing, and those of America still a dream, the release of civilization from this nightmare of militarism would have been impossible. Britain did not win the war, but without her command of the sea, her financial support, and her army to take over the main burden of the struggle from 1916 onwards, defeat would have been inevitable. The United States did not win the war, but without their economic aid to ease the strain, without the arrival of their troops to turn the numerical balance, and, above all, without the moral tonic which their coming gave, victory would have been impossible. And let us not forget how many times Russia had sacrificed herself to save her Allies; preparing the way for their ultimate victory as surely as for her own downfall. Finally, whatever be the verdict of history on her policy, unstinted tribute is due to the incomparable endurance and skill with which Germany more than held her own for four years against superior numbers — an epic of military and human achievement.

BIBLIOGRAPHY

THE appended list is, of course, far from a complete list of the books which have been read or consulted during the eleven years since the war. Its purpose is to indicate those of main historical significance. It comprises those sources from which facts or quotations have been drawn for use herein, or which have directly helped in forming one's picture of the war. During these years one has also been privileged to see a number of documents, British and foreign, which have not yet been published or utilized, and to gather the personal evidence of those who participated in critical actions and in the taking of important decisions. Such sources, where they have contributed to the narrative, are referred to as either "Unpublished Documents" or "Personal Evidence." Although it is not yet possible to give a fuller identification, all such sources have been recorded and privately catalogued for the eventual use of historical students.

In concluding this preface to the Bibliography I take the opportunity to acknowledge the great debt which all serious students of the war owe to the *Army Quarterly*, and especially its "Notes on Foreign War Books." This feature during the past ten years has been invaluable as a signpost and searchlight amid the vast and confusing mass of material that has been published. No periodical, military or historical, in any country has kept or marked so clear a track for students of the war.

BIBLIOGRAPHY

CHAPTER I

ORIGINS

J. W. Headlam-Morley, *The Outbreak of War. Foreign Office Documents* (1926)

G. P. Gooch and H. Temperley, *British Documents on the Origins of the War*, Vols. I–V (1927)

Haldane (Viscount), *Before the War* (1920)

Grey of Fallodon (Viscount), *Twenty-Five Years, 1892–1916* (1925)

G. Buchanan, *My Mission to Russia* (1923)

H. Wickham Steed, *Through Thirty Years, 1892–1922* (1924)

R. W. Seton-Watson, *Sarajevo* (1926)

G. P. Gooch, *Recent Revelations of European Diplomacy* (1927)

H. W. Wilson, *The War Guilt* (1928)

B. Hendrick, *The Life and Letters of W. H. Page* (1922–25)

P. Renouvin, *Les Origines Immédiates de la Guerre* (1925)

R. Poincaré, *Au Service de la France*, Vols. I–IV (1926–27)

M. Paléologue, *An Ambassador's Memoirs* (Eng. trans. 1923–25)

German Foreign Office, *Die Grosse Politik der Europäischen Kabinette, 1871–1914* (1926) [Eng. selection and trans. in 4 vols. *German Diplomatic Documents, 1871–1914*, 1928–]

K. Kautsky, M. Montgelas, and W. Schücking, *Die Deutschen Dokumente zum Kriegsausbruch* (1919) [Eng. trans. 1924]

A. von Tirpitz, *Memoirs* (Eng. trans. 1919)

The Kaiser's Letters to the Tsar (Eng. trans. 1920)

M. Montgelas, *The Case for the Central Powers* (Eng. trans. 1925)

K. Lichnowsky, *My Mission to London, 1912–1914* (1918)

Generaloberst Helmuth von Moltke. Erinnerungen, Briefe, Dokumente 1877–1916 (1923)

W. von Schoen, *The Memoirs of an Ambassador* (Eng. trans. 1922)

Diplomatische Aktenstücke zur Vorgeschichte des Krieges, 1914 (1919) [Eng. trans. *Austrian Red Book*, 1920]

Conrad von Hötzendorf, *Aus meiner Dienstzeit*, Vols. I–IV (1922–25)

Czernin, *In the World War* (Eng. trans. 1920)

How the War Began in 1914, Being the Diary of the Russian Foreign Office . . . July, 1914 . . . Published by the Russian Soviet Government (Eng. trans. 1925)

S. Sazonov, *Fateful Years, 1909–1916* (Eng. trans. 1927)

Un Livre Noir, diplomatie d'avant guerre d'après les documents des archives russes (1922–23)

CHAPTERS II–VII

GENERAL

W. S. Churchill, *The World Crisis*, 4 vols. (1923–27)

John Buchan, *A History of the Great War*, 4 vols. (1921)

Oxford and Asquith (Earl), *Memories and Reflections* (1928)

G. Arthur, *Life of Lord Kitchener*, Vol. III (1920)

Esher (Viscount), *The Tragedy of Lord Kitchener* (1921)

C. à C. Repington, *The First World War, 1914–1918*, 2 vols. (1920)

W. R. Robertson, *From Private to Field Marshal* (1921); *Soldiers and Statesmen, 1914–1918* (1926)

Beaverbrook (Lord), *Politicians and the War, 1914–1916* (1928)

N. Macready, *Annals of an Active Life* (1926)

C. E. Callwell, *Experiences of a Dug-Out, 1914–1918* (1921)

C. P. Lucas, *The Empire at War*, 3 vols. (covers war effort of Dominions and Colonies)

Royal Engineers' Institute, *The Work of the R.E. in the European War, 1914–1919*, 9 vols. (1921–27)

War Office, *Statistics of the Military Effort of the British Empire, 1914–1920* (1922)

R. van Overstraeten, *Des Principes de la Guerre*, Vol. II (Vol. II covers World War)

C. Seymour, *The Intimate Papers of Colonel House*, 4 vols. (1926–28)

J. W. Gerard, *My Four Years in Germany* (1917) [U.S.A. Ambassador]

E. Ludendorff, *Urkunden der Oberste Heeresleitung, 1916–1918* (1920)

Kuhl, *Der Deutsche Generalstab in Vorbereitung und Durchführung des Weltkrieges* (1920) [French condensed trans. by Douchy, *Le Grand État-Major Allemand avant et pendant la Guerre Mondiale*]

M. Erzberger, *Erlebnisse im Weltkrieg* (1921) [French trans. *Souvenirs de Guerre*]

J. V. Bredt, *Die Belgische Neutralität und der Schlieffensche Feldzugsplan* (1929) [excellent summary in *Army Quarterly*, July 1929]

E. von Falkenhayn, *General Headquarters, 1914–1916 and Its Critical Decisions* (Eng. trans. 1919)

Stürgkh (Graf), *Im Deutschen Grossen Hauptquartier* (1921) [intimate impressions and pen-portraits by the Austrian military representative]

Zwehl, *Erich von Falkenhayn* (1925) [contains extracts from diary]

Groener, *Das Testament des Grafen Schlieffen* (1927)

H. von Hentig, *Psychologische Strategie des Grossen Krieges* (1927) [criticism, usually acute, of the German war policy and strategy]

L. Gehre, *Die Deutsche Kraftverteilung während des Weltkrieges* (1928) [gives location of all German divisions on fifteenth and last day of every month]

Bauer, *Der Grosse Krieg in Feld und Heimat* (1922) [intimate revelations of the German Supreme Command during the war]

M. Schwarte, *Der Grosse Krieg, 1914–1918*, 11 vols. (1921–   )

Buat, *L'Armée Allemande pendant la Guerre de 1914–1918* (1920)

WESTERN FRONT

J. E. Edmonds, *Military Operations, France and Belgium*, Vols. I–V (1922–30) [*British Official History*, Vols. I–II, 1914; III–IV, 1915; V, 1916]

The Despatches of Lord French, 1914–1915 (1917)

French (Viscount), *1914* (1919) [a record of his command, distinguished by inaccuracy]

J. H. Boraston (Ed.), *Sir D. Haig's Despatches, 1915–1919* (1919)

G. A. B. Dewar and J. H. Boraston, *Sir Douglas Haig's Command, 1915–1918* (1922)

H. L. Smith-Dorrien, *Memories of Forty-Eight Years' Service* (1925) [covers, if with extreme reserve, his service as corps and army commander in the first phase]

C. E. Callwell, *Field-Marshal Sir Henry Wilson*, 2 vols. (1927) [extracts from an amazingly unreserved diary, 1914–1919]

F. Maurice, *The Life of General Lord Rawlinson of Trent* (1928) [covers the whole war]

J. Charteris, *Field-Marshal Earl Haig* (1929)

Huguet, *Britain and the War* (Eng. trans. 1928) [impressions of French representative at British G.H.Q., 1914–15]

C. E. W. Bean, *The Australian Imperial Force in France, 1916* (1929) [Australian Official History]

J. Monash, *The Australian Victories in France in 1918* (1920)

A. W. Currie, *Canadian Corps Operations during 1918* (1920)

A. A. Montgomery, *The Story of the Fourth Army* (1920) [for last half of the 1918 campaign]

A. de Schrÿver, *La Bataille de Liége* (1922) [by the chief of staff of the fortress]

Deguise, *La Défense de la Position Fortifiée d'Anvers en 1914* (1921) [by the Belgian commander]

E. Menzel, *La Vérité sur l'Évacuation d'Anvers en 1914* (1925)

C. Merzbach, *La Vérité sur la Défense de Namur en 1914* (1927)

Duvivier and Herbiet, *Du Rôle de l'Armée de Champagne et des Forteresses Belges en 1914* (1929) [effect in detaining German forces]

Les Armées Françaises dans la Grande Guerre, Tome I, Vol. II (covers operations up to eve of the Marne, 1914); Tome VII, Vol. I (covers period 18th June–25th September, 1918) [French Official History]

B. E. Palat, *La Grande Guerre sur le Front Occidental*, 12 vols. (1921–   )

P. Renouvin, *Les Formes du Gouvernement de Guerre* (1929) [relations between Government and commanders in France]

R. Poincaré, *Au Service de la France*, Vol. V. *L'Invasion, 1914* (1929)

Lanrezac, *Le Plan de Campagne Français et le Premier Mois de Guerre* (1920)

V. Margueritte, *Au Bord du Gouffre* (1920) [French plan for 1914]

F. Engerand, *La Bataille de la Frontière (Août 1914) Briey* (1920) [French plan for 1914]

Percin, *1914: Les Erreurs du Haut Commandement* (1922) [French plan for 1914]

Tanant, *La Troisième Armée dans la Bataille. Souvenirs d'un Chef d'État-Major* (1928) [special light on the opening battles of 1914]

Toussan, *Historique des Corps de Cavalerie Commandés par le Général Conneau du 14 Août, 1914 au 2 Mars, 1917* (1924)

E. Valarché, *La Bataille de Guise* (1928)

A. Grouard, *La Conduite de la Guerre jusqu'à la Bataille de la Marne* (1922) [an acute criticism by a famous military critic who gave the French General Staff an unheeded warning of the German plan]

Camon, *L'Effondrement du Plan Allemand en Septembre 1914* (1925)

Mermeix, *Joffre — 1e Crise du Commandement; Le Commandement Unique*

Rousset, *La Bataille de l'Aisne* [Nivelle offensive, 1917]

P. Painlevé, *Comment j'ai nommé Foch et Pétain* (1924)

Laure, *Au 3ème Bureau du troisième G.Q.G. 1917–1919* (1922)

L. Madelin, *La Bataille de France* (1918 campaign)

Koeltz, *L'Offensive Allemande de 1918* (1928)

Jean de Pierrefeu, *G.Q.G. Secteur I*, 2 vols. (1921); *Plutarque a menti* (1923)

N. Domège, *En Marge de Plutarque*

Mordacq, *Le Commandement Unique. Comment il fut réalisé; La Vérité sur l'Armistice*

Reichsarchiv, *Der Weltkrieg 1914–1918*, Vols. I, III, V, VI (1924–29) [German Official History, covers 1914]

Reichsarchiv, *Antwerpen, 1914* (1921) [German Official Monograph on siege]

Reichsarchiv, *Ypres, 1914* [German Official Monograph, Eng. trans. 1919]

Crown Prince Rupprecht of Bavaria, *Mein Kriegstagebuch*, 3 vols. (1928)

Krafft von Delmensingen, *Die Führung des Kronprinzen Rupprecht von Bayern auf dem Linken Deutschen Heeresflügel bis zur Schlacht in Lothringen im August 1914* (1925) [light on opening battles in Lorraine]

Die Schlacht in Lothringen (1929) [Bavarian Official History]

German Ex-Crown Prince, *Meine Erinnerungen aus Deutschland Heldenkampf* (1923)

Generaloberst Helmuth von Moltke. Erinnerungen, Briefe, Dokumente 1877–1916 (1923)

W. Foerster, *Graf Schlieffen und der Weltkrieg* (1920)

Kluck, *The March on Paris, 1914* (Eng. trans. 1920)

Army Quarterly, October 1921, *General Ludendorff on the German Plan of Campaign, August 1914* (extract from letter)

The Memoirs of Prince Max of Baden (Eng. trans. 1928) [especially for light on last phase of war]

Final Report of Gen. J. J. Pershing (1919)

First Army Report (printed 1923)

Shipley Thomas, *History of the American Expeditionary Force* (1920)

R. L. Bullard, *Personalities and Reminiscences of the War* (1925)

J. G. Harbord, *Leaves from a War Diary* (1926)

J. W. Thomason, *Fix Bayonets* (1927)

J. T. Dickman, *The Great Crusade* (1927)

Hunter Liggett, *Commanding an American Army* (1925); *A.E.F.* (1928)

T. M. Johnson, *Without Censor* (1928)

T. C. Lonergan, *It Might Have Been Lost* (1929) [extracts from British Official documents dealing with Pershing's struggle to preserve the national unity of the A.E.F.]

RUSSIAN FRONT

(See also Chapter III, Scene 2)

Reichsarchiv, *Der Weltkrieg, 1914–1918*, Vol. II (1924); Vol. V (1929) [German Official History, covers 1914]

E. Ludendorff, *My War Memories* (Eng. trans. 1920)

P. von Hindenburg, *Out of My Life* (Eng. trans. 1920)

A. von Cramon, *Quatre Ans au G.Q.G. Austro-Hongrois* (French trans. 1922)

M. Hoffmann, *The War of Lost Opportunities* (Eng. trans. 1924); *War Diaries and Other Papers* (Eng. trans. 1929)

Russian Historical Commission, *La Grande Guerre. Relation de l'État-Major Russe* (French trans. 1927)

Conrad von Hötzendorf, *Aus meiner Dienstzeit*, Vols. IV–V (1925–26) [covers 1914 campaign]

François, *Gorlice, 1915* (1922) [the 1915 break-through]

A. Arz, *Zur Geschichte des Grossen Krieges, 1914–1918* (memoirs of Conrad's successor)

J. E. Edmonds in *Army Quarterly*, July 1921, *The Austrian Plan of Campaign, 1914, and Its Development*

K. F. Novak, *Der Weg zur Katastrophe* (French trans. 1920) [Conrad's evidence]

Buat, *Hindenburg et Ludendorff Stratèges* (1923)

Camon, *Ludendorff sur le Front Russe 1914–1915* (1926)

Y. Danilov, *La Russie dans la Guerre Mondiale, 1914–1917* (French trans. 1927)

Sukhomlinov, *Erinnerungen* (1924)

B. Gourko, *Russia in 1914–1917* (Eng. trans. 1918)

A. Knox, *With the Russian Army, 1914–1917* (1921); *Hindenburg's Second Offensive in Poland* (in *Army Quarterly*, July 1921) [Lodz]

C. E. Callwell, *Experiences of a Dug-Out, 1914–1918* (1921)

C. Maynard, *The Murmansk Venture* (1928)

ITALIAN FRONT

L. Cadorna, *La Guerra alla Fronte Italiana* (1921)

Capello, *Note di Guerra* (1920–21)

Vigano, *La Nostra Guerra* (1921)

A. Tosti, *La Guerra Italo-Austriaca, 1915–1918* (1925)

Kuntz, *La Psychologie du G.Q.G. Italien sous le Général Cadorna* (1923)

A. Krauss, *Die Ursachen unserer Niederlage* (1921)

A. Arz, *Zur Geschichte des Grossen Krieges, 1914–1918* (1924) [covers 1917 and 1918]

A. von Cramon, *Quatre Ans au G.Q.G. Austro-Hongrois* (French trans. 1922) [the chief German representative]

Kerchnawe, *Der Zusammenbruch der Oester-Ungar: Wehrmacht im Herbst* (1921) [Austrian documents]

J. F. Gathorne-Hardy in *Army Quarterly*, October 1921, *A Summary of the Campaign in Italy and an Account of the Battle of Vittorio Veneto* (by the British Chief of Staff)

R. H. Beadon in *Army Quarterly*, January 1925, *An Operation of War* (British move to Italy after Caporetto)

BALKAN FRONT

Wolfgang Foerster, *Graf Schlieffen und der Weltkrieg*, Part III (1921)

O. Landfried, *Der Endkampf in Macedonien, 1918* (1925)

Nedeff, *Les Opérations en Macédoine. L'Épopée de Doiran, 1915–1918* (1927)

Feyler, *La Campagne de Macédoine*, Vol. I, 1915–1916; Vol. II, 1917–1918 (from Serbian and Greek sources)

Jouinot-Gambetta, *Uskub ou du Rôle de la Cavalerie d'Afrique dans la Victoire* (1920) [final break-through]

Robert David, *Le Drame Ignoré de l'Armée d'Orient* (1928) [especially political side]

Les Armées Françaises dans la Grande Guerre, Tome VIII, Vol. I (1928)

Œhmichen, *Essai sur la Doctrine de Guerre des Coalitions. La Direction de la Guerre, Novembre 1914–Mars 1917* (1927) [Joffre's influence on Salonika campaign]

Sarrail, *Mon Commandement en Orient, 1916–1918* (1920)

L. Villari, *The Macedonian Campaign* (1922)

THE DARDANELLES

(See Chapter IV, Scenes 1 and 2)

PALESTINE

(Including Egypt and Arabia)

G. MacMunn and C. Falls, *Military Operations, Egypt and Palestine* (1928) [British Official History]

C. E. W. Bean, *Official History of Australia in the War*, Vol. I.

H. S. Gullett, *Official History of Australia in the War*, Vol. VII (1923)

A. P. Wavell, *The Palestine Campaigns* (1928)

R. M. P. Preston, *The Desert Mounted Corps* (1921)

T. E. Lawrence, *Revolt in the Desert*

T. E. Lawrence in *Army Quarterly*, October 1920, *The Evolution of a Revolt*

W. T. Massey, *The Desert Campaigns* (1918)

M. Bowman-Manifold, *An Outline of the Egyptian and Palestine Campaigns* (1922)

G. E. Badcock, *History of the Transport Services of the E.E.F.*

Army, Navy and Air Force Gazette, June 18, 1927

Reichsarchiv, *Yilderim* (1925)

Kress von Kressenstein, *Zwischen Kaukasus und Sinai* (1922) [covers the period 1915–1917]

Liman von Sanders, *Five Years in Turkey* (Eng. trans. 1928) [covers 1918]

Rafael de Nogales, *Vier Jahren unter dem Halbmond* (1926)

MESOPOTAMIAN FRONT

F. J. Moberly, *The Mesopotamia Campaign, 1914–1918*, Vols. I–IV (1923–1927) [British Official History]

Report of the Commission on Mesopotamia (1917)

C. V. F. Townshend, *My Campaign in Mesopotamia* (1920)

Erroll Sherson, *Townshend of Chitral and Kut* (1928)

Keisling, *Mit Feldmarschall von der Goltz Pascha in Mesopotamien und Persien* (1922)

Rafael de Nogales, *Vier Jahren unter dem Halbmond* (1926)

Schraudenbach, *Muharebe* (1926)

Gleich, *Vom Balkan nach Bagdad* (1922) [light on siege of Kut]

R. H. Dewing in *Army Quarterly*, January, April, July 1927, *Some Aspects of Maude's Campaign in Mesopotamia*

Edmund Candler, *The Long Road to Baghdad*

L. C. Dunsterville, *The Adventures of Dunsterforce* (1921)

W. Marshall, *Memories of Four Fronts* (1929)

C. E. Callwell, *Life of Sir Stanley Maude* (1920)

NAVAL

J. S. Corbett, *History of the Great War* (*Naval Operations*) Vols. I–III (1920–21)

H. Newbolt, *History of the Great War* (*Naval Operations*) Vol. IV (1928)

486 BIBLIOGRAPHY

C. E. Fayle, *Seaborne Trade*, 3 vols. (1920–)
A. Lawrens, *Précis d'Histoire de la Guerre Navale* (1929)
W. S. Churchill, *The World Crisis*, 4 vols. (1923–27)
Jellicoe (Viscount), *The Grand Fleet, 1914–1916* (1919)
J. E. T. Harper, *The Truth about Jutland* (1927)
G. Campbell, *My Mystery Ships* (1928)
W. S. Sims, *The Victory at Sea* (1920)
R. Scheer, *Germany's High Seas Fleet in the World War* (Eng. trans. 1920)
G. von Hase, *Kiel and Jutland* (Eng. trans. 1926)

AIR

W. A. Raleigh, *The War in the Air*, Vol. I (1922) [Official History]
H. A. Jones, *The War in the Air*, Vol. II (1928) [Official History]
C. F. Snowden-Gamble, *The Story of a North Sea Air Station* (1928)
A. Rawlinson, *The Defence of London* (1923)
E. B. Ashmore, *Air Defence* (1929)
E. A. Lehmann, *The Zeppelins* (Eng. trans. 1928)
H. Ritter, *Der Luftkrieg* (1926)
Keller, *Die Heutige Wehrlosigkeit Deutschlands im Lichte seiner Verteidigung gegen Fliegerangriffe im Kriege, 1914–1918* (1926) [German Air Defense Organization]

PRESS AND PROPAGANDA

E. T. Cook, *The Press in War-Time* (1920)
C. Stuart, *Secrets of Crewe House* (1920)
N. Lytton, *The Press and the General Staff* (1921)
C. E. Callwell, *Experiences of a Dug-Out, 1914–1918* (1921)
H. D. Lasswell, *Propaganda Technique in the World War* (1926)

ECONOMIC AND HOME FRONT

M. Consett, *The Triumph of Unarmed Forces, 1914–1918* (1921)
R. H. Gretton, *A Modern History of the English People, 1910–22* (1929)
A. Hallays, *L'Opinion Allemande pendant la Guerre, 1914–1918* (1923)

CHAPTER III

SCENE 1. THE MARNE

J. E. Edmonds, *Military Operations. France and Belgium*, Vol. I (British Official History)

Reichsarchiv, *Der Weltkrieg, 1914–1918*, Vols. III and IV (1926) [German Official History]

Kluck, *The March on Paris, 1914* (Eng. trans. 1920)

J. E. Edmonds in *Army Quarterly*, January 1921, *The Scapegoat of the Battle of the Marne*

Militär Wochenblatt, September 18, 1920 (court of inquiry on Col. Hentsch's rôle)

M. von Poseck, *Die Deutsche Kavallerie in Belgien und Frankreich, 1914* (1922)

Baumgarten-Crusius, *Marneschlacht, 1914* (1919); *Deutsche Heerführung im Marnefeldzug, 1914* (1921) [fuller extracts from Col. Hentsch's report]

Bülow, *Mein Bericht zur Marneschlacht* (1920) [French trans.]

Zwehl, *Maubeuge-Aisne-Verdun* (1921)

Helfferich, *Weltkrieg*, Vol. II

Tappen, *Bis zur Marneschlacht*

François, *Marneschlacht und Tannenberg* (1920)

Foerster, *Graf Schlieffen und der Weltkrieg*, Part I (1920)

Kuhl, *Der Marnefeldzug, 1914* (1920) [French trans.]

Crown Prince Rupprecht of Bavaria, *Mein Kriegstagebuch* (1928)

German Ex-Crown Prince, *Der Marnefeldzug, 1914* (1927)

Hausen, *Souvenirs de la Campagne de la Marne en 1914* (French trans. 1922) [Saxon Third Army Commander]

Reichsarchiv, *Das Marnedrama, 1914* (1928–29) [German Official Monographs, in five parts. Extensive summary in *Army Quarterly*, July 1928, January, April, October 1929, January 1930]

Müller-Loebnitz, *Die Sendung des Oberstleutnants Hentsch* (1922) [Official account of Hentsch's mission]

Generaloberst von Moltke. Erinnerungen, Briefe, Dokumente, 1877–1916 (1923)

Palat, *La Victoire de la Marne* (1921)

Dubail, *Journal du Campagne*, Vol. I, Ière Armée

J. Charbonneau, *La Bataille des Frontières et la Bataille de la Marne vues par un Chef de Section* (1929)

Mémoires du Maréchal Galliéni, Défense de Paris (25 Août–11 Sept., 1914) [1926]

Clergerie and Delahaye d'Anglemont, *Le Rôle du Gouvernement Militaire de Paris de 1er au 12 Septembre, 1914* (1920)

Marius-Ary le Blond, *Galliéni parle* (1920)

Les Armées Françaises dans la Grande Guerre, Tome I, Vol. II (1927) [French Official History]

Toussan, *Historique des Corps de Cavalerie Commandés par le Général Conneau du 14 Août, 1914 au 2 Mars, 1917* (1924)

J. de Pierrefeu, *Plutarque a menti* (1922)

Hirschauer and Klein, *Paris en État de Défense, 1914* (1928)

H. Carré, *La Véritable Histoire des Taxis de la Marne* (1921)

Boëlle, *Le 4e corps d'Armée sur l'Ourcq* (1925) [light on Maunoury's part]

Dubois, *Deux Ans de Commandement sur le Front de France, 1914–1916* (1920) [light on Foch's part]

Bujac, *Le Général Eydoux et le XI Corps d'Armée* (1925) [light on Foch's part]

De Castelli, *Le VIIIe Corps en Lorraine Août–Octobre, 1914* (1926) [light on French right wing and on loss of St. Mihiel]

Army Quarterly, October 1922, *Another Legend of the Marne, 1914*

Private Evidence

CHAPTER III

SCENE 2. TANNENBERG

Reichsarchiv, *Tannenberg* (1927) [German Official Monograph]

E. Ludendorff, *My War Memories* (Eng. trans. 1920)

P. von Hindenburg, *Out of My Life* (Eng. trans. 1920)

Army Quarterly, October 1921, *An Echo of Tannenberg*

H. von François, *Marneschlacht und Tannenberg* (1920); *Tannenberg* (1926)

Y. Danilov, *La Russie dans la Guerre Mondiale* (French trans. 1927)

M. Hoffmann, *The War of Lost Opportunities* (Eng. trans. 1924); *Tannenberg wie es wirklich war* (1927); *War Diaries and Other Papers* (Eng. trans. 1929)

E. Ironside, *Tannenberg* (1925)

Russian Historical Commission, *La Grande Guerre. Relation de l'État-Major Russe* (French trans. 1927)

Noskov, *Militär Wochenblatt*, August 1, 1926 (a Russian view)

A. Smirnoff in *Army Quarterly*, April 1926, *A New Light upon the Invasion of East Prussia by the Russians in August 1914*

CHAPTER IV

SCENES 1 AND 2. THE DARDANELLES

C. F. Aspinall-Oglander, *Military Operations, Gallipoli*, Vol. I (1929) [British Official History]

The Final Report of the Dardanelles Commission (1919)

Ian Hamilton, *A Gallipoli Diary*, 2 vols. (1920)

C. E. Callwell, *Experiences of a Dug-Out, 1914–1918* (1921)

J. Masefield, *Gallipoli* (1923)

Wester Wemyss (Lord), *The Navy in the Dardanelles Campaign* (1924)

E. Ashmead-Bartlett, *The Uncensored Dardanelles* (1927)

W. Marshall, *Memories of Four Fronts* (1929)

Compton Mackenzie, *Gallipoli Memories* (1929)

Liman von Sanders, *Five Years in Turkey* (Eng. trans. 1928)

H. Kannengiesser, *The Campaign in Gallipoli* (Eng. trans. 1928)

Reichsarchiv, *Dardanellen, 1915* (1927)

Turkish Official History, *Campagne des Dardanelles* (1924) [extensive summary in *Army Quarterly*, January and April 1926]

Army Quarterly, October 1929, *The First Turkish Reinforcements at Suvla, August 7th–9th, 1915* (from Turkish sources)

Times, February 14, 1925, *The Suvla Bay Failure. New Evidence*

S. Sazonov, *Fateful Years, 1909–1916* (Eng. trans. 1927) [shows Russian attitude]

Les Armées Françaises dans la Grande Guerre, Tome VIII, Vol. I (1928) [French Official History]

Private Evidence

CHAPTER IV

SCENE 3. THE GAS CLOUD AT YPRES

J. E. Edmonds, *Military Operations. France and Belgium, 1915*, Vol. III

Les Armées Françaises dans la Grande Guerre, Tome III (1927)

Huguet, *Britain and the War*

C. E. Callwell, *Field-Marshal Sir Henry Wilson*, Vol. I

Volonté (Paris), April 25, 1929, account of Gen. Ferry's warning

Hanslian and Bergendorff, *Der Chemische Krieg* (1925)

Falkenhayn, *General Headquarters, etc.*

Unpublished Documents

Private Evidence

CHAPTER IV

SCENE 4. LOOS

J. E. Edmonds, *Military Operations. France and Belgium, 1915*, Vol. IV

Les Armées Françaises dans la Grande Guerre, Tome III (1927)

Army Quarterly, July 1924, *The Fight for Hill 70* (from German sources)

Crown Prince Rupprecht of Bavaria, *Mein Kriegstagebuch* (1928)

Palat, Vol. IX. *Les Offensives de 1915*

Huguet, *Britain and the War*

Oxford and Asquith, *Memories and Reflections*

Maurice, *The Life of General Lord Rawlinson of Trent*

J. Charteris, *Field-Marshal Earl Haig*

Private Evidence

CHAPTER V

SCENE 1. VERDUN

Reichsarchiv, *Die Tragödie von Verdun, 1916* (1926–1929) [German Official]

Wolfgang Foerster, *Graf Schlieffen und der Weltkrieg*, Part III (1921)

German Ex-Crown Prince, *Memoirs*

Crown Prince Rupprecht, *Mein Kriegstagebuch*

Zwehl, *Maubeuge-Aisne-Verdun*

Ludwig Gehre, *Die Deutsche Kraftverteilung während des Weltkrieges* (1928)

De Thomasson, *Les Préliminaires de Verdun, Août 1915–Février 1916* (1921) [contains numerous documents]

Pétain, *La Bataille de Verdun*

J. Poirier, *La Bataille de Verdun* (1922)

A. Grasset, *Verdun, le Premier Choc à la 72ᵉ Division* (1926)

B. E. Palat, *La Ruée sur Verdun* (1925)

CHAPTER V

SCENE 2. BRUSILOV OFFENSIVE

For sources see RUSSIAN FRONT

CHAPTER V

SCENE 3. THE SOMME

C. E. W. Bean, *The Australian Imperial Force in France, 1916* (1929) [Australian Official History]

J. Charteris, *Life of Field-Marshal Earl Haig*

Maurice, *Life of Lord Rawlinson of Trent*

Dewar and Boraston, *Sir Douglas Haig's Command*

J. F. C. Fuller, *Tanks in the Great War*

Army Quarterly, January and July 1924, *The German Defence during the Battle of the Somme* (July 1)

Army Quarterly, January 1925, *Mametz Wood and Contalmaison, July 9–10, 1916*

Army Quarterly, October 1925, *Delville Wood, July 14–19, 1916*

Army Quarterly, October 1926, *The German Defence of Bernafoy and Trônes, July 2–14, 1916*

Palat, *Bataille de la Somme*

Schwarte, *Der Grosse Krieg*, Vol. II

Reichsarchiv, *Somme-Nord 1 Theil* (July 13); *Somme-Nord 2 Theil* (July 14–31)

Rupprecht, *Mein Kriegstagebuch*

Constantin Hierl, *Der Weltkrieg in Umrissen* (1927) [German methods of defense]

Unpublished Documents

Private Evidence

CHAPTER V

SCENE 4. THE GROWING PAINS OF THE TANK

C. and A. Williams-Ellis, *The Tank Corps* (1919)

A. Stern, *Tanks, 1914–1918. The Log Book of a Pioneer* (1919)

J. F. C. Fuller, *Tanks in the Great War* (1920)

D. G. Browne, *The Tank in Action* (1920)

E. D. Swinton, *Tanks* (*Encyclopædia Britannica*, 1922)

W. S. Churchill, *The World Crisis*

Evidence given before the Royal Commission on Awards to Inventors

Evidence given in the case of *Bentley v. The Crown*, 1925

Unpublished Documents

Private Evidence

CHAPTER V

SCENE 5.   RUMANIA SWALLOWED

For sources see RUSSIAN FRONT, also

E. von Falkenhayn, *Der Feldzug der 9 Armee gegen die Rumanen und Russen, 1916–1917*, 2 vols. (1921)
M. Sturdza, *Avec l'Armée Roumaine, 1916–1918*

CHAPTER V

SCENE 6.   THE CAPTURE OF BAGHDAD

For sources see MESOPOTAMIAN FRONT

CHAPTER V

SCENE 7.   JUTLAND

The Admiralty, *Official Documents and Despatches, Battle of Jutland* (1920)
J. S. Corbett, *History of the Great War (Naval Operations)* [1921]
Jellicoe (Viscount), *The Grand Fleet, 1914–1916* (1919)
C. Bellairs, *The Battle of Jutland* (1920)
R. Bacon, *The Jutland Scandal* (1925)
H. W. Wilson, *Battleships in Action* (1926)
J. E. T. Harper, *The Truth about Jutland* (1927)
W. S. Churchill, *The World Crisis, 1916–1918*, Part I (1927)
R. Bacon, *Mr. Churchill and Jutland* (1927) [in *The World Crisis: A Criticism*]
E. Altham, *Jutland (Encyclopædia Britannica)*
R. Scheer, *Germany's High Seas Fleet in the World War* (Eng. trans. 1920)
G. von Hase, *Kiel and Jutland* (Eng. trans. 1926)

CHAPTER VI

SCENES 1–4.   ARRAS, MESSINES, PASSCHENDAELE, CAMBRAI

B. E. Palat, *La Grande Guerre sur le Front Occidental*, Vol. XII (1927)
Rousset, *La Bataille de l'Aisne*
R. Normand, *Destructions et Dévastations au Cours des Guerres* (1929)
W. S. Churchill, *The World Crisis*

Dewar and Boraston, *Sir Douglas Haig's Command*

J. F. C. Fuller, *Tanks in the Great War*

Reichsarchiv, *Flanders, 1917* (1919)

E. Ludendorff, *My War Memories*

Rupprecht, *Mein Kriegstagebuch*

C. E. Callwell, *Field-Marshal Sir Henry Wilson*

F. Maurice, *The Life of General Lord Rawlinson of Trent*

Laure, *Au 3ᵉ Bureau du troisième G.Q.G.*

Mermeix, *Nivelle et Painlevé — 2ᵉ Crise du Commandement*

P. Painlevé, *Comment j'ai nommé Foch et Pétain* (1924)

Unpublished Documents

Private Evidence

CHAPTER VI

SCENE 5. CAPORETTO

For sources see ITALIAN FRONT

Also Private Evidence

CHAPTER VII

SCENE 1. THE FIRST BREAK–THROUGH

E. Ludendorff, *My War Memories*

Rupprecht, *Mein Kriegstagebuch*

Wolfgang Foerster, *Graf Schlieffen und der Weltkrieg*, Part III

Albrecht Philip, *Ursachen des Deutschen Militärischen Zusammen-bruch, 1918* (1925) [summary of parliamentary inquiry]

Kuhl, *Entstehung, Durchführung und Zusammenbruch der Offensive von 1918* (1928)

Schwertfeger, *Die Politischen und Militärischen Verantwortlichkeiten im Verlaufe der Offensive von 1918* (1928)

Bruchmüller, *Die deutsche Artillerie in den Durchbruchschlachten des Weltkrieges* (1921)

Joachim, *Die Vorbereitung des Deutschen Heeres für die Grosse Schlacht in Frankreich im Frühjahr 1918* (1927)

Fehr, *Die Märzoffensive 1918 an der Westfront* (1921) [reveals Wetzell's influence on Ludendorff's strategy]

Kuhl, *Der Deutsche Generalstab*

German Ex-Crown Prince, *Memoirs*

M. Erzberger, *Erlebnisse im Weltkrieg*

E. Gugelmeier, *Das Schwarze Jahr* (1917) [food conditions]
Rudolf Binding, *A Fatalist at War* (Eng. trans. 1928)
Laure, *Au 3ᵉ Bureau du troisième G.Q.G.*
Koeltz, *La Bataille de France, 21 Mars–5 Avril, 1918; L'Offensive Allemande de 1918*
L. Madelin, *La Bataille de France*
Dewar and Boraston, *Sir Douglas Haig's Command*
C. E. Callwell, *Field-Marshal Sir Henry Wilson*, Vol. II
F. Maurice, *The Life of General Lord Rawlinson of Trent*
C. Falls, in *Nineteenth Century*, October–November 1921
C. à C. Repington, *The First World War, 1914–1918*, Vol. II
J. Charteris, *Field-Marshal Earl Haig*
Seymour, *The Intimate Papers of Colonel House*, Vol. III
Unpublished Documents
Private Evidence

CHAPTER VII

SCENE 2. THE BREAK–THROUGH IN FLANDERS

Additional:
La Bataille des Flandres d'après le Journal de Marche et les Archives de la IVᵉ Armée Allemande (9–30 Avril, 1918) (1925) [French trans. of captured documents]
Unpublished Documents

CHAPTER VII

SCENE 3. THE BREAK–THROUGH TO THE MARNE

Additional:
Unpublished Documents
Personal Evidence

CHAPTER VII

SCENE 4. THE SECOND BATTLE OF THE MARNE

Additional:
Les Armées Françaises dans la Grande Guerre, Tome VII, Vol. I (French Official History)
Zwehl, *Die Schlachten im Sommer, 1918* (1922)
Private Evidence

CHAPTER VII

SCENE 5.   AUGUST 8

Additional:
A. A. Montgomery, *The Story of the Fourth Army*
J. Monash, *The Australian Victories in 1918*
M. Daille, *La Bataille de Montdidier* (1922) [French share]
C. Falls in *Army Quarterly*, July 1928, *An Aspect of the Battle of Amiens, 1918* (French coöperation)
Unpublished Documents
Personal Evidence

CHAPTER VII

SCENES 7 AND 8.   ST. MIHIEL AND MEUSE–ARGONNE

Final Report of Gen. John J. Pershing
First Army Report
Frederick Palmer, *Our Greatest Battle* (1919)
R. L. Bullard, *Personalities and Reminiscences of the War*
Hunter Liggett, *Commanding an American Army; A.E.F.*
T. M. Johnson, *Without Censor*
J. G. Harbord, *Leaves from a War Diary*
J. T. Dickman, *The Great Crusade*
Wellmann, *Das I. Reserve-Korps in der Letzten Schlacht* (1925)
Passaga, *Le Calvaire de Verdun* (1928)
Personal Evidence

INDEX

ABERNON, ADMIRAL d', his account of Turkish raid on Russian ports, 146.

Achi Baba, 160, 161, 164.

Admirals and generals, 271, 272.

Aehrenthal, Count, Austrian Foreign Minister, his Bosnian deceit, 18.

Aeroplanes, use of, 81, 313–319.

Africa, the war in, 80.

Agadir incident, 20.

Aisne, the, the Germans retreat to the line of, 64, 100; French offensive and defeat on, 328.

Albania, set up as new state, 20, 21.

Albert, King of Belgium, 65, 67.

Alexander III., Tsar, 6.

Alexandretta, Gulf of, plan for landing in, 119.

Alexeiev, Gen. Michael V., Russian command transferred to, 135.

Allenby, Gen. Sir Edmund, at Vimy Ridge, 300; takes Jerusalem, 306, 307; in Arras campaign, 324; defeats Turks at Megiddo, 382, 439–448.

Allied Council at Versailles, 306.

Allies, first effort to obtain unity of action among, 199; principle of simultaneous general offensive adopted by, 199; growing sense of depression among, in 1917, 297; reject German peace move, 297; strength of (Nov. 1916), 298; Supreme War Council of, 364, 365; military executive committee of, 365, 366; their relative numbers, 365, 366; breakdown of arrangement for mutual support, 367, 368; initiative definitely and finally passes to, 375; final operations of, 375–378, 385, 386. See also Allied Countries by name.

Amara, 140.

Americans, arrival in France, 372, 374, 386, 420, 423; placed at disposal of France, 373; at Château-Thierry, 373, 417; erase St. Mihiel salient, 376, 449–460; attack in the Meuse-Argonne, 378–380, 461–469; pressure of, on Lorraine front, 383.

Amiens, 398, 399, 402, 404; the battle of Aug. 8, 1918 (German "black day") at, 429–438.

Anderson, commander of division in battle of Ypres (1915), 176.

Antwerp, fall of, 64–67.

Anzac, 123, 124, 161, 163, 168, 171.

Anzac Corps, 242, 243, 247.

Ardennes, the, 461.

Argonne Forest. See Meuse-Argonne.

Armentières, 408.

Armies, 36–42.

Armistice, appeal for, 378, 379; terms of, 383–385; terms accepted by Germany, 386; fundamental cause of, 471–473; immediate causes of, 473–476.

Armistice Day, 470.

Arras, 67, 399; and Lens, French offensive between (1915), 130, 131; French offensive at (1917), 321–329.

Artois, French victories in, 134, 187, 190, 196, 198.

Aspinwall-Oglander, General, reference to his official history of the war, 150.

Asquith, Herbert Henry, 141; and the tank, 253, 254.

Aston, Brigadier-General, lands with marines at Ostend, 84, 85.

Aubers Ridge, British attack toward, 131.

Augustovo forests, defeat of Russians in, 125.

Australia, the, attacks Admiral von Spee at the Falkland Islands, 78.

Australia, navy of, 80.

Australians, at Gallipoli, 161, 168; in France, 242–244, 328, 334, 375, 434–437; in Flanders, 408; in Palestine, 446, 447.

Austria-Hungary, Bismarck's policy toward, 4–6; annexes Bosnia and Herzegovina, 18; opposed to Serbian aims, 20; proposes attack on Serbia, 21; war feeling in, 21; in Serbian crisis, 23, 24; receives support of Germany, 24, 25; ultimatum to Serbia, 25, 26; orders general mobilization, 31; attempts to crush Serbia, 70; conquers Serbia, 137, 138; offensive in Trentino, 224; forces of, in the campaign against Rumania, 264–266; collapse of, 382.

Austro-Hungarian army, 39.

BAGHDAD, captured by British, 207, 267, 270.

Bailleul, taken by Germans, 409.

Balfour, Arthur J., 312.

Balfourier, Corps commander, 177, 178.
Bapaume, 205.
Bartenbach, Capt. von, Chief of the German Flanders flotillas, 210.
Basra, 139.
Battles, length of, 214.
Bauer, Major, artillery expert, 95.
Beatty, Admiral Sir David, traps German squadron off Dogger Bank, 79; in command of Battle Cruiser Fleet in battle of Jutland, 209, 275–295.
Beaucourt-sur-Ancre, taken by British, 247.
Beaumont-Hamel, taken by British, 247.
Beersheba, 307.
Belgium, invaded by German troops, 35, 54, 55; German plan to manœuvre through, 46, 47; manœuvres in, 65–70.
Below, Gen. Fritz von, in command in East Prussia, 111, 113.
Below, Gen. Otto von, in the Somme sector, 247, 248; at Caporetto, 360.
Berchtold, Count Leopold von, Austrian Foreign Minister, in Serbian crisis, 23–25; his responsibility for the war, 33.
Berlin, preparation for bombing of, 386.
Berthelot, Philippe, 64.
Besika Bay, 160, 162.
Bethmann-Hollweg, Theobald von, becomes chancellor, 19; opens negotiations for Anglo-German agreement, 19; in Serbian crisis, 30, 31.
Bibliography, preface to, 477; the, 478–495.
Bieberstein, Baron Marschall von, German Ambassador at Constantinople, 143.
Binding, Rudolf, quotations from his diary, 400, 401.
Birdwood, Lieut.-Gen. Sir William R., at Gallipoli, 163, 168; commander of Anzac Corps, 243; in Somme offensive, 244.
Birmingham, the, in battle of Jutland, 290, 291.
Bismarck, Count Otto von, his policy, 4–6; dismissal of, 6.
"Black day," of the Germans, 375, 429–438.
"Black Hand," Serbian secret society, 22.
Blaireville project, 321.
Bliss, General Tasker H., of Versailles committee, 365.
Blücher, the, sunk in North Sea, 79.
"Blücher" attack, 373.
Boehn, commander of German Seventh Army, 420.
Boisdeffre, Gen. de, French negotiator, 7.
Bolsheviks, overthrow Kerensky, 304.
Bosnia, annexed by Austria, 18.
Bössau Lake, 111.

Botha, Gen. Louis, his services to British cause, 80.
Boulogne, 65.
Bouvet, the, sunk in battle of Jutland, 152.
Breslau, the, evades British, 77, 144.
British, military system of, 41, 42, 69; in battle of the Marne, 58–61, 86–92, 98, 99; attempt to raise siege of Antwerp, 66; in defense of Ypres, 67–69; attack at Neuve-Chapelle, 126; their new armies brought into action, 135; take over Arras front, 202; in Somme offensive, 204; capture Baghdad, 207, 267, 270; defeat Turks and invade Palestine, 208; in offensive campaign of 1916, 227–248; their naval strategy, 272, 273; state of their fleet in May 1916, 274; in battle of Jutland, 275–295; take Vimy Ridge, 300; strength of in 1917, 301; take Messines Ridge, 302, 330–336; attack at Ypres, 302; in Arras offensive, 321–329; at Passchendaele, 337–343; their raid at Cambrai, 344–356; break Hindenburg Line, 380; their change from offensive to defensive (March 1918), 388; at German offensive of March 1918, 396–402; at German Flanders offensive (April 1918), 405–410; at the German offensive of May 1918, 411–418; at Amiens (Aug. 8, 1918), 429–438; at Megiddo, 439–448.
Bruchmüller, Colonel, "battle-piece" producer, 391, 400.
Brusilov, General, his 1916 offensive, 202–204, 224–226; succeeds to supreme command, 304.
Brussels, occupied by Germans, 55.
Bucharest, fall of, 261, 266.
Bukovina, the, 203, 225, 226, 304.
Bulair, 147, 160, 161, 170, 173.
Bulgaria, throws off Turkish suzerainty, 18; in war against Turkey, 20; opposed by Serbia and Greece, 21; entry into war arranged, 133; enters war on side of Teutons, 137, 138; collapse of, 377, 475.
Bullard, Maj.-Gen. Robert L., commander of American Third Corps, 464; at St. Mihiel, 464; put in charge of Second American Army, 467.
Bülow, Bernhard von, German Chancellor, supports Holstein, 10; calls for conference over Morocco, 14; letter of Emperor to, 15; repudiates Emperor's Daily Telegraph interview, 19; replaced, 19.
Bülow, Gen. von, in the battle of the Marne, 62, 86, 87, 93, 97, 98.
Butler, R. H. K., 435.
Byng, Gen. Sir Julian, in battle of Cambrai, 345–347.

CADORNA, GEN. COUNT LUIGI, on the Isonzo, 135, 136, 208, 305; proposal of, 298; superseded, 306, 361; at Caporetto, 359–361; of Versailles committee, 365.

Calais, 65.

Cambrai, 205; use of tanks at, 258, 259, 303; British offensive at, 344–356.

Cameron, Maj.-Gen. George F., commander of American Fifth Corps, 456, 464; at St. Mihiel, 457; at the Meuse-Argonne, 464; replaced, 467.

Cameroons, taken by Allies, 80.

Campbell, D. G. M., in 1916 campaign, 240; in 1918 campaign, 414.

Campbell-Bannerman, Sir Henry, government of, 16.

Canadians, in France, 375, 434, 435.

Capello, General, at Caporetto, 359.

Caporetto, Italians defeated at, 203, 306, 357–363.

Caprivi, German Chancellor, 9.

Carden, Admiral, his plan for forcing the Dardanelles, 121, 149; his caution, 151; superseded in command, 151.

Carpathians, the, 125, 132.

Castelnau, Gen. de, new French army under, 64; outflanking attempt of, 66; Chief of French General Staff, 220; sent with full powers to Verdun, 220, 221.

Castor, the, in battle of Jutland, 288.

Cavan, Lord, 247, 362.

Champagne, French offensive, 134, 187, 190, 196–198.

Channel ports, 64–66.

Chantilly Conference (Dec. 5, 1915), 227; (Nov. 1916), 297, 322.

Charleroi, battle of, 59 n.

Charmes, gap of, 94.

Charteris, General, biographer of Haig, 389.

Château-Thierry, Americans at, 373, 417.

Chelius, Gen. von, 32.

Chemin des Dames ridge, 59 n., 303, 411–413.

Chrétien, General, 221.

Chunuk Bair, 168.

Churchill, Winston S., First Lord of the Admiralty, 66; dispatches marines under Aston to Ostend, 84, 85; promotes idea of tank, 118, 253, 254, 256; opposed to wasting man-power in France, 120; advocates Dardanelles Expedition, 121, 149, 150; shelved, 141; quarrels with Fisher, 150.

Clemenceau, Georges, on the American forces, 466.

Cointet, Col. de, Chief of the French Intelligence, 413.

Combles, 245, 246.

Communiqués, the practice of issuing, 45.

Compiègne, "tongue," 373, 374; armistice signed in Forest of, 386.

Congreve, commander of British Thirteenth Army Corps, 236.

Constantine, King, withdraws consent to help force the Dardanelles, 147.

Convoy system, 310.

Coöperation and coördination, 36.

Courcellette, taken by British, 246.

Coutanceau, General, Governor of Verdun, 218.

Cradock, Admiral Sir Christopher, his squadron defeated by von Spee's cruisers, 78.

Crown Prince of Germany, in command of Fifth Army between Metz and Thionville, 57.

Ctesiphon, battle at, 141.

Daily Telegraph, London, Emperor's interview in, 19.

Danilov, directs Russian strategy, 104.

Dardanelles Expedition, 119, 121–124, 146–159. *See also* Gallipoli.

Delcassé, Théophile, sacrifice of, 14.

Delmensingen, Gen. Krafft von, Rupprecht's Chief of Staff, 56, 358.

Delville Wood, 241.

Derrfflinger, the, damaged in North Sea, 79.

Diaz, General, supersedes Cadorna, 306, 361.

Dickman, Maj.-Gen. James T., commander of American Fourth Corps, 456; at St. Mihiel, 457; quoted on St. Mihiel, 458; transferred to First Corps, 467.

Dinant, 59.

Dobruja, the, 206, 262, 264.

Dogger Bank, 79.

Douaumont, Fort, 217.

Driant, Colonel, 218.

Drum, Gen. Hugh, St. Mihiel plan formed by, 451; Chief of Staff to Liggett, 467.

Du Picq, Ardant, 45.

Dual Alliance, 12.

Dubail, General, 218.

Duchêne, General, Commander of the Sixth French Army, 413, 416.

Duff, Commander-in-chief in India, 268.

Dunajec sector, German attack on, 131, 132.

EAST PRUSSIA, Russian operations against, 70, 71, 103–114.

Eastern and western schools of thought, 118, 154.

Ebert, succeeds Prince Max, 383.

Economic forces, 44.

Edgeworth, Richard, his device, 252.

Edmonds, General, British official historian, 101, 189, 195, 410.

Edward VII, King, his part in making the *Entente Cordiale*, 13; as cause of irritation to the Emperor, 15, 16; visits Francis Joseph, 19.

Einem, Gen. von, Commander of German Third Army, 420.

El Kantara, repulse of Turks at, 117.

Elbing, the, sunk in battle of Jutland, 288.

Emden, the, destruction of, 78.

Emmich, Gen. von, at Liége, 54.

Entente Cordiale, 13.

Enver Pasha, 117, 143–145, 159, 160.

Eren Keui Bay, 152.

Erzberger, secures peace resolution, 319.

Espérey, Gen. Franchet d', Commander (succeeding Lanrezac) of Fifth French Army, 63; in the battle of the Marne, 91–93, 96–98; story of, 350; defeats Bulgaria, 377.

Estiénne, Colonel, 255.

Evan-Thomas, Admiral, in battle of Jutland, 277–281, 290.

Eyncourt, Tennyson d', Director of Naval Construction, 254, 259.

Falkenhayn, Gen. Erich von, determines to reduce Antwerp, 64; plans strategic trap, 67; his policy, 115, 116; realizes that long war is inevitable, 116; on the importance of the Dardanelles, 119; his strategy, 124, 131, 133, 134; produces new form of attack, 200; sees England as arch-enemy, 200; superseded by Hindenburg, 203; in command against Rumanians, 206, 264–266; on the purpose of the battle of Verdun, 215; his downfall, 226.

Falkland Islands, naval battle off, 78.

Fashoda, 12.

Fère-en-Tardenois, taken by Germans, 416.

Ferry, General, 177, 178.

Festubert sector, French attack on, 131.

Financial resources, 44.

Fisher, Sir John, First Sea Lord, 15; urges plan for landing on German coast, 119; and the Dardanelles Expedition, 148; quarrels with Churchill, 150.

Flanders, the break-through in, 403–409. *See also* Belgium; Ypres.

Fleets. *See* Germany; Great Britain.

Flers, 245.

Foch, Ferdinand, on moral element in command, 45; in effort to turn German flank (1915), 67; and French, 68; in the battle of the Marne, 82, 96, 97; his unreasoning optimism, 120; in control in Flanders, 180–184; his armistice terms, 383, 384; made Commander-in-Chief of the Allied armies, 372, 409; and the second battle of the Marne, 423–428; and the Amiens attack, 430, 432; urges change of plan for Americans at St. Mihiel, 452, 453.

Foerster, Colonel, critic, 215.

France, Bismarck's policy toward, 4–6; in military convention with Russia, 6, 7; in Fashoda incident, 13; passes three years' service act, 21, 22; spirit in, in 1914, 22; mobilization ordered, 33; frontier of, 46, 49; her plan of operations at beginning of war, 49, 50.

Franco-Prussian War, 4.

François, Gen. von, commander of German forces in East Prussia, 110–113.

Franz Ferdinand, Archduke, murder of, 22, 23.

Frauenlob, the, sunk in battle of Jutland, 288.

French, invade Upper Alsace, 55; invade Lorraine, 55–57; in Somme offensive of 1916, 204, 227–248; 1917 offensive of, 300; mutinies and desertions in armies of, 300, 301; defeated on the Aisne (1917), 328; at the German offensive of May, 1918, 411–418.

French, Sir John, supports French plan of war, 51; and Lanrezac, 59, 60; and Foch, 68; in the battle of the Marne, 99; opposes Dardanelles plan, 119; his unreasoning optimism, 120; at Neuve-Chapelle, 126; gives place to Haig as Commander-in-Chief, 135; strategy embodied in, 148, 149; in Flanders, 181–184; relations with Smith-Dorrien, 183.

Freyberg, Lieut.-Com. B. C., 163.

Fricourt, 205, 235.

Fromelles, 242.

Fuller, Colonel, draws up plan for tank raid, 345–347.

Furse, W. T., in 1916 campaign, 240.

Gaba Tepe, 122, 160–163.

Galatea, the, at battle of Jutland, 277, 278.

Galicia, the Teutons in, 71; Eastern, taken by Brusilov, 226; Russians driven from, 304.

Galliéni, Gen. Joseph, Military Governor of Paris, directs blow at German right flank, 61–63; in the battle of the Marne, 82, 83, 88–93, 100, 101; proposes landing of British forces at Salonika, 120; writes regarding Verdun forts, 218.

Gallipoli, 122, 149; expedition sent to, 156–158; the landing on, 159–174. *See also* Dardanelles Expedition.

Gallwitz, Gen. von, references to, 382, 458.

Gas, first used by Germans at Neuve-Chapelle, 129, 130; shells, 129, 326; discharged from cylinders, 130, 179; chlorine, 130; used by Germans at

Ypres, 130, 175–181; used by British at Loos, 190–192; mustard, 340.

Gaza, attacked by British, 208, 307.

Geddes, Sir Eric, First Lord of the Admiralty, 385.

Generalissimo, demand for, 387; appointment of Foch as, 409.

Generals and admirals, 271, 272.

German army, organization and training of, 36, 37; moved by great moral impulse, 37; the general staff of, 38; artillery of, 39; railway communications of, 39.

German East Africa, conquest of, 80, 308, 309.

German Empire. *See* Germany; William II.

German Southwest Africa, conquered, 80.

Germans, invade Belgium, 54, 55; enter Liége, 54; enter Brussels, 55; assume offensive at Verdun, 201, 214–223; proceed against Rumania, 206, 207; naval strategy of, 273; state of their fleet in May 1916, 274; in battle of Jutland, 275–295; make peace move (Dec. 1916), 297; their new Hindenburg line, 299, 300, 322–324, 327; new defensive methods of, 302, 339; at Cambrai, 303; their relative numbers, 365, 366; their offensive of March 1918, 370–372, 387–402; their offensive in Flanders (April 1918), 372, 403–410; their break-through to the Marne (May 1918), 373, 411–418; their offensive of July 1918, 374–428; their "black day," 375, 428–438.

Germany, Empire was the creation of Bismarck, 4; alliances of, 4–6; change of policy of, from internal to external expansion, 8; friction of, with Great Britain, 8, 9; growth of her naval ambition, 9; rejects Chamberlain's proposals for alliance, 10; and Tangiers, 14; extends German control of Turkish army, 21; clamor for universal suffrage in, 21; war spirit in, 21; assures support to Austria, 24, 25; in the Serbian crisis, 26–30; begins mobilization, 32; ultimatums of, to Russia and France, 32, 33; declares war on France, 34; her ultimatum to Belgium, 35; invades Belgium, 35; her fleet, 42, 43; her plan of war, 45–49, 54; strategy of her naval command, 74, 75; her war on the sea, 77–79; proclaims waters round British Isles war zone, 79; her oversea colonies seized by England, 79; development of her resources, 116; her campaign of 1915, 124, 131–134; strategy of, 124; her submarine campaign, 210–213; forces of, in the campaign against Rumania, 264–266; forces of, Nov. 1916, 298; peace resolution of, 319; general strike in, 320; her plan for 1918, 368–374; abandons hope of victory, 376; appeals for armistice, 378; revolution in, 382, 383; becomes republic, 383; fleet mutinies, 383; accepts terms of armistice, 386; cause of her sudden collapse, 471–473.

Geyer, Captain, training handbooks compiled by, 391.

Ginchy, 244.

Gneisenau, the, in battle in the Pacific, 78; destruction of, 78.

Goeben, the, evades the British, 77, 144; sent to Constantinople, 143; report of her sinking, 146.

Gommecourt, 230, 321.

Gonnelieu, 355.

Goodenough, Admiral, 279, 280, 288, 290.

Gorizia, 208, 305.

Gough, Gen. Sir Hubert, in 1916 campaign, 230, 237, 243–245, 247; at Passchendaele, 341.

Gouraud, General, 421.

Gouzeaucourt, 355.

Grand Couronné de Nancy, 62, 94.

Grandmaison, Col. de, 49.

Great Britain, Bismarck's policy toward, 5, 6; in Egypt, 6; friction of, with Germany, 8, 9; offers alliance with Germany, 10; in alliance with Japan, 12; in Fashoda incident, 13; recognition of her occupation of Egypt, 13; gives Germany warning of possible *rapprochement* with France and Russia, 13; trawlers of, fired on by Russian fleet, 14; holds out hope of assistance to France, 16; draws nearer to Russia, 16, 17; loses independent influence in crisis, 17; uncertainty of Government of, 34, 35; delivers ultimatum respecting neutrality of Belgium, 35; enters war, 35; her fleet, 42, 43; her part in plan of war, 50, 51; her Expeditionary Force, 58, 67, 68; "New Armies" of, 69, 236; her sea-power, 73–79; sea strategy of, 75, 76; Ministry of Munitions, 127, 128; munition manufacture in, 127–129; formation of National Ministry in, 141; "Kitchener's Army," 198; Military Service Act, 199; change of Government in (Dec. 1916), 297; political handicaps in, 367; her navy the most important factor in determining the result of the war, 471–473.

Greece, in war against Turkey, 20; combines against Bulgaria, 21; breaks treaty with Serbia, 138; her attitude toward Dardanelles Expedition, 147.

Grey, Sir Edward, quoted, 17, 19; in Serbian crisis, 27, 30.

502 **INDEX**

Gröner, Colonel, Chief of the Field Railways, 115.
Grünert, General, 107.
Guillemont, 244.
Gumbinnen, 70, 105–107.

Haber, inventor of gas, 179.
Haig, Lieut.-Gen. Sir Douglas, in battle of Ypres, 67, 68; at Neuve-Chapelle, 126, 127; on the machine-gun, 128; succeeds French as Commander-in-Chief, 135; at Loos, 186–198; quarrels with French, 195; and the Somme campaign, 227–247; approves of use of tanks at the Somme, 257; subordinated to Nivelle, 299; and the Passchendaele offensive, 337, 338; and the Cambrai offensive, 347, 348, 353, 355; hastens appointment of generalissimo, 367; relies on arrangement with Pétain for mutual support, 367, 389; value of surprise underrated by, 390; his proposals for armistice terms, 383, 384; and Lloyd George, 388, 389; his historic order of the day (April 12, 1918), 403; Amiens attack proposed by, 430, 431; urges change of plan for Americans at St. Mihiel, 452.
Haldane, J. A. L., Viscount, his mission to Germany, 20; the Territorial Force due to, 42; shelved, 141; in 1916 campaign, 240; commander of British Sixth Corps, 326.
Hamilton, Sir Ian, 68; in command at Gallipoli, 121–123, 156, 157, 161–174.
Hamilton-Gordon, commander of the British Ninth Corps, 334.
Hankey, Lieut.-Col. Maurice, Secretary of War Council, urges attack on Constantinople, 148; memorandum of, 157; and the armored car, 253.
Hare, at Gallipoli, 164, 165.
Harington, Chief of Staff to Plumer, 302.
Harper, at Cambrai, 351.
Hartlepools, the, naval raid on, 79.
Harvey, Major, in battle of Jutland, 278.
Hausen, commander of German Third Army, at the Marne, 86, 95.
Hazebrouck, 372.
Heligoland, ceded to Germany, 6; a shield to German naval bases, 75.
Helles, Cape, 122–124, 160, 164, 170.
Henderson, Arthur, speech of, 233.
Heneker, British division commander, 414.
Hentsch, Colonel, in battle of the Marne, 83, 84, 98.
Herr, General, 217.
Herzegovina, annexed by Austria, 18.
Hindenburg, Field-Marshal Paul von, placed in command on the Eastern front, 71, 72; defeats Russians at Tannenberg,

103, 108–113; appointed Commander-in-Chief, 107; refuses to withdraw to securer line in rear, 206; supersedes Falkenhayn in supreme command, 203.
Hindenburg Line, 299, 300, 322–324, 327, 350, 376–381, 452, 458, 461, 462, 467.
Hines, commander of the American Third Corps, 467.
Hipper, Admiral, in command of Germany's Battle Cruiser Fleet in battle of Jutland, 275, 276, 279–283.
Hoffman, Lieut.-Col., attaché with Japanese army in Manchuria, 38, 108, 109; of the German Eighth Army Staff, 71, 107; declares that Dardanelles must be kept closed, 124; his diary quoted, 125; in control of Eastern front, 304; approached nearer than any other general of the war to military genius, 369.
Holden, Sir Capel, Director of Mechanical Transport, 254.
Holstein, Baron von, dominant factor in Germany's refusal of English proposals of alliance, 10, 12; and Tangiers, 14.
Holt, Benjamin, inventor of agricultural tractor, 250, 252, 253.
Holtzendorf, Admiral von, Chief of the German Naval Staff, 210.
Hood, Admiral, in battle of Jutland, 281, 282.
Horne, Gen. Sir Henry, commander of British Fifteenth Corps, in 1916 campaign, 236, 240.
Hötzendorf, Gen. Franz Conrad von, his promptings to war, 23, 25; his responsibility for the war, 33; his plan of campaign, 52; assumes offensive against Italy, 203, 204; deposed, 204.
House, Col. E. M., 318; his report on war spirit in Berlin, 21; unofficial ambassador, 296, 297; and the armistice terms, 384.
Howitzer, the, 38, 55.
Hoyos, Count Alexandre de, 24, 25.
Hubbard, Major S. T., of the American Expeditionary Force, 412.
Hughes, Australian Prime Minister, 434.
Huguet, Lanrezac's Chief of Staff, 59.
Hunter-Weston, Maj.-Gen. Aylmer G., in command of British division at Gallipoli, 163–172; in command of Eighth Corps, 236.
Hutier, Gen. von, 398.
Huy, 60.

Indefatigable, the, sunk in battle of Jutland, 279, 293.
Independent Air Force, 313, 319.
Inflexible, the, attacks Admiral von Spee, 79; in Dardanelles Expedition, 152.
Ingenohl, Admiral von, 79.

Invincible, the, sent against Admiral von Spee, 78; destroyed in battle of Jutland, 283.

Irresistible, the, sunk in Dardanelles, 152.

Ismailia, repulse of Turks at, 117.

Isonzo, the, 136, 202, 208, 305.

Isvolsky, Alexander P., Russian Foreign Minister, 18.

Italians, on the Isonzo, 208; defeated at Caporetto, 357–363.

Italy, joins Germany and Austria in Triple Alliance, 5; a doubtful partner, 17; decides on neutrality, 35; joins the Entente, 117; declares war against Austria, 132; her first campaign, 135, 136; the break-through in, 304–306.

JACKSON, H. C., at the Chemin-des-Dames (May 1918), 413.

Jaffa, taken by British, 307.

Jameson raid, 8.

Japan, in war with China, 8; in alliance with Great Britain, 12; enters war, 80; takes Tsing-tao, 80.

Jellicoe, Admiral Sir John R., commander of the British Grand Fleet in battle of Jutland, 77, 209, 210, 275–295.

Jemal, commander of the Turkish Fourth Army, 441.

Jerusalem, capture of, 306, 307.

Jeudwine, commander of British division at Cambrai, 354.

Jevad, commander of the Turkish Eighth Army, 441.

Jilinsky, General, 103, 104, 106, 110.

Joffre, Gen. Joseph, Chief of the French General Staff, 49; in French retreat and battle of Marne, 60, 64, 82, 83, 86–92, 97, 100–102; his unreasoning optimism, 119, 120, 134, 187; in Artois-Champagne offensive, 187, 188; rebukes Galliéni, 218; his calmness, 222; and the 1916 offensive campaign, 227, 228, 238, 246; gives place to Nivelle, 299, 322.

Jutland, battle of, 271–295.

KANNENGIESSER, GENERAL HANS, 145, 160.

Kavanagh, commander of the British Cavalry Corps, 348.

Kemal, Lieut.-Col. Mustapha, 160, 168, 169.

Kemmel Hill, 372, 409.

Kerensky, Alexander, 304.

Keyes, Admiral Sir Roger, plan of, 123; at Gallipoli, 167; his raids on Zeebrugge and Ostend, 311.

Kiderlen-Wächter, German Foreign Minister, dispatches gunboat to Agadir, 20.

Kiel Canal, 75.

Kiggell, Chief of Staff to Haig, 135, 234, 347, 348.

Kitchener, Lord Herbert, muzzling of the press due mainly to, 45; his intuition of German plan, 51; grasps probable duration of war, 69; his call to arms, 69; advocates plan for landing in Gulf of Alexandretta, 119; his views on German lines in France, 120; and the Dardanelles Expedition, 121, 123, 148, 149, 155; his view of the machine-gun, 128; his loyalty to France, 154; endorses Loos offensive, 187, 189; and the tank, 253, 254.

"Kitchener's Army," 199, 227.

Kluck, Gen. Alexander von, 61, 62, 85–93, 98.

Kress, Lieut.-Col. von, 144.

Krithia, 170, 172.

Krüger, Pres. Paul, the Emperor's telegram to, 9.

Kuhl, Gen. von, Kluck's Chief of Staff, 98; Crown Prince Rupprecht's Chief of Staff, 392; disclosures of, 417.

Kum Kale, 122, 161.

Kut-el-Amara, 140, 141.

LADERCHI, commander of the Italian Ninth Corps, 362.

Lake, Lieut.-Gen. Sir Percy, in Mesopotamia, 268.

Landships Committee, 254.

Langle de Cary, Com. de, 221.

Lanrezac, General, suspects character of German advance, 58; and Sir John French, 59, 60; in the battle of the Marne, 86, 88.

Lansdowne, Lord, quoted, 15.

Lateau Wood, 352.

Law, A. Bonar, demands evacuation of Gallipoli, 123.

Lawrence, Col. T. E., 331, 443, 444, 447.

Le Cateau, 60, 61, 86.

Lechitski, commanding the Russian Ninth Army at Czernowitz, 225.

Lecquis, General, 363.

Lemberg, taken by Germans, 72, 132.

Lenin, overthrows Kerensky, 304.

Lens, and Arras, French offensive between, 130, 131.

Lettow-Vorbeck, Gen. von, in command in German East Africa, 80, 308.

Lichnowsky, Prince Karl Max von, German Ambassador in London, 30, 34.

Liége, in Moltke's plan, 48; occupied by Germans, 54.

Liggett, Gen. Hunter, commander of American First Corps, 456, 464; at St. Mihiel, 457; quoted on St. Mihiel, 458; at the Meuse-Argonne, 464, 465; transferred to command of First Army, 467.

Ligny-en-Barrois, American Headquarters at, 452.

Limpus, Admiral, ex-chief of Naval Mission to Turkey, 145.

Lion, the, Beatty's flagship in battle of Jutland, 278, 280.

Lloyd George, David, warns Germany, 20; opposed to wasting man-power in France, 120; advocates sending British forces to Balkans, 120; at head of Ministry of Munitions, 127; promotes Stokes Gun, 128; personality of, 141; objects to plan for use of army in Dardanelles Expedition, 155; protests against the premature use of the tank, 257; replaces Asquith as head of Government, 297; seeks interallied executive committee, 367; and Haig, 388, 389.

Loans, American, 311–313.

Lodz, 73.

Loos, attack at, 186–198.

Lorraine, invaded by French, 55–57; offensive, preparations for, 385, 386.

Luck, Austrians attacked near, 203, 225.

Ludendorff, Gen. Erich von, at Liége, 54; Chief of Staff of Hindenburg, 71–73, 107; defeats Russians at Tannenberg, 103, 108–113; his strategy of decision, 124; First Quartermaster-General, 203; on effect of the tank, 250; reorganizes German man-power, munitions, and supplies, 299; orders new line of defense, 299, 300; failure of his operations in the West, 368, 369, 374; his operations in the West, 370–374; informs Emperor that peace negotiations should be opened, 375; decides to appeal for armistice, 378; resigns, 382; his plans for offensive of March 1918, 391, 392; his limitations, 400; and the Flanders offensive (April 1918), 403–405; on the "black day," 429, 430.

Lusitania, torpedoing of, 79.

Lutzow, the, Hipper's flagship in battle of Jutland, 278, 285.

Luxembourg, entered by German troops, 34.

Lys, the, battle of, 403–410.

"Maastricht Appendix," 48.

Macedonia, war over, 20, 21.

Machine-gun, the, 38, 127, 250, 252, 253.

Mackensen, Gen. von, in command of German forces on Russian front, 109–113, 131–133; in charge of Serbian campaign, 137; his operations against Rumania, 206, 264–266.

Magdeburg, the, sunk in the Baltic, 274.

Magdhaba, Turks defeated at, 208.

Mametz, capture of, 235.

Mangin, Gen. Charles, 40; at the second battle of the Marne, 424, 425.

Marne, the, retreat to, 58–61; battle of, 61–64, 85–102; controversy about battle of, 82, 83; battle of, a psychological victory, 83; primary cause of the victory of, 83–85; the breakthrough to, 411–418; the second battle of, 419–428.

Martinpuich, taken by British, 246.

Marwitz, Gen. von der, 351.

Masefield, John, his *The Old Front Line* quoted, 232.

Masurian Lakes, 105, 125.

Matthews, Colonel, at Gallipoli, 167.

Maubeuge, fortress of, 59 *n*.

Maude, Lieut.-Gen. Sir Stanley, in Baghdad campaign, 207, 268–270.

Maudhuy, General, in command of Tenth French Army, 67.

Maunoury, General, in the battle of the Marne, 61–63, 87, 88, 90–93.

Max, Prince, of Baden, called to be Chancellor to negotiate peace move, 378; hands over to Ebert, 383; memoirs of, 474.

Maxim, Hiram, inventor of machine-gun, 250.

Maxse, British division commander, 240.

Maxwell, commander in Egypt, 172.

Megiddo, victory of, 382, 439–448.

Menin road, 340, 341.

Mesopotamia, British operations in, 139–141, 207, 267–270.

Messines Ridge, capture of, by British, 302, 330–336.

"Methodical progress," 243.

Meuse-Argonne, battle of, 460–469.

"Michael" attack, 369, 370, 393, 404.

Michich, General, splits Bulgarian Army, 377.

Milner, Lord, 371, 383.

"Mobilization," 77.

Mole, L. E. de, his tank model, 252.

Molodeczno, 225.

Moltke, Count Helmuth von, Chief of German General Staff, assures Austria of German support, 31, 32; his responsibility for the war, 33; his arrangements for two-front attack, 34; his modification of Schlieffen's plan of attack, 47, 48, 54, 56, 60, 61, 63; at battle of the Marne, 85, 94, 95, 8, 102; selects Hindenburg and Ludendorff for the eastern front, 108.

Monastir, capture of, by Allies, 138.

Monro, Sir Charles, declares for evacuation of Gallipoli, 123; honored, 124.

Mons, battle of, 59 *n*.

Montagu, of Ministry of Munitions, 257.

Montauban, 205, 235.

Montdidier, 398.

Montfaucon, 464, 466.
Moreuil Wood Ridge, taken by Germans, 399.
Morhange-Sarrebourg, battle of, 55, 57.
Morland, commander of the British Tenth Army Corps, 236, 334.
Morocco, recognition of right of France to occupy, 13; settlement over, 20.
Mudra, in command of First German Army, 420.
Mudros, 154, 156, 163.
Munich, proposed advance on, 386.
Munitions, English, 44, 127-129; French, 44; German, 44.
Murray, Sir Archibald, French's Chief of the General Staff, 90; defeats Turkish forces, 208; succeeded by Allenby, 306.

NAMUR, Germans appear before, 55; the reducing of, 59, 59 n.
Narocz, Lake, Russian attack at, 202, 224.
Nasiriya, 140.
Nassau, the, in battle of Jutland, 288, 289.
"Nation in Arms," 36.
Neuve-Chapelle, British attack at, 126, 129.
New Guinea, seized by New Zealand expedition, 80.
New Zealand, expedition of, 80.
New Zealanders, at Gallipoli, 161, 172; at Messines, 334.
Nicholas, Grand Duke, 70, 72, 73, 125; defeated at Tannenberg, 104; superseded, 134.
Nicholas II, Tsar, Emperor William's hold on, 8; and Emperor's draft treaty, 14, 15; abdication of, 304.
Nicolai, Colonel, at Constantinople, 160.
Nivelle, General, succeeds Joffre, 299, 322; Haig subordinated to, 299; his handicaps, 299; his policy, 299; defeated on the Aisne, 328.
Nixon, Lieut.-Gen. Sir John, in Mesopotamia, 140, 141.
Northcliffe, Lord, in campaign for munitions, 127; appointed Director of Propaganda in Enemy Countries, 319.
Northey, in East Africa, 308.

Ocean, the, sunk, 152.
Odessa, raided, 146.

PALAT, GENERAL, on Verdun, 222.
Palestine, British operations in, 208, 366, 439-448.
Passchendaele, use of tank at, 259, 260; battle of (third battle of Ypres), 302, 337-343.
Peace movements, 319, 320.
Péronne, 238.
Pershing, Gen. John J., American Commander-in-chief, 450, 452; places

American troops at Foch's disposal, 373; erases St. Mihiel salient, 376, 450-460; protests against armistice, 384; insists that American army be used as a whole, 454; in the Meuse-Argonne, 461-469.
Pétain, in defense of Verdun, 202, 220-223; his policy, 301; his "elastic defense," 420, 421; and the second battle of the Marne, 420-425; agrees to proposed change of plan for Americans at St. Mihiel, 452.
Piave, the, 306, 361, 362.
Plans of war, 45-53, 57, 60; French plan for countering German invasion, 57, 58. *See also* Schlieffen, Count.
Plumer, Major-General Sir Herbert C. O., 183; captures Messines Ridge, 302, 330-336; at Passchendaele, 341.
Pohl, Admiral, replaces Ingenohl as Commander of High Seas Fleet, 79.
Poincaré, Pres. Raymond, quoted, 22.
Poland, occupied by Teutons, 71, 72, 133.
Pommern, the, sunk in North Sea, 291.
Portuguese, at German offensive of April, 1918, 404-408.
Posen, the, at battle of Jutland, 288.
Potiorek, military governor of Bosnia, 22, 23.
Pozières, 244.
Presan, General, Rumanian Chief of General Staff, 266.
Press, muzzling of, 45.
Princess Royal, the, in battle of Jutland, 279, 288.
Prittwitz, General, on Eastern front, 70, 105-107; superseded, 71, 108.
Propaganda, 45; German, 116, 305; British, 319; among the Italians, 362; peace, 381; Allied, effectiveness of, 474.
Przemysl, taken by Russians, 125; retaken by Germans and Austrians, 132.
Psychological forces, 44, 45.
Pulteney, Lieut.-Gen. W. P., commander of British Third Army Corps, 236, 348.
Putz, General, 178, 180.

Q-SHIPS, 212.
Queen Elizabeth, the, 169, 171.
Queen Mary, the, sunk in battle of Jutland, 279, 293.

"RACE TO THE SEA," 64, 100.
Rafa, Turks defeated at, 208.
Ramsey, David, his self-moving car, 251.
Rapallo conference (Nov. 1917), 364.
Rathenau, Dr. Walter, 116.
Ravelsberg Ridge, taken by Germans, 409.

Rawlinson, Gen. Sir Henry, in charge of relieving force, 66, 67; in the 1916 campaign, 231, 237, 239, 240, 244, 247; and the Amiens attack, 431.

Raws, Lieut. J. A., 244.

Reading, Lord, his mission to United States, 312.

Refet Bey, 445.

Reims, and second battle of the Marne, 419–425.

"Reinsurance Treaty," 5, 6.

Rennenkampf, General, advances into East Prussia, 70; driven out of East Prussia, 71; at Tannenberg, 104–114.

Reparations, 384.

Repington, Col. Charles A., military correspondent of the *Times*, public outcry for munitions initiated by, 127.

Reschadieh, the, taken over by England, 143, 144.

Rhodes, Sir Cecil, 8.

Riga, captured by Germans, 304.

River Clyde, the, at Gallipoli, 161, 165.

Robeck, Admiral de, and the Dardanelles Expedition, 121, 123, 151–153, 156, 157.

Robeida, Albert, writings and drawings of, 252.

Roberts, Lord, 42, 50, 63.

Robertson, Sir William, Chief of the Imperial General Staff, 135, 207; endorses Loos offensive, 186; and the tank, 258; his views on Mesopotamia campaign, 268, 269; succeeded by Wilson, 365, 366.

Romani, Turks defeated at, 208.

Ross-Smith, in Palestine, 443.

Royal Air Force, 319.

Rumania, attached to Triple Alliance, 5; offered to Bulgaria, 21; encouraged to enter the war, 142; enters war on side of the *Entente*, 203, 206, 226, 261; takes offensive against Transylvania, 206; defeated and overrun by Teutons, 206, 207, 264–266; army and equipment of, 262; counsel of Allies as to her action, 262, 263.

Rupprecht, Crown Prince of Bavaria, 56–62, 94, 95, 300.

Russia, Bismarck's policy toward, 4–6; in military convention with France, 6, 7; begins to build new Balkan alliance, 21; popular unrest in, 21; her part in plan of war, 51–53; orders mobilization, 29–31; annexation of Constantinople and the Dardanelles the corner-stone of her policy, 150; disapproves of efforts of Allies to force the Dardanelles, 150, 155; collapse of, 303, 304.

Russian military system, 40, 41.

Russians, fire on British trawlers, 14; invade East Prussia, 70–72; defeated at Tannenberg, 71; thrown back on

Warsaw, 72, 73; retreat of (1915), 131–134; their offensive under Brusilov, 202–204, 224–226; attack Germans at Lake Narocz, 202.

Russo-Japanese War, 13.

Russo-Turkish War of 1877, 4.

"ST. GEORGE" attack, 372, 393, 404.

St. Gond, 82, 96.

St. Mihiel salient, erased by Americans, 376, 449–460.

St. Nazaire, 65.

Sakharov, commanding Russian Eleventh Army near Tarnapol, 225; near Brody and Lemberg, 225.

Salisbury, Lord, weakness of his government, 11.

Salonika, British consider sending troops to, 153–155; significance of surrender of, 475.

Salonika Expedition, 138, 139.

Samoa, seized by New Zealand expedition, 80.

Samsonov, General, enters East Prussia, 71; defeat of, 71, 104–114.

Sanders, Liman von, at Gallipoli, 159–161, 170–173; in Palestine, 444–446.

Sarikamish, battle of, 117.

Saros, Gulf of, 160, 161, 163.

Sarrail, General, in the battle of the Marne, 95; in Salonika Expedition, 138, 139.

Sarrebourg-Morhange, battle of, 94.

Sazonov, Sergius D., in discussions preceding the war, 27–32; suggests internationalization of Constantinople, 150.

Scapa Flow, British naval base at, 74, 77, 385.

Scarborough, naval raid on, 79.

Scharnhorst, the, in naval battles with English, 78.

Scheer, Admiral, in battle of Jutland, 209, 210, 275–285.

Schlieffen, Count, his plan of German attack, 46–48, 56, 60, 61, 63, 115.

Scholtz, Gen. von, in command of German forces on Russian front, 105, 111.

Schulenberg, German Crown Prince's Chief of Staff, his plan of attack, 392.

"Scrap of paper," 35.

Sedan, 469.

Seeckt, on the eastern front, 131, 132.

Seely, General, in 1916 campaign, 231.

Serajevo, crime of, 22, 23.

Serbia, in treaty with Austria, 5; in war against Turkey, 20; combines against Bulgaria, 21; ultimatum of Austria to, 25, 26; conquest of, 137, 138.

Seydlitz, the, damaged, 79.

Shcherbacher, Gen. Dmitri G. commanding Russian Seventh Army at the Strypa, 225.

Silesia, 125.
Smith-Dorrien, Gen. Sir Horace, at Le Cateau, 60; relations with French, 183.
Smoke screen, the first, 191.
Smuts, Gen. Jan Christien, in campaign against German East Africa, 308.
Snow, General, 176; forecasts counterstroke to Cambrai by Germans, 354.
Soissons, taken by Germans, 416.
Somme, the, battles of, 204, 205, 223, 227–248.
South Africa. See Transvaal.
South African War, 41.
South Africans, at Delville Wood, 241.
Southampton, the, in battle of Jutland, 288, 290, 291.
Spain, her agreement with Italy, 5.
Spee, Admiral von, defeats British squadron, 78; defeated by British, 78.
Spincourt, 222.
Spitfire, the, 288.
Stanislau, 304.
Stein, Moltke's deputy, 56.
Stern, Major Albert, 258, 259.
Stevin, Simon, landships of, 251.
Stirling, Captain, in battle of Jutland, 291.
Stokes Gun, 128.
Sturdee, Admiral Sir Frederick C. D., defeats the Germans off the Falklands, 78.
Submarine, the mastering of, 309–311.
Submarine campaign, 209–213, 296, 297; policy of unrestricted, 212.
Sultan Osman, the, taken over by England, 143, 144.
Summerall, replaces Cameron as commander of the American Fifth Corps, 467.
Supreme War Council, 364, 365, 389.
Suvla Bay, 122–124, 173.
Swinton, Col. Ernest, originator of tank, 118, 253–259.

Tagliamento, 361, 363.
Tanga, 80.
Tangiers, incident of, 14.
Tank, the, conception of, 118; and Ministry of Munitions, 128; first use of, 205, 245; name of, 249, 251; a British production, 248; evolution of, 250–255; effect of, 250; French, 255; premature use of, at the Somme, 255; use of, at Cambrai, 258, 259, 303, 344–356; trials of, 258, 259; use of, at Passchendaele, 259, 260, 340; at Arras, 328; in the Amiens attack, 432; in the Meuse-Argonne, 464.
Tannenberg, battle of, 71; legends connected with, 103–114.
Tarnopol, 225.
Taxicabs, episode of, 93.

Thiepval, 244, 246.
"Three emperors' alliance," 5.
Thursby, Admiral, 169.
Tirpitz, Admiral Alfred von, creator of German navy, 9, 42; and submarine campaign, 209.
Tisza, Count Stephen, 23, 25.
Togoland, occupied, 80.
Tombeur, in East Africa, 308.
Townshend, General, in Mesopotamia, 140, 141, 267.
Transvaal, the Emperor's attitude toward, 8, 9.
Transylvania, 206, 261.
Trench deadlock, reactions of, 117, 118.
Trenchard, in charge of Independent Air Force, 313, 319.
Trentino, Austrian offensive in, 202, 224.
Triple Alliance, 5–7, 17.
Tritton, Sir William, 255.
Trônes Wood, 240.
Tschirschky, German Ambassador to Austria, 24, 25.
Tsing-Tao, taken by Japanese, 80.
Turkey, railway concessions in, 8; Revolution in, 18; in war with Bulgaria, Serbia, and Greece, 20; recovers territory in Europe, 21; enters war on side of Central Powers, 116; strikes at Russia and Great Britain, 117; asks Germany for secret alliance against Russia, 144; offers Russia a Turkish alliance, 144; admits passage of the Goeben and the Breslau through the Dardanelles, 144, 145; moves toward war, 145; her fleet raids Russian ports, 146; collapse of, 381, 382. See also Dardanelles Expedition.
Turks, defeated by Murray, 208; defeated by Allenby, 439–448.

U-boats. See Submarine; Submarine campaign.
United States, enters the war, 296; her first aid, 311–313. See also Americans.
Unwin, Commander, 161.

Valturio, his wind-propelled war chariot, 251.
Van Deventer, in German East Africa, 308.
Vaux, Fort, 202, 217, 221, 223.
Venizelos, Eleutherios, Greek Prime Minister, places forces of Greece at disposal of Entente, 147; proposes to land troops on Gallipoli peninsula, 155.
Verdun, battle of, 201, 214–223; recovery of ground at, by Guillaumat, 303.
Versailles Executive Committee, 365, 366.
Villers Guislain, 355.
Vimy Ridge, taken by British, 300, 326.
Vinci, Leonardo da, 251, 252.

Virton-Neufchâteau, battles of, 58.

Vittorio Veneto, 306.

Von der Tann, the, in battle of Jutland, 279.

WALDERSEE, Assistant Chief of German General Staff, 24, 107, 108.

Wangenheim, Baron Hans de, German Ambassador at Constantinople, 117.

War of 1914–1918, fundamental causes of, 3, 4; immediate causes of, 18, 24; the main personal causes of, 33; psychological symptoms of, 81; can be viewed in the perspective of history, 470; won by no single country, 476.

Warsaw, 72, 73.

Watts, H. E., in 1916 campaign, 240.

Wells, H. G., his tank-story, 252.

Wemyss, Admiral Sir Rosslyn, 123.

Wetzell, Major, adviser of Ludendorff, 358; his plan of attack in 1918, 392, 393.

Weygand, General, of Versailles committee, 365.

Whitby, naval raid on, 79.

Wiesner, conducts investigation of Sarajevo crime, 23.

William I, German Emperor, 4.

William II, German Emperor, accession of, 6; and Prince of Wales (Edward VII), mutual antipathy of, 7; his ultimatum to Great Britain on railway concessions in Turkey, 8; his interference in Russo-Japanese affairs, 8; his attitude toward Transvaal, 8, 9; proclaims himself protector of all Mahomedans, 9; "saw too many things at once," 9; his responsibility for the war, 11; attempts to break up

Franco-British entente, 13, 14; presents draft treaty to Tsar, 14, 15; looks for alliance with Turkey, 16; his *Daily Telegraph* interview, 19; gives support to Austria, 24; visits Norway, 24; in the Serbian crisis, 26; on the "black day," 429. *See also* Germany.

Wilson, Gen. Sir Henry, 51, 64; quoted on Kitchener's army, 69; his influence, 135; and Robertson, 186; proposes that British army should be divided into two groups, 187; succeeds Robertson as Chief of the Imperial General Staff, 365, 366.

Wilson, Lieutenant, 255.

Wilson, Pres. Woodrow, ultimatum of (April 1916), 209; his neutral policy, 296; invites Allies to state war aims, 297; his speeches, 319; refuses to negotiate with military autocracy, 320; leaves decision of armistice terms to generals, 383, 384.

Woollcombe, commander of the British Fourth Corps, 348.

YANUSHKEVICH, chief of Sazonov's General Staff, 30, 31; made assistant of Grand Duke Nicholas, 104.

Ypres, defense of, 68, 69; gas cloud at, 175–185; third battle of, 302, 337–341. *See also* Passchendaele.

Yser, the, 66–68.

ZEEBRUGGE, 311.

Zeppelin raids, 80, 313.

Zwehl, General von, on battle of Verdun, 215, 222; his comment on the tank, 250.